Foreword

This story is about discovering I was no more than a trick of the light. Before the nature of my particular delusion became apparent, ghosts wandered through my wounded heart, forever homeless and hungry. These shadows, these shells, these murmurs, and rumours were with me all the time. We were so close, these shadows and I, that I believed we were the same thing. We were as close as nerve endings and the pain and pleasure they carry.

I went to India in search of something and found Nothing. I wanted to discover who I was, but I discovered who I was not. I tried to run away from myself, but my 'self' ran away from me, and I was left standing, empty of everything and full of Nothing. I would later hear and read of this state when I encountered the work of Nisargadatta Maharaj, Ramana Maharshi, Mooji, Papaji, Adyashanti, Gangaji, David Carse, and many others.

What was revealed perhaps deserves a story like

'Indiana Jones and the Temple of Doom'. Instead, the closest I can get is **'Swami Premananda and the Temple of Whom.'**

Indiana Jones faced much peril on his adventure. Snakes, thicker than a dinosaur's thudding jugular and quicker than a mongoose's pulse, watched him struggle. They licked their mirthless lips, anticipating his fall into oblivion. Due to the pen of his creator, he succeeded in his quest. In my case, I had to cut free from the past and escape from myself.

Indiana had the far easier search because everyone knows you can't run away from yourself. But what happens if you stop running, turn around, and run toward yourself? This is what I did by asking a simple question. In the middle of all the intellectual noise and the story-telling of the mind, the emotional turmoil and tangle of my relationship with the past, this is what I asked.

Who am I?

I was in the ashram of Swami Premananda. He answered with Silence, and I fell into Nowhere and Nothing. Indiana Jones acquired Something and became Somebody. I lost Everything and became Nobody. The door to the Temple of Whom had opened.

You may not be able to run away from yourself, but you can certainly ask yourself a sincere question.

Who am I?

Life is your guru. Everyone who ever loved you or hurt you brought you here. Each cold glance from unknown strangers and the most intimate embrace of love brought you here. Sadness and joy were the stones on the road beneath your feet. Hurt, confusion, clarity, and comfort rose to meet you as you travelled the road, and each in their way brought you here. What you've run from and what you've run toward has brought you here, so share this journey with me. Explore this question with me.

Who Am I?

We begin this story in the air as our plane descends toward Madras Airport. We're going to the distant ashram of Swami Premananda for the festival of Shivaratri, where Swami will — but wait. I'm getting ahead of myself. Let me just say we need to get to the ashram in a hurry.

Swami Premananda

&

The Temple Of Whom

Written by Paul Donaldson
Copyright @ 1994 Paul Donaldson

CHAPTER ONE
Falling

Above the city of Madras, Southern India, 1993

***

Falling.
Falling.
Falling.
On wings of fire, I fall to the earth.

The sun is intense, reflecting off the curve of the engines. From the window of this plane, the city of Madras looks like a plate of clay and marble dropped and broken into fragments from high up in the sky. Madras is speckled white and cream and red and studded with shabby patches of green where trees have slowly shrugged off the concrete, giving the impression of spinach jutting through old teeth. Mother Nature is slowly pushing through the concrete as if to see what has been heavily upon her for the last few centuries.

She surrounds Madras, modestly pulling her hem close to the city's outskirts. Her dress is a patchwork of shabby green fields and coffee-stained soil. Within the city, there are places where the earth has been gouged away and cleared for construction. Madras is rebuilding itself even as it decays.

Tendrils of sun-baked earth reach into the surrounding countryside, pulling commerce closer. Looking out of the window of this passenger plane, which skittishly bucks, high on turbulence, I wonder what life is like down there and imagine barefoot travellers with rolls of rupees tucked away, hidden from sweating shopkeepers, stubby brown toes cheekily peeking from open-toed sandals. I imagine people with the thin solace of a few rupees, passing shops where the more fortunate or industrious sip chai, reading the morning papers. The papers will be crisp until the heat wilts them and then crisp again when even the humidity has to hide from the unbearable heat. I imagine lots of slightly harassed brown fellows in white shirts and women wearing saris of green and red, and purple. The cloth will be veined with gold-like thread. My mind summons an image of beggars with knees like clubs and legs like sticks, sadhus with eyes of honey and dusty feet with soles like leather.

All of them are down there in the city of Madras.

I can scarcely contain my eagerness to discover if India's reality will rise to meet my hopes. My expectation of it is high. Part of me thinks India is a dream in vivid colour. Intensely three-dimensional with subtle hints of a fourth carried on the wind, fragrant with incense. In this dream, the naked eye alone can't see India. It must press itself like an engraving on the optic nerves to never be forgotten.

My knowledge, or perhaps that should be ignorance, of India has been informed by Kipling (the writer, not the cakes, though it may not seem to be the case if you saw me now) and old movies about the Raj when any Indian character of note was usually played by a white man who had been coloured in for the part. Very often, even the characters of little import were also white. If I hadn't been drawn to some of the notable spiritual figures born in India, my knowledge would have remained as shallow as the face paint used in 'Carry On Up The Khyber' to turn the actor Bernard Bresslaw into the character of Bungdit Din.

Not that I'm claiming any depth of knowledge now. My view of India will remain a finger painting of a place with infinite complexity and profound simplicity, of which I'm in awe.

So is Lesley, my partner. She's added to my expectations of India through the literature she avidly consumed through the years. The speed at which she does it is impressive, particularly since she retains much of the information. Imagine falling from a great height with just a parachute and an instruction manual. As you plummet, the rate at which one would have to read the manual is the speed at which she reads. At least, that's how it appears to me. In my case, I would have just licked my finger to turn the first page when the manual would become more useful as a blotter than a set of instructions.

Our plane drops, suddenly flipping my stomach. I hear Lesley take a sharp intake of breath. I lean across her to see out the window, blocking her view.

'Do you want to have a look?' I ask, looking at her.

'No,' she replies, her voice just a little strained. 'I'll look when we land. Or crash. Whichever comes first.'

She doesn't mind flying but is quite literally shaken by turbulence. I pat the back of her hand, her slender fingers gripping the armrest as if it were the edge of a cliff. The blood has been squeezed from her knuckles, and her veins look rigid, contoured over her bones.

I return my gaze to the view from the window. Dark

shadows nestle between buildings, square and rigid with modernity, panes of glass glinting in the sun. Older buildings, humbler and shabbier, stand next to them, hunched up like old aunties shoved into the edge of a family photograph at the last minute. Some structures look ancient, giving Madras the look of time all a tumble and jumbled up.

The plane drops. Lesley's hand clamps onto my arm. I sit back in my seat and smile reassuringly, enjoying our approach to the airport. The seesaw sensation of rising and falling forces my stomach muscles to tense, as if a big warm hand is holding me in my seat.

'Won't be long now,' I say cheerfully. 'Landing is the best bit if you ask me.'

'I agree, but this bit isn't landing. This bit is strapped in a metal tube, rushing toward the earth. And what happens when we hit the runway? Are we safe at that point?'

'Yes.'

'No. We're not. Think about it. We fall out of the sky, land on an enormous pair of rollerskates, and hurtle down the runway. We're not safe until we stop.'

The plane lurches, giving a tremendous drunken heave upwards. Lesley grabs my hand. If she squeezes any harder, the marrow will squirt out like toothpaste.

She might appear nervous at this moment, but she's not a fearful person. She just doesn't like falling out of the sky. So, I sit back, wanting to look relaxed for her. But, without the distraction of the window, I toon start to feel a little anxious. The plane groans as if it's just remembered something unpleasant. Metal is creaking a little too loudly, and I hear cups and cutlery rattling as if with fright. I close my eyes. It sounds like we're on a large drinks trolley.

The plane drops like a stone. Lesley grinds my knuckles so hard that I must look like I'm passing a kidney stone. She's very pale and flinches when the engines bellow as if they, too, are trying to void something a little too large for comfort. Aeronautical horsepower rears its head. We rush on, riding the rising of each hot-scented gust of turbulence. The belly of the plane drops again and again, and we're plummeting, buttocks clenched, teeth clamped, and eyes closed.

I'm aware of other noises. Behind us, incessant chatter comes from the other passengers, mainly migrant workers returning home from Saudi. They talked throughout the flight as if the very act of staying in the air depended on it. For most of our journey, it's been like sitting in the only call centre in Babel. Not even the increasing roar of the engines or the ground coming up toward us can stop them.

And here it comes!

WHUMP!

The wheels thump on the runway — once — twice — and then rush along the hot tarmac, throwing stones roughly up against the wings. The stones rattle like rain while the engines roar and the brakes bite. Our speed drops until we're rumbling slowly along the runway. The grip on my hand softens. Lesley releases her breath with a long heartfelt sigh, and our eyes meet. She says just one word, and it's full of wonder.

'India.'

Her face is full of light at this. She turns away from me to look out the window at the country that has been the birthplace of many spiritual personages. It's almost as if there's something in the water or the air. I hope it's not just down to spicy food. If so, my feeble attempts at meditation have been a waste of time. I peer past the back of her head to see the rolling runway and tufts of unkempt grass huddling untidily along the edge of the tarmac. A goat is lunching lazily on some foliage. Behind the goat, I see a fence and, beyond that,

Madras. Even further away, eight thousand three hundred and fifty-six kilometres away, is the place we left several days ago.

England.

There it is. Hunkered down behind the white cliffs of Dover, dreaming of the past. It barely noticed when we left. Instead, it gave us a cold, wet kiss of rain, perhaps hurt that we could so easily shrug off our natural shores for India's warm and exotic embrace.

***

Even before the plane's hot, fat, smoking black wheels stop rolling, we hear seatbelts unbuckling behind us. I reach for my lap belt, but Lesley puts her hand over mine.

'Wait,' she says. 'Stay in your seat. There'll be a dash for the exit, and we don't want to get trampled.'

Sod that, I think, feeling claustrophobic. A hot fug of hair oil, sweat, vomit and the odious farts of strangers makes me feel queasy.

'Let's make a run for it,' I say, unbuckling, ' before — '

A surge of shouting behind us cuts me off. I crane my neck around and see an avalanche of battered suitcases, brown arms, white teeth and round eyes rapidly approaching. I pull my neck in to avoid getting a valise in the trachea as a portly, perspiring man, the head of the herd, scrambles past, dragging a battered portmanteau. People are pulling, pushing and rolling their belongings and each other down the aisle. I've never seen anything like it. It's like a hole suddenly appearing in the fuselage at 20,000 feet and people being sucked in and spat out—all in less than seven seconds. The only difference is this lot are less organised than anything suddenly being blown out of a hole.

'What the feck was that?' I ask Lesley as the last

passenger tumbles past my seat.

She rolls her eyes. 'I know. It was like this when I went to Sri Lanka. It was like the pilot had suddenly jammed the brakes on, and everybody shot forward like those dummies they use to test what happens if you don't wear a seatbelt.'

We pull our luggage from the overhead locker and shuffle toward the open door. I step over a solitary sandal abandoned in the aisle. The way the other passengers ran for the exit, I'm surprised it's not got the stump of a foot in it. I doubt anyone would have stopped if it had. But, wow — look how bright the sun is coming through the doorway. I squint, but the light is searing. And the heat, when it hits me, is like a bucket full of hot fog, full in the face. It's like opening an oven door.

'God,' I mutter, taken aback. I stand at the top of the stairs with the hot breath of India on my face. I hesitate while my heart flutters, but then — I succumb to the heat of its embrace. Seduced down to the marrow sizzling in my bones, I descend. The handrail's hot enough to fry an egg while the egg's still in the hen. I try not to use it. Safely on the tarmac, I wait for Lesley. I take her suitcase and carry it with my own toward the Arrivals Hall.

Inside, the air conditioning blows us cold kisses, a luxurious relief after the brief blast of heat. Ahead of us, an old woman wearing a green sari trimmed with silver thread struggles with two suitcases. The smaller one she holds by the handle. The other, she drags along the ground, jerking it forward with every small step.

Lesley catches up with her and takes hold of the heavier bag. The woman looks up, wide-eyed, and clutches the handle tighter. Pulling mightily, she glares at Lesley.

'Let me help you with this,' Lesley says.

The old lady nods and walks beside Lesley, who quickly

struggles to pull the case along the ground. I'm already burdened with the bulk of our luggage, so I can't help but speculate why it's so heavy and decide her husband is inside having a nap. Finally, we reach a large open space where people are lining up in front of several cubicles, and Lesley hands the case back. The old woman bows slightly and disappears into the midst of other passengers.

'Have you got the passports?' I ask.

Lesley takes them out of her handbag and hands mine to me. I look inside at my picture to make sure I still resemble myself. The bespectacled brown face peering back is ample proof that I do. I close it and lead Lesley toward a disorderly line that meanders to passport control. A man in uniform scrutinises each passenger and the documents which vouch for them. The official at the head of this queue looks as if helping anybody is a long way down the list of unpleasant things he wants to do before lunch. This isn't the only queue, but a quick look at the others shows them to be no more inviting. All of them are moving at a snail's pace.

Lesley sighs. 'This may take some time.'

'Yes. I think you're – '

I don't finish my sentence, but my mouth remains open. A man in the queue beside ours just picked his case up and walked forward, passing the people in front of him. He puts his luggage down and smiles politely at his new neighbour.

There's bound to be trouble. I look at the people, so blithely skipped, expecting one of them to berate him, but — nothing happens. I'm utterly baffled by this. In England, queue jumping can lead to a punch-up. So, when another man, a very brown man in a shirt so radiantly white it can be seen from the moon, walks past Lesley and me, I'm *absolutely* outraged. He puts his bag down, takes out a hanky and wipes his face.

'Did you see that?' I blurt, barely able to contain my

indignation.

'See what?' She mumbles. She's rummaging through her bag.

'That — that — ' Several expletives jostle in my mouth, desperate to be heard, but I restrain myself. The pressure of not swearing makes the word I eventually manage to get out virtually burst into being. 'That — *man!*'

She looks up.

'What, man?'

'That one! And that one! There! Him! They just skipped the queue. They just picked up their bags and went up the line about eight places and — look! There goes another one!'

Noting the look of outrage on my face, Lesley pats me on the arm.

'Indian queues are a law unto themselves,' she says reassuringly. 'It was the same in Sri Lanka.'

'You never mentioned this before. You told me you were held at gunpoint on the way from the airport, but you never said anything about this particular madness.'

'As anecdotes go, being held at gunpoint seemed a little more interesting than queue-jumping, so I might not have brought it up at the time. But, that was when — oh — here we go, we're moving. Quick!'

We pick our bags up and move forward. Two steps. That's right, two. One for each foot. Not the man behind us, though. He keeps going another fifteen. By now, I'm speechless. The humble queue and the ability to wait with patience and dignity is a sign of civilisation. Once we lose patience, we turn the line sideways, making an excellent firing squad. Not that I approve of capital punishment for queue jumping. Not for a first offence, at any rate. I think a minor flesh wound would be sufficient in such a case.

'This is ridiculous!' I grumble. 'If the animals had queued

like this to get on the Ark, Noah would have let them bloody well drown.'

'Calm down,' Lesley says. 'It'll be our turn soon enough.'

'We should walk to the head of the line right now. We should do it. We've got another 300 kilometres before we get to the ashram.'

'Feel free. But you'll still have to wait because I'm going to wait my turn.'

Naturally enough, time passes, but as we all know, time is stubborn. Try to make it hurry along, and it'll stop to watch you. Eventually, though, even time itself gets bored and moves on. We make it to the desk. We hand our documents over, they get stamped, and we're through. We stride across the concourse and closer to the exit where India awaits.

'We'd better get some money for the taxi south,' Lesley says.

'Yeah. There's a sign over there for the *bureau de change*.'

'Great. Can you sort it out while I have a quick cigarette?'

'Okay.' I leave the bags with her and follow the directions on the sign. The exit from the concourse, leading out to the street, is crammed with people. I suck in a deep breath. Plunge into the crowd. Shuffle and squeeze my way through. My skin prickles. Humidity places a pillow over my glistening face. Strangers are pressing against me, a wall of bodies is boxing me in, their voices like an orchestra tuning up, a rising din of strange music. I push through the babbling crowd and see palm trees — distant mountains. The sky is *too* blue and way too big. I feel unsure of myself and don't know which way to go.

Small hands come at me, empty and accusing and pitiful. I move through a gaggle of children into the openness of the street, where the sun is raw and intense. A man steps away from his cab and opens the door, beckoning toward the dark interior. I back away, waving him off and walk on to the *Bureau de Change*. Entering feels like taking refuge. It's calm and quiet, and the temperature drops to its knees, presumably, where it can beg forgiveness for trying to boil me alive earlier.

I'm not the only one appreciating this quiet space. The Bureau Cashier is also enjoying it. Without the noise and heat of the world outside, he's had time to concentrate on being *very* annoyed. Or at least, this is the impression I've got because my sudden appearance seems to have ruined the moment for him. From behind the glass window of his cubicle, a small, dark figure with glossy hair made darker by the oil glistening on it watches me with a sour expression curdling his face. Then, after a second or two, when it becomes apparent that I wish to use his services, his face becomes professionally blank.

'I'd like to change some Travellers Cheques, please.'

He puts three sheets of paper and places them before me. Perusing them, I pat my pockets for a pen. In most other circumstances, this would prompt the offer of something to write with, a pen or pencil, quill or even a banana dipped in squid ink.

Not here. No.

'Can I borrow one of your pens?' I ask, pointing to the neat row of biros in his shirt pocket. I can see that he's far from happy. His face has assumed the look of a man whose new toupee has just farted. He puts a biro on the counter with a sigh, and now I'm irritated too. I fill the form in and very carefully place the pen, with exaggerated exactitude, back on the counter.

He snatches it up and says, 'Vast butt.'

'I'm sorry?' I say, shocked at such outrageous rudeness.

'Pisspot!' he snaps.

I glare at the little shit as he stabs a finger toward my passport, firmly clenched in my hot hand.

'Piss-pot,' he repeats emphatically. 'Piss-pot!'
'Oh! Passport! Yes. Here you are.'

***

The short journey back to Lesley was less daunting now that I knew what to expect. She's sitting where I left her and is talking to a couple of Indian gentlemen who appear to be giving her directions. On seeing me, she waves, and so do the two men. They depart as I approach.

'Did you get the money?' she asks.

'Yes,' I say, picking up our bags.

'Those men were very helpful.' she says, but I don't hear much of what follows. Instead, I'm running the disagreeable encounter with the cashier through my mind. A series of devastating put-downs have occurred to me, too late to be of any use but satisfying in their pungency. By the time we leave the airport, my mind has turned to what we need to do next. Our destination is 300 Kilometres to the South, so we'll need a reliable taxi and driver.

A long line of suitable-looking vehicles is lined along the pavement, but the drivers look less promising. Nevertheless, I have a reasonable list of characteristics needed in a driver for such a long journey, and I'm determined to stick with it.

Which of them isn't ferocious, feeble-minded, fraudulent or flatulent? Looking at them, I have no idea. One gives me the feeling he already has a body in the boot. The driver beside *him* looks so old that *rigour mortise* may be the only thing keeping him on his feet. Beside him is a man with eyes so piercing that they're gazing at each other fondly over his hawk-like nose. His companion steps forward and waves a chunky set of keys. By this time, I've lowered my expectations so much that I'm about to hire him, but only because he looks like his ransom demands would be entirely reasonable if anything goes wrong.

'What on earth are you doing?' Lesley asks.

'I'm sorting out a driver for us.'

'I've already done it.'

'What? How?'

'Those gentlemen I talked to when you went to get some money. They told me where to go to ensure we got a reasonable price and a reliable driver. I told you this in the airport, but you weren't listening.'

'Sorry. Where do we go for the taxi?'

'Follow me.'

Within a few minutes, Lesley sorted it out. Our driver is a young man with a quiet, dignified demeanour and an honest-looking moustache.

'So, do you know where we're going?' I ask him.

'Yes.' He nods, quietly confident. Christopher Columbus gave his crew the same kind of reassuring nod before setting off to find India.

'Great!' I say and then have a moment of doubt. 'So — when you say you know where we're going, does that mean you know where the ashram is?'

'Yes,' he says. A little head waggle accompanies this.

'Right. Brilliant. So, when you say you know where it is —'

Lesley gently propels me toward the car. 'Just get in the taxi. You can interrogate him on the way. In the meantime, we're getting nowhere standing here.'

The taxi is a cream-coloured Morris Oxford III. The seats are comfortable and wide, vibrant with red leather upholstery. The lavishly polished chrome trimmings make it feel like a car that is cherished and pampered like a pussycat. Lesley slides along the roomy back seat and makes herself comfortable. I enter the front while the driver puts our luggage in the boot. I roll the window down, feeling like James Dean, then put my elbow out and burn myself on the chrome sill, like Mister Bean. The driver gets in the car and looks at me. I understood his expression to mean, 'Are we ready?'

I nod. The big diesel engine suddenly starts and growls assertively beneath the creamy curve of the bonnet. We take off so fast that I assume he spotted an angry wasp on the accelerator and stamped on it. Within seconds he's honking at bikes and boys and girls and goats and cars and trees, and when nothing else is in sight, he honks himself.

I look back at Lesley to convey my surprise at this peculiar behaviour. Back in England, using your horn gratuitously is an offence. In India, it seems to be obligatory.

'It's a lovely car, isn't it?' she says.

I nod enthusiastically. 'It reminds me of the cars you see in old films.'

'Like in *Casablanca*?

'That's right. I can see Humphrey Bogart riding around in one of these.'

'Yes. It would look quite at home parked outside Rick's Café Américain, would it?.'

I can but agree. Mind you, if our taxi driver had been there, the classic scene would have sounded like this:

"Of all the gin joints in all the world, you have to **BEEP! BEEPITY! TOOT!** in mine.'

***

I feel we are driving into a country made up of myth and mystery, a place attached somewhat tenuously to the present. How could it be otherwise? India is vast and has so much history, people, and beliefs that it drags itself into the future like a sack of treasure and old bones. The present is only a veneer. For thousands of years, the sun has baked the dry walls, bleaching the colour away, quietly crumbling history into something the street sweepers sweep into the gutter. It glances off windows and glints on silkily curved cars. Mind you, the sun may be supreme and above us all, but it still winks at us from the polished chrome of our bonnet.

I watch the city, vibrant and loud and riotous with colour, grinding its way past the windscreen until the view softens into the vegetation of the countryside. We become one of the vehicles seen from the air. Something small on a journey away from the big city. Some say the name 'Madras' comes from a Portuguese phrase, *'Mae de Deus'*, which means *'mother of God.'*

Ahead of us, humidity blurs the horizon like tears in the eyes of a mother when her child leaves.

CHAPTER TWO

The Awkward Silence of God

I once came within waving distance of Pope John Paul. I was thirteen years old and lived in a grey slab of a tower block. It had all the charm of a pauper's gravestone and was named in honour of a dead man. The Pope flew past James Connolly Tower in a helicopter on his way to Phoenix Park in Dublin. The year was 1977. Hundreds of thousands of people went to see him. Having been raised a Catholic, I should have welcomed his visit too. But, instead, I stayed in bed. My mum waved. My two brothers, Tony and Jason, may have waved, but I didn't see them, being under a thick grey woollen blanket, my head firmly wedged into the warmth of my pillow.

Southern Ireland was a very Catholic country. God and Guinness were in the blood, and each day at six o'clock, a call to prayer rang out from the television. A church bell, or at least a recording of one, gave a clear and solemn sound to remind people it was time to say a prayer. It was known as 'the Angelus'. Most people took it as the time to get up and have a piss before the next programme came on.

Each Sunday, from our fourth-storey flat, I saw people on their way to attend the church service. They were dressed in their best clothes. I say best, but this was in the seventies, so they still looked awful, but they did at least make an effort. The faithful and the dumbly compliant flapped along in big flared pants to pay homage to God, drop a few coins in the collection boxes and mumble along with the prayers.

At that point in my life, I lived in Ireland in Ballymun. Ballymun was nailed to the ground like the lid of a coffin, hammered in place by seven depressingly grey tower blocks. These colossal concrete pile drivers were embedded in the earth to ensure it didn't get any ideas about growing grass. They were fifteen stories high. There were also nineteen blocks of eight stories that seemed to hunch in their own shadows, like unemployed troglodytes waiting outside the labour exchange in the cold wind when the rent was due. Ten more blocks of four stories were built, possibly because some concrete was left over, and the demand for gravestones had fallen. Hundreds of semi-detached houses were also built in the area so the people in the towers could see what a normal, ordinary house looked like.

We lived in one of the towers.

Ballymun was known as the 'Heroin Capital of Ireland' because of the many addicts using it to muffle whatever sounds of anguish the heart makes when living in a place like Ballymun. We were unaware of its reputation when we arrived at the foot of our particular tower block. But, like Dorothy when she first arrived in Oz, I knew something wasn't quite right.

It certainly wasn't Kansas, though, if you took enough heroin.

No, not even then.

Being part Irish and part Jamaican, what would the residents of Ballymun make of us? Would they think we were Jam-rish, perhaps? Or Iri-can?

No.

The Irish decided we were niggers.

This was pointed out to avoid confusion within minutes of our arrival. I was sitting on our luggage at the foot of James Connolly Tower, waiting for Ma, Tony and little brother Jason to return. They were carrying boxes up to the flat, which was to be our new home. Three men standing around a small car started shouting.

'Go back to where you came from!'

I looked around, wondering who they were addressing before realising it was me. I was shocked and hurt, but it didn't register as racism. More than anything, I was appalled at such atrocious manners. I looked over at them for a minute, making eye contact as if seeing I was a conscious human being would make a difference. It didn't. They carried on.

My full name is Paul Andrew Martin Donaldson. I chose 'Martin' to honour Martin Luther King and his non-violent approach to racism. So, in respect of this and a sincere wish not to be beaten up, I lifted my head high and turned away. I treated them as if they were dogs barking at the moon.

Perhaps, to balance things out, on the other side of the world, there was a young man whose skin was blacker than mine. His hair was bushier by far. He was the saint I'd meet in the future. If someone told him to go back to where he came from, he could have assured them he'd never left. He came from God. There was nothing but God. Where else could one go but toward God from God within God and by the grace of God?

Even in Ballymun.

***

At this point, let me tidy the story up a little by providing a brief chronology.

I was born in England on the 28th of January, 1966. My older brother is called Tony. A younger brother joined us seven years later. After leaving our father, our mother took us to Ireland, and we lived for two years in a one-bedroom flat. I went to a Christian Brothers school, where I had a little trouble because of the initial reaction to my colour, but it soon settled down, and I felt like I was one of the lads. This acceptance wasn't because of the 'Christian' nature of the school. It was because I could take a beating from the teachers with as much stoicism as any of the other children incarcerated in the education system as it was then.

Once I was settled in that school for a few months, Ma brought Tony to the school where he would be enrolled. I went with them on that day. As we passed through the school gate, faces appeared in the windows, pressed against the glass. Some of the windows opened, and we heard the jeers and taunts.

> *'Blackie.'*
> *'Nigger.'*
> *'Go back to where you came from.'*

Monkey noises can be quite endearing, but not when they're directed at you. Ma turned us around and took her boys away. Some part of us was left in that gateway, like dried blood at the scene of an accident. Despite this notable incident, I felt we were generally accepted where we lived. Tony went to work in a Builders Merchants, where he seemed to feel quite at home and enjoyed earning a wage.

In 1977, we moved back to England. It was after Elvis died, but that had nothing to do with the decision. We hadn't been living in Ireland on some witness protection scheme, hiding out from the wrath of the King of Rock and Roll. No, it was because Ma couldn't seem to settle anywhere, no matter where we went.

Back in England, Ma rented a house in Old Trafford, Manchester, until a drunken Pakistani forced his way into the place, saying it belonged to his dead mother. This startling intrusion prompted a swift return to Ireland. Barely six months had passed, but somehow everything had changed. We were no longer welcome. Ballymun took one look at us and spat us out. Our faces may have been acceptable in the working class cul de sac of Kennedys Villas, but not in Ballymun. I'm not sure why it was different. Perhaps it was because 1975 saw us living in the heart of the city, whereas Ballymun was more like the arse.

So there I was, in Ballymun, a twelve-year-old standing on the trembling cusp of puberty. Like a remarkably naive eighteenth-century explorer on the edge of uncharted territory, I had little idea of what lay ahead. Still, I felt reasonably sure that good manners and sensible shoes would see me through.

***

I clip shades onto my spectacles to stop the sun from painfully glancing off my retinas. The driver overtakes a gaily painted juggernaut, its horn blasting like a dinosaur with a toothache. Seated in the back, Lesley leans over and puts a hand on my shoulder, her mouth to my ear.

'Do you think the driver will mind if I smoke in his car?' she whispers.

'No,' I say, 'I don't believe it would bother him.'

It doesn't, and as if to prove it, he pulls into a gas station as soon as Lesley lights the cigarette. The smell of warm leather from the upholstery mingles with hair oil and the stench of diesel fumes. I see Lesley's eyes, wide and round over the glowing tip of her cigarette, as she realises where we are.

Saint Peter standing by the gates of heaven, puts down the book he's reading and puts his fingers in his ears. We are expected soon, somewhat singed but perfectly acceptable nonetheless.

Rapidly she stubs the cigarette out in the ashtray.

Saint Peter sits back down again.

Having dealt with the possibility of immolation, we relax. We've been in the taxi for a few hours, so getting out and stretching our legs is a relief. We walk to a nearby wall and sit. The bricks are hot but not uncomfortably so, and Lesley can smoke without the risk of waking up in a tree. I sit with her while the driver refuels the car. He does this quickly but then opens the car's bonnet, which concerns me. Is there something wrong? I walk over and, like him, put my head under the shade of the upraised bonnet. The engine's heat surges into my face, so I stand back. He continues looking into the hot, greasy-smelling pit that houses the engine.

'Everything okay?' I ask.

He looks up and smiles. He pats the car.

'Good engine,' he says.

Trying to look like I'd know a good engine when I saw one, I peer into the abyss of dark metal, twisted into pistons and mechanical things about which I know very little. Sagely, I nod like a *connoisseur* of hot, smelly metal things. But, really, I'm hoping this isn't the boot because the luggage doesn't look well if it is. The driver seems to approve of my interest. He wipes a long, thin piece of metal with an oily rag and smiles at me again. I presume it's a dipstick, and he's not about to challenge me to a duel with his little rapier.

He may be thinking the same thing about me.

***

Trudging up the concrete stairwell of our tower after being verbally abused, I felt very low. The sharp smell of concrete was in the air. Specks of dust drifted in the pale light that came through a scratched window of Perspex. I was carrying a box of my comics. Two girls, who I thought were about 12 years old, came down the stairs and passed by me. I was instantly smitten with one of them and smiled at the vision of female loveliness as she and her friend approached.

Wistfully I thought, 'How lovely she is.'

They passed, and I heard them snicker behind me. One of them shouted up.

'Nigger!'

They ran the rest of the way down, laughing.

I was crushed. My heart was mashed to mush, and then I had a minute or two of embarrassed anger and, oddly enough, shock. I hadn't known such a lovely face could have an ugly thought behind it. I carried on up the stairs with my box of comics. It felt much heavier than before, and I was glad to put it down inside the flat. I stood momentarily, resting my head on the wooden door below the spy hole.

'What is wrong with these people?' I wondered in dismay. 'Why do they look at me and just see colour?'

What was wrong with them — was the same thing that was wrong with me. We all thought I was a brown, twelve-year-old boy with an afro and glasses, but I'm something else entirely. I wouldn't find this out until many years later, on a moonlit night in Southern India.

***

A cool draught comes through the open window of the taxi. We're travelling on Route 45, a road that stretches like a long lazy yawn toward hills of purple and blue. The sky is utterly perfect, a sun-saturated blue. It's delightful. Dreamlike. Drowsy. Mind dissolves into the loveliness of it all — sniff—?

What's that odour?

There's an odd smell in the car. It's not unpleasant, but something about it smells familiar. I lean closer to the open window, smiling at the warm wind buffeting my face, and let the scent fill my nostrils. Then, I close my eyes and take a deep lungful of whatever it is. Turning to Lesley, I ask if she knows what it is.

She says, 'Hmm?— oh yes, the villagers defecate in the fields, and the sun dries it out.'

'You're joking.'

'Seriously. What doesn't fertilise the soil blows away in the wind. No pun intended. If you're not careful, it can lead to a nasty eye infection.'

Rapidly I roll the window up. I haven't come all this

way just to be seasoned with a fine coating of dehydrated village crap — but within minutes, I'm sure I've got a grain of dehydrated turd festering in my eyes. They're itchy and don't feel right. And god, I'm so hot with the window up. Glumly, I roll it down, but the dust from the road irritates my eyes even more, so I roll it back up. This heat is unbearable, baking me brown like a bun. I roll the window down. My eye stings ferociously. Up with the window. The driver makes winding motions with his hand, indicating I roll it down. I do this — reluctantly, moving my seat into the incline position, hoping to stay away from the rush of dried crap in the hot air. Despite my concern, I drift, softened by the heat and lulled by the engine.

***

Every time I left that flat in Ballymun, I used up a measure of courage and optimism. If I went down the stairs, I braced myself for when I passed other children because it turned out the amoebic wit of the two girls wasn't an exception. The lift could be just as bad, the idea being that you shouted 'Coon' just as the door closed in my face. Usually, it was children of a similar age to me, but adults could be just as bad.

The days began to grind away at me, drilling down deep. Darkie!' drifted down from the balconies. 'Jigaboo!' leapt from the windows of cars and buses as they passed. 'Nig-nog!' nipped at my heels as I walked to the library. The possibility of physical violence sniggered behind me until I returned to the warm sanctuary of home laden with books about history. I read about Rorke's Drift thinking it was like Ballymun in reverse.

I'd never encountered sustained hostility to the fact of my existence before, and I struggled with it physically, emotionally and intellectually. I didn't know how to handle it. If I ignored it, it kept happening. If I confronted it, it kept on happening. If I laughed at it, it kept on happening. If I got upset, it kept on happening. The upset was something I kept to myself. I don't remember crying. Crying wasn't something I did. Even as a child, I favoured a stiff upper lip over one that trembled. Crying would have been pointless anyway, in that it wouldn't change the situation and would have left me feeling unmanned. I couldn't control the reaction of the external world to me, but I'd do my best to control my internal reactions to what lurked outside my door.

My brothers shared my experience to one degree or the other, though Tony didn't go out much, and Jason was too young to go out on his own. None of us spoke to Ma about what was happening. She had enough on her plate raising three boys alone, and we didn't wish to add to her worries. We also thought she wouldn't understand how awful life became because she didn't care what colour anybody was. She proved it by having three brown children despite being as white and Irish as they come. Her family, large and very Catholic, lived beside Guinness's Brewery. Her father had been a wagon driver, delivering the black stuff. Her mother got a pension from the Brewery when he died. She also got one from the Army because he'd been a soldier. They lived between the foul stink of the River Liffey and the pungent punch in the nostrils that was the smell of hops coming out of the Brewery.

Ma left Ireland when she was sixteen because of a sense of adventure. Considering where she came from, I'm surprised she didn't leave just for a breath of fresh air. She met my father, a long, lean, handsome Jamaican, and they were together for maybe ten years before they split up. Of course, like most stories about people, it was far more complicated than that, but that's all this story requires. Dad was a good man who deserved better than to lose his children. By the time we moved to Ireland, he was a sharp memory, a dull ache in the past I rarely spoke about under the assumption he must have done something wrong. For the record, he hadn't. Ma made a rod for her own back by not staying with him.

Despite the evidence presented thus far, I remember feeling optimistic about our future in Ireland. I assumed the Irish would get used to us, and the hostility would finally calm down. It didn't. I was permanently puzzled by how people reacted to the colour of my skin because they were reacting to something that wasn't me. Brown is a colour an artist could scrape off his palette. I was something else.

Perhaps this planted a singular, most precious seed in the darkly hidden furrows of my brain.

If I'm not this skin, am I what this skin contains?

Each night to the intermittent sound of rubbish clattering down the metal chute that ran through the tower like a rattling hollow spine, I spoke to God, asking for help. Then, finally, I'd fall asleep to the sound of the distant day rolling toward me like a grey boulder, coming to crush my spirit once more.

Or maybe that noise was just the rubbish chute swallowing its pride.

***

I wake with a gasp. The driver's tapping out Morse code on the horn. Peering through the dusty windscreen at the road, stretching for miles without a single vehicle in sight, I wonder what the man is beeping. I see it, then —an old woman, stooped and grey-haired, walking toward us on the other side of the road. She's got a large bundle of sticks on her back. The driver honks again, just to be sure she sees us.

I sit back, reassured by his vigilance, and realise my eyes no longer hurt. Warm, content and smiling with relief, I enjoy looking at the small dusty villages we pass through. These are dotted and, in some cases, possibly dumped along the road. They're higgledy-piggledy places, lifted, shuffled around and dropped in the dust, almost identical to each other in their untidiness and architecture. Yet, it's still all quietly exhilarating. This internal vibration is an undercurrent, like the subtle vibration of the car. I feel it even when it slows down and idles to let a cow pass. Everything is exciting, even people driving goats in front of them. Others with vast bundles of stuff wrapped in coloured cloth are fascinating. The bundles are balanced on the head or a bone-curved back or piled onto rickety wooden handcarts. In England, it would be a circus novelty act. In India, it's merely a man coming back from the market.

Smoke from small cooking fires by the side of the road rises into the sky so vast it could swallow all creation and still have room left for pudding. The enticing smell of food fills the car as we rush by. Mouth-watering scents hitch a lift to the next village, where they dance with other aromas. Chapatti and masala, puris and sambar make lovely couples as they tango across my tastebuds.

My face is slippery with sweat. My clothes are damp and cling like heavy sloughing skin.

Lesley asks the driver, 'Where are we now?'

The name he gives will soon become another milestone hidden in the undergrowth of a thousand other thoughts and observations.

***

The temperature in the car is utterly ridiculous. It's like an oven. I lean out the window to cool my face but burn my arm on the metal. This is supposed to be the coolest part of the year. I lick the burn mark on my arm, wondering if we're having a heatwave. It certainly seems like it. The road ahead quivers as if unsure of itself, shimmering as if to dissolve. With such heat, we've had to stop frequently to purchase coconuts from men selling them by the side of the road. They open the large green fruit by chopping the top off deftly with a machete, the sharp edge glinting as it flashes through the humid air. We drink the coconut water through thin green straws and, in this way, avoid becoming dehydrated.

***

The flat in Ballymun had a balcony, which was a little blessing. It allowed us to be outside without the drawbacks of being outside. It didn't matter how many drunken revellers were rambling home in the evening, stumbling in speech and foot, because we were out of the line of fire. Tony and I regularly stood leaning against the concrete balcony wall. The hard surface was always cold, no matter how warm the day had been. We felt safe, looking out over Ballymun as the summer evening gathered itself to draw a veil over the estate.

Nighttime gave me plenty of time to think. I used to stand on the balcony, thinking about the dark shape hunched low to the ground behind the tower block facing ours. That shape was Ballymun Comprehensive School. I'd be going there when the summer holidays ended, and the thought filled me with dread. I remembered when Ma tried to enrol Tony in a similar school and how that turned out, with pupils leaning out the window shouting, nigger.

That happened when I was eight or maybe nine.
Now I was thirteen.
Unlucky for some.

***

Ulundurpet is approximately 150 kilometres from Tiruchirappalli and is also easier to spell. We're on a street packed with colour, noise, dust, heat, babbling tongues and curious glances. Groups of men are standing around conversing. One man uses his hands to illustrate some point and then waggles his head as if the conversation is so good the rest of the body wants to join in. Some of the men listening to him are so exquisitely lethargic that all they manage is a reluctant wiggle of the head in response to his. I see these things in detail because we move *soooo* slowly. A large cart, which looks to have been hastily hammered together from wood and optimism, is in front of us. The cart, creaking arthritically along the road, pulled by a bullock, is stacked high with bundles of cloth. From the lack of urgency in man and beast, I suspect this is the local 'One-Day Delivery Service', meaning that whatever he's delivering will turn up one day.

The paint-flaked pastel walls of Ulundurpet have drained the impetus out of our journey. Our southward rush has slowed to the lazy swinging hammock of bullocks balls. Other vehicles have stacked up behind us, honking furiously despite the apparent futility. Other bullocks stroll in the other direction, absent-mindedly swishing flies away with their tails.

Lesley taps me on the shoulder and says, 'Why don't you buy a pair of sandals here?'

I reply. 'I'm fine as I am. Let's just keep going.'

'No. We're going nowhere at this rate. So you may as well use the opportunity to get something comfortable.'

She's right. I should have bought a pair of sandals in England, but I thought they looked very effeminate. I'm not sure I'd want to point this out to Leonidas or any of his Spartans at Thermopylae, but sandals don't look very masculine. However, now I'm in India, the lightweight pumps I've got on are getting more uncomfortable by the hour.

'You're right. Driver? Can we pull over at a shoe – eh - sandal shop?'

He nods and, seeing one up ahead, stops the car on the side of the road opposite it. I rummage around in my pockets for where I've stuffed the rupees. While I'm doing this, the cart turns into a side street. The rest of the traffic leaps forward like a rabid dog let off its lead. The funereal pace rises exponentially to one which may well cause funerals.

Suddenly, I'm aware of being surrounded by a foreign culture rushing around us like a river. I feel anxious, as if I'll be carried downstream if I step out of the car. Regardless, I dash into the road, dodging trucks and bikes, provoking a tumult of honks and ring-a-ding-dings. Finally, leaping over a steaming splodge of freshly deposited bullock dung, I reach the other side of the road and step inside the shop.

The shopkeeper, quite a small man, has watched my progress, and he smiles in greeting, presumably pleased I made it.

'Hello,' I say. 'Do you sell sandals?'

He steps aside, gesturing with a broad sweep of his arm toward at least a hundred pairs displayed on racks attached to the far wall.

'Oh,' I say. 'Of course, you do.'

You can say many indelicate things about a man with big feet, but I know of only one that is true. That is, they have trouble buying sandals in Ulundurpet. Nothing on display will fit me. I seem to be one of the ugly sisters in a land full of Cinderellajis. The shopkeeper looks down at my feet, looks back up at me, appears dubious and then waggles his head a little. What might be a gesture of apology flutters across his fingers as he considers the enormity of the problem. I think he's stumped.

'They are very — big,' he says, delivering his expert opinion in a grave tone.

He turns from me and enters the back of the shop through a curtain-covered doorway. I hear boxes being tumbled and dragged across the floor before he emerges, holding a pair of sandals which, in his hands, look huge. I expect he never thought he'd sell them unless Bilbo Baggins popped in on the way to Mordor. The man looks so happy to have found a pair he thinks will fit me that I feel obliged to accept them without trying them on. Besides, my feet must stink after being boiled and fermented in the pumps I was wearing. So, I leave with them held in my left hand. I'm about to run through the traffic, but someone grabs my right hand before I can move. It's the driver. Seeing how I crossed the road earlier, he's taking no chances. I feel like an idiot as he guides me across, but I'm too polite to refuse. A little bit of my pride is left in the road, flattened like a discarded milk carton, but I see the funny side of the little episode.

'Did you get a pair?' Lesley says from behind a cloud of cigarette smoke.

'Yes. I did. Luckily, the shop's got a range of sizes. Small, medium, large and embarrassingly big.'

The driver gets in. His door slams. He starts the car up. I can smell bullock dung. Or maybe it's my pumps.

***

Back on the road again. We make good time, but I'm hungry and need a toilet stop.

'Should we stop for some food?' I ask Lesley, who's fanning herself with her straw hat. Her eyes are closed.

'Remember, we're supposed to be fasting.'

'Oh — yeah. I forgot.' It's traditional to have a period of fasting during Shivaratri. It only lasts 24 hours, but I baulk at the idea now that I'm hungry.

'I'm half Irish,' I say. 'We don't do fasting. Well — not unless the spuds run out.'

'I think you'll find there is a difference between a famine and fasting.'

'Tell that to my stomach. I need a snack to keep me

going.'

'Okay, we'll get some tea. I could do with a little something myself.'

So, I tell the driver, 'We need to stop.'

'You want to stop? Here?'

'No. We need tea and toilets.'

'Ah. Tiffin. Okay. Soon.' He points into the distance.

I close my eyes. Even though I was asking about food, I need a toilet more than anything, but I find it too embarrassing to ask directly. I even cringe when buying toilet rolls. We could stop, and I could pop behind a tree, but I'm not interested unless it's fitted with tissue, a flushable toilet, a sink to wash my hands and possibly a newspaper to read. Some people are fussy eaters, but I'm fussy in — the other direction. I used the convenience back at the airport, but that was many coconuts ago.

I drift off, carried away to other pastures by the heat, but an abrupt change in the soothing rhythm of the car rouses me. The driver turns in to a walled courtyard and pulls up beside a two-storey yellow building. The door and windows are tucked under the shade of a long veranda, and, oddly enough, a peacock is strutting toward us, magnificent plumage held stiffly behind him.

I trot past the bird looking for the cafe toilet. Lesley is going in the other direction, looking for a cup of tea. What I presume to be the toilet block is a little distance away from the main building. The block looks old, but its apparent decrepitude doesn't bother me. I enter the gloom. Water drips down the walls like in a cave. A thin film of liquid on the ground gives it an air of dungeon *chic*. Underfoot is slippery with mould. Carefully, I walk further in and find an old man with bright eyes looking out from behind a crooked nose. He's leaning on a broom in such a way as to suggest it's holding him up.

Good God, he's *ancient*.

'Hello,' I say.

He nods.

I point to the cubicles to explain my presence in what feels like his cave. I feel pretty uncomfortable with him being there, but — oh, well—duty calls.

Water. Drip. Drip. A liquid metronome drips in the background. Bright eyes follow my progress toward the first cubicle. I enter. There's a hole in the floor where the toilet should be. A moment of disappointment before I step back out under the gaze of Methuselah, who still leans upon the brush. An embarrassed smile from me. Nothing from him. The next cubicle and — what's this? There's another hole in the ground? I *'tut'* and step back into the gaze of the Keeper of the Broom, who now looks a little confused.

I don't need to step into the last cubicle because I can see yet *another* hole. I stand, looking into it, held in a baffled silence broken only by the methodical water drip.

Where the hell is the —?

— Oh

No —

These holes are the toilets.

I can hardly believe it as I stand and gawp at the gap. The hole now looks like a chasm. I'm baffled at the mechanics of how to use this thing. I'm supposed to lower my standards, loosen my dignity and hold onto the wall while — hang on a minute!

Where the *fuck* is the door?

I turn abruptly to look at the old man with the broom as if I might catch him sneaking out with it. He's not even looking at me now. Instead, he's slowly sweeping the water on the floor, with immense concentration, as if he were a Zen Master about to sweep the water into a neat pile.

I leave. I don't run because I'd probably slip, adding to my embarrassment. There's no way I can go to the toilet under these conditions. No. Not in a hole in a cubicle. Not in a million years. Not with a man with a broom standing outside, hoping for something more interesting to happen than the dripping of water. But above all, I need a door. I need some barrier between the stranger and me. I don't believe in communal crapping. I can't make myself that vulnerable in front of someone I don't know. I reject the notion on a visceral level.

Outside, the peacock steps daintily aside as I approach the cafe. I join Lesley inside at a table with three pop bottles on it. The driver's sitting at the counter talking to the staff while a large ceiling fan rotates slowly. It doesn't provide much draught but gives the flies something comfortable to sit on.

Lesley says, 'I decided not to get tea.'

'Oh?'

She nods. 'We better err on the side of caution and only drink bottled water until we reach the ashram. We don't want to get a tummy bug.'

'Not if it means using a toilet like the one I've just been in.'

She pulls a sympathetic face. 'Oh, dear. Wasn't it clean?'

'It wasn't a toilet. It smelled like one, but it wasn't. There were no toilets in it. Nothing but holes in the ground.'

She laughs. 'What were you expecting? Why do you think the villagers go by the side of the road?'

'I don't know. I'd not thought about it. I just presumed a cafe would have a toilet.'

'It does. But not the sort you're used to.'

'Look — a toilet can't be a toilet unless it's got a toilet in it, can it?'

'Yes, it can, and it is. A hole in the ground is quite

sufficient to qualify as a lavatory.'

'Well, all I can say is, I'm glad we haven't come here to play golf.'

'Don't be silly. Go back and use it. Otherwise, you'll make yourself ill.'

'No. I won't. I've got a library card. I've got a driver's licence. On the way here, I ate a packet of polo mints at twenty thousand feet. Once a man reaches that level of sophistication, he needs a door.'

Lesley shakes her head. 'When in Rome — ' she says, with an air of knowing weariness.

'Do as the Romans do. Okay. If we pass the Coliseum, I'll nip out and have a crap —'

'Shhh. The driver's coming over. He's been asking for directions.'

The driver sits down on the chair opposite me. The other patrons are peering at us with undisguised curiosity.

'Excuse me,' Lesley says, pushing her chair away from the table. 'I need to powder my nose.' She looks at me pointedly to encourage me to use the facilities, but I ignore the hint and speak to the driver. She rolls her eyes and departs.

'So,' I say. 'you got directions?'

'Yes,' he says.

I wait for him to share them, but he doesn't. An awkward silence opens between us. For me, this is nothing new.

I had the same problem with God and Myself. It all started in Ballymun.

***

Sometimes, when I went to bed, I'd close my eyes tight and pray. So intense was my longing to be heard my hands would be clenched in knuckle white clumps of fingers. For some reason, I equated earnest prayer with effort. I have no idea why I presumed speaking to God should require the same effort it took to get the lid off a jar of pickles. Had anyone asked me where God was, I would have said, 'God is everywhere.'

Everywhere — except the last few millimetres that I had to bridge by trying very, very hard.

When I was about seven years old, Tony and I used to play football with our friends outside our house in Manchester. One lad, a fair-haired, freckle-faced, generously fed child, was always in goal. I remember him for one reason only. He contorted his body into the most fantastic shapes in a futile attempt to stop the ball from slamming into the wall we used as a goal. While the ball bounced away, he always held whatever ridiculous pose he was in and looked at us in disbelief. It was as if to say, 'I don't know how the ball went past me. Just look how hard I was trying.' But, of course, we all knew he had no intention of trying to stop it. The ball was hard and stitched with leather, the kind of stitches that held Frankenstein's head onto his neck. It was hard, like a calf muscle, and he was soft and plump like a pudding. Nevertheless, he was so intent on looking like he was attempting to stop the ball that sometimes he ignored it altogether, and it slowly rolled past him.

Maybe, like him, I was trying too hard. I put so much effort into talking to God that I never actually listened for a reply. Would it come with a choir of angels? A deep voice? A blinding light? Or would it roll right by me, unnoticed, as I mumbled another Hail Mary?

I had no idea. All I knew was each morning, I woke up with Ballymun Comprehensive lurking at the far end of Summer, waiting for me. I'd cover my head and roll over, burying my face in my pillow, chasing sleep as it departed. I chased it as if it were a train, and I had somehow gotten off at the wrong stop. People in solitary confinement have been known to talk into the toilet bowl to hear another voice coming back at them. Prayer began to feel like that as I waited for God to get us out of the scheisse.

Saints and philosophers speak of the Silence that is God.

I must say that Silence wasn't the one I felt between God and myself. No — mine was the sort of awkward silence, like that of two strangers in a lift. Or a cafe beyond Ulundurpet with a peacock in the car park and no loo in the toilet.

***

The silence between the driver and myself is very uncomfortable. His limited English has been exhausted, and my — whatever his language is — is non-existent.

But I try again.

'Do you get many passengers who want to travel this far?'

The driver looks baffled. A smile slips into shyness, and he looks at the table, gathering his wits for a reply, and mumbles apologetically, 'My English is very small.'

Our attempts at polite conversation make the language barrier higher and wider. Each vowel is another brick. Every second syllable slaps the mortar thickly into any gap where the light of comprehension can shine through.

Finally, he points at me and asks, 'England?'

'Manchester', I reply, wondering if he's heard of it.

'Ah! Manchester United?'

'Yes! That's right. Alex Ferguson?'

'Georgie Best!'

'Eric Cantona?'

'Ryan Giggs.'

'Very excellent,' he says with a slight head wobble.

We settle into a silence that fits like an old pair of slippers. This shared thing between us seems to show that we don't need a religion, politics, philosophy or even hugs to break down the barriers. We just need to grunt in the same general direction, and everything will be okay. The driver finishes his drink, nods to me and leaves. He's walking in the direction of the non-toilet. I get my little notebook out from the thigh pocket of my shorts to record the day's events so far. Before we left England, I had decided to keep a diary, which became this book.

Lesley returns, trailing the scent of *Rive Gauche* and tobacco, the olfactory equivalent of smouldering passion and just —well, smouldering.

'How's the diary going?' she asks, sitting down. The chair scrapes along the floor as she pulls it in.

'Okay,' I say, sliding it over to her so she can look.

***

I didn't keep a diary in Ireland. I wanted the experience to go away. Having a record of it was the last thing I needed, and besides, life has a habit of leaving its marks all over you anyway. For many years, I had a small scar on my throat from when a man swung at me with a knife. As diary entries go, that might seem like it would have been a bad one, but it wasn't. I remember it as the only time a stranger tried to help in Ireland. I was walking down the street with Jason, our younger brother, who was, I think, seven years old. He was too young to go to school on his own. A middle-aged man passed us and shouted, 'Niggers!' He was wearing an oversized black coat which resembled something the Grim Reaper would have worn when originally auditioning for the job.

I put Jason behind me and shouted, 'What is wrong with you? You fucking idiot!'

The man snarled and came at me, flailing a clenched fist. I ducked and swung at him but missed, just as he had. At this point, a passing stranger called out in warning.

'He's got a knife!'

I stepped back as it cut the air on its way to my jugular. Without him, I may never have lived long enough to discover that I do not exist.

But wait — I'm getting ahead of myself again.

***

Back in the car now, and the cafe and the peacock are far behind us. We pass men, wiry and weary, sweating and straining, hacking into the road, which has been baked hard by the sun and compressed by the hot crush of endlessly rolling wheels. Slender women in saris, covered in dust, haul the debris away. None of them looks up as the driver honks and toots and blithely adds another layer of dust to their beautiful brown skin.

After many hours we reach the bridge across the Cauvery River on the outskirts of Trichy. The driver points through the windscreen to a hill that dominates the skyline. A fort has been built on the ancient feature, though it looks like it's grown out of the rock itself. On top of that is a temple crowning the structure. The temple complex is integrated into the fort, like war and peace in the affairs of man. Known to the locals as Malaikottai, it's more widely known as the Rock Fort.

'Ashram. Twenty — maybe thirty minutes,' the driver says.

He looks more relieved than we do. It's been a long journey. At the mouth of the bridge, we all get out of the car to enjoy the view. We walk a little way across the bridge to stretch our legs. The river itself is almost dry. Narrow ribbons of water run lazily by the banks, and we see men, backs glistening, washing dhotis. Colourful cotton squares have been laid out to dry on the hot boulders. The voices of those men flow beneath the bridge as if the river is muttering to itself. Behind us, a juggernaut rumbles past, rudely belching black smoke, a dyspeptic dragon of hot metal and rubber. Grit trickles a trail from its rear. I watch it cross the bridge and disappear down the road we came from, and I wonder how I got here. Once upon a time, I wouldn't cross the room to see the Pope, and now here I am, five thousand miles from home and looking for a Holy Hindu.

The driver calls out to us.

'Well, here we go,' I say to Lesley, gripped with eager anticipation. She quickly squeezes my hand, and we get back in the car. It coughs politely, the engine starts, and we roll forward, hungry tyres crunching crushed rock on hot macadam.

Halfway across the bridge, the driver stops the car and gets out.

One of the tyres is hissing like a Python.

***

The sun is low in the sky, and now we're part of the machinery that churns in the guts of Trichy. Traffic curdles and spreads and then eases like muscles flexing. Hot oil and polished chrome, dust and eye-watering pollution, rusting hinges and unhinged mystics mingle in the rush hour at the end of a very ordinary day in Trichy.

To the side of the road, an accident. A pulse of compassion goes out to the victim, but I'm glad we're driving away. I don't want to be touched by this sadness.

The evening is coming swiftly.

People rush in the gathering dusk.

City chaos, unfolding and collapsing in on itself

We follow the giant moon into the countryside, which swallows us.

And there, in the belly of the night, we see the light of the ashram, a warm glow that defies the cold indifference of the stars above us.

CHAPTER THREE
Something Sacred This Way Comes

The taxi swings off the rough stone road to the ashram and takes us through the open gates. The graceful arc of our headlights illuminates a line of trees leading to a cluster of huts. Bright pinpoints of light festoon the trees on which wires lazily loop through the limbs. On this electric wire, the glass buds of Christmas lights glow and twinkle through the leaves. The air is sweet and swollen with devotional songs. Each face we pass is little more than a pale blur softened by the risen moon.

We pass a large open-sided structure with hundreds of people sitting beneath a roof of thatched banana leaf. They're singing and clapping their hands, pushing the tempo and being drawn along with it. It's going so fast that it feels like it will fall over itself. Tambourines and small bells shake like birds shaking the rain off their feathers. The precise tap and thump of the *tabla* run through and around the legs of this communal devotion, bringing it home to the heart.

Small stones are rattling beneath our taxi, thrown up by the wheels until we slow down and roll to a halt outside a building with a flagpole outside of it. This, we discover, is the Prayer Hall which is why there's so much activity around it as devotees walk to and fro. We step out of the car into the warm evening air and briefly become the centre of attention as people look to see who we are. I feel self-conscious about being the object of attention, but they lose interest quickly and resume their conversations.

Being observed and then wholly ignored leaves me feeling lost and far from home. The devotional songs are for Shiva and the Divine Mother, not Jesus and the Virgin Mary. The Catholic God of my childhood must be shaking His head and wondering where He went wrong.

'What do we do now?' I ask, almost to myself, looking past the crowd and back down the road to where the large marquee is.

'I've no idea,' Lesley says. 'Will you pay the driver and thank him? I'll go and find out where we're staying.'

On cue, the driver puts our luggage at my feet. I thank him and pull a bundle of warm rupees from the money belt around my waist. I'm still not used to the money. It looks, feels and smells odd. Due to the exchange rate between sterling and domestic currency, I have what seems like an obscene amount of cash. The English have a slang term for money. They call it bread. What I have in my hand feels like a whole loaf. As I peel rupees off my stash, I feel like a high roller in Las Vegas.

Counting out the correct amount for the fare will take forever, so I extract a large handful of notes which I judge to be enough to pay the fare. I roll these into a smaller bundle. It's about the size a giant dung beetle could reasonably push around on a long walk. I pay the driver with this, and he nods graciously. Then, it occurs to me that I should tip him, so I take another bundle of rupees from the wad of notes in my hand and give this to the driver.

He smiles hugely before slipping back into a more humble demeanour.

His reaction has me thinking, 'damn! Just how much have I given him? Maybe I *should* have counted the money.'

The driver reaches into the car and pulls a document from the glove compartment.

'What is it?' I ask.

'Ressit.' he replies.

I'm confused. 'Press it? Press what?'

'Ressssit,' he says, enunciating with the precision of a man speaking to a Labrador that may be able to lip read.

I shrug. 'Sorry. I don't understand.'

'Ressss eat,' he says again. 'Please. For you, isn't it? Ressss eat for taxi.'

'For the taxi?'

'Yes.Yes. For taxi.'

'Hang on. Are you telling me you're giving me a receipt for the taxi? My God, how much money have I given you?'

'What? But — but, is fare.'

'I know. It might seem fair to you, but I don't want your car. That money I gave you was a tip. For you. And your family. Put your kids through college or something. So you keep the money *and* the car.'

Now he appears to be speechless. He's looking at me with his mouth slightly open. His head begins a little wiggling momentarily as if building up the impetus to reply, but then it subsides. His mouth closes, and he stands there, looking at me with — well, I'm not quite sure *what* the expression is.

And then I think —

'— oh, wait. You're giving me a receipt for paying the fare?'

His face lights up. 'Yes. Fare for taxi. Ressit.'

I laugh at myself and my misunderstanding as I wave

away the offer of a receipt.

'It's okay,' I say. 'I don't need one.'

'But —?

'Paul?'

I turn at the interruption. It's Lesley. Beside her, wearing a red sari, is Satya Mataji, a friend of Lesley's from a long time ago. They both look pleased to be in each other's company again. I've met Mataji, but only once, which was very briefly when Mataji passed through England.

'And how is Paul?' Mataji asks. I notice she's holding a torch.

'I'm fine,' I say. 'How is yourself?

'Fine. Thank you. Let me help with your bags.' She takes hold of one and begins leading us away. Lesley asks her to wait. She thanks the driver for looking after us, to which he waggles his head and smiles shyly.

I echo her sentiment, but the receipt in his hand pops up again at the sound of my voice.

'Okay. If it makes you happy, I'll take it.' I stuff it into a pocket and extend the other hand to shake his. Then, remembering this isn't quite the done thing as the right hand is used to wash one's bottom after going to the loo, should you find one, I wave instead and then hurry off after the ladies. Following them, I reflect on waving etiquette and wonder if, in India, the gesture is similar to saying 'goodbye, and incidentally, I wipe my ass with this hand.'

We only walk for a minute before we're away from the bright lights and in darkness. Mataji illuminates the path before us with her torch. Behind us, a devotional song, scented with incense, swells in the heart.

'When do we get to see Swami?' I ask. I've seen his picture and heard the stories about him, but I've never seen him in person. Lesley has, but me, never.

'Later,' she says. ' It's a hectic time of the year for all of us in the ashram. There are hundreds of people here now, but thousands will have passed through by the time the festival is over.

This is to be expected, as we've arrived during Shivaratri. It's one of the few religious festivals in the Hindu religious calendar, celebrated during the hours of darkness. This is symbolic of when darkness and ignorance are overcome with the help of Lord Shiva. Shiva burns up the 'God' of desire to liberate us from the agitation it creates within the mind. This agitation distorts our perception and confuses us. It even makes some people think we're a piece of meat, making noises at both ends for a few years before being buried or burned when the noise stops.

Without desire, the mind is still, and we begin to see our true self, the limitless, formless, unchanging self or the soul.

Shiva is represented in several ways. One of these is a Lingam, which is shaped like an egg and represents the formless aspect of Shiva. Artisans all over India make and sell lingams to sell to devotees. Nature will sometimes form one by using the wind, the rain, and the sun when it has a few thousand years to spare.

They also grow within Swami Premananda.

***

Lesley met Swami in 1984. I lived in Ireland then, so it was well before my path crossed hers. She'd heard about a saint visiting the United Kingdom and decided to pop along and have a look. So with a friend of hers, called Gina, they travelled from England to Wales. Oddly enough, Lesley had seen the meeting place while meditating but hadn't realised it was an actual place until that day when they arrived. This may have been Peculiar, but it was entirely in keeping with the tone of her life at that point. Both Lesley and Gina had been experiencing many things which could be viewed as spiritual or supernatural. Despite this, Gina was entirely unprepared for what happened next.

She recognised him.

He'd been walking through her dream life since she was a child. So to see this figure, who she assumed only existed in her sleep, was shocking. Indeed, it didn't take long for the two friends to realise they were in the presence of someone extraordinary. They continued to seek him out as he travelled around the country.

Driving back from seeing him, this time in London at a temple somewhere in Wimbledon, they were on the M1 motorway heading back to Manchester. Gina was sleeping, her seat reclined. Lesley was driving. She enjoyed this, particularly at night when it was quiet, and she had the road to herself, motoring along, chain-smoking and being followed by the August moon. Her window was open slightly to whip the smoke away. She was tired but content, or at least she was, until Swami Premananda stood in the middle of the road. No — not standing, but *floating* —ahead of the car, standing a few feet above the white lane line with his arms extended in blessing. He kept an exact distance, travelling eighty miles an hour while moving backwards.

Gripping the steering wheel in her left hand, she slowly reached over and gently shook Gina with the other.

All this time, Swami Premananda was there, chuckling away to himself.

'Wake — up,' Lesley urged with a deliberate calmness. She didn't wish to startle her passenger.

'Hmmmmm?'

'Wake up for a minute,' she repeated.

Her friend yawned. 'Are we nearly there?'

'No. Not quite — sit up, will you?'

Gina sat up and suddenly jumped in her seat.

'What! What is it?' Lesley asked, her panic spurred by Gina's.

Through her fingers clamped over her mouth, Gina said, 'You're not going to believe this.'

Oh — but she would.

'Swami's floating backwards in front of the car,' Gina said, pointing at the saint they had left behind in London several hours ago. If Gina had known she'd see him in two different places at the same time a few years later, she might not have been so surprised to see him flying backwards down the M1.

Yeah — Swami Premananda, not only was he a saint, but he also had a sense of humour.

***

Satya Mataji led us toward her koothi, a circular hut of baked earth with a concrete floor and a roof of coconut palm leaf. This is where she lives. Candlelight and shadow jostle each other as we enter. A statue of the Goddess *Meenakshi* stands on a small table to the left of the doorway. The shadows of her delicate hands move, choreographing the dance of light and darkness around us. Silvery light flickers upon her fingers. Garlands of fragrant flowers hang around her neck, and incense heavy like summer blossom fills the air.

Swami Premananda gave this beautiful statue to Mataji in 1992. To do this, he piled garlands of flowers and fluttered petals into Mataji's outstretched arms. The figure of Meenakshi appeared from God knows where, an abrupt heaviness in her arms beneath the pile of fragrant offerings.

Lesley whispers, 'Are you sure this is alright? I mean, us staying here. I feel as if we're intruding.'

It sounds weird because she's talking about imposing on a statue, but I feel the same way. Meenakshi has a presence that might be a trick of the mind, but —

Mataji smiles and says, 'I'm sure she won't mind. Besides, it was Swami himself who put you two in here. So you may as well make yourself at home.'

I look around. There isn't much else in the room. Against the wall is an old kitchen table that serves as a desk, a chair tucked under like a lamb suckling. An old wardrobe stands beside a simple cot bed. Until we get something similar, we'll be sleeping on the ground. I consciously avoid thinking about what things may skitter, scurry and crawl across it during the night.

Mataji takes us through a doorway to a small kitchen area where a few cooking things are neatly arranged. There's also a small gas burner and a couple of pots. A small fridge hums to itself. I walk over to it, hoping to find something effervescent and cold in a bottle with icy dewdrops slinking down the frosted glass.

I open the fridge door. The light doesn't come on, but I can see a few simple ingredients with which to cook. I close the door, and it gives a slight shudder as if it found my disappointment somewhat distasteful.

I notice we share the roof with another dwelling. A wall that is little more than head height separates the two humble homes. A single bulb hangs from a long flex directly above the wall. Feeble light glows from the bulb, which looks both plump and brittle.

The back door is open. I see moonlight on the trunk of a small banana tree. The large leaves look as if they are waiting to brush the heads of those who leave the koothi this way, as if the tree were an amateur phrenologist reading skull bumps. Mataji opens another door and shows us the bathroom and toilet. Unfortunately, the toilet is a hole in the ground, and the bathroom is a bucket and matching water butt. Oh — crap, I think. I was hoping for something better. Surely *somebody* in India has got an *actual* toilet. The cafe with the peacock in the car park had disappointed me, but I assumed the ashram would have modern, pristine bathrooms. This isn't good. In fact, awful. Granted, it's spotless, but I won't use it, and that's that. There'll be a modern hotel in Trichy, the city closest to the ashram. I'll go there.

'Make sure you keep the lid on the water butt,' Mataji says, lifting the lid so we can see it's two-thirds full of water.

'Why's that?' Lesley asks.

'It stops the snakes, lizards and frogs getting in it.'

Oh — great. I envision myself running through the ashram with my pants flapping around my ankles, being chased by a lizard, a frog on my head, and a boa constrictor tied in a neat bow around my balls.

'Right,' Mataji says, firmly replacing the lid, 'who wants a cup of tea?'

If you're English, tea is always a welcome and well-placed comma in the narrative of your life. It takes the edge off all sorts of tribulations. For instance, in 1773, when American rebels threw prodigious quantities of tea into the waters of Boston Harbour, the British reacted with alarm. What they should have done was add milk and sugar. Rather than having a revolution, the Americans would merely have felt somewhat refreshed after having the world's largest cup of tea.

Oh well, never mind.

***

***

Back in 1977, God was moving mysteriously in Ballymun within the awkward silence that followed my prayers, and I was disillusioned. I began to seriously wonder about the nature of God for the first time. Why was I being ignored?

I'd been a relatively well-behaved child. I didn't do the things that some other boys did, like pulling the legs off spiders. This wasn't just because insects gave me the heebie-jeebies, and I shuddered at the thought of actually handling one. I didn't want to inflict pain consciously. Sure, I'd kill spiders. I'd smack them hard with a shoe because anything with that many limbs would be up to no good. Obviously. Had someone told me about Shiva and all His arms, I would have advised smacking Him as well with the admonition that one can't be too careful.

But that was back then. That was when I lived in a concrete tower block, and I looked out at the world with my face pressed against a window that was too high for anyone to clean the outside. The people outside, down there, baffled me. Why did they have to be so hostile? I bore them no ill will, so I was at a loss as to why they seemed aggrieved at my existence. I was a peaceful child with a strong sense of fair play and without aggression toward any colour, creed or race — except perhaps the Germans.

Before arriving in Ballymun, like many of my generation in England, I spent a lot of time shooting imaginary Germans. In the 1970s, when the memory of the Second World War was vibrant in our blood, we re-enacted it in the playgrounds and our houses. The conflict was regularly replayed in the movies and television and retold in books and comics. I remember upwards of thirty children defending the sandpit in school during playtime, and it was nothing unusual. The Germans may have surrendered in 1945, but my war with them continued until 1974, and that was only because I started to feel very self-conscious about shouting 'Bang!'

I also discovered the war had ended thirty years ago. This information was a great shock when I read it on the back of a comic. Like Hiroo Onada, a Japanese soldier who surrendered in 1974, I was initially stunned. Without a doubt, the implications were far more significant for him than for me, but I was only eight years old. Also, I had only been pretending to shoot people, whereas he had done it for real.

Oops.

I couldn't imagine God holding any of this against me. After all, I didn't approve of actual violence. I'd never even been in a fight, except for one occasion when a girl threatened to punch me. I was eight. My reaction was to gallantly hold out my hand for her to shake in the spirit of peace and friendship.

'Boys don't hit girls,' I said.

She looked pretty pleased with this information and continued to do so as she enthusiastically slapped the face off me.

I didn't retaliate. I didn't even point my finger and go, 'Bang!'.

But when God repeatedly ignored me, I felt I had no choice but to cock my finger and point it at heaven.

— bang!

***

Our tea is hot and sweet. We sit on the floor listening to the sound of devotional songs being sung outside, and when we speak, we speak in whispers.

'Do we get to see Swami soon?' I whisper.

Mataji shakes her head. 'Later. He's in his koothi now.'

'And what about the lingams? When will they come?'

'It could be any time, but in the past, he's always left it until pretty late,' Mataji leans forward conspiratorially and beckons us closer.

We lean in.

Quietly, she asks, 'Why are we all whispering?'

We burst out laughing.

'It's the candlelight,' I say. 'It's like being in church.'

Candlelight can do that to me. It can bring back the feeling of intimacy and awe I had as a child, sitting in the house of God. I recall a stillness of breath and the sense of ancient secrets grinding together under the flagstones. The murmuring congregation and the priest holding up the Eucharist are all in my bones. I remember the shuffling of feet as people rose from their knees and the smell of soap and tobacco as the priest drew a cross on my forehead. He told me I came from dust, and to dust, I will return. The cross was made of ash from burnt palm leaves. As well as a reminder of mortality, it also represented grief. Grief that we sinned before the eyes of God and so were thrown out of the Garden of Eden.

There will be ash on the ashram over the next few days. This ash is called vibhuti, and like the lingam, it's closely associated with Shiva. This is because Shiva burned the God of desire into ash, removing the agitation that confuses the mind.

I think of vibhuti as the Hindu equivalent of holy water in that it's used to sanctify, but it's so much more than this. Vibhuti also has antiseptic qualities. This is counter-intuitive because one essential ingredient of vibhuti is cow dung. The cow *is* sacred in India, and the dung is purified by fire, hence the ash — but I still find the idea odd. Nonetheless, vibhuti has a delightful scent because prayer and incense are two constituent parts. Like holy water, it is a product of the priestly class.

However, the vibhuti Swami Premananda gives to his devotees is not a product of anything so mundane. Instead, that exudes out of the pores of his skin, sometimes at an alarming rate. At least, that's what I've been told. I've yet to see this happen for myself.

'What about the vibhuti?' I ask. 'Will it come tonight?'

Mataji shakes her head. 'No. It'll probably come three or

four days after the lingams.'

'It comes out of his skin?'

'Yes. Have you not seen any of the pictures?'

'Some, but they weren't very clear. Lesley's told me about it as well, of course. But I'm looking forward to seeing it for myself.'

Lesley adds. 'It's unnerving when you see Swami breathing, and he's got powder coming from his mouth, like a mist.'

Mataji says, 'I've watched him materialise things for years now, and you get used to it, but now and then, I'll just be left speechless. But Swami says, what's important isn't what we call miracles, but what is in here.' She places her hand on her heart.

'True,' I say. 'But I'd still like to see the vibhuti when it happens.'

'Well, he'll be standing in front of you, and it doesn't get much clearer than that.'

Despite my attempt not to do so, I yawn like a hippo.

'You two must be exhausted after your journey.' Mataji says. 'Get some rest while you can. You may be up all night waiting for the lingams to come. Probably best to take a shower as well.'

Lesley pats me on the knee. 'Go on, sweetheart. You go first. I want to catch up with Mataji.'

I stand and stretch and yawn again before leaving the girls to their quiet conversation. In the kitchen, I close the door behind me. I feel hot and weary. My t-shirt's stuck to my back, and I can taste salt on my upper lip. The thought of sluicing the dust and grit from the long day off my tired body is delicious. I undress quickly, leaving my clothes in the sort of pile that suggests I have vanished, and my clothes dropped where I stood.

I step into the shower, which is dark inside. The intense light of the moon puts the single naked electric bulb to shame. The moonlight comes through a small opening in the wall through which I can see a banana leaf. The soles of my feet prickle with the slightly rougher texture of the ground. I shiver at the drop in temperature. Closing the rickety shower door does nothing to change this. A draught comes through even though there isn't a breath of wind outside.

Tentatively, I lift the lid off the water butt and peer in, looking for snakes, lizards and frogs. Lions, tigers and bears, too. Without my clothes, I feel particularly vulnerable and wish I'd done this search before getting undressed. I see my reflection in the water, wide eyes set in a brown face, looking like someone looking for reptiles. Seeing nothing in the container that looks like it could swallow a mongoose, I put my hand in to test the water, which feels lovely. Warm and clean. A delicious sense of anticipation floods through me.

Whistling something suitably warm and tropical, I reach for the small bucket. With it firmly gripped in both my hands, I slowly submerge it. The warm liquid gently rises toward the lip of the water butt, lapping the sides, until it suddenly sloshes into the open mouth of the bucket. I chuckle. It feels so satisfying, and I smile, raising the bucket over my head and tip it —

My testicles shoot up and slam into my skull as a torrent of icy water cascades down my body.

'Jesus Christ!' I squawk, feeling my toes crunch as they dig into the wet ground.

'Are you okay in there?' Lesley calls from the other room. 'You made a sort of — squawking noise?'

I can't speak for a second or two until I wrench my breath back to where it belongs.

'I'm all right,' I croak, shivering, gripping the bucket so

hard it's warping.

Lesley enters the kitchen and closes the door behind her.

'You don't sound fine. What happened?'

'This bloody water is freezing!'

'Really? It shouldn't be. It's still hot out here.'

'Well, it isn't in here. Oh, bugger — my head hurts. I think my testicles may have hit something important on the way up.'

'Pardon?'

'Nothing. I've not brought in a towel. Can you pass one to me?'

She goes back to the other room and comes back. I step out into the rough embrace of a big towel and start drying myself off.

'Thanks.'

'You're welcome.' Lesley says, gathering up my clothes. She puts them into a cotton wash bag. She's also brought some fresh clothes for me to put on. It's a Punjabi suit that I bought in England. I step into the trousers, which feel odd because they're loose in all the wrong places.

'Do you feel any better?' Lesley asks, smiling.

'Yes. Much. But that water was a bit of a shock. I can't understand why the water was so cold. I tested it, and it felt fine.'

'I should have warned you. It was like that in Sri Lanka. It's something to do with the difference between your hand and your body's core temperature. You'll get used to it.'

***

In November 1984, Swami Premananda invited Lesley and Gina to stay with him in a devotee's house in Columbo, Sri Lanka. They were vaguely aware of a civil war unleashing the usual evils, but it didn't loom large when they made their plans to travel. After all, their invitation came from a saint who was, oddly enough, celebrating his birthday. What could go wrong? So, off they went, landing in Colombo wearing matching turquoise jumpsuits, like Patsy and Edina from Absolutely Fabulous. Seeing the heavy military presence at the airport was disturbing, especially as the soldiers had matching accessories, but they were designed to kill and maim. Needless to say, they were relieved to be picked up by Donald Wallace, one of Swami's devotees and taken to the relatively large house of the Sri- Lankan devotee.

Whilst staying in Colombo, they went off by train to visit a place called Bentota further down the coast for a few days. On their return, they took a rickshaw whose driver insisted he left them at the bottom of the road that led to the large house they were staying in. He refused to take them to the door and drove off quickly. As it was getting late in the evening and a considerable distance to walk, they set off, pulling their suitcases behind them.

For the first ten minutes, they happily chatted despite the strain of the luggage. Despite the setting sun, they weren't worried. The locals seemed quite friendly, even inviting the girls in. Then, pausing to wipe the sweat from their brows and shake their stinging hands, rubbed sore by the suitcase handles, they saw another person waving them over in the doorway of a house.

Lesley smiled back and waved as they moved along the street.

'They're very friendly, aren't they? That must be our fourth invitation in the past ten minutes.'

'They're a bit *too* friendly if you ask me,' Gina replied. 'I'm not stepping foot in any of these houses. Let's keep walking.'

Someone else beckoned, a dark stranger with white teeth

and wide eyes, and he looked scared.

Gina clutched her bag tighter. Lesley pulled her suitcase along a little faster.

'Is it just me, or do they all look worried?' Lesley asked.

'They *do* look worried. Something's not right here.'

An old lady, frantically beckoning from her doorway, finally convinced them to stop. So they went over to her.

'Hello,' Gina said.

'What are you doing?!' the woman asked.

'We're returning —'

The woman flapped her hands in front of them. 'Never mind what you are doing! They will shoot you if they see you.'

'What!? Who?'

'The soldiers! There is a curfew. It would be best if you got off the street. There's a civil war going on.'

This nugget of tourist information shook Lesley and Gina, as you can imagine. They'd been looking forward to a cup of tea and a slice of Swamiji's birthday cake. However, the thought of being gunned down made the latter seem less appealing, even if their desire for tea and wisdom remained firm. So, frightened but looking '*Absolutely Fabulous, darling,*' they continued to the devotee's house.

Off to see the wizard —

Looking out for Lions and Tamil Tigers and Government Bears with rifles. Despite the danger, they reached the house without further incident.

All's well that ends well.

***

Oh, my. All was not well. The towers of Ballymun stood mute with the mystery of why they were built. Immense, angular, and grey, the seven largest ones were a modern Stonehenge, an unnatural imposition on the horizon. One day, people will look back at them and wonder what unfathomable fuckwit built them. What sort of primitive mind thought it was a good idea to stack thousands of strangers on top of each, like odd shoes collected from the side of the road and gathered in boxes for disposal? Like bones waiting to be archived by a coroner's apprentice. Or unsolved crimes that gather dust as they remain forlorn and unsolved. In the concrete filing cabinet that was Connolly Tower, we'd been erratically filed and forgotten. Nobody had even bothered to file us away alphabetically.

Why build those damned towers? Was it to provide jobs for architects, builders, social workers, police officers and drug dealers? Or were they supposed to align with the pale light of a dying sun so that aged astronomers could read the future? Might they have been the architectural equivalent of chicken bones to be read by the wise or demented? I had no idea, but I was sure of one thing. They weren't built with the people who had to live in them in mind.

I also knew everything above our flat was a mystery because I didn't go there. During the night, I sometimes felt the pressure of what was above us, nine floors of untold stories, bearing down like inclement weather approaching. I also knew everything below our floor was a potential threat. Stepping into the lift was a fall from grace when it worked and sluggishly descended.

But home?

Home was safe.

Home was where we were fed and clothed and kept warm by our Ma. In return, we held our troubles to ourselves. What we were going through was something beyond her experience and ours. If we walked out with her, we were given immunity from verbal abuse, so she never saw what happened when we were outside on our own. However, she knew something was up because things started to change in Tony, her eldest boy. He was seventeen.

He rarely left the flat after the first few months. Instead, he spent a lot of time sitting in his room painting. It was as if the world had become such a hostile place, rejecting him so thoroughly, that he was *trying to appease it by caressing it with colour. He sat in front of a small canvas, smaller than the windows from which we peered. He stroked this with the smooth horsehair of a paintbrush, like a boy stroking a wounded animal.*

I have this image of us. Tony is painting, the smell of oil paint and cigarette smoke curdling in his room. Ma is cooking, making a stew, the delicious and comforting smell filling the house. Blondie's singing on the radio. Young Jason is in his room, bouncing up and down on the bed like it was a trampoline, and I'm standing by the front door, getting ready to go out. I'm going to the library. I needed my books, tickets, and a hardened carapace over my sense of self. What will this cost me? How much of my capacity for joy will be taken away from me to do this?

Whatever the cost, I always shrugged myself into my anorak and went out. I held my head up and made my face impassive or smiled. Both were meant to convey that I was impervious to the taunts, insults, and scornful laughter, but my abdomen was locked tight like a fist, holding in my despair and tumourous, cold anger. These people who mocked me will be the little fuckers with whom I'd have to go to school. The adults who scorned me would be the god-damned teachers.

So, as bad as it was, I hoped the Summer would never end.

***

Sleep.

I tried.

The candles have gone out. Mataji is breathing softly on her bed. Lesley's on the floor, sleeping on a mat, and I'm beside her on another. The room's dark now that the electric light is cold. I don't know how long it's been since we fell asleep. Time has become fluid, bubblegum melting, sweetly stretched. I drift, carried along on a stream of consciousness. Unknown to all but God, I slip into unconsciousness.

Further downstream, my consciousness breaks the surface

once more. Images flow into ideas, rolling over like dolphins, becoming emotion, surging into tumultuous feelings, becoming driftwood in the stillness behind the mind.

Listen, heart.

Hear devotional songs, alive with drums pounding for muscle and bells shaking for flight.

Closer, much closer, breath, soft, rhythmic, reassuring.

I also hear —

Something moving?

Suddenly awake, I peer up at the strips of woven bamboo leaves that make up the roof supported by thick tree limbs, still enclosed in the bark. The noise again, rustling — I hold my breath, alarmed, picturing a giant lizard. Rodents don't bother me, but I'm concerned it might freak Lesley out. Hopefully, she won't hear it in her sleep.

'Can you hear something?' she whispers.

So much for that.

Calmly, I say, 'It's just a bird. Don't worry about it.'

She remains silent. The music outside stops.

Another rustle. A prolonged, rather loud rustle, like a sack being dragged through a hedge.

Lesley asks, 'What kind of bird has got four legs?

'Two ducks. Go back to sleep.'

'Hmmm. I'm not convinced, but — okay. Two ducks it is.'

She nods off, slipping easily into gentle breathing. I remain where I am until long after the rustling stops. Then, quietly, I creep out to the veranda into the moon's luminescence, which bathes everything I can see. Soft yellow light from candles flickers in the doorways of other humble dwellings. I stoop and take my sandals off. The earth is warm and intimate beneath my feet. I'm calm and at peace but intrigued by the peculiar atmosphere.

It's as if the world is waiting to exhale.

The devotional songs begin again, drawing me toward the heart from whence it came. I walk toward the large open-sided hut we passed in the taxi earlier this beautiful evening. Hundreds of people have gathered, singing songs that feel poignant with longing for the sacred. I watch beneath a palm tree in shadow, content to stay on the periphery, feeling invisible. When, at last, I look up between the large leaves of my sheltering, up into the firmament, there are thousands of stars.

Light in the eyes of the Beloved.

***

Sri Lanka, November 1984

Lesley and Gina eventually found Swami Premananda in Colombo and celebrated his birthday with his family and some of his devotees. Many of these were from England. Two couples lived in London, Stephen and Adrienne and Donald and Linda. There was also a couple from Birmingham, Naren and Rekha.

Interestingly, Swami was as joyful as a child in the morning, beautiful like Krishna, laughing and playful, but as wise as the oldest sage by the evening. With the threat of violence all around him, he kept them safe. He embodied peace at a time when many howled for blood. Everything he did, was for other people. He took nothing for himself, and everything given to him, he gave away.

The ashram in Matale, which Swami had founded in 1972, had been burned down during the internecine rioting in Sri Lanka in 1983. As someone who advocated peace and unity,

Swami was an obvious target. It meant great hardship for Swami, his family, and his devotees. They took shelter where they could, and sometimes it was less than salubrious. Lesley recalled one place they stayed on their brief visit to Sri Lanka, where cockroaches scurried up the walls and along the ground with their black, angular legs of spiky jiggery-pokery. On another occasion during their visit to Bentota, Lesley and Gina accepted a lift in a canoe from two piratical-looking men to visit an ancient Buddhist temple in a mangrove swamp. Then, the monsoon broke with comical but potentially fatal consequences, and a deluge of rainwater threatened to sink them. The men handed them empty pots and urged them to bail out the water quickly. The water outside the canoe was rising as fast as the water outside.

It was frightening at times, but it was worth it to have experienced the love of the *'Mae de Deus'*, a sublime impersonal love that emanated from Swami Premananda. It was in his eyes like warm honey pouring into one's broken heart. It forgave all you had done. It knew all you had endured, and if grief, shame, or anger came sobbing into the light, that sense of something sacred washed these things away with the salt of your warm tears.

***

I open my eyes. It's pitch black, and Lesley's shaking my arm.

'Paul, wake up.'

'What is it?'

'Mataji's outside waiting for us. It's time to go.'

I sit up, rub my eyes and look around. Slowly the light of the moon reveals the open doorway as my eyes adjust.

'Okay,' I say, getting to my feet. 'What time is it?'

'8.30 pm. Here, take a sip of this.'

'What is it?'

'Some tea. It's hot, so be careful.'

Grateful, I take the tin mug and sip tentatively.

'Thanks. Lovely, that.'

'You're welcome. Okay, let's go. Don't forget your camera. Oh — and Mataji's given us some cushions to sit on. Yours is by the door, so grab it on the way out.'

Mataji leads us to the large hut with the banana leaf roof, where hundreds sing in unison and clap along. We're joined by Adrienne, who Lesley first met in Sri Lanka with Gina. She'll be staying in Mataji's koothi as well. She's walking ahead of us, just behind Mataji. Lesley and I hold hands for as brief a time as it takes for the heart to thump a dozen heartbeats before giving a little squeeze and letting go.

'I can't believe we're here,' Lesley says.

'Me neither. It's magical.'

'Isn't it. I'm a bit worried, though. It's been ten years since I last saw Swami in Sri Lanka.

'What are you worried about?' I ask, surprised to hear her say this.

'It's silly, I know, but what if he doesn't recognise me? He's such an important part of my life, but it's a long time—.'

'What?' I shout as her voice is drowned out by the singing, suddenly surging forward into a louder, faster tempo. The tabla are doing their best to catch up.

We see Mataji and Adrienne step out of their sandals. We remove ours and leave them beside an honest-looking tree. The soft grass prickles and whispers beneath our bare feet as we walk to the crowd's edge and wait for the singing to abate.

'I'm afraid you two will have to split up,' Mataji says,' Paul, you go over there to the left where all the men are. Lesley, you and Adrienne must sit with the ladies over on the right.'

I feel cheated. Lesley and I have come so far together that it doesn't seem right that we can't share this experience sitting side by side. She disappears into the crowd. I turn toward the stage at the front of the marquee. I can see it from where I stand because people mainly sit on the ground, but I want to get closer to the stage. It seems pretty impossible with so many people tightly wedged in the way. When Swami turns up, I'll have to observe him from this far away.

Whoa—

Strong, warm hands on either side of me take my arms and pull me forward. Two men are virtually lifting me off my feet.

'Wait—'

One of the men says, 'The Mataji, she told me you must go to the forward, isn't it? Very good seat we give you. No problem.'

They leave me standing close to the stage, balancing like a heron among the devotees. I smile apologetically at my neighbours and sit down, wedging myself like an extra marshmallow in a candy box. I'm still holding my cushion, so, smiling apologetically again, I have to press against the strangers to give myself enough leverage to push it under my bottom. I look like I'm competing in a cushion rodeo for a few seconds as I wriggle about to get comfortable.

When I finally settle and look around, I feel like I'm in a sea of people. Heads bob up and down, and voices wash over me like waves on a beach. To my right, on a rocking chair, there's an old gentleman, a white man frosted with silver hair. His face is kind. Slender glasses give him a thoughtful look, and in his arms, a child rests his head on the old man's shoulder. Thin arms loop lazily around the aged neck. The child observes everything, eyes taking it all in until their eyelids slowly close.

I look to my left. An Indian gentleman smiles at me, nodding his head as he claps and sings lustily along with the bhajans. His voice and all the others are bouncing off the bamboo leaf roof. I clap along and let it carry me forward into the night. It seems to go on for hours. On and on we go until my legs are aching and my palms are tenderised from clapping. My throat becomes dry and cracked from singing, but I can live with all this. What I can't accept is the very uncomfortable, contradictory mingling of numbness and pain emanating from my arse. I look at my watch more as a distraction than through any genuine desire to know what time it is. A little more than one hour has passed. Oh, Lord. What will the pain be like if this goes on much longer? The cushion I'm sitting on feels like a small bag of cement. I have to shift position every few minutes, but it becomes excruciating.

The appeal given by Jesus during the Sermon on the Mount comes to mind.

Turn the other cheek.

***

A few words of misplaced and unwanted advice came from the doorway of one of the eight-storey blocks.

'Hey! Niggers! Fuck off back to Africa.'

'Just ignore them,' I said to Tony. It was dark, and the night soft with a cold drizzle. We couldn't see who was shouting at us. Not in that poor light. Not where they were standing, in the shadowy open mouth that led into the block's foyer. But we could hear them laughing like hyenas.

Tony stopped. It took me by surprise. I turned to look at him, and his eyes met mine.

'Fuck it,' he said, turning toward the pack. The orange tip of the

cigarette he had been smoking waved back and forth as he sprinted away from me.

'Whoa!' I called after him as if he was a runaway horse. He galloped on, and I pounded after him.

The laughing hyenas stopped laughing. I could see the dark figures scrambling over each other, trying to escape. Tony slowed down and turned back to me, gasping for air.

'That was nuts,' I said, laughing. 'But did you see those idiots run?'

He nodded and took a last look at where they'd been.

'Let's go,' he said.

I fell into step beside him, proud of my big brother. My legs were shaking, and my heart was thumping, but I felt like I was walking beside Mohammed Ali.

From behind us, the laughter resumed from the shadows.

A chant, the lullaby of the lynch mob, stalked us.

'Nigger. Nigger. Nigger'

Tony flicked his cigarette into the wet grass.

Like a snake, it hissed before its light went out.

***

The devotees are no longer singing. They are, instead, doing the usual things familiar to crowds all over the world. Coughing, yawning and sneezing, scratching and looking around, talking and waving to people they know. From where I sit, I can see Lesley and Adrienne, so I do a little waving myself. On stage, a gentleman holds up his hand for silence. Someone behind me is shushing his neighbours, urging them to listen.

'The Doctor is announcing the Swami. Be quiet!'

I look at the man on stage, who I now know is a medical professional thanks to my neighbour's pronouncement. Then, presuming Swami Premananda will arrive soon, I get on my knees to improve my field of view and ease the pain in my bottom.

Where is Swami?

I look among the crowd standing just outside the marquee. Like most Tamils, Swami Premananda is relatively small, but unlike his countrymen, he's got an afro, so I'm looking for that. I expect to see it moving along among the people like the dorsal fin of a dolphin.

Many people are now quietening the crowd by hushing each other.

The Doctor on stage taps the microphone and blows into it. The accompanying loud 'whump!' of breath makes me wince. He clears his throat by 'harrumphing', then waggles his head a little. He indicates toward the microphone with an open hand while looking off-stage. Someone calls out instructions or confirmation, and he holds his hand up to show he understands.

The Doctor taps the mike lightly, and it 'thuds' hugely from the speakers, waking the child snuggled into the warm neck of the old man with silver hair. The child looks around sleepily before laying his head back down.

One more cough, one more definitive, emphatic throat clearing from The Doctor and he is ready to speak. I should think so too. The only way he could clear his throat more thoroughly would be to pull his trachea out and run it through with a pipe cleaner.

***

Before I met Lesley, I began reading a book by Howard Murphet. It was about an Indian 'saint' called Sai Baba. Fascinated but sceptical, I read accounts of people miraculously healed by Baba and many impressive stories of devotees being positively transformed through his benevolent influence. I can't say I liked the look of Sai Baba, but something about what I was reading resonated deep within me. For a little while, the flickering light of hope grew. Could it be that people like him walk among us? Is the human race seeded with these divine souls guiding us back to sanity?

It was a reassuring possibility, but then I thought, 'Who is this person writing such a book? Why should I take his word about anything?' I wanted to believe what I was reading but wouldn't let that desire lull me into believing just anything. The more I read, the more sceptical I became until I was mildly contemptuous of the author and the level of gullibility he assumed in his readers. Where is the proof? Any idiot can make stories about miracles and divine manifestations and materialising sacred objects, and what's this?

Sai Baba's got scented powder coming from his fingertips.

Yeah, right.

What kind of a dick-head will believe anything like that?

Halfway through the book, I stopped. I looked at the picture of Sai Baba on the front and said the following:

'If people like you exist and things like this happen, I want to see for myself. If this is true, then I want to know. But if it's a lie, I'm not going to waste my time with it.'

I tossed the book about Sai Baba over my shoulder.

***

On stage, The Doctor speaks in Tamil. I've no idea what he's saying. I want him to get on with it and then get off. I'm still hoping he's introducing Swami Premananda and hoping it's soon because my arse is hurting so much I can hardly bear it.

I look around at my neighbours. None of them seems to be experiencing the pain I'm trying to endure. They must have buns of steel. Most are smiling, excited at the prospect of what is to come. Others are waiting patiently or straining forward for a better view, their heads bobbing up and down and around, trying to see past those in front of them. A few have the eagerness of greyhounds in their expressions. Others, like the old man near me, have none of this. Instead, he looks to be quietly contemplating. People are praying, singing devotional songs, or silently meditating all around me. So much devotion and piety, and here I am thinking, my arse *really* hurts.

After ages, The Doctor finishes and steps down from the stage, followed by a smattering of polite applause. I crane my neck, looking for Swami, but I don't see him. Instead, I hear the jingle of bells. Four of the young girls who live in the Ashram come on stage. They perform an intricate traditional dance, bells jingling on their wrists, bare feet thudding on the wooden floor. It's very charming. I look over to where Lesley's sitting. She smiles at me, tilting her head as if she were laying it on my shoulder.

I wave to her.

***

After the dancing, a band sets up on stage. According to one of the people sitting nearby, they're excellent. I don't know how he can tell. The noise crashing out of the speakers is rattling my teeth. All the band members sit cross-legged with their instruments on their laps, which looks quite odd as the music's lively. Their heads are waggling metronomes, and their hands and fingers are possibly about to burst into flames with the speed of their plucking, banging, tapping and strumming, yet they're utterly still below the waist. It looks like someone gave them an epidural before they came on stage, and it's working well. The singer, in particular, gets my attention. He's got one finger jammed in his ear so he can hear himself above the noise. I'm tempted to put both of mine in mine, so I can't. It's *way* too loud, and the genuine passion he's singing with is making my head hurt.

***

About eighteen months before coming to India, I was in the flat of a young man called Thomas. He played the guitar, and I played bass, so with the usual optimism of musicians worldwide, we decided to have a jam session. The one-in-a-billion chance that this cross-pollination of styles would yield fame and fortune had us grabbing a few bottles of beer and heading up to his flat. It was a very short-lived acquaintance, but I owe him this. He was the one who first told me about Swami Premananda. Thomas had a photograph of the saint on a coffee table. But, of course, I had no idea at the time who the smiling figure in the red robe with the afro was.

'Who's that?' I asked.

Thomas said, 'That's my guru.'

'Your what?'

'My guru. You know, like — he's my teacher.'

I must have looked dubious because he felt the need to explain more.

'He's a great saint. He's helped me with things, man.'

'Yeah?'

'Sure. Here, look— '

He reached behind the picture and took out a little oblong thing, a pinkish wad of paper that had been neatly folded. 'This is from him.'

He carefully opened the packet, and I saw some grey powder in it.

'You want some?'

I held my hand up to ward it off. 'No. I don't do drugs, mate.'

He laughed. 'It's not what you think it is. This is vibhuti. I put some on my forehead when I try to meditate.'

I wasn't too sure what to say. This was like saying I rub powder on my elbows when I try to concentrate. Of course, it's rude to call someone an idiot to their face, but that didn't stop me from thinking about it.

Wait a minute — vibhuti? That word sounded familiar, and then I remembered where I'd seen it. Vibhuti was mentioned in the book about Sai Baba, and I'd told Baba that I didn't want to just read about saints. I wanted to meet one.

'It sounds crazy,' Thomas said as if hearing himself for the first time. 'But it's true. He heals people.'

'Oh — that's nice. Does this Swami bloke have a practice over here? Like a treatment room or something?"

'No, man. He's in India. And I don't mean he's like a doctor or something like that. I mean, he heals them, like Jesus.'

I was too polite to point out Jesus didn't exist except as the corporate logo of the Catholic Church. I'd stopped believing in Jesus back in Ireland shortly after I'd begun to question the motives of his Dad.

'You have to meet my friend, Lesley. She's the one who told me about him.'

And she's obviously, quite mad, I thought. But I *was* intrigued, despite my scepticism. The mention of vibhuti coming so close after reading about it in the Sai Baba book was interesting enough to get my attention. So, I agreed to meet Lesley. Oddly, I couldn't get her out of my mind. Inadvertently, I began to use her name when speaking to other women. The desire to meet her was a constant undertone, like a phone ringing in the distance, like I just *had* to meet her, and then there she was.

A couple of weeks later, she was sitting in a comfortable armchair, cigarette held between two slender fingers, smoke lazily rising like something trained by a snake charmer. Her eyes kept a warm smile. She didn't look at all mad, guru or not.

'Hi,' I said, feeling my eyes smiling and brim full of warmth for her.

And then, as if by magic, we were sitting in a marquee looking at each other, waiting on Swami Premananda.

***

A lady of a certain age graces the stage now. She's singing something spiritual, but I'm too uncomfortable to appreciate it. We've been waiting for hours. I want to get up and walk about, but I won't. I don't want to miss anything, so I accept the pain with an effort of will. I manage to further diminish my discomfort by throwing myself wholeheartedly into appreciating the vocal performance of the lady on stage. I do this to such a degree that when she reaches her dénouement and puts her hand on her heart with a demure waggle of her head, I clap along like a demented seal. I would have been only mildly surprised if I had been hit in the face with a cold, wet fish.

***

So, I told Sai Baba I was not interested in reading about Holy men, strange tales of vibhuti, miracles, and manifestations. If things like this exist, I want to see them with my own eyes. Shortly after, I see a picture of Swami Premananda and am introduced to Lesley. She wasn't a saint, but she certainly knew one. Through her, it became easy for me to believe in miracles.

Is sacred ash tumbling from his fingertips?

Why not?

Anything is possible.

I began to think of myself as a devotee of Swami Premananda. Then it gradually dawned on me that I didn't — or rather, *couldn't* believe in him. How could I? I'd never met him. Whatever faith I had in Swami Premananda was actually faith in Lesley. She thought he was a saint, and I believed in her intelligence, integrity and intuition. So I talked of Swami Premananda like she did, but the words were only on my lips because they were on hers.

***

I feel like an imposter because I'm not like everyone here. They're devotees of Swami Premananda, but I'm not. I'm sitting here with the ghost of the boy from Ballymun who listened in vain for God to reply to his prayers. He wanders in the empty architecture of my bones, a lonely figure lost in the dead and compressed layers of my history. He's curled up in the pit of my stomach, sleeping in the wound in my heart, and he warns me not to be fooled into thinking there is a God who cares.

Minutes tick by into hours, and the hours pace the earth restlessly. The night goes on and on.

I've got the oddest feeling.

I feel a Presence

It's coming this way.

I turn to look over my left shoulder. I can't see Swami

Premananda, but I know he's there. It's impossible to see past the devotees thickly pressed together before me, but I can feel an energy coming from beyond them. The word now comes, passed through the crowd like a surge of electricity. *'Swami is here.'* The singing grows louder, more urgent, almost falling over itself with longing for the sacred. I look at the stage. Many of the children who live in the Ashram are there, singing. Most are relaxed. A few look bashful. One is wholly consumed by the words she sings. Her face is held up towards the heavens as if thirsting for water, and hundreds of voices join in this songful prayer. The clamour is growing and waning, swelling and falling. As beautiful as it is, this song is not graceful but heavy, like a mother's belly, clumsy with its weight. Clapping hands, hold it up and push it forward.

I still can't see Swami Premananda, but his presence surges through the crowd. I can feel him approaching, walking through the dense crowd toward the stage. Heads are craning around, trying to catch a glimpse of him, and there's something in the air like the moment between a flash of light and the rumble of thunder. The moment dissolves into something timeless, an ever-expectant moment through which history passes unnoticed.

No!

I recoil from this.

I will *not* be drawn into this, and I *will* judge it dispassionately. I shall not be carried along in the arms of other people's excitement. My rational mind will observe Swami Premananda and —

— *my heart is beginning to melt.*

I resist. I set my jaw firmly and grip my mind like a fist. Do something — camera! Where's my camera? I pick it up and steady it.

I will not be swept away.

The camera flashes, whirring once, twice, three times, and I stop, tears from my left eye streaming down my face because —

— my heart knows this.

I'm in the presence of something sacred.

I'm struck dumb.

My silence amid the noise deepens as I see his bushy hair moving through the crowd. Then, rising out of the people surrounding him, he walks onto the stage.

Swami Premananda, red-robed, exuding love and compassion, looks out upon his devotees.

My intellect offers no shelter from this light, only shadows.

I weep in His Presence.

How to explain —?

The breath of life blows through me. It sings an old familiar refrain, but not from memory. The song has no history but is only ever sung in the *now*. It's supernatural but also the most natural thing, and I am lost before it, and gladly so. I'm deeply touched by something I don't understand but accept.

Love

Simple

Garlands of fragrant flowers are placed around Swami Premananda, and he sits in a wooden chair. He's looking at us, and I am shocked to see the expression on his face. He's suffering. Christ. This is *not* what I expected. I'd imagined Swami would turn up and be a beatific figure, a gentle lamb holding his arms out in blessing, but this is not that. Instead, this is a raw, exposed nerve of spiritual power coming from someone who looks very human in the severity of his discomfort. And yet, the love radiating from that figure up there is overpowering.

Within him, the lingams are moving. I hadn't imagined this would be painful for him, but it is. Look at his eyes. I can see the pain — but also compassion for me as if he understands what made me who I am. He turns his head in my direction, and I feel him look at me, into me, and through me like a light shining through the darkness.

The Silence within me recognises this.

The uncommon miracle's first lingam falls from his mouth into a cloth on his left hand.

I'm shocked. Stunned, I witness the pain of this birth over and over. One after the other, for hours in which time contracts and dilates, something sacred happens while the world holds me suspended in mute incomprehension.

He's the one in pain. His discomfort is obvious, yet waves of love and compassion flow from him.

He holds each lingam above his head for us to see.

The world is spinning, the hands clapping, the voices singing, cameras flashing —

Swami Premananda calls his mother, who is nearby. She goes to him and holds her child's hand, and I think of Jesus Christ and His Mother, seeing that relationship through new eyes. We see the nails that pierced His hands and feet but forget that while it was His Body, it was Her Heart.

Swami begins to sing. His voice is ragged but strong, like frayed cordage. He rasps a song of devotion as tears flow from my right eye. I think how odd it is to cry from only one eye at a time. Later, when I weep for myself and those I love, the tears flow only from my left eye. But no matter which eye the tears stream from, they come from the same place. The waves of compassion coming from Swami Premananda reach down into the well of my sorrows and draw them up toward the light.

I don't know how long this lasts, but eventually, people

are called forward for a blessing.

I get to my feet and, barefoot, carefully walk through the crowd to where Lesley's sitting. I kneel behind her, placing my arms around her shoulders. She leans back against me. The display of obvious affection isn't something we usually do in public, being quite modest in such matters, but this is far from a typical night. I feel all of us have shared something more intimate than the comforting warmth of a loved one. Of course, I'm assuming everyone had a similar experience because it felt so overpowering, but it's more likely each person had an experience unique to them. For some, it may even have been quite ordinary, but my world has been shaken. I wonder how Lesley is.

She says, 'I'm exhausted, but I feel wonderful,'

I see Mataji gesturing for us to come forward toward the stage.

'What's she saying?' I ask.

'Go forward,' Lesley replies. 'She wants us to go to the stage.'

I help Lesley to her feet. I'd much rather sit back down to observe whatever happens next and process what I just experienced. But, feeling I should go forward, I follow Lesley threading her way through the little warm hummocks of people singing and praying. I can't look at Swami Premananda as we get closer because I don't want to stand on anyone. When we're clear of the crowd and go up the few steps to the stage, we have to kneel, so I still can't look at him properly. Instead, I'm looking at his brown feet peeking from his red robes. Saints have ordinary toes. The hard knot of the uncommon miracle, the lingam, is on my head now and is being held there firmly. By the time my mind grasps at this moment, it's already gone.

We move on, and others take our place as we leave the

hut's noise and energy.

I feel raw, emotionally.

Unable to speak, I sit with Lesley on a small bank by the honest tree where our sandals still wait for us.

The sun has risen.

Morning is yawning, and we need a cup of tea.

***

Sunlight spills through the window slats of the koothi. We sit on the floor, munching digestive biscuits and sipping sweet tea. The mind wanders back through the night, tiptoeing through the experience, unsure what to make of it. We don't spend too much time discussing what happened during the night. In my case, this is because I don't know what to say. The experience was so completely removed from my everyday life that I can't yet explain it to myself, let alone another person. There's also the feeling that it was so intimate that to discuss it in front of other people will somehow sully it.

After a long time in this peaceful silence, Mataji asks if I managed to get any good pictures.

'I'm not sure,' I say, speaking from behind a mouthful of crumbs. 'I found it hard to take pictures while Swami was in pain.'

Lesley says, 'Poor thing must have been in agony. Did you see the size of the lingams?'

'Yeah,' I say, feeling reverence and awe, which lasts until a lump of digestive plops into my tea. Normally, I'd consider this a disaster, but in light of recent events, the fact that my tea will now have a disgusting sludge lurking at the bottom of the cup is less traumatic than usual. I watch it swirl and come apart. The universe is unravelling in my teacup—the entropic dance of life. Putting my cup down, I yawn mightily.

'I've got to put my head down,' I say, lifting my heavy eyelids to look at Lesley and Mataji.

'Don't let us keep you awake,' Lesley says. 'I'm going to finish this tea, have a cigarette outside the Ashram gate and then I'll be off to sleep too.'

I nod.

Mataji concurs. 'It's been a long night. Sleep well, Both of you.'

I crawl over to my mat and lie down with a long, deep sigh. Then, I roll over and off the edge of consciousness into my absence.

CHAPTER FOUR

In The Cradle of Myself, I sleep

Mataji wakes us up. I groan, unhappy with being disturbed. I feel like I've only just closed my eyes. I can hear Lesley stirring sleepily. There's another voice as well. I lift my head and see Adrienne sitting on a yoga mat. She said she would join us in the koothi, so she must have done so while I was sleeping.

Mataji's saying, 'We must go to the prayer hall.'
'What's the rush?' I ask.
'Swami is giving a lingam blessing.'
Adrienne says, 'I've just come from there. If I were you, I'd bring a cushion because you might have to wait a while.'

***

Hundreds of abandoned sandals are outside the Prayer Hall, waiting for their owners. Very few have been neatly placed. Most look like they have been removed midway through the owner's cartwheeling past. Lesley takes hold of my arm for balance and removes hers. As she does this, she looks past the Prayer Hall to where the large open-sided marquee hut still stands. It's empty now. Some devotees are dismantling the roof.

Mataji says, 'It'll be gone by this evening.'

'It's quite sad when you think about it,' I say, observing the activity.

'What is?' Lesley asks.

'I can think of loads of people who need to experience something like we did there last night. Something to get them out of the mental rut they're in.'

'I used to think that way, but seeing Swami bringing up a lingam isn't for everyone.'

'Well, I'm not surprised when you say it like that. You make it sound like a fur ball.'

Lesley places her sandals neatly together as we laugh. I waggle mine off my feet, and they plop onto hers. She rearranges both pairs so they sit tidily in tandem.

'Furball or not, 'I say, 'seeing something like that is such a shock to the system it might show some people there's more to life than they think. It could take the blindfold off.'

'Oh, I don't know. Some people want to believe there *isn't* more to life than what they can see or touch. Or what they've been told. It's a source of comfort for them.'

'Yeah. I suppose so. I wish I could have my family here at least.'

'They might not have gotten anything out of it. Not like you did. I think you have to be ready for it.'

The night appeared briefly in my mind. 'Actually, I'm not sure I was ready for it myself. I've not even figured out what I experienced. It was incredible, but — what exactly does it mean?'

'It doesn't have to mean anything.'

'I know that, ' I say, and then contradict myself by adding, 'but it *does* mean something. Because of last night, everything is different even though everything on the surface is the same.'

Mataji laughs. 'Good luck explaining *that* one to friends and family. Come on. We better go inside.'

Lesley and I follow along, picking our way across the footwear.

She says, 'If you think last night was hard to get your head around, wait until you see what happens when the vibhuti comes. The way it pours from his skin is something else.'

Mataji calls over her shoulder. 'That won't happen for a few days.'

'Good. I need a break from anything weird to get my equilibrium back.'

'Or possibly, your blindfold?'

'Yeah,' I say, smiling, 'maybe even that.'

The Prayer Hall, long and wide, is filled with devotees. The scent of flowers and incense perfumes the air. The pale blue walls are adorned with portraits and photographs of saints. At the far end is the wooden chair Swami sat in to produce the lingams. It's empty now. Swami isn't here yet, so I sit on the left with the men while Lesley joins the women on the right.

Looking at the pictures and prints and paintings, I think about my mother and a picture she had of Jesus with his hand on his heart. She keeps it in the hallway. His heart is exposed and bleeding. I'm so used to seeing that particular image that the visceral nature of it has been lost to me until now. It conveys a sense of my suffering being his. But this image also has a sense of peace, as if these things will pass.

I had long ago dismissed Ma's belief in Jesus Christ because I considered Jesus a lie imposed on the world by a morally bankrupt church and resurrected by Hollywood.

They put flesh on the bones and turned Jesus into a beautiful hippie, but if someone like Swami exists, why not Jesus?

***

Ma couldn't understand why I turned my back on the church. I was, after all, raised a catholic, and she took it as a personal failure on her part that I strayed away from the flock. It was more accurate to say I didn't so much stray as run in the opposite direction.

'Why won't you come to Mass?'

I rolled my eyes heavenward from behind the comic I was reading. It was a question Ma had asked many times since we moved to Ballymun.

'Because, Ma, God doesn't exist. It's all made up.'

'Well, if God doesn't exist, how do you explain Jesus the Son of God.'

'Christ,' I muttered.

'What's that? Take that comic away from your face when I'm talking to you!'

I put the comic down. 'I can't explain Jesus, Ma. Maybe he's an orphan? I don't know, but I'm not going to Mass.'

Ma shook her head. 'Well, I won't force you. Any of you. You or Tony. I just pray you'll see the error of your ways and return to God's church.'

She took Jason by the hand and led him out the door. Before Jason disappeared, he turned around and stuck his tongue out at me. As an argument, it made far more sense than the one Ma had used. I'd stopped going to Mass months ago, but now and then, she felt the need to remind us that we ought to go because that was what God wanted.

My view of this was that God could fuck right off.

Or, if you like, I chose to flock off because I could no longer be part of that particular herd of sheep.

I'd given up on God not just because my prayers were ignored but because everyone's prayers were ignored. I saw the world on the news and knew my troubles were a drop in the ocean, but so what? God could move mountains. All I wanted was a removal van and a new address. It wasn't like I was asking to go on a Witness Protection programme like, say — Judas. I just wanted people to stop calling me 'nigger' and desist from occasionally throwing things at me. It seemed like such a simple thing for an omnipotent God to do, but He plainly didn't think so. What seemed like a rather callous lack of interest in my troubles made me want to know more about God. Not in the way someone who loves God desires to find out more. No. It was more about someone who has a serious complaint about the service and wants to know who is responsible.

I was a Catholic, and the Catholic Church was a self-proclaimed authority on God. So what better place for me to start my search? So I began to read about it. I decided to start with the Pope. He was, after all, the representative of God on earth.

This simple act of looking at the popes throughout history had an unexpected consequence. It resulted in the death of God, albeit temporarily.

Oops.

I discovered many, if not all, of the popes were less Christian than Pontius Pilate. If cleanliness is next to godliness, then at least Pilate had the virtue of washing his hands, which placed him closer to God than, for example, Pope Urban VI, who complained that he didn't hear enough screaming when his Cardinals were tortured. Many other popes were just as bad, launching murderous crusades across Europe and into the middle east. It was very sobering to read about all the plotting, stealing, adultery, murder, orgies, and squandering of wealth in which the church indulged. They even re-wrote the bible, cutting out parts that didn't agree with their grim purpose of achieving temporal power. I felt like a lamb suddenly discovering the benevolent shepherd works for the abattoir.

The church sold indulgences to forgive the rich while condemning the sins of the poor. It suppressed science and labelled it heresy as it elevated dogma above spirituality. It revealed itself as a potent political tool and an obscenely profitable business.

My disillusionment happened quickly, like a window shattering. My cynicism went deeper with each bloody footprint I found leading to the present day. Faith requires trust. Trust needs a reason. Reason dictated that an organisation with such an ungodly history knew less about God than I did. It also meant everything about it was suspect.

The Bible was a lie.

There were no saints.

God was dead.

Jesus on the cross was a corporate logo.

In the Bible, God threw Adam and Eve out of the Garden of Eden. I went one better and threw God out of Ballymun. It wasn't an idyllic backwater of creation. It was a grim tower block; a grey middle finger raised to any sense of the aesthetic, but I wedged God into the refuse chute that clattered through the spine of the edifice and shoved Him down. I did this because I was bright enough to see the lies but too dumb to know the truth.

I wasn't turning my back on God, just the cartoon-like portrait of him drawn by the Vatican and Hollywood.

***

The walls of the Prayer Hall have retained the morning chill. At least two hundred of us are still waiting for Swami to turn up. To pass the time, I look at and think about the portraits along the length of the blue walls. I don't know which, but one of them is a portrait of Swami Paramaguru, who predicted the birth of an important spiritual being within the lineage of one of his devotees. Her name was Thaiyalmuthu, and Swami Paramaguru told her the birth would happen within a few years of his own death.

A few hours ago, I wept in the presence of this 'important spiritual being,' whose birth was foretold.

Thaiyalmuthu was the grandmother of Swami Premananda.

If Swami Premananda is a saint and I'm not deluded, both of which are possible, then perhaps there's more than a grain of truth in the stories about Jesus. It could be closer to the truth to think that Jesus isn't just a benevolent freak of nature or the only Son of God, but he's one of many. Jesus was no shepherd, and we're not his sheep. We are brothers and sisters of these divine beings without realising it. That would seem to be the consistent message of the holy men and great spiritual teachers, that we are unconscious of our true nature, and they're politely reminding us. I think of the words they use. Those words are enlightenment, self-realisation, awakening, and the end of illusion. What is meant by this? What is this *self* that is realised? From what sleep do we awaken? What is the illusion, and what remains when it no longer dances before us, mesmerising our senses?

With no fuss and no fanfare, Swami Premananda appears. He's come from a doorway at the far end of the Prayer Hall. A curtain veils the door behind and to the right of his wooden chair. He's talking to someone. His bushy hair accentuates the movement of his head when he gives a little head waggle. I smile to myself. When I first saw a picture of Swami, I was amused at seeing a saint with an afro. It was like thinking of Buddha with a Mohican.

I'm happy to see Swami up there, but I'm also wary of him, as I would be, had I accidentally stepped on a live wire and then found myself treading the same ground. Yet, despite this instinctive reaction to the power I sense emanating from him, I soon relax. The atmosphere is so calm I soon feel soothed by his presence as he walks along the front of the Hall, placing a lingam on the bowed heads of the devotees before him. He holds it in place briefly. I hear a man behind me ask, 'When can I have a blessing?'

The reply, also behind me, informs the fellow that these blessings are only for those leaving today.

'But — today *I* am leaving the Swamiji.'

'Then you must go to the front. Go now. Quickly.'

There's some little shuffling behind me as a man gets to his feet. Then, he walks along the centre aisle, combining humility with alacrity due to the speed of his legs and the waggling of his head.

The guiding voice behind says, 'That fellow, he is fortunate. If he were not at the front for these blessings, then he would have no blessing at all.'

This seems reasonable. What kind of fool wouldn't walk a few yards for a blessing? As the fortunate fellow sits, I see a familiar face peering along the row of devotees. Our taxi driver's sitting up front waiting for a blessing. I thought he left yesterday, but he's obviously changed his mind.

We leave the Prayer Hall shortly after this, and I ask Lesley, 'Guess who I've just seen?'

'No idea?' she replies, looking for our sandals.

'The driver!'

'Who?'

'Our driver. From yesterday. The taxi?'

'Oh? I thought he left yesterday. You *did* pay him, didn't you?'

'Yeah. Of course. It looks like he's hung around to get a blessing.'

'Aww. That's nice.' Lesley bends down to retrieve our sandals and lobs mine to me.

'Thanks. Hey! Here he is now with Mataji.'

Mataji's leading him over to us, and — he's holding a piece of paper in his hand, which is funny because that's what he was doing the last time I saw him.

Mataji asks, ' Could one of you sign this receipt for the

driver? Without it, he won't get paid. It's to say you've been delivered safely and are happy with the service.'

'Oh — ' I say lamely. 'So it's not a receipt for the car?'

Lesley looks at me, puzzled. 'Why would you think it's a receipt for the car?'

'Because -— never mind. I'm sorry for delaying you, mate.'

The driver graciously waves away any inconvenience and says something which Mataji translates.

'He says it's okay, and he's had a blessing from Swami, so everything is fine.'

***

Back in the koothi, Lesley puts the kettle on. Mataji and Adrienne have gone off somewhere, so we sit on the little verandah, waiting for the water to boil.

I ask Lesley if I'd ever shown her the pictures of me when I was younger and had an afro like Swami.

'No. I can't imagine you looking like that. As long as I've known you, your hair's been short.'

'I had a 'fro, and it was massive.'

'How old were you?

'Fourteen and still living in Ballymun.' I hear a trace of bitterness in my voice and consciously attempt to dismiss it.

'That would have been in the early eighties? Before I met Swami?'

'Yeah. I looked at a picture of myself a few years ago and realised how odd I must have looked. My hair just looked wrong. Imagine a small ornamental tree moving along the pavement, wearing flared pants and glasses. Like a short-sighted sapling.'

'Oh, dear. It couldn't have been that bad, could it?

'Yes. It could — and was.'

'Then why didn't you go to a barber?'

'I was too self-conscious by then. I imagined myself sitting in a barber's chair and people gathering around as if it were a freak show. Remember, this was when I couldn't walk down the road without being stared at. Besides, there was nowhere to get it cut. There were no black people, so there was nobody with experience cutting hair like mine. Eventually, I cut it off myself, but not because I knew how ridiculous it looked. No, it was because I'd gone into a shop and been ignored by the staff serving everyone but me. I was too polite to shout or push in. Eventually, the boss saw me and said, "Can someone help this young lady?"'

'He thought you were a girl?'

'Yeah! I looked around to see who he was talking about, and it *was* me. I already felt bad enough with all the other abuse hurled at me by strangers, so looking like a girl on top of that was too much for me to cope with. I went home and locked myself in the toilet with the scissors. When I came out, I was minus the afro. I've had it short ever since.'

The kettle whistles, and Lesley gets up to make the tea.

While she's gone, I think about my afro. Children, in particular, were fascinated by it, which was quite disturbing whenever I got on a bus. If a baby were sitting on their mum's lap on the seat behind mine, nine times out of ten, the infant would be elbow deep in my afro within seconds. I'd turn around looking cross, and the mum sometimes had the decency to apologise and look embarrassed. One time I got home and discovered the remains of a well-gnawed toffee.

Lesley comes back with two cups of tea.

'Thanks,' I say, putting it on the veranda wall to cool in the shade. I tell Lesley what used to happen to me on the buses in Dublin.

'Swami gets vibhuti in his hair,' she says to make me feel better but adds, 'I expect it's easier to wash out.'

'When you said 'Swami' just then, I got a little jolt. It's like my brain doesn't know what to do with the idea that he's real. It can't settle until he's been explained away.'

'I know what you mean. I was like that myself after I met him for the first time. But, my appreciation of what he is keeps changing. It gets deeper, I suppose. Or more subtle, maybe. Does that make sense?'

'Yeah. It does. I see Swami differently now after meeting him.'

'In what way?'

'Well, to begin with, he didn't freak me out before, but he does now.'

Lesley laughs. 'There's nothing unusual in that.'

'Before Thomas introduced me to you, he said he sometimes had to turn his picture of Swami toward the wall because it made him feel really self-conscious when he wasn't behaving himself.'

'Yes, I know. He used cocaine sometimes. I never touched the stuff myself, but I knew that Thomas did. He knew Swami would disapprove of using drugs like that. The thing is, Swami is honest but not judgemental. He'll point out your error and show you the right way to conduct yourself by his good example, but it is up to you to decide what to do. It's your drama, and Swami just wants to help you choose which role you play in it.'

I nod. I like that. 'Thomas never met Swami, did he?'

'No. Why?'

'Because up until this point, Thomas and I had the same relationship with Swami. The photograph was our point of contact. I used to sit and look at it. His eyes seemed to have an element of gold in them. I guess it was a trick of the light, but they reminded me of honey. It comforted me, and like Thomas, I sensed that he knew I was there. Maybe it was wishful thinking? I don't know, but it was something of which I was in control. I could turn the picture to the wall or put it away if I wanted to, but now I've met Swami, the dynamic has changed. Now — he's stepped from behind the glass and out of the photograph, and he's real. Too real, almost. And now it's not just *me* looking at *him*. Instead, he's looking at *me*, and that's an altogether different sensation.'

Lesley appears to be thinking about this, and in relative silence, I hear the quiet, studious buzz of insects in the dry grass. I pick my mug of tea up and feel the heat in my fingers. It's still too hot. I put it down, stand up, stretch, yawn, and feel my bones crack. Birdsong is in the air, carried by the scent of flowers. Children are laughing nearby, but I can't see them. I hear the scrape of Lesley's cup as she lifts it from the wall and takes a tentative sip at her brew, even though it must be scalding. Finally, the cup is placed back down.

'So, how did you get it out?'

'Get what out?' I ask.

'The sweet. From your hair?'

'Oh. I can't remember. I might have cut it out. But, hey — you know what's odd? At this moment in time, proof that someone sacred lives among us is probably no more than a hundred yards away. He might be washing rice to feed the children. He might even be in another country, floating backwards down the M1 motorway in front of one of his devotees' cars — I don't know. Whatever he's doing, if it's true that he is what he seems to be, I should, at the very least, be thinking about it and what it means. But, instead, what *am* I thinking about —?'

I don't give Lesley long enough to reply.

'—toffee in my afro', I say. I sit back down and shake my

head in wonder. 'Why are my thoughts so mundane in the presence of someone so exceptional?'

'To be fair,' Lesley says, 'there probably aren't too many people in the world right now thinking about afro toffee. I expect you're the only one.'

We chuckle, but despite the silliness, I feel it's wrong, or at least somehow out of step, for my mind to be occupied with things that aren't spiritual, especially here in the ashram. This is, after all, no ordinary day — hang on a minute. It *is* a normal day. That's possibly the most disturbing thing of all, in a way. Despite what I saw and experienced, nothing has changed.

Or has it?

My mind starts to chase its tail around this thought.

I pick my tea up again and, this time, manage to have a small sip without scalding myself.

'We need to go into Trichy,' Lesley says. 'I can't spend another night on the floor without something softer to sleep on. We'll get some camp beds.'

'You didn't sleep well?'

'No. I would have slept better propped up in the wardrobe.'

'Oh? I didn't think this would be a problem for you. Didn't you and Gina sleep on stone floors in the Ashram in Sri Lanka?

'We did. But if I'd had a cot bed then, I would have slept in it, not underneath it. Besides, that was ten years ago. I've picked up a few more aches and pains since then.'

'Okay.'

'We also need to buy some food. And some pillows, too."

'Good idea.'

***

Tiruchirappalli is a very, very busy city by the look of it. We see this as passengers in a taxi with Lesley, Mataji, Adrienne, and a young man who has taken time out from his studies to see Swami. Back in England, he was preparing for his exams when the opportunity to see Swami came along, and he jumped at the chance, which shows that not even a student dentist will look a gift horse in the mouth. He's dressed in shorts and a white shirt and looks comfortable, unperturbed by the heat. I look and certainly feel dishevelled, wondering why my knees are sweating.

Passing through the outskirts of Trichy into the heart of the city, we see the gears of industry, commerce, education and religion locked together and turning to grind the city through another day. The traffic's very noisy, as expected, and raises a lot of dust into the air, pungent with fumes and the smell of food. The colours are vivid, as if they've soaked up too much sunlight, and it's spilling back out. Bikes flit between vehicles of dusty chrome, rubber and glass scorching to the touch. Stubborn grass reaches between the broken slabs of blistering pavements as if the weight of humanity is squeezing the grass through the gaps, like spinach between teeth.

Consumerism shouts from billboards and belches from exhaust pipes. It bursts out of shop fronts like full bellies bulging over trouser tops. It smiles coyly from the better class of shop but still lingers without shame by their open doorways. It pouts and gives knowing looks to those who want things they can't afford. The unsubtle work of advertising agencies shamelessly extols the virtues of bigger, brighter, sexier, faster, cooler, hotter and cheaper goods.

We alight from the taxi in a densely populated market area heaving with people, sounds and smells. A substantial portion of Trichy's 750,000 people seems to be here, politely besieging the fruit and vegetable stalls. Adrienne, Lesley and I give Mataji some of our valuables to keep safe, and she leads us into the milling crowd. The young dentist goes off on his own. Over her shoulder, Mataji tells us, 'Swami buys supplies for the Ashram here. We try to grow as much as we can, but with so many mouths to feed, it's not possible to be self-sufficient for now.'

The ashram feeds, clothes and educates hundreds and hundreds of children. I understand this to be immensely time-consuming, and I appreciate Swami's involvement in their care, but something in me finds this disappointing. I don't want Swami to be squeezing vegetables to see how fresh they are. I want him to be walking on water or doing something else miraculous. The idea of the extraordinary doing something so ordinary and mundane seems to me to be quite remarkable in itself.

Mind you — what *is* ordinary in any of this? Here I am, so infinitesimally small compared to the sun that I scarcely exist. But at the same time, compared to the atoms in this body, I *am* the cosmos. I came from nowhere, and nothing squeezed into physical existence through a woman's body, who responded to this imposition by feeding me, keeping me warm and wiping my bottom. The biggest mystery in my life is not why a Sri Lankan saint buys bananas here or anywhere else. The question mark hangs over my relatively sudden appearance of us all between a stranger's legs and all that ensues after the midwife slaps up.

I don't know if the question was answerable in the market while shopping, but before I found the answer, my mind wandered off like an untethered balloon.

There's so much with which to be distracted. Trichy's not a place you can move through without being touched. You taste it and smell it and feel it. The visceral rumble of traffic sometimes will shudder up through the soles of your feet.

Beneath the mellow sweetness of fruit lurks the faint putrid stink of fallen vegetables, trodden underfoot and mashed into the ground. Blink away the mean, thin-lipped stench of pollution which stings the eyes. Step over the crushed petals of fallen flowers, slumming in the gutter with discarded cigarette cartons. Livestock grunt and swish insects away with indolent tails. People move fluidly, gracefully, channelled suddenly down narrow streets from generous open spaces and back again. The faces hold curiosity, friendliness, indifference and amusement in their expressions. Some dumbly see while others observe and know and keep what they know to themselves. We hurry along like ducklings behind Mataji, paddling upstream as the life of this market flows around us. Everyone seems to be selling stuff, buying or moving away from stuff to get to other stuff. Money changers call out like crows. Horns honk distantly like departing geese as sweat rolls down my face. All this happens in heat so fearsome that shadows hide beneath the awnings.

'Here we are,' Mataji says.

We're outside a shop called Mangal-Mangal. It's a relief to step inside the cool interior.

Adrienne points to display cases with jewellery glittering behind the glass.

'Aren't they beautiful?' she says.

Lesley, who wears no jewellery other than a necklace Swami materialised for her years ago, leans forward and has a look. 'Yes. Gorgeous — ' she says.

Hearing this, one of the sales assistants seems hopeful until she continues her sentence.

' — now, where are the cheap spoons?'

He deftly diverts himself in the direction of another customer.

Mataji approaches the counter and asks for what we

need in Tamil. When I hear someone speaking any language other than English, part of me thinks they're just making it up. But, of course, having lived in the ashram so long, Mataji speaks Tamil fluently. She can certainly ask for spoons and little brass plates, a small bell, and other things, so we can do a little abhishekam with these when Lesley and I return to Manchester. A large round tray and a brass bucket are added to a neat pile of brass items placed on the counter. Mataji also asks for a white conch shell to pour water during the ritual. I'm particularly taken with this last item.

The Indian Ocean has caressed and battered, rolled and moulded it with restless tides. It would have had a giant predatory sea slug living in it once, but that has long gone. The conch is empty, but what remains, where the opening is curved like a delicate ear, is the memory of warm water whispering inside. I pick it up and listen to it. It's got all the tactile pleasure of a father's thumb in a baby's hand. It fits perfectly in mine, and I hold it up to better appreciate its loveliness. The shell appears pearl-like and bone-like, a perfect boundary between the land and the ocean, with regular nodules and grooves to intrigue and delight the whirling ridges of my fingertips. While doing this, Adrienne calls Mataji away to the other end of the shop. Lesley sits herself down on a wooden stool.

The gentleman who collected all these things from different shelves and cupboards waits for my approval. I nod, put the conch down, and he produces a pencil stub to compile a list.

'Thanks,' I say, looking at it after he's given it to me. It makes no sense, but I presume it's a bill. 'How much?'

He waggles his head and begins picking my stuff up, conch, and everything else.

'Wait!' I say, thinking he's putting it back, 'I want that

stuff, mate. Don't take it away!'

He pauses and points to a man sitting behind another counter. I turn to look, and the rest of my goods are whipped up and away as I do so.

'Hey — ' I go over with my chit and wave at the counterman. 'That guy over there just took my stuff away before I could pay him.'

He puts his hand out for the list, peruses it, looks bored, and then looks back up at me as if he thinks one of us might be an idiot, and he's got a strong feeling it isn't him. To my relief, the goods reappear, carried by the young man from 'over there.' He rattles it all down between us on the counter.

'That's mine,' I say, pointing to the pile, particularly the white conch.

The man with my list looks down at my goods and then back up at me through thick black lashes. He waggles his head as if this whole thing may be problematic, but with the grace of God, he may be able to help me.

'How much?' I ask.

The man appears to blanch as if I'd borrowed his spacesuit and promptly farted in it.

Mataji, noticing the chaos I've introduced into what should be a simple transaction, steps up beside me.

'This good gentleman will work the price out for you,' she says. Then, in Tamil, she says something to the gentleman with the list. He nods and begins to scrutinise the goods, giving the act an air of solemnity.

He tells me the price.

'Fine,' I say, reaching for the rupees.

Sotto voce, Mataji says, 'You should haggle.'

'Oh? — that's too expensive,' I mumble.

The cashier shrugs. His heart isn't in it. I'm already boring him. He knows I'm going to roll over straight away on

101

the price. He's right. I hand the money over. The man counts it rapidly, using a tiny rubber thumb thimble to flick mechanically through the notes. The rupees are placed into a drawer, and the drawer is slammed shut. He gives me a receipt.

'Thanks,' I say, reaching for my goods, but another man promptly whips them away.

'Hey! Hang on, mate. They're mine!'

This man looks confused until Mataji speaks in Tamil to clear up the confusion. To me, she says, 'You can't take anything yet. Go to that counter, show the gentleman your chit *and* receipt, and he'll wrap everything up. *Then* — you can take your goods.'

Finally, with the things I'd purchased wrapped in the wilted pages of old newspapers, we step out into the naked heat of the sun. I can scarcely believe the heat. Soon my shorts are clinging and chafing. Heat radiates out of the legs like a set of exhaust pipes. To make things worse, the brass implements begin to bake through the paper and become uncomfortable to hold.

At the very least, the shorts will have to go. Most of the other men around us are dressed in a length of cotton wrapped neatly around their midriff. It begins below the belly button and goes down to the knees. This simple garment called a dhoti looks just the very thing for this climate. I'll have to get a couple of those before the day is out because I'm so uncomfortable with the chaffing.

On the way back to our taxi, we stop at the stall where Swami buys produce for the ashram. Lesley buys a bag of plums that are virtually steaming in the heat, reminding me of the other reason I want to be rid of my shorts.

Watching the exchange, I wonder why someone who can produce objects out of thin air would need to do any shopping at all.

'Why does Swami buy fruit when he could just materialise it?' I ask.

'It's already been materialised,' Mataji says, 'on a tree or in the ground. The farmer harvests it, and we pay him for his labour and providing he's paid a reasonable sum, this is a fair exchange.'

Lesley joins us. She's holding a paper bag with six plums inside and a giant watermelon tucked under her arm. Adrienne's got some bananas and grapes. We continue our journey back to the car.

'Damn,' Lesley says, stopping for a moment. 'I've forgotten to get pillows.'

'Don't worry,' Mataji says. 'I'm sure you can borrow some in the ashram.'

'Okay. I've had enough of shopping for now.'

We carry on back toward the taxi, and I resume my conversation with Mataji.

'So, if Swami won't materialise food out of thin air, what about money?'

'What about it?'

'Why doesn't he just make money for the food appear out of nowhere?'

'Because that would be wrong.'

'But why? What harm would it do?'

'Money has to come from somewhere. So even if Swami made it appear out of nowhere, somebody somewhere has to pay the price for it. Money is, after all, a form of energy. It's generated by someone using their life energy.'

We reach the taxi where the trainee dentist is waiting with the driver. Our things are stashed in the boot. Then, after a brief stop to buy foldaway camp beds and a pair of dhotis for me, we start the journey back to the Ashram. We sit in silence with the windows open and warm air rushing in. The heat is enervating, but it doesn't stop me from thinking.

Why not make money appear out of nowhere?

If he can make other things appear, then why not this?

***

I think this is why. One man goes to a bank and deposits £1.00. The bank can give that same £1.00 out in loans to nine different customers, meaning eight of those pounds don't exist. So — people borrow money the bank doesn't have, but the debt must be paid back with 'real' money. The bank can then lend the money they received in payment for the money they never had, and the cycle of money for nothing continues.

The banking system is based on 'materialising' money out of thin air.

Governments have shackled every man, woman, and child to vast black holes of debt by borrowing money from private banks. Most of the money borrowed never existed at the source. Interest is charged on the imaginary loan, and the debt becomes even more astronomical. No amount of labour can cover it, but the debt isn't meant to be paid off. Its purpose is to keep humanity in perpetual enslavement to debt.

People vote for a new government every few years hoping it'll represent them. Instead, the new administration 'borrows' more money. Humanity continues to work in service to those who control the supply of money. The wealth nations generate is given to those who thrive on the suffering and unimaginable corruption the banking system perpetuates.

So, why doesn't Swami Premananda make money appear out of nowhere and use it to fund his ashram?

I'm sure you can work it out for yourself.

***

***

Our arrival in Ballymun had coincided with the Summer holidays, but Summer ended, and the day which filled me with dread rolled around. It was the day when I had to be enrolled in Ballymun Comprehensive. Ma took me over one morning just before the start of the school year. I was immensely relieved when we got into the school without anything bad happening, but I put that down to the fact that the other children hadn't started yet. Ma spoke to the headmaster and asked for his assurance that I would be looked after and not have any trouble because I was 'half-caste.'

The principal, Mr Cannon, was a generously proportioned gentleman who looked like he could give you a thunderous punch, should he wish to do so. He towered over Ma and me.

To Ma, he said, 'Don't you worry. I won't tolerate any bullying in this school. Not even for a mingyit. This young fella here will be fine.'

'Good,' Ma said, 'only you know what lads can be like.'

'I do indeed, Mrs Domican. They can be rather rumbunctious.'

'I'm sure your school is lovely, Mister Cannon, but let me tell you why I'm worried about my son coming here.'

'Would you like to sit in my office?'

'No. Here's fine. I won't keep you long.'

'That's quite alright.'

'Well, now y'see, we used to live in a place called Kennedys Villas. It was in 1975. And when we arrived, I put Paul in school, a Christian Brothers one where they gave the kids a good hiding if they misbehaved. Then I took the eldest, that's Tony, he's at home now, painting, and we went up to the school where I was going to enrol him. Now — listen to this, 'she said as if Mister Cannon wasn't, ' — as soon as we entered the school driveway, the children were all out of the windows shouting the most disgusting things at my boys. I've been brought up very respectable, like yourself, so I won't lower myself and repeat what the little bastards — sorry — I mean — children were

saying.' Her hand came up as if to ward off a barrage of questions that Mister Cannon wasn't asking.

I piped up with, 'They said to go home nigger.'

'That's right! The little bleeders!' Ma said, her righteous anger getting the better of her momentarily. She recovered her composure and placed one hand on her chest as if the expletive had been nothing more than a soft belch. 'They were shouting ', we don't want any of you lot here' and 'Go back to where you came from.'

'I can assure you, Mrs Domican, that woul —'

'I'm born and bred in Dublin, Mr Cannon, but my boys are all English. And I can tell you I was so ashamed of my country that it could be so cruel to somebody they don't even know just because they're half-caste. I couldn't send my boys to a school where they'd pick on them because of their skin. That was why I took Tony away from that school. As a result, Tony never had a chance of getting a formal education.'

'Or an informal persecution,' I added, muttering, 'lucky sod.'

Ma went on. 'Tony was only thirteen at the time, the same age as Paul is now. Mister Cannon — I want your personal guarantee that my son Paul will be okay in your school.'

'I can give you my word, Mrs Domican. Your child will be safe with us. Such behaviour as you've met in the past would not be tolerated here. The mingyit something like that happened would be the last mingyit the perpetrator would have in this school. We treat all our boys alike here.'

Mr Cannon turned his attention to me. He put the two shovels that were his hands behind his back and rocked back and forth on his black brogues. The leather creaked like a weighted hangman's noose as he said, 'Now, young man. Do you have any questions about your new school?'

I wanted to ask what were the chances I'd be lynched before lunch — but thought it far more reasonable to ask what a mingyit was

He looked at Ma and back at me. 'You don't know what a mingyit is?'

'Eh — no. Not really.'

'A mingyit is a unit of time. Sixty mingyits make an hour.'

'Oh? You mean a minute?'

'Yes. That's what I said. A mingyit.'

He looked at me as if to say, I don't mind you being brown, but I won't tolerate you pretending to be thick.

***

As soon as we enter the koothi, I head straight for the kitchen, undress and wrap one of my newly purchased dhotis around my hips. It feels good but slumps down and lands at my feet after only a few seconds. Bending, I pull it back up, tie the ends together tightly, and then make for the other room to go and show Lesley. The damn thing slips down to my knees before I reach it.

How do I keep this thing up without buttons, belts, braces, or strings? I bunch the top of it so I can tie the ends together. It's so tight I feel like a novelty balloon tied in the middle. I manage to get through the door this time and show Lesley. The dhoti remains in place, but I hear gravity chuckling in anticipation.

'It suits you,' Lesley says.

'Thanks. It's such a relief after wearing shorts.'

'Great. Pop the kettle on, will you? I'm parched.'

I return to the kitchen, but while I'm trying to light the gas burner, my dhoti unravels and swoons to the floor.

'Oh, for crying out — ' I grab it and tie it up with a large knot resembling a pair of rabbit ears protruding from my hip. It looks ridiculous.

I hear a stranger's voice come from the other room. I look around the door and see a young man called Rajesh. He smiles shyly and returns my greeting.

'Do you know where Mataji is?' he asks.

Lesley says, 'I think she's with Swami, maybe? When we got back from Trichy, she went looking for him.'

Rajesh nods. 'Do you have everything you need?'

'Yes. Thanks. But maybe you can show me how to wear this so it doesn't fall off?'

While he demonstrates how to secure the garment at my waist, Lesley asks if I can go and find some pillows for us.

'I'll finish making the tea,' she adds.

I follow Rajesh out the door. He goes one way, and I go another. Instead of using the path, I walk through the prickly grass, past modest shrubs and beneath small trees where dappled shade slips from my bare shoulders as I pass by.

I look toward the Prayer Hall to my right and my heart thumps.

Swami Premananda.

He's standing on the steps talking to devotees, making them laugh. The sight of him shakes me. I put my head down, feeling a strong urge to walk faster. What a peculiar thing this is, to have come so far to see him, and now I want to run away.

How to describe the feeling I had when seeing him?

***

Within weeks of meeting, Lesley and I thought it would be interesting if we meditated together. So, in her flat, we lay in front of the gas fire, covered ourselves with a blanket and stuck a large amethyst crystal on the floor just beyond our stockinged feet. Above our heads, Lesley had placed another large amethyst. Side by side, we lay. She put her right foot against mine, and I placed my left hand over her right hand, and that was that. All the stuff to do with crystals was her doing. She knew how to use them, and I trusted her.

We waited. Nothing happened. I just lay there, letting my mind wander. I wondered how long I'd be lying there. Lesley could meditate for hours. My attempts at meditation generally turned out to be a prelude to nodding off, and I was a little concerned about obliterating her meditation with an impromptu bout of industrial snoring.

A couple of years after leaving Ballymun, I'd tried to meditate. I had no technique other than instinct and a need to find peace within myself. I lay on my bed, consciously slowing my breath, hoping it would release the tension in my abdomen. I kept a lot of my stress locked in there. After some time, God knows how long, I noticed the clock on the wall slowing down. The gap between each spasm of the minute hand was getting longer and longer until —

The clock remained still.

Time had stopped

I lay in the gap between seconds

My body wasn't breathing

Panicking, I sat up, and the clock ticked. Time started again. The *mingyits* returned to normal. This was on the 23rd of June, 1986. I know this because I had watched Barry McGuigan boxing in Las Vegas on television earlier that night. Barry had a big heart, and I cried mine out when he lost. I knew what it was like to be beaten. Twelve months later, I'd leave my house with a metal bar tucked up my sleeve and murder in my heart.

I don't know.

Four years after the night that time momentarily forgot itself, I lay on the floor with Lesley to meditate once more.

'Can you see anything?' Lesley asked, startling me. I'd forgotten she was there.

'No,' I replied quietly. I didn't want to talk. I wasn't expecting anything to happen, but if it did, I didn't want it to have been influenced by anything we might say. I also felt very peaceful lying beside Lesley. Even though we'd only known each other for a few weeks, she felt oddly familiar. So, being warm and comfortable, my focus moved within my body from the left to the right and then forward and back, tasting the experience of my physicality—the heat and weight of myself, the softness and solidity, all in great detail.

How odd we must have looked on the floor between two crystals. Bemused by this image, I visualised myself as a miniature man looking up one of my nostrils and saw it as a cavernous hole. Huge draughts of air were being sucked into it. Somehow, over time, I became loosened within myself and whimsical, watching shapes, colours, and sounds rising giddily and falling into each other. Thoughts swooped like nightingales. The knot of mind was slipping. Drifting away from the mooring

Not thinking but seeing thoughts —

Wondering where Lesley is?

I know where *I* am.

I'm on the side of a pyramid under a blue sky and blazing sun.

Oh — wait. Lesley's inside the pyramid. How do I get to her? I don't know, but maybe if I walk along here. Careful, now. Don't slip. I'm very young. Younger than she is.

I start to rise and feel the breathless exultation of flying, as in a dream.

I'm rising into the air, lifting myself with an act of will, going up and up. But then, I'm falling into the sky, going faster and faster, and — suddenly, I'm scared because I realise I'm not in control. This is too much. Too fast. But something else is pulling me upward. I try to force myself back down — but up I go — hurtling — faster, faster, faster — oh — fuck — I'm pulling backwards, desperate to get back to the ground. Oh,

God! I look down, and the earth is thousands of feet below and still falling away. The pyramid's a small square and getting smaller.

Up I go —

Shit! I sit up in a panic, and Lesley does too.

'Jesus!' she gasps, her hand on her heart. 'You frightened the life out of me!'

'Sorry,' I said, feeling like an idiot.

'What did you see? What made you jump?'

I can't answer. Not at first. I was so relieved to find myself sitting on Lesley's floor and not *'falling'* upwards that all I could do was sit in silence.

When I could speak, I said, 'I'll tell you what I saw in a minute. What about you? Did you see anything?'

'Yes,' Lesley replied. She grimaced and rotated her right shoulder.

'You okay?'

'I think I've pulled a muscle.' She reached over to a small table, took up her cigarettes, pulled one out, and lit it. Then, after placing her pack beside her with the lighter neatly on top of it, she began.

'I was in a pyramid,' she said. ' I was doing some sort of ritual, but I knew you were outside. You were too young to participate in whatever I was doing. I went out to look for you, and I saw you looking around, looking for me, maybe? I don't know. I don't think I was in my body. Anyway, I took your hand because I wanted to show you how to fly. I started to rise but *really* fast, bringing you with me, but you were frightened. You kept pulling back, and I kept pulling you up. Hmmm —' She takes a contemplative drag on her cigarette and blows the smoke out slowly before adding, 'I wonder if that's when I hurt my shoulder?'

That was the first and last meditation we had together

like that. I was freaked out as well as intrigued. I drew back from repeating the experience because it was a bit *too* weird.

And that feeling of falling too fast into the sky?

Well — that's the feeling I had when I saw Swami Premamanda standing on the steps of the Prayer Hall.

Too much.

Too fast.

***

The prospect of going to school in Ballymun was so appalling that I could hardly breathe. My abdomen was clenched as if waiting for a sucker punch. The only way I could sleep was to release another source of tension beneath the sheets, rubbing until it got better.

I kept telling myself that I shouldn't worry so much. I'd been a pupil in an Irish school less than two years ago. Basin Street Christian Brothers School had literally been hammering an education into rough working-class children for over 150 years. Like the other children, I was hit with sticks, leather straps, lengths of bamboo, chalk dusters and the occasional shoe by various teachers. But, unlike a lot of my classmates, I never cried or even winced. I played football, could be funny, never picked on anyone, and a teacher could bounce a duster off my head without me blubbing. That was a recipe for success in Basin Street Christian Brothers, or it seemed to be because I got on well in that school.

In the short time we'd been away from Ireland, a revolution in their approach to education had come about. Someone in authority had discovered an instruction book for a twelve-inch ruler and realised it wasn't just for smacking children. It was a controversial approach to education, but the authorities decided to try it so, in Ballymun Comprehensive, the teachers couldn't hit you. Although this may have been a good thing, I took no comfort from it. I wasn't worried about the teachers. I was worried about the other pupils. The children of Ballymun had proven to be either indifferent or hostile to our presence. This was made clear in my brief encounters with other children I passed each day. So, what would it be like being locked up with them for almost eight hours a day? If the experience of trying to enrol Tony in a similar school was anything to go by, then it would be hell indeed. No matter how often I reassured myself that I'd already sampled life in an Irish school and survived intact, my thoughts kept dwelling on that morning with Tony and Ma.

Go.

Home.

Niggers.

And then, out of the gloom came a ray of hope for me.

It came in the form of a television series called Roots. It was based on a book of the same name by Alex Hailey. It told the story of a young man called Kunta Kinte, who was forcibly taken from Africa and sold as a slave in America. Both the book and the series were phenomenally popular. Like most of Ireland, Ballymun tuned in to watch this powerful saga, which related how corrosive racism is and some of the different ways in which it devastated lives. I watched it with the intensity of a castaway searching the horizon for a ship. When it was finished, I followed Tony out onto the balcony. He needed a cigarette, and I just had to talk about what we had seen.

'That was fantastic,' I enthused.

'It was okay,' Tony said. 'Quite interesting, actually. I didn't realise all that stuff went on back then.'

''What? You mean slavery?'

'No, Not that. I knew there were slaves, but I didn't know they branded people with hot irons like cattle. Disgusting. And they were raping the women to breed more slaves, just like they were livestock. Those people were sick.'

'Yeah. But on the bright side, it'll make things better for us, won't it?'

'How?'

'It'll give the idiots in Ballymun an education. That's how. It'll

let them see the effect racism has. It destroyed the lives of millions of people. Like the holocaust.'

'You think so?' Tony looked dubious.

'Yeah. Of course. What kind of idiot would watch a programme about racism and come away from it thinking, 'd'ye know something? That racism? It's fucking brilliant!'

We laughed at the very idea.

'Yeah,' Tony said, clearly thinking about it.' You might be right.'

'I hope so. I've got to go to school in a couple of days, and I'm dreading it. So anything which makes these people think twice about calling me coon*, has got to be good, hasn't it?'*

I was wrong. In the morning, Ma sent me to get some milk, bread and butter. When I stepped out of the lift, two men were standing there.

'Jaysus!' one of them exclaimed. 'Would you look at that? It's Kunta Kinte!'

They were still laughing as the doors closed. The lift took them up into the cold guts of the building, and I walked out into the rain. By the time I got back, the name 'Kunta Kinte' had been shouted from a balcony. It fell on my shoulders like effluent dumped from the blunt end of a pigeon. I couldn't believe that a story sympathetic to the plight of people suffering from the effects of racism seemed to have worsened our situation.

***

Oh Good. Swami's not standing outside the Prayer Hall anymore. I pass by with two pillows tucked under my arm, somewhat embarrassed by my earlier instinctive reaction to him. Back in the koothi, I toss the pillows onto our sleeping bags. I can hear Lesley in the kitchen, filling the kettle. Mataji's sitting on her bed writing. I'm reluctant to disturb her because Swami gave her the task of recording and collecting his words for his devotees. Nonetheless, I announce that I've just seen him.

'Did you speak to him?' Mataji asks, her pen hovering above the page. 'Nope. Swami was talking to some devotees outside the Prayer Hall when I passed.'

'Were they French?'

'No idea. Why?'

'Some of the French devotees are leaving today. Swami's kept them waiting since this morning.'

'Oh? Is that because he's busy with Shivaratri and everything.'

Mataji chuckles. 'It's a busy time, Yes. But that's not why he delays people. He does it on purpose. He gets everyone rushing around, and then he doesn't turn up.'

'But — if they're leaving the Ashram, don't they have flights to catch?'

'Probably. Usually.'

'What happens if they miss the plane?'

'They won't. Swami Premananda's got an uncanny sense of timing.'

'But why? What's the point? Why wind people up?'

Mataji shrugs and smiles. 'People wind themselves up. He just provides the key. They don't *have* to use it.'

I sit on my camp bed. 'So, does annoying people go on the list of miraculous events then?'

She laughs and puts her writing to one side. 'No. If anyone ever writes one, many things could go on the list, but messing with your travel plans probably won't be on it. Though maybe it should be.'

I raise my eyebrows by way of a question.

'Think of the journey from here to the airport. How many roads will you travel down? How many intersections and unforeseen events? A lot. But, you'll still get to where you're going and on time, even if he delays your departure.'

'But why would he do that?'

Mataji shrugs. 'Perhaps it's his way of saying he knows the road ahead of you.'

'He can see into the future?'

'Yes. Over the years, my time with Swami Premananda has led me to believe he can.'

'Tea?' Lesley asks, popping her head around the kitchen door.

'Oh yeah,' I say.

Mataji goes back to what she's writing. I'm left with my thoughts about the bushy-haired saint. I think about the night of Shivaratri, sitting with my own ghost curled in my belly, warning me not to be fooled into thinking there is a God who cares.

But then Swami Premananda appeared, and the ghost in my heart was struck dumb. I had brought two reliable chaperones, my intellect and pride, to ensure I didn't give myself away cheaply. I had intended to observe the tiny Sri Lankan from a safe distance inside my head, or so I thought, but instead, they just looked on with bewilderment while I wept. My heart, it seemed, had an intelligence all of its own and humility too. It stepped out from behind the cold cogitation of the brain and knew him for what he was.

Swami Premananda was a spiritual being.

It wasn't the strange spectacle of the lingams being produced that made me think this way. The sense of 'knowing' that recognised Swami Premananda for what he was came before any thought. I also knew this recognition of his innate spirituality changed everything. I just didn't realise how much or in what way. Like when your child is pushed out into the light, tiny fingers clenched in outrage at being evicted from the amniotic Eden, everything changes at that moment, and there's no going back. Even though the child is part of *your* drama, you're no longer the most important person in it.

Beneath me, my camp bed creaks as I roll onto my side and put my face in the warm nook of my arm. I think about what I saw and felt emanating from Swami Premananda. I stay like this until Lesley comes through with the tea. Then, while waiting for it to cool, something occurs to me.

Why think about the spirituality of Swami Premananda?

Surely the thing which matters is my spirituality, not his? He could be the Son of God but would my knowing that fact make *me* any more spiritual? I could have a comprehensive knowledge of the life and times of Swami Premananda and still be an asshole. His being spiritually enlightened wouldn't bring me peace. The only way for that to happen would be for me to experience whatever it is that fills him with light.

I take a tentative sip of my tea. The surface of it looks glossy with the sugar in it. I burn my lips and, irritated, put it back down.

How do I experience whatever it is that fills Swami Premananda with light?

And who, I wonder, is this 'I' that I keep referring to?

***

It's late in the evening. From the corner of my eye, I see something black with a lot of legs moving slowly beside Lesley's thigh.

I gasp. 'Look at the size of that!'

Lesley rolls off her campbed, bounding up and away, almost falling over Adrienne, asleep on another camping bed. I pad across the floor in my pyjamas to look at the insect about the size of a matchbox.

Across the other side of the koothi, Mataji lifts her head from her pillow.

'Don't worry,' she says. 'It's just a cockroach.'

I jump back. As a child, I lived in a house full of cockroaches, and I never saw one this big. My skin isn't just crawling with revulsion. It's virtually churning all over my back.

'It — can't be a cockroach. It's too big.'

'That's actually quite small,' Mataji replies, totally unconcerned. 'We get bigger ones than that.' She yawns and lays her head back down.

I step back even further.

'No *way* is that a cockroach. It can't be!' I look over to Mataji. 'Can it?'

The Roach stops its glacial, cold-blooded movement as if to ponder this question. Long, creepy, sticky-out things are slowly waving in front of it. My skin is on the verge of shedding my body and hiding in the kitchen.

Lesley recovers her composure enough to speak.

'Would you mind getting it off my bed?'

'What! No chance. I'm not going near it.'

'You told me you lived in a house full of them. Surely you can sort this one out?'

'I didn't live *with* them. You make it sound like we were flatmates. The house was infested.'

'Well — you still need to sort it out.'

'Okay. Okay. Just give me a minute to figure out what to do with it.'

'Just put it outside — '

'Outside? Outside! It's not a bloody pussy cat! I can't just pick it up by the scruff of the neck and pop it outside! This could take any of the cockroaches I've ever seen before and use them as clogs.'

'Shall I get you some paper to pick it up with?'

'No. Get me a chair and a whip,' I reply, thinking of a

lion tamer.

'What?'

'Nothing. Where's the broom?'

Mataji yawns and asks, 'Would you like me to get rid of it?'

'No! I'll sort it out. Just give me a second.'

'Okay,' Mataji replies, rolling over to face the wall.

Lesley hands me the broom and adds, 'You do know they can fly, don't you?'

'What?'

'They can fly.'

For a moment, I can't speak. 'Really?'

She nods and adds, 'So if I were you, I'd hurry up. For all we know, it's doing a pre-flight check right now.'

I brace myself. I'm going cold at the thought of it taking off and flying into my face.

The cockroach resumes its progress, moving forward with zen-like slowness, long creepy antennae still waving in the air. Tentatively, I step closer, holding the brush like a lance. The roach is almost at the edge of the bed, and my mouth is dry.

With all the grim slowness of blood coagulating, the thing walks forward on skinny limbs, which are spiky, angular, and utterly alien. The legs, thin and black like cadaverous pallbearers, carry the body forward. I shudder as the two creepy-looking filaments of cockroach curiosity, waving hypnotically in front of this little monster, stop.

'Can you get on with it?' Lesley says. 'I want to get back to bed.'

The cockroach apparently thinks she's talking to it because it moves forward and steps over the edge of the bed. It waits there upside down just because it can. Then it falls. It lands, *'clack!'* on its carapace, leg-things scurrying in the air.

I leap forward to crush it with the end of the broom, but —

It does a backflip. It lands on its legs, all eight of them and then starts to sprint like Usain Bolt.

Arrgghhh! It's coming in my direction! I leap back, prodding the ground before it in a blind panic. It swerves left and right, coming closer — and just before I embarrass myself by jumping into Lesley's arms, it does a handbrake turn. It's heading for the wardrobe. Humiliated by my retreat, I give chase —

***

In 1975, just before we moved to Ireland for the first time, we lived in a rented house in Corby Street, Manchester, England. I didn't like the place because the upstairs was creepy even in the daytime, and I was convinced 'something' lived under the bed. In addition, I sometimes heard footsteps in the attic during the night, like something was trying to be quiet up there. After seeing a television programme featuring something similar, I imagined a hunched, malevolent presence on top of the wardrobe.

In this house, I first realised world war II had ended thirty years ago. I read it on the back of a comic. From this house, Tony and I made the journey each morning to Gorton Cathedral to clean the brass and gain favour in the eyes of God. Jason was a baby when we moved to this house. Barely had he taken his first few steps when we had to leave because of a cockroach.

I woke one night with a terrible thirst. I got up and leapt from the bed to the door. This leap ensured that whatever lived under the bed didn't grab my ankles. I walked out onto the landing. The light was always left on. Creeping down the creaky stairs that creaked like an old man's cartilage, I opened the door to the living room. It was very dark inside. Heavy curtains kept the light of the moon at bay. I could hear something like dry leaves rustling. That's odd, I thought, reaching out and flicking the brown bakelite switch that clunked and lit up the room.

Cockroaches

Everywhere

Climbing up the walls. Moving across the floor, obscene abdomens rubbing along the carpet, they drag their shadows behind them. Some were sitting on the sofa watching the cold dead screen of the television. Slowly they waved coal-black antennae as if in worship or perhaps to bring it back to life.

Cockroaches —

— everywhere.

I could feel them through the soft skin of my bare feet, seething under the floorboards, about to boil up out of the ground.

I ran back upstairs and leapt onto my bed, shivering.

By the time morning came, they'd gone. Slipped back through the cracks in the underworld from which they had crawled. I was mightily relieved they seemed to have an aversion to daylight. At least that's what we thought until a family friend photographed Ma and Baby Jason. He's sitting on her lap. Both of them, smiling at the camera, unaware of the cockroach crawling up the white woollen baby blanket. When Ma looked at the photograph some weeks later and saw the cockroach, her protective outrage propelled us out of the house. It pushed us over the water to Ireland. This was how we ended up living in Dublin for the first time. We lived in Kennedys Villas, in the shadow of a lunatic asylum where the sane people drugged, lobotomised and electrocuted those who were insane.

We had a small ground-floor flat beside St Brendan's Psychiatric Hospital. Despite the high walls surrounding the hospital, I could easily imagine the 'mad' people those walls held at bay escaping and running amok. In the nighttime, especially when fog from the River Liffey rolled in surly and cold-shouldered, I fearfully imagined those walls were holding back the living dead. Tony had shown me a picture in one of his magazines devoted to horror movies where the undead were walking across a field.

It turns out zombies may have been closer to the truth. The medical establishment in Ireland experimented with insulin-induced comas, chemical coshes such as Temazepam, lobotomies and electroconvulsive therapy. Being 'disturbed' in Ireland wasn't easy. Those who were judged insane were dreadfully dealt with in a country which had the dubious distinction, at one point, of locking up more of its people per head of population than Russia under Stalin.

Some individuals in St. Brendan's may have thought they were Stalin, but this doesn't make it any less of a shameful statistic. They also had their fair share of cockroaches, but I don't remember seeing any in our flat. One of them had already altered the course of our future by popping up in a family photo. Without that 'roach', we wouldn't have lived near an insane asylum. I wouldn't have gone to Basin Street Christian Brothers School, where it was normal for teachers to speak about the love of God one minute and then smack you with a sawn-off broom handle the next.

***

I'm holding the broom like an assegai and pointing it at the bottom of the wardrobe. The cockroach has been under there for five minutes. Adrienne's *still* asleep. Mataji has nodded off, and Lesley's back on her bed.

'You can't stand there all night,' she says.

'I won't be able to close my eyes knowing that thing is crawling around.'

'I don't think it's coming back out. Go and lay down. You can see the wardrobe from your bed. If it *does* come out, you can get it.'

I put the broom down and lay on the sleeping bag on the bed. I settle down to watch the gap with a sandal in my hand, remembering the walls crawling with cockroaches. A photograph of a roach sitting silently with the baby.

If God is everywhere, then God is roaches too.

In which case, I'll smack God with this sandal if He comes out from under the wardrobe.

Again I shudder.

But this is not the past. A saint sleeps within seventy yards of where I am now. The night is quiet and warm and forgiving. The sound of breathing, the gentle lullaby of life, soothes me. My eyelids are heavy like curtains, and they fall. Outside, the moonlight.

In the cradle of myself, I sleep.

CHAPTER FIVE
Moon Graffiti Moses

Early morning. I'm awake because I'm cold. I fell asleep last night on the lightweight sleeping bag I've used as a cover. Despite my pyjamas, I feel chilled to the bone, so I get into the bag and hunker down until everything below my nose is covered. I hear a sloshing noise in the kitchen—Lesley's washing clothes. Mataji and Adrienne are nowhere to be seen, but their beds are neatly made, which suits me fine because I'm going to lay in mine until I warm up. The sound of the water is soothing, and I drift pleasantly — wait!

I leap out of my bag and away from the wardrobe.

The cockroach!

Where's the broom handle? It's gone! I snatch up a sandal and stalk the bottom of the wardrobe. The cockroach is nowhere to be seen. I get on my hands and knees to look underneath — from a distance, of course. No roaches. I take the bottom end of my sleeping bag and shake it well. Confetti of crumbs falls out.

'Are you alright?' Lesley asks, poking her head around the door. She's holding the missing sweeping brush.

'Yeah,' I say. 'I was just wondering where the cockroach went?'

'No idea,' she replies, 'but it's not here now. Would you like a brew?'

'Yeah. Thanks. I'm gasping.'

'Great. Call me when it's ready. I'll be hanging the washing up and sweeping out the kitchen.' She goes out into the yard, and I'm left with an empty kettle. I remove the lid to fill it and then remember there isn't a tap. So I go to the water butt. That's empty too.

'There's no water,' I call out, a little peeved.

Lesley answers in a voice that sounds a little bit stilted, like that of a ventriloquist.

'I know. I used the last of it to do the washing.'

I look into the yard and see she's got three pegs between her teeth as she uses a fourth to hang a cheesecloth shirt on the line.

'Be a love and fill the water butt, will you? Take the two big plastic urns in the kitchen. If you take those to the pump, it shouldn't take long.'

Each container is two feet high, and neither has a handle on its bulbous girth or gaping mouth. On my way to the pump, I pass a man with two urns like mine. They dangle from the end of each arm. His face has an endearing predisposition to smiling. As we pass, his eyes twinkle, and he reveals a set of perfect white teeth.

The pump, a hand-cranked contraption that goes *ratchet-krunk* as the handle is pushed and pulled up and down, draws water up from two hundred feet below ground, rattling dramatically like a rusting and seaweed slick anchor chain on a frigate. I don't fill my containers to the top. Instead, I leave a generous void, assuming I'll have a better grip if the neck is dry.

The journey back to the koothi sees me sloshing along, slopping water all over my legs and drenching my sandals, which become abrasive from the damp sand particles. By the time I pour what remains of the water into the water butt, I'm irritated. Filling it like this will take forever, and I *still* haven't had a cup of tea.

My *chagrin* is also a source of irritation in itself.

Surely, I should be in a good mood?

There's a saint somewhere nearby, and it seems God is not dead. The sun's shining. We're in an ashram devoted to love, truth, devotion, purity and wisdom. The sweetness of life at this moment should make me immune to minor irritations, yet here I am — annoyed that such a simple task is not as easy as it looks. I return to the pump, passing the man I saw earlier in his garden, watering his plants. I nod to him. He presses his palms together in a humble *Namaste.*

I begin the — *ratchet-krunk, ratchet-krunk* —, and the water gushes from the mouth of the pump.

'It is better if you fill them.'

I turn to see who is giving this counter-intuitive advice. Behind me stands the same man with his two containers.

'I will show you.' He vigorously pumps water into an urn until it sloshes over the brim. Now he shows me how to grip, putting his fingers on the inside of the open neck and his thumb outside. I do as he has shown me, making a huge difference. The water increases my grip and no longer sloshes about.

I'm very pleased and compliment him on how lovely his garden is.

'The seeds I have planted in such a way that they will grow and blossom into the words, *Divine Love.*'

'How lovely. I'm not much of a gardener, though I once grew a potato on my window sill. It became a biohazard.'

The man waits politely for me to continue with my story, but we both realise there isn't one, and an awkward silence ensues until he breaks it.

'Have you been here before?

'Yes. This is my second trip.'

'This is excellent. What year did you visit?'

'Oh. I thought you were asking if I've been to the pump before. No. I've — I mean, no. This is my first visit to the Ashram.'

'Okay. This is splendid also.'

'Thank you. How long have you lived here?'

'Long time. I came with Swamiji almost —' he waggles his head as if counting up silently and using his ears as extra digits,' — nearly ten years ago. This area was desert, growing nothing—stones and thorn bushes. Swami began to clear the land and lay foundations. Planting trees and sinking wells. Now it is beautiful.' A wiggle of his head emphasises the last word, and he gestures, like screwing a lightbulb into a socket, as he says, '— this is why I plant the seeds, to blossom into divine love.'

When I return to the koothi, Lesley's already made the tea. We sit on the veranda with it, the air thick with blossom and lazy with the bumbling hum of insects drunk on pollen. True to his words, the gardener goes back and forth, tending the flowers. The sound of water pouring onto the soil becomes a slow liquid metronome soothing me.

The garden in the ashram isn't like Eden. Swami doesn't throw people out for eating the fruit. There are snakes, though. The children are taught to recognise them and to be wary. Then, when they're old enough and wise enough, the children pick them up and crack them like a bullwhip. Death is instantaneous.

It makes more sense to throw the serpents out of Eden

and leave the people in peace.

What kind of idiot would throw out the people instead of the snake?

***

Whatever it was that clattered down the chute in James Connolly Tower on Monday morning took a long time to land. I was already awake, watching cold light cut through the gap in my bedroom curtain to dissect the gloom. I lay there watching it on the ceiling. Motes of dust moved upon the air, swirling like minuscule shoals of fish when I exhaled heavily. Today was the day I'd be going to school.

When I was a child, living in Corby Street with cockroaches, I believed something lurked beneath my bed, waiting to grab an ankle or two if I got up during the night. My fear disappeared as I got older. I realised the safest place to be, sometimes, was actually under the bed itself. I wished I could have hidden away when the alarm clock in Ma's room started to ring. The sound was muffled as she put her hand on it, and there was a clatter as it fell off the bedside table. A muffled curse. Bedsprings. The clock was silenced. Ma was getting up to make my breakfast. A meal for the condemned — pupil.

I was frightened of walking toward Ballymun Comprehensive and being cruelly rejected by the mocking barbs of the other children. It happened to Tony, and now it was my turn. When it happened to our brother, we were with Ma, who had decided to turn away from the school to protect him from what lay ahead.

I'd be on my own.

Not even tumbleweed for company.

I rolled out of bed, feeling damned, abandoned by God. At this point in my life, I no longer prayed but still spoke to Him. It may be said that monologue was a form of prayer, but it wasn't. I was angry with the Almighty, and this was me shouting at the dead tone after the phone was put down, cutting me off. I didn't verbalise my words because that would have been insane. But maybe a little insanity was what I needed if I was to believe in a God who seemed to belong in St Brendan's Psychiatric Hospital. How could a God of Love allow such unhappiness in the world, of which mine wasn't even a drop in the ocean?

What was wrong with God?

What was it that had sent Him into the realms of madness?

Perhaps He had read some of the Catholic Doctrine.

Now, there was something to drive any sane being over the edge of sanity.

In the 16th century, the Church declared that people are born with the urge to do wrong. This tendency had been inherited from Adam, the Original sin being his.

God said don't touch a particular fruit, traditionally depicted as an apple. Despite this, Adam took a bite, and the Cult of the Vatican subsequently condemned humanity. Of course, the inability to differentiate between evil and being a bit peckish should have disqualified the pushers of Catholic Doctrine from being an authority on anything, but sadly it didn't.

Usually, Eve gets blamed for Adam's transgression because she suggested he partook in the forbidden fruit. It wouldn't stand up in a court of law because there were no witnesses other than Adam, and we know how unreliable he is because he's the idiot who ate the apple. Satan was involved, of course. Found guilty of passing along the world's worst dietary advice to Eve, he was turned into a snake for his trouble, and snakes can't talk.

The disobedience of Adam was passed down to every human being, a sort of genetic predisposition to sin. So, despite a 'watertight' alibi, humankind was born guilty as sin. As alibis go, sitting in a sac of amniotic fluid, listening to your mother's heart pulsing through your barely formed veins is a pretty good one, but not as far as the Church was concerned. Guilty until proven innocent was the credo.

Who was holding humankind responsible for the sin of Adam?

God was.

And what solution did the God of Infinite Wisdom and Compassion come up with?

He sent his Son to be publicly tortured and executed.

What?

Perhaps the nature of being infinite means putting things into perspective is a little bit tricky. Maybe the divine power of creating galaxies with a shrug leads to a tendency to be somewhat heavy-handed. So instead of our humble apology, God settled for a sincere execution. The apparent cruelty of God throwing His child to the sharks just so He could forgive the sharks for the appetite and teeth He gave them is, at the very least, an interesting approach to parenting.

That wasn't a God of love.

He was utterly mad.

He was the lunatic who secretly gave Moses two tablets of stone with ten commandments carved on them when all He had to do was write on the moon in giant letters,

'BE NICE — OR I'll DROP THIS ON YOU.'

So — I should have continued to pray to God? I'd have to have been insane.

And that was why I no longer prayed. It was also why I told God to fuck off as I rolled out of bed that morning. I could smell bacon and hear the radio in the kitchen. Ma was singing softly.

'Fly me to the moon —'

***

Sitting in the Prayer Hall with at least two hundred devotees listening intently to Swami Premananda, this question is on my mind.

Who am I?

He's sitting on his ornate chair in the far-left corner. Beneath the red robes, his feet are resting on a cushioned stool. Questions are asked of him, and he answers, talking at length.

His voice, a peculiar mix of gravel and honey, is ragged due to the passage of the lingams on Shivaratri. Nevertheless, he seems to enjoy making his devotees laugh with some of his replies. The way he waggles his head from side to side, the motion exaggerated by his bushy hair, brings to mind a sagacious teddy bear.

I find the spiritual conundrums posed by the devotees to be pointless. What's the point of asking, *'How do ' I ' get rid of my bad karma'* when you don't know who this 'I' is?

Who am I?

I'm fascinated by this simple question. Most of the time, the desire for an answer is a gentle but persistent thing, tantalising the mind. But sometimes, the need for an answer drives me with the persistence of a salmon swimming upstream. So I sit and hold Swami Premananda and this question in my heart. I do this to convey my question's sincerity, but I later realise that it was my mind with its smug trickiness setting a test.

Can Swami Premananda answer my question without me asking it?

I sit like this until my attention wanders to graze elsewhere in the paddock. I'm not interested in what Swami Premananda's saying to the other devotees—being near him now feels like basking in the sun. So I tell myself his words aren't meant for me. They're for the *other* devotees.

My ego this morning is a big fat, overfed cat licking its furry fundament. It's a wonder anyone can hear Swami Premananda speaking over the sound of my ego purring. By the time I pull my attention back, the talk has turned to the eventual emergence of spiritual government. My instant reaction is scepticism and then amusement. I can believe in miracles, but the idea of a government not owned by those few individuals who own the media and the banks stretches credulity a little too far.

Swami decides it is time for a break, so I return to the koothi. Mataji's sitting on the floor with a pile of books and papers. She's in front of the large metal wardrobe under which the cockroach ran.

'Hello,' she says. 'I wondered where everyone went.'

'We went to the Prayer Hall to listen to Swami.'

Mataji looks alarmed. 'Really? Swami asked me to write down all his words when he did Satsang. I better get over there.'

'Don't rush. He's left the Prayer Hall for now. He'll be back in a while.'

'In that case, I'll carry on. I'm sorting out some of these books. I thought I'd donate them to the ashram library. If there's any which interest you, take them.'

All the books are about spirituality, and I take a couple. Mataji opens the doors of her wardrobe and takes more books out. I stand back, wary of the cockroach. It's probably gone, but what if it's in there trying her sandals on?

'Why're you writing down Swami's speeches?'

'Because he asked me to do it, mainly — 'the wardrobe muffles her voice. ' — but it's hard to keep up with him.' I hear a dull clunk from within, and Mataji pulls out a weighty hardback book and puts it with the others. A wisp of hair dangles in front of her face. She tucks it behind her ear.

'Why not just use a dictaphone?'

'I do, but I also write what he says by hand to ensure I get it all down correctly. One thing I've learned from Swami after all these years is this. If he asks you to do something, there's *always* a good reason.'

'So, do you write down the questions people ask?'

'When I'm there. Yes. Why? Have you any questions for Swami? You never know. It may end up in one of the books we publish.'

Yes, I've got a question.
The only one that matters.
Who Am I —

***

Walking through the gates of Ballymun Comprehensive, accompanied by sniggers from other lads starting at the same time as me, I felt a little relief. There had been nothing more than quiet, snide laughter and the occasional whispered question to disturb me.

'Is that Kunte Kinte?'

No, it isn't, I thought as I joined the herd of teenage boys, my head held high and my satchel hanging low. I'd sharpened my pencils so diligently they could penetrate the hide of a rhino if need be. If I had to defend myself, I would go down fighting or, at the very least, scribbling.

At the main entrance to the school building, teachers shepherded us into an area that served as a modest library. We were told to sit on the floor, and soon, about a hundred and fifty boys were being addressed by the formidable Mister Cannon. He gave a welcome speech, a cross between an exhortation to do well and a promise to deal severely with any boy who landed before him for any breach of discipline. It was all going well until he said, ' — the mingyit this happens, you'll regret it.'

'Mingyit?' whispered a spotty-faced boy beside me. 'What the fuck is a mingyit?'

A boy on the other side of him with a blue school bag the size of a coal sack replied. 'I don't know. Something serious — I t'ink.'

I leant forward and told them, 'It's a minute.'

They both looked at me as if surprised I could speak English.

'Roight,' said the spotty boy, 't'anks.'

This brief exchange made me feel good until I heard a hushed voice behind me explaining, ' — the nigger says a mingyit's a minute.'

'Will ye feck off? That makes no sense.'

'I just heard him sayin' it!'

'Jaysus, he can't even speak English.'

'Who?' Kunte Kinte?'

'No. Not the darkie. I mean that big bollocks talking now. The headmaster.'

Mister Cannon and his big voice boomed on as I blushed with anger and embarrassment. Lots of the lads knew each other from nursery onwards. I envied their easy familiarity with each other as they stared at me. This bovine curiosity didn't bother me too much. It reminded me of the dumb unselfconscious gaze of livestock peering over a fence. Over the past few months, I'd seen enough of it to assume it would happen wherever I was. It was almost possible to forget the eyes looking at my skin and hair. What got under that skin were the lads that looked at me, whispered something to their friends and then sniggered.

I had no intention of being a victim in school. I wouldn't be bullied. Reluctantly, I told myself the first one who tried it would get a smack in the mouth. Admittedly, this was quite ambitious, seeing as I'd never been in a fight before, apart from with a girl who slapped the face off me when I was eight.

Trouble came early. A teacher took us down a corridor and left us waiting outside the classroom for our head of year. One of the lads, Padraig, a dark-haired boy who frequently jerked his head spastically to get his fringe out of his eyes, asked, 'How do you stop a nigger from drowning?'

He answered his own question: 'Take your foot off his head.'

I pushed him into the wall. The situation had arisen where I was supposed to punch Padraig in the mouth, but I was horrified. I didn't want to hurt him. I didn't want to hurt anyone. I didn't want anyone to hurt me.

'Hey—!' Padraig cried out, apparently mortally offended. 'Calm down! It's just a joke, for fuck sake!'

I was taken aback because he looked genuinely surprised at my reaction, as did everyone else. After a moment of shocked silence, they *laughed at me. I felt like an idiot. Being made fun of was one thing, but being laughed at was much worse. The classroom door being opened by the teacher released the tension in the air. A red-faced ginger-haired man beckoned us in. I sat at the back, only half-listening to what he said. I was perplexed. If I didn't react to racist language, it chipped away at my self-respect. It made me question my courage. On the other hand, if I did respond, I was laughed at, which felt a lot worse.*

I resolved not to act with hostility to any racist remarks. If it was good enough for Martin Luther King, the American Civil Rights leader assassinated in 1968, it was good enough for me. I'd chosen my middle name in honour of Martin Luther King because he was one of my heroes, so it wasn't a great stretch to conclude violence wasn't the way to go in future. I'd defend myself against physical force, but I'd not be the aggressor. I told myself violence never solved anything, though anyone who's ever swatted a mosquito knows this is untrue. It's also true that you can't swat every mosquito you encounter because there're too many of them, which neatly sums up the situation I found myself in.

There were so many minor incidents of ignorance concerning my colour it was impossible to confront everybody, so I gave up. I was overwhelmed by what felt like a tidal wave of stupidity. All things considered, though, the day went well compared to what I'd expected. At least I made it into the school, which was more than Tony managed when he was my age.

My stress level settled into background anxiety.

On my way home, nobody called me nigger even though I expected it with every footstep. When I entered our flat, I almost felt like I was just one of the lads. I knew this wasn't the case when I took off my jacket and found the name 'Kunte Kinte' written on the back and a globule of spit. I wiped it off before anyone in the house saw it.

I kept my anger and shame, and sadness to myself.

***

***

Swami steps back into the Prayer Hall to resume his discourse. He looks at me, and suddenly, as if a light is pouring into the murkiest depths of my past, I feel shame. Even though his eyes hold no reproach, it's too much for me. It's so uncomfortable that I get up, walk outside, and sit on an old, small wall to hear his honey gravel voice speaking. The gentleman who was referred to as 'The Doctor' on Shivaratri night is translating. The Doctor tells us Swami will help us to stay on the spiritual path.

Looking back on my life, I wonder if it's more accurate to say I occasionally trip over the path rather than walk along its length. My sense of shame comes again, but with it, there are questions.

Am I this?
Am I this feeling?
Am I all the bad things I've done?
Am I all the good?
Am I the footsteps I left behind me?
I close my eyes and ask Swami Premananda.
What am I?
Who am I?

***

I was very pleased with myself. Summer had slinked off to warm some other part of the world, and Autumn settled itself onto Ballymun, blowing the dead leaves across the car park and raining nightily. The dark and inclement weather meant I could move around Ballymun, bundled up in my oversized anorak with the hood up, without being noticed. Tucked under a blanket of darkness, I felt safe. If nobody can see you, nobody can call you coon. The denizens of Ballymun had even been considerate enough to smash the street lights, which should have lit the pathways across the green which led to the library. How very thoughtful.

The grey slabs of the concrete path were sprinkled with glinting confetti of broken glass, which crunched underfoot. Fresh rain pattered on my hood, and my face was wet, but I was happy. Under my arm, four good books in a plastic bag, and a packet of warm toffees snug in the palm of my hand.

One of the books in my bag was called To Hell and Back, about Audie Murphy and his experience in the Second World War. Another book was about Martin Luther King and the Civil Rights Movement. Tucked between those two was a book that might have some sexy bits. I wasn't the most diligent of students, but I intended to study this with the sort of intensity usually reserved for the likes of Sherlock Holmes when looking for clues. I also had a book on UFO abductions, which I thought Tony might like.

When I reached the bottom of the tower, I was more than a little surprised to hear what sounded like a horse whinnying indignantly. I backtracked a little and looked around the corner of the building, and there, in the middle of the car park, was a horse. It was caught in the beam from one solitary but bright light as if in a circus ring. Sitting on the horse was a boy smoking a cigarette. He looked like the Marlboro Man before his balls dropped. The pony had a bridle but no saddle and looked bloody miserable. Off to the left, just out of sight, I heard someone laughing, and then another small horse trotted into view with two other lads on its back. Marlboro boy flicked the butt of his cigarette up and away, and off went the trio, trotting out into the night.

When I got upstairs, Ma was in the living room watching Blankety-Blank. Jason was asleep on the sofa. He'd been playing with one of his action men before he went asleep and had nodded off with it in such a way that it was digging into his cheek. I gently tugged it from under his head and left it on the sofa beside him.

Tony was on the balcony, looking out and smoking. He nodded to me in greeting before returning his attention to whatever he'd been looking at.

'How're you doing?' Tony asked.

'Not too bad,' I replied. 'How about yourself?'

He shrugged and flicked his cigarette butt into the air. It rose like a distress flare and then plummeted into the night.

'I'm alright,' he said, but we both knew he wasn't. He hardly ever went outside. The hostility of the place got to him. He was a prisoner in the sky, where the pigeons circled like sharks and dropped their guts on the people below. Day after day, night after night, Tony remained in the tower. Rapunzel grew her hair. Tony painted. He painted portraits of his face, getting older and sadder while poisoning himself with nicotine and gallons of Coca-Cola. The rare occasions he ventured out to the shops convinced him that staying in was the better option.

Below us, we heard the distinctive clatter of horses' hooves. I looked over the balcony and saw the three young lads gallop across the car park on the horses.

'Look at those gobshites,' I said. 'Where've they got those horses from?'

'There's a horse trading fair in North Dublin,' Tony replied.

I looked at him, surprised that he knew this.

He shrugged, almost by way of an apology. 'It was on the news a couple of days ago. Ponies go cheap.'

'You're sure they weren't talking about budgies?'

'They said it was a healthy alternative to heroin.'

Ballymun was the Heroin capital of Ireland. Ironically, 'Horse' is one of the street names for heroin. A campaign aimed at keeping children away from drugs was launched in Britain. It had a straightforward slogan.

Just Say No

For the children below us, it was 'Just Say Neigh.'

'Do you get much hassle?' Tony asked. He looked at my school, perhaps thinking of the day he tried. Not being able to go had a profound effect on his education.

'I get some hassle but not as much as I thought.'

'That's good,' he said.

'It's ironic because I was dreading going to school here, but in a way, it was just what I needed. I get out of this tower and laugh with lads my age. They take the piss out of me occasionally, but it doesn't feel malicious for the most part. Besides, they also laugh at Jews, women, homosexuals, Protestants, the 'handicapped', Pakistanis, dead people and pensioners. They laugh at each other, and I get to laugh at them too.

'That's good,' Tony said without much enthusiasm. He coughed and then spat over the balcony. 'You're just like one of the lads, eh?'

'Fuck, no. It's uncanny, but as soon as I start thinking I am just one of the lads, someone says something that reminds me I'm not. And that's just my classmates. And that increases as soon as I enter the corridor and interact with the rest of the school. As for walking home, that's just the same as when we first got here. I may or may not get home without being told to go back to Africa or being called Kunta Kinte, but in either case, I'm bracing myself for it, and that's almost as bad. In fact, it's worse. So — not like one of the lads. No.'

Tony nodded. 'I know what you mean about waiting. I went to the shop for ciggies while you were in school. It felt like walking through a minefield and waiting for something to go off. Waiting for one of the people I passed to turn around and call me a nigger and — ' Tony shook his head, looking lost in thought. 'I don't understand why they do that. What's wrong with them?' He looked at me as if I might have an answer.

I shrugged. I knew as well as Tony that the kindness of strangers in Ballymun seemed to be reserved for others who were also strangers to us.

'I get less hassle from the lads who know me,' I said. 'Once they get to know you, there's less antagonism. I think that's because you become a person to them rather than just a colour. And, to be fair, I think if most people knew what it felt like to be treated the way they treat us, they'd stop. They're just ignorant, that's all.'

'So you think they insult us because they don't know what it's *like to be us?"*

'Yeah.'

The rain started up again, so I stepped back and dug my hands deep into my pockets. I was feeling cold and about to step back inside when Tony spoke again.

'You're wrong. The people down there insult us because they don't want to know us. They don't give a shit how it feels. It feels good to them. That's all that matters. We're nothing to them.' *He placed his hands on the concrete balcony and gripped it tightly. He leaned back and drew forward as he spat into the rain.*

'Nothing,' *he muttered.*

Such troubled times.

But how could I blame the Irish for not knowing who I am?

I had no idea, either.

***

Who am I?

I'm sitting outside the Prayer Hall, asking Swami Premananda the same question. Even though I have no answer and don't know if there is one, I feel content with the sense of solitude and stillness on the little wall on which I'm sitting. Then, a young couple walks to the window nearest to me and stands looking through to where Swami is seated. They speak softly to each other. I don't understand the words, but I can hear the reverence in their voices. I watch them for a couple of minutes, hoping they'll go away, trying not to be irritated by this intrusion of my solitude. Then, unwilling to share the space, I get up and stroll around to the back of the Prayer Hall.

There's an open door. I go in because it appears to lead to another quiet space. I also need some shelter from the sun. I find myself in a little room, veiled from the rest of the Prayer Hall by a length of material. I can hear Swami talking on the other side, and, feeling like a naughty boy, I move forward stealthily and peer through a narrow gap curtain. I see people in the hall. I'm wholly hidden, and I'm right behind Swami.

His chair's right in front of me to the side. I can see his left hand as he gesticulates, emphasising his point. I move back slowly and lower myself to the ground to sit cross-legged. I'm almost breathless in my desire to stay silent and out of sight.

I sit for a long time, enjoying the peace. Eventually, I begin to wonder —

'Does he know I'm here?'

Swami turns and looks at me through the veil.

The hair on the back of my neck stands on end.

He turns back to the devotees and continues his discourse.

I'm disturbed by this. Did Swami Premananda just read my mind? I've been asking him to show me who or what I am, on the understanding that he can, if he wants, read my mind, but this is different. What just happened isn't me lobbing a thought to him, wondering if he'll catch it. This is him picking up the thought as easily as a discarded magazine in a waiting room. I'm freaked out. I get up and go outside to my little wall. The couple have gone, and once more, I'm alone with my thoughts — well, almost alone if what just happened is anything to go by.

Soon, the wall burns the back of my legs, so I sit forward, moving my calves away from it while I review the past few minutes. Swami Premananda looking at me through the veil had to have been a coincidence. Or maybe not? I don't know. I have an intense desire to find out. It's almost an ache, but I won't ask him. I've been projecting the same thoughts at him, on and off for hours, like the tap-tapping of Morse code.

Who am I?
What am I?

If he can help me find that out, he's welcome to read my mind. He can even colour in the pictures if he wants. And if he can't, and it's all for nothing, I've also lost nothing.

In the same way that I don't want to listen to what he's saying, I also don't want to speak to him. I want to look at Swami Premananda, but not out of adoration. It's something akin to an immense curiosity, the root of which is possibly my ego which is still purring away. I recognise Him as being different somehow, but I still don't understand what he is. His existence is like a Rubik's Cube for the mind. It keeps going back to try and figure out the solution to what he is but keeps coming back with no satisfactory explanation.

I wonder if, when he comes out of the Prayer Hall, he'll see me? I imagine him smiling and waving, asking how I am. After all, he knows I'm here, doesn't he? So maybe there's something special about me? Or is that my ego talking? Of course, it is — and do I *really* believe he's a mind-reader? Or have I just suspended my disbelief because some part of me is enjoying the drama of feeling a little different from others?

Whoa —

I make a determined effort to stop my mind from twittering to itself, but it's like trying to stop the wind by holding up a dandelion.

To my great disappointment, Swami leaves the Prayer Hall through the front door, thus avoiding me. Usually, he goes through the back door, where I'm sitting. I feel snubbed like he's deliberately avoided me. My ego stops purring, and now I feel like a fool. My energy drains away. Deflated, I go back to the koothi, check that there are no cockroaches, and lie down on my bed with a great sigh. My mind returns once more to what happened. Having the well-thumbed, grubby sections of my brain available for someone to look at makes me feel ashamed, but I take comfort from three things. First of all,

I'm no better or worse than anybody else. Secondly, I assume Swami has seen worse minds than mine. And last of all, perhaps I'm wrong about the whole thing?

This last thought runs along the grooves of my brain, panting like a lab rat, looking for a button to push, one that will provide some gratification in the form of a definitive answer. The lab rat smashes into the big glossy button marked 'coincidence.'

It must have been

Maybe

I know I'm warm, comfortable and tired, thinking about the mind being where the body isn't, and the voice of my body fades away.

Sinking into mind

        Drifting off to sleep

Sleeping off to drift

                slinking off to drink

    mind enough to

shrouds

        memories

drifting upon

                    something dark

scurrying

        scuttling across the floor

  skinny black legs

      barbed like vicious spears

 cockroaches

No No No No No No

There's a rush of warm breath on my face.
Startled, I wake. I sit up and look around.
  'Hello? Who's there?'
  Nobody.

I'm all alone. I roll over. Peer under the bed. It's too small for anyone to be underneath, but I still need to look. I see my sandals. That's all. Dust. Nothing else.

I sit up, heart thumping.

Who woke me?

I sit with this question for a long time until I hear footsteps outside the koothi. Mataji enters, holding a sheaf of papers. 'Hello,' she says. 'I thought you'd still be asleep.'

'I was. I was having a nightmare, and then someone blew in my face and woke me up.'

'Oh? Who?'

'No idea. There was nobody here.'

'It could be Swami. He can be very playful in his way.'

I tell her what happened in the little room at the back of the Prayer Hall.

'Is it possible he was reading my mind?' I ask.

'Yes. It certainly is. Anything is possible.'

'It's not uncommon for him to do these things,' Mataji says. 'Lesley must have told you loads of stories about him. Things she witnessed.'

'She has, but they were just stories.'

'You didn't believe them?'

'That's not what I meant to say. What I mean is, when Lesley shares those stories, they're neat little anecdotes of weirdness in other people's lives, but now that weirdness is becoming my own experience of life.'

'Does it bother you?'

'No. Not really. However, I do wonder if it's all just in my head. And I don't know what to do with these experiences that I may or may not be having.'

'Why do anything?'

'I don't know. I feel like they mean something.'

'Then they do. What would you like them to mean?'

'Nothing.' I said, shrugging, dissembling, not admitting that I wanted them to mean I was in some way special.

'Then it doesn't mean anything. Just move on. It's enough that you're aware.'

'But that could apply to anything?'

'That's right.' Mataji sits down on her bed. It creaks. She looks thoughtful and then says, 'Swami doesn't want followers. He's not the Pied Piper. He wants people to follow themselves — meaning, their own 'Self' or 'Soul' and not him. But to do this, they need to know *what* that self is. So, don't get hung up on the physical phenomena. Instead, concentrate more on the space within which that happens.'

I look around the space in the koothi, none the wiser.

Dubiously, I say, 'Yeah?'

'Yes,' she says, smiling. 'It might help to remember this. Swami likes people to question things, but he also likes when they can recognise the answer when it comes. Sometimes the answers are so subtle you can't help but wonder if you're fooling yourself. You think the answer needs to be more obvious, but it doesn't matter how obvious it is if you're looking in the wrong place.'

Mataji begins to sort through the papers she's got in her hands and then pauses.

'You might be making the mistake of presuming Swami Premananda is reacting to whatever you were doing. But, as much as I believe he knows what's in my heart, he doesn't need to know the inner workings of you, me, or anyone else. All that's necessary is that he moves at exactly the right time. And if he does move, for want of a better expression, according to the Will of God, then his timing can't be anything other than perfect in whatever he does. And if that movement or action answers a question for you, then so be it.'

She goes back to her task.

***

Lesley's sitting on a small wall outside the ashram, smoke from her cigarette slowly rising, uncoiling, a lazy loop of grey fog.

'Hello there,' she says with a smile, looking at me from beneath the brim of her floppy straw hat.

'Hi,' I replied. 'I wondered where you'd gone.'

'I went for a walk with Adrienne after Satsang and then went looking for you.'

'I was fast asleep.'

'I know. You were in such a deep sleep I thought it best to leave you.'

I sit with her, and we watch the world doing nothing much. A villager comes along the road, sandaled feet crunching the dirt. He passes by, leaving us with a glimpse of a shy smile. Another comes along on a rickety black bike, bony brown knees rising and falling as he pedals past. Time ambles along in his wake. This moment is too perfect to be rushed along.

Here comes a young man on a bicycle. It's a *bone shaker*, a heavy black contraption held together with rust, string and optimism. The wheels rattle like bedsprings in a bin, rolling down a slope. Oddly enough, he's got an aged gentleman perched on the handlebars. Both men look at us as if having an octageNarenan instead of a bell is nothing unusual. If not for the noise of the wheels, their slow progress would be hypnotic. The effortless grace of their unhurried pace takes them slowly down the road.

'Do you think that,' Lesley says, ' that pensioner actually wanted to be on the bike, or was he just crossing the road at the wrong time?'

'I don't know. He certainly looked happy enough.'

'Probably glad it wasn't a bus.'

I notice Lesley scratching small red marks on her arm. Against her pale skin, they look livid.

'You've been bitten?'

'I think so. It's really itchy.'

'Don't scratch.'

'It's hard not to. I was going to ask Mataji if she's got some cream I can use, but she disappeared after satsang.'

'I was just talking to her. I was telling her about — ' I fill Lesley in on what happened earlier at the back of the Prayer Hall and also the manner in which I woke. '— and so I opened my eyes, and guess who was there?'

'Swami?'

'No. Well, not in person. Possibly not even there at all,'

'What?'

'I mean, there was nobody there. So between that and what happened in the Prayer Hall, I was a little freaked out for a while.'

'It reminds me of when Gina and I went to see Swami in Wimbledon, near London. He was at the front of this hall, surrounded by loads of devotees. We waited ages to talk with him, but it got so late that we decided to leave. There were so many people we thought there was no way we'll get to see him. It was a long drive back to Manchester, and we both had work in the morning —.'

She pauses to bat at a giant fat-bottomed bee who seems intent on pollinating her straw hat.

'— little sod. Where was I? Oh, yes. We decided to leave, but we both cried out just as we reached the exit. I had my hand over my right eye, and Gina had a hand over one of her ears. Some force had jabbed at both of us to get our attention. We turned around, and one of Swami's helpers looked directly at us. He waved a finger from side to side and mouthed, 'Don't leave.' So, we stayed, and then Swami saw us. There's no doubt he can project his will wherever he wants.'

'Weird.'

'Considering what happened to Gina and me, you're lucky to have been woken with air blown at you. You could have been woken up with a slap in the face.'

***

Back in the past, a few days after Lesley and I had that meditation, something peculiar happened in my chest. My heart was not my own, quite literally. In her presence, my heart or something in its vicinity whirled like a windmill of light behind my breastbone. It turned and spun ever faster, becoming a luminous wheel of light. This isn't a figure of speech. I mean this, literally. As we spoke, there was a peculiar dialogue between my heart and hers. Apparently, they were old friends and were catching up. I felt it was happening regardless of Paul Donaldson or Lesley Capucho-Paulo. We became ever closer, trying to catch up with this secret dialogue of the Heart.

***

The sun, high in the blue sky, casts shadows, turning us into sundials as we walk to the Prayer Hall to watch an abhishekam. This Hindu ritual can take many forms, but in this instance, it involves the ritual washing of a statue. Morning, noon and night, this act of devotion is a deep heartfelt pulse within the Ashram. A regular, rhythmic reminder of the Sacred. Attendance isn't obligatory, but generally, they are well attended.

We enter the Prayer Hall and sit among the devotees. The Abishakem begins, accompanied by a mantra spoken strongly and clearly by the Mataji performing the ritual. Many devotees join in, but I merely mumble along, fumbling with the pronunciations and dropping the rhyme clumsily. It reminds me of being in church.

I close my eyes, my mind running to the past while my body sits in the present. I was an altar boy. So was Tony. He was twelve. I was seven. In the morning before school, we helped a Franciscan monk called Brother Jerrod, who gave us a delicious soup to warm us up. He also made coffee so strong that Jesus would have risen on the second day and not the third had he taken a sip before the crucifixion.

In the Prayer Hall, the ringing chime of bells barely disturbs me. I'm thinking of the *thurible*, a brass ball on a long chain, incense smouldering inside. Back and forth, it swung, chain clinking and the scent of Olibanum wafting through the air. The nose has a better memory than the mind. It brings me back to when I believed the *'Body of Christ'* was contained in a wafer. Now, decades later, I think the sacred *'something'* is here in a Sri Lankan Saint.

A tumult of little bells being rung vigorously brings me back to the now. An arathi, a brass implement like a candle holder, is being held up, and in response, we hold our hands up to the five points of flaming light, camphor burning brightly, and take a blessing from it.

I managed to sit cross-legged on the floor through the ritual. It's a pose that makes me feel spiritual when I get into it and arthritic when I get out. Shifting to a more comfortable position, resting on my knees for a while, I wave to Lesley, sitting with the women, peaceful and mellow, full of light and warmth. Up ahead, garlanded with fresh flowers, the beautiful golden statue of Lord Krishna lures the eye with its honey lustre. Many believe Krishna and Christ are very similar, but the Catholic Church won't entertain the possibility that they could be the same. The belief that Jesus is God's only son will not change anytime soon. Having another *'son of God'* with the same message of love and tolerance at least a thousand years before the first heretic was burnt doesn't sit well with the Vatican.

Talking snake?

Millions of animals fitting into a small boat?

A woman being made from a rib?

I used to believe all of that. I even used to think the God of all creation was a single parent, firing blanks for billions of years, with the one notable exception of Jesus.

Am I any less deluded now, sitting before a statue of Krishna Swami Premananda materialised in 1978, a year after I arrived in Ballymun? That would have been one year before the Pope flew in a helicopter over the towers, the junkies and a few bewildered, sad ponies. Across the other side of the world, Swami Premananda was quietly teaching his devotees about humility and the simple love of purity. For much of that time, I lay in bed, my head under my pillow, listening to the tower swallowing the bones of God in the dead of night.

Sitting in the Prayer Hall, reflecting on the past, I wonder if I just swapped one form of madness for another.

Perhaps I have.

Swami Premananda enters the Prayer Hall unannounced. He steps from behind a veil that covers a doorway. I was behind that curtain yesterday, and he had looked at me through it. The hair on my neck had risen, and I'd walked out, spooked by it. Perhaps because of that, I now have a new sense of his power. Even though he's quite small, it's like watching a herd of buffalo approach. I hunker down, surrounded by other devotees and watch his progress as he approaches. He touches the head of a white-haired lady with his palm and continues walking. Devotees turn their faces to follow his. Down the aisle, swiftly he moves. He turns slightly and is — damn, he's coming this way. A mild panic erupts before me. People scramble to get out of the way.

I hear someone saying, 'Don't touch his feet!'

Much bottom shuffling. People slide to the side, making a furrow for him to tread along through the devotees.

Voices insist *nobody* must touch his feet.

I don't *want* to touch them, thank you very much.

But look! Here they are, those very feet, whispering along beneath his red silk robe, coming closer. I shuffle to my left to get out of the way. I'm almost oblivious to my neighbour's hot, clammy bulk as I squash up against him.

Don't touch Swami's feet —

I don't wa — oh, crap! His foot brushes against me. It's almost a kick. Oh damn! What have I — Wait! What's this? His hand is firmly upon my head, warmly rooted, and now it's gone. He's walking further along toward the open doors of the Prayer Hall. Light is streaming in. He stops, turns, and comes back down the aisle, back to the door through which he entered.

I can still feel the warmth of his hand on my head.

Later, Lesley and I are walking near the Dharamsala. The smell of food is delicious.

'Swami gave you a blessing,' Lesley says. 'When he put his hand on your head.'

'It didn't feel like a blessing. At one point, I thought he was trying to dropkick me out of the Prayer Hall.'

'He touched you with his feet?'

'Yeah. I tried to get out of the way, but he barged right past me. People were saying not to touch his feet. Did I drop a clanger? Some awful foot-based faux pax?'

'No. I don't think so. Of course, it's considered bad form to touch the feet of a saint without permission, but it looked like he deliberately went over to you, so I'd say it was a blessing.'

We continue walking. The subtle hum of honey bees hums in the air. The water pump goes 'ratchet-krunk.' One of the older children works the handle so his friends can fill their cupped hands. The sun is intense, making the faraway colours of heaven and earth swoon into each other. The far end of the ashram wavers, becoming liquid. The planet's molten core is boiling up through my sandals.

***

Evening comes, and the heat subsides. Like the warm dark shadow of an owl sitting on its nest, night settles comfortably on the Ashram. The candles by Meenakshi flicker and glow, honeying the air, shivering shadows over the flower petals by Her feet. Lesley and Adrienne murmur, sleepily sharing memories of when they spent time with Swami Premananda in Sri Lanka.

I'm on my camp bed, looking up at the banana leaf ceiling where a tiny gecko rustles. It sounds like he's trying to eat a bag of crisps without anyone noticing. My eyelids are heavy. I'm trying to push them back up. I want the world to keep pouring itself into me while I lay in wonder.

Something sacred looks at us through the eyes of other people.

The thought is a flash of lightning in the darkness.

Stillness.

I am gone.

CHAPTER SIX
Do Hedgehogs Hug?

It's five in the morning. The goose-pimpled skin of my arms feels rough as I rub warmth into them. We're up early to join the early morning meditation. Slipping out into the silent moonlight, we go over to the Prayer Hall. I'm hopeful that being near Swami Premananda will deepen my meditation. I may not attain a state of bliss, but perhaps I can put my mind in the shallow end of cosmic consciousness. If not, I'll settle for just feeling mellow.

Inside, where the candlelight jitters the shadows and the floor is cold and hard on the soft soles of my feet, I sit as comfortably as I can. My belly is empty, but the emptiness feels good. It feels tight and pious, and I'm confident the meditation will be nourishing. So, I sit and wait for my mind to settle. Within minutes, perhaps seconds, it wanders off. I drag it back, but away it goes again to graze outside the paddock. I bring it back—

My head falls forward.

Oops. I think I was snoring.

When the mind can't settle, it's known as *Monkey Mind.*

Mine is peeling a banana and looking for Tarzan. I'm irritated by my lack of mellowness, but I keep trying. Finally, my effort moves beyond *Monkey Mind* into *Cow Mind*, monotonously chewing the cud of my brain. I want the universal Om, but all I can manage is the opposite, which is Moo.

I hear little noises. People cough. They sneeze. They shift position. They whisper. But that's nothing to the sound of my head as I breathe. Huge draughts of air noisily rush through my nostrils as if worked by bellows. Gastric juices begin to churn.

My head jerks back up with a porcine grunt.

I return to the koothi, accompanied by the moon. The sun is peering over the horizon, probably wondering where the undignified grunt came from. Tired, hungry, and disappointed, I snuggle into my sleeping bag.

Lesley comes back when the sun is up.

'Guess who I've just been talking to?' she asks.

'No idea,' I say, pushing the sleeping bag to my feet.

'Rekha.'

'Who?'

'You know, Rekha, she's married to Naren? They were among the first devotees of Swami in England. I told you about them. Remember?'

'Oh. Yes. I do. Didn't we visit them in Birmingham when one of the ladies from the ashram came to England on a little tour?'

'That's right.'

'How is Rekha?'

'She's fine. She might pop in later. She's here with Naren. Would you like a brew?'

'Great.' I hold my arms out to Lesley, and she walks over. In the warmth of a hug, we slowly rocked from side to side. It's a moment of contentment, a meditation in itself, which is somewhat spoiled by Rekha sweeping through the door with a colourful swish of silken sari. She throws herself onto the nearest cot bed with a dramatic sigh.

'Good morning Paul,' she says. 'How are you?'

'Fine,' I reply, 'long time no see. You're looking well.'

'I don't know why,' she replies, rolling her eyes and fanning herself with her hand. 'You'd think I'd be able to take this heat, being as I'm of Gujarati extraction, but it's awful. I forget how hot it gets in-between visits to India.'

Lesley, who loves the sun, says, 'It's a lovely morning.'

'Yes, it is, isn't it?' Rekha says reluctantly. 'It's lovely. Too hot, but it will do for now. Lesley, my dear, has Mataji said when the vibhuti will come? I meant to ask you earlier when we met, but I forgot.'

'No, but I think it'll be within the next few days. Maybe even today.'

'Oh, that's a bother. I was hoping to go into Trichy. I just *have* to go shopping.'

'Me too. We're running out of stuff ourselves. We need food and some more toiletries.'

'Food? Forget food,' Rekha says, sitting up. 'I need some new suitings.'

'Suitings?' I ask.

'Yes. Suitings. You'd know them as saris, Paul. They're so cheap here I'd have to be utterly mad not to take some back to England.'

***

Soon, we're in Trichy, with Mataji guiding us. She's asked Swami if the vibhuti would come today, and he assured her it wouldn't. So she walks between Lesley and Rekha, and Naren walks behind with me. Her presence is comforting as we walk busy, unfamiliar streets packed with people.

Many of the shops don't have windows. Instead of glass, they have open fronts. At night, grilles and boards are put up for security. The advantage of not having a large display window hits me in the face as I stop and stand outside a shop that does have one. The heat bounces off it, misting my glasses. I remove them to wipe the lens with my T-shirt. A droplet of sweat splashes onto them as I look down. Naren waits for me as I do this. Losing sight of each other in such a busy street would be easy.

He points at the blue sky and smiles. 'It almost makes you miss the rain.'

'Yeah, almost,' I reply, laughing.

Like Rekha, Naren is also of Gujarati extraction, but I'd say they are more English than I am. He has a warm, scholarly air and walks with his hands behind his back as if to stop fidgeting. I don't know either of them too well, but I like them very much. Naren and I follow along and catch up with the others as they enter a sari shop. I stop to look in the window but stand back this time, not wanting my glasses to steam up. The exquisitely dressed mannequins behind the glass hold their hands as if asking for something. Beggars come to mind, and I turn my back on them. Within moments the reflected heat burns my neck — for feck sake — this heat. It's like doing the conga with a dragon standing in line behind me.

All the people rushing by are making me feel even hotter. I can almost smell their warmth. Their loose-limbed, graceful flow has friction all of its own, generating more heat. It's the claustrophobic heat of an unwelcome embrace. I feel dizzy. Look to my left. A cow ambles along the pavement, aloof on the hoof and doe-eyed, tail lazily waving at the flies following its bony rump. Velvet ears twitch the insects away from the soft stickiness inside the fluttering fold.

I raise my arm to wipe my overheated, slick forehead. Naren points to my waist. Raising my arm lifted the hem of my T-Shirt and exposed the utility belt around my waist.

'Paul, you need to be careful. There'll be pickpockets here, no doubt. I hope you've nothing in there that can't be replaced.'

'Damn. I better be careful. It has everything — rupees, my passport and a camera. I've even got a sachet of Imodium.'

'You're having tummy trouble?' Naren asks. He's kind enough to look concerned rather than laugh, which is what I would have done.

'No,' I reply. 'I brought it just in case. Though if I lose everything to a pickpocket, I just may sh -'

The cow drops a steaming bolus of manure onto the road.

***

There was more than a whiff of bullshit in Ballymun every time I went to school and listened to Mister Cardigan, the poor man whose job was to talk about religion and the love of God. When he spoke of Religion, what he meant was Christianity. Every other faith was considered superstition and an informal invitation to burn in hell. My Catholic upbringing had left me with much the same opinion, though I thought that burning seemed like a bit of an over-reaction by God to the non-believers. Indeed, a light singeing and a stern warning to stop being a dick would have had the same effect if delivered with thunder and lighting. But, of course, after a few months in Ballymun, I considered Christianity a superstition to be lumped in with all the others.

Listening to Mister Cardigan waffle on about the love of God was like listening to someone talk about their imaginary friend. I could scarcely contain my contempt. I'd taken the time to learn about the dark history of my religion with its absurdities and contradictions of its God and considered the teacher a well-meaning fool. It's possible that turning my back on the man-made God allowed me to consider the possibility of God, made Man.

***

Oh, God! Shopping is *so* dull. We've been at it for an hour, and Rekha's striding off toward more 'suiting' shops. Naren, trailing in her wake, has a parcel under each arm. Having had enough of this, Lesley, Mataji and I go in the opposite direction. We'll meet them later by the taxi which brought us.

Mataji brings us into the cool interior of the Femina Hotel. Outside, the traffic honks at itself. Inside, the superior air-conditioning smugly hums. You could keep a dead dolphin behind the desk for months before it went off. I'm so happy to feel the delicious chill as we're shown to a table in the restaurant. Drinks are brought to our table, tea for Mataji and Lesley and a cold bottle of effervescent pop for me. I gulp it down until my tonsils feel like they're being dissolved in acid. Then, with a loud gasp, part pleasure and part pain, I clunk my empty bottle onto the table.

'God, I needed that.'

'Looks like it,' Lesley says. 'Would you like another?'

'No thanks. I suspect it'll make me belch like a bullfrog.'

'Thanks for sharing.'

Mataji says, 'Have some tea. It's better for thirst. All that sugar will make you want to drink more.'

'True. I'll get some *'chai.'* I look around for a waiter while Lesley and Mataji talk about temples. Raising my hand a little to gesticulate for service, I'm bemused by how quickly a waiter appears.

'Have you been shot out of a cannon?' I ask.

He looks confused. Lesley seems a little embarrassed and is covering her face with one hand.

'The *Mutiny*', she whispers.

'What? Oh — sorry. Tea, please.'

He goes to get my brew. I hope he didn't think my remark about being shot out of a cannon was meant to offend. During the Indian Mutiny of 1857, the British executed many Indians by strapping them onto the mouths of cannons. They then fired, killing them indiscriminately to terrorise the population into staying subservient to the Empire. Again, I hope the waiter didn't make the connection.

When my tea turns up, it's delicious and doesn't taste like piss, so it looks like my stupid comment went unnoticed. I occupy myself by looking out the window at the traffic, only half listening to the conversation.

I hear Mataji say, '—the temples at Madurai are within easy travelling distance.'

Lesley's smiling at the prospect and says, 'I'd love to see them. I read about Madurai before we left England. And if we get time, we can even go further afield.'

An excursion off the ashram doesn't appeal to me. I think we should stay and be around Swami, and I'm about to say so when, under the table, Lesley puts her hand over mine.

'Wouldn't it be great to go south and see Vivekananda's Rock?' she says. I admit the idea has some appeal. I have a great fondness for Swami Vivekananda. I read many of his texts searching for a God to replace the one I dumped in Ballymun. That search brought me to Swami Premananda, and though I may not have found God, it feels like God has found me when Swami looks my way. So with that in mind, I decide I want to stay at the ashram rather than go touring.

But, the look on Lesley's face brings me up short. This little excursion means a lot to her.

'What do you think? So long as the vibhuti isn't coming tomorrow, we'll leave early in the morning?'

'Yeah,' I say. 'That'd be great.'

She squeezes my hand before putting her own back on the table. She's all aglow with anticipation.

Feck —

***

As if living in Ballymun, dealing with racism and losing my faith in everyone's imaginary friend wasn't enough to deal with, my body began sprouting hair in once smooth places. In particular, it grew on my legs, which worried me immensely because I mistakenly thought this was premature 'hairiness' brought on by my being, how you say — 'over familiar' with myself.

I was in the first year of a new school with hundreds of other lads, all strangers to me, ricocheting around the corridors, propelled by their testosterone. Eventually, my colour became less of an issue. Fewer people reacted adversely to my presence, and as the weeks and months passed, I began to feel as if the worst was behind me. Then, the leg hair started to grow, and I woke up with feet too big for me. And spots. It may not seem too much of a problem, but it was a disaster to me. It felt like I'd escaped a firing squad by climbing over a wall, only to find another firing squad waiting on the other side. I was gutted. My body was changing, but not in a good way. In the eyes of others, as far as I was concerned, it made me look even more ridiculous and more of a target for ridicule.

Many of my classmates had spots, and their voices were changing like mine. We all had the gangly clumsiness of teenagers, but nobody else seemed to be growing hair on their legs like me, apart from one lad so huge and hirsute, he might have been a bear on the run from Dublin Zoo. His voice hadn't just broken; it was shattered. The fragments fell down the back of his throat and landed deep in the pit of his belly. When he spoke, the noise rumbled up from the depths of a set of balls that probably wouldn't have looked out of place, dangling from the back of a horse. The noise made the rest of us sound like 45's played back on 78. If he got any hassle from the other lads, he just growled, and it stopped soon enough. The size of this boy also helped. There was no way I could be as intimidating as he could. For one thing, my voice hadn't broken yet. So if I got angry, my voice went up in pitch, and I sounded like someone vigorously rubbing a balloon.

I decided to shave them to avoid being singled out for ridicule due to my hairy legs. I'd never shaved anything before, but how difficult could it be? So I set to work in the bathroom one Saturday morning, using a disposable razor Tony had left on the side of the sink. It was easy at first, but halfway through the first leg, I began to have doubts. First, it became painful as I scraped a trough through the shaving foam I'd sprayed myself with. I hadn't been expecting pain to be part of the exercise and became increasingly alarmed when I saw blood smeared into the shaving foam where I'd nicked my skin. I was sorry I'd started, but if there's anything worse than being the only boy with really hairy legs, it would be the boy with only one hairy leg. I carried on grimly. More scraping. More nicks. More tissue ripped and carefully placed onto the little cuts.

Ma knocked on the door, tapping rapidly.

'Are you alright in there?' she asked.

'I'm fine,' I replied, trying to sound nonchalant and, considering the amount of paper on my legs, trying not to rustle.

'You've been in there for ages. What are you doing?'

'I'm — ' I couldn't say what I was doing. Ma would think I was mad. 'I'm having a bath.'

'I didn't hear any water running.'

'Look! Just leave me alone. I'll be out in five minutes. Okay?'

She walked away, muttering.

I left the bathroom as quickly as I could. Little bits of tissue fell from the bottom of my trousers like confetti throughout the day. God stood by, watched me flounder with puberty and struggle with racism, and must have known of the lonely ache in my heart.

They say God moves in mysterious ways.

I did, too, for a couple of hours until my trousers stopped chafing my legs.

No matter how God or I moved, the world was no better for it.
In fact, it sucked.

***

Swami's sitting in his ornately carved wooden chair. He's speaking about spirituality to those gathered in the Prayer Hall. I'm only half-listening to him, content to be in his presence. I like the way the big bushy hair exaggerates his head waggles. I don't know what he's been talking about, but he's holding his hand out in front of him, palm upwards as if weighing something.

'What to do?' he says, sugaring his words with a big smile. 'The devotees take my disciples away to Trichy and fill them with the ice cream.'

People are laughing at this gentle ribbing, and Swami chuckles too. I don't. I feel uneasy.

'My disciples are getting fat,' he says. 'No work is getting done.'

This is so obviously untrue it might explain why everyone's so amused—everyone except me. I may not have been paying attention to what Swami said before, but now I'm all ears. I feel sure Swami's referring to our trip off the ashram tomorrow morning. I look over to where Lesley is sitting, expecting her face to mirror my concern, but *she's* laughing too. My gaze roams over the devotees, searching for Mataji. She's standing at the entrance to the Prayer Hall by the open door and looks amused, too, just like Lesley, just like everyone else but me.

I look back at Swami and begin to doubt myself. Was he referring to us when he spoke? Lesley's known him for years. Mataji has lived and worked in his ashram for over a decade. I've only been around him a few days, so could it be that I'm the only one who understands that he doesn't want us to leave the Ashram tomorrow? It seems a little ridiculous, but now it occurs to me — maybe *I'm* the one who's supposed to stay in the ashram.

That's it! That must be why Lesley and Mataji are unconcerned by what he said.

Satsang ends, Swami leaves, and the devotees trail out of the Prayer Hall. I hurry to the double doors wide open to the sunshine and catch up with Lesley by a palm tree. She's leaning on it to steady herself while putting her sandals on.

'I'm not going with you tomorrow,' I blurt.

'What? Why?'

'Swami just said we shouldn't go — or at least he hinted at it.'

She puts her hand on my arm. 'Sweetheart, he's joking.'

'I don't think so. I think he was serious.'

She looks lost for words for a moment. I begin to doubt myself. I even feel a little foolish.

'Paul, he was laughing with the devotees. He's just teasing. Being playful — '

'I'm not going,' I say firmly.

Tears well up in Lesley's eyes, surprising me. I step forward, but she stops me by raising a palm. She looks at me, her eyes searching for — I don't know what. Then, she turns abruptly and walks away.

'Lesley?'

I follow her, stumbling over sandals and pushing past devotees, trying to pick up their footwear. She walks faster.

'Lesley!'

It's not like her to react like this. My resolve begins to crumble. I'll go to Madurai and — I stop. Anger is rising. How can she walk away from me just because I don't want to go off and see a temple? Above anyone, Lesley should understand why I want to stay here. I want to be near Swami. She knows very well the profound effect he has on people.

I stalk off in the other direction, irritated and embarrassed at the little scene we made. I notice some devotees looking at me, and I feel judged as if I've done something wrong—a hot flush colours my cheeks. I feel trapped. What should I do? If I go with Lesley tomorrow, I'll feel bad, feeling that I've been coerced into it by tears, but if I don't go, I'll still feel bad. And what am I thinking? Lesley has never used tears to make me do anything. She's not that kind of woman. But wait — staying here isn't even my idea.

Swami said he didn't want us to leave the ashram. It's his idea. Or is it? He hasn't *actually* told me to stay in the Ashram, has he? This could easily be my ego seeing something which isn't there. Think about it. Why *would* Swami want *me* to stay in the ashram? There's no good reason I can think of except — what if he can see something in me which is pure and untouched by the life I've lived?

I see myself now in a red robe, calm and gentle.

What if —

And I catch my breath at this idea.

What if we've come to see a saint, but the truth is, the saint wants to see me?

***

The hair on my legs grew back, and my voice dropped, as well as a couple of other things. One was a large cabbage, and the other was a well-sprung mattress. Both narrowly missed me as I walked along the pavement at the bottom of the tower block where we lived. Ma had sent me to the shop for groceries when the cabbage exploded in front of me. It smashed into the ground with such force I would have suffered a severe head or neck injury, possibly turned into a cabbage by a cabbage. Of course, having been the focus of much racist hostility, I considered this to be the same. I stopped dead, covered in bits of cabbage shrapnel, and raised my fist toward someone's head, peering seven stories up from a window.

'What the fuck?! Hey! Arsehole! What are you doing? You racist son of a — Ma?'

'Paul, stop that language and go back to the shop. I forgot to ask you to get teabags.'

Incredulous, I looked up the side of the tower block at my mother, who had used a root vegetable to get my attention.

'Jesus Christ! You nearly killed me!'

'Don't be exaggerating. And don't be taking the Lord's name in vain like that!'

'But — ' I shook my head and turned back toward the shops.

'Paul!'

I turned back and looked up at Ma.

'What?'

'Bring back another cabbage!'

This was in the days before mobile phones, but I strongly suspect that if Ma had owned a mobile — she would have thrown that instead.

A few weeks later, walking by the same spot, a huge mattress landed, end on, in front of me with a massive 'whump!' I leapt backwards, viscerally terrified as the force of the impact made it fold in on itself. It closed like a giant mouth, a big pair of fabric lips which sprang open hungrily with a rubbery 'flubbery-dub'.   Another couple of steps, and it would have hit me and broken my neck or back. Laughter was coming from one of the floors at the top of the tower, but I couldn't see anyone. I assumed it was coming from whoever launched the mattress out of a window, but maybe it was just God mocking me. My legs shook as I went up the stairs, having narrowly avoided an entry in the book of ludicrous fatalities. When I got home and told Ma what had happened, she was appalled.

"The little bleeders,' she said. 'Throwing a mattress out of a window? How could anyone be so stupid? God watch over you and protect you!.'

'I don't think God's interested, Ma.'

'Don't say that. God will look after you.'

'Well, he seems to have stopped you from throwing vegetables at me out the window, so maybe you're right.'

'You can mock all you want, but God was looking out for you today, Paul.'

'If he didn't raise his hand to stop the assassination of JFK, Martin Luther King or Gandhi, then I'd have to be an idiot to think he saved me from a king-size Sleep Easy mattress.'

'You should say a little prayer of thanks.'

I didn't. God and I weren't on speaking terms. I wasn't even angry with God anymore because it was pointless. God was infinite. 'Tutting' in the general direction of infinity wasn't going to make much of an impact. Besides, I had gone past the stage of blaming God for anything.

God made food.
Man made famine.
God wasn't the problem.
We were.
God made Gravity.
He didn't throw out the mattress.

***

The thought of staying in the ashram for the day has become one of staying in it for years. I walk the grounds to burn up my anger. It ebbs away slowly until a terrible jolt of grief thumps me in the chest. It's the thought of Lesley returning to England alone. It's an idea I can only approach warily before the sense of loss drives me away from it.

But look — *look* where I am! I'm in the ashram of a saint who could show me the truth behind this flesh and these bones. I could become a truly good person. He could make me whole and pure and free me from the past. I don't have a massive ego, which is the sort of claim the ego would make, but I feel oppressed by it regardless of how big it may or may not be.

Yes, stay here in the ashram.

Swami, teach me how to be like you.

Once more, the dull electric thump of heartrending pain at the thought of leaving Lesley.

I swallow this. Force it down. The pain cracks the shell of my reserve, allowing ancient grievances to emerge. They uncoil and claw their way up, dragging my past up from deep waters, bitter with memory. Finally, I stop and slump down onto a rock, the weight of my head resting in my hands. My life grinds away within me, an undertow of quiet despair, a tightly repressed and painful scream of anguish, rejection and abandonment, grief and rage, sullied innocence.

I cry, sobbing up my heavy heart, fat tears dropping and splashing onto the dust of the ashram path. I'll stay in the ashram with Swami as my teacher.

I'll purify myself.

Turn my back on the world and lead a spiritual life.

My sobbing subsides.

Around me, the world quietly chuckles.

It knows I'm fooling myself even if I'm not aware of it.

This is nothing new.

***

* * *

On my way back to the koothi, I feel utterly drained. I've calmed down, but I'm unsettled at being overcome by emotion. I'm not an overly emotional person, and it's not like me to be so broken up. Lesley's reaction outside the Prayer Hall is also odd. She's a warm, loving person but is not given to emotional outbursts either. Calm and sweet-natured, she isn't one for crying over a minor setback. It's natural that I should feel emotional, seeing as I can see the brick wall in front of us, should I decide to stay in the ashram. However, I can't understand why Lesley is so emotional because she's got no idea what I'm thinking.

I thought she'd be glad that I now fully understand why she's spent years in the wilderness, so to speak, holding onto Swami Premananda even though he was thousands of miles away. She wanted me to meet him, and now I have. Lesley should be happy for me, which I guess she has been until today, but for some reason, she's all upset. It seems pointless to visit a temple when I feel God is here, not there.

She never even gave me a chance to explain. That in itself is unlike her. Whatever's going on, I'm sure she'll feel better once I explain myself. Make her feel better. Make myself feel better.

I enter the koothi and nobody's home. Lesley's straw hat's on my bed beside some of the stuff we bought in Trichy. Then, I hear a cup clatter in the kitchen.

'It's only me,' I call out.

'The kettle's just boiled. Would you like a cup of tea?'

'No thanks — .'

Behind me come the words, 'I'd love one, but I daren't.'

I turn and see a man called Ian, whom we've met several times in England. I didn't know he was in the ashram.

'Hi,' I say, wishing he'd go away.

'How lovely to see you both. Mataji said you two had

finally made it to the ashram. Thought I'd drop in and say hello.'

Lesley enters the room and greets him with a smile, asking after his wife and children.

'They're all fine,' he says. 'Still back in Blighty. But I'm feeling a little under the weather. Food goes in one end and comes out the other without stopping.'

I wish he'd sod off out the other end of the koothi in much the same way, but he doesn't.

'Oh dear,' Lesley says.

'Yes. Get out of the way if I start running toward the toilet.'

'Paul, do you have any Imodium? It might help Ian.'

He gives me a sympathetic look. 'You poor thing, don't tell me you've had this too? Are you still suffering?'

' No. I don't — I mean, my bowels are fine. I carry the medication in case of emergencies. I'll get it for you.'

'Thank you, but no. I've already taken a dose. I'm just waiting for it to start working. I only — where did you get that?'

Eagerly he strides over to my bed and picks up the white conch shell we purchased in Trichy. It's on the bed beside Lesley's straw hat.

'I've just *got* to get one like this,' he says, clutching it to his chest. 'Ours is far too big. You've met my wife, haven't you? Yes, of course, you have. Her hands are so small she can barely hold the one we've got. She's like a doll.'

'Take it,' Lesley says, instinctively generous.

What? I think, dismayed. But I want it!

'That's very kind, but no — ' Ian says.

Thank God, I think.

'Go on,' Lesley insists. 'Please. You can send us the one you don't want in the post.'

No! Don't! -

'Oh, I couldn't!' he gushes, clutching it to his chest.

That's right. You can't because I bloody well want it.

But he can. He can, and he does. He leaves with the conch and a large slice of cold watermelon that had been chilling in the fridge.

I'm very disappointed, but I refrain from saying anything. There are other things we need to discuss.

Tentatively, I begin. 'Lesley—?'

She replies without looking at me.

'Yes?'

Now Ian's gone, the polite social mask has fallen, and I can see she's still upset.

'Lesley, I —

Rekha enters through the open door. One end of her newest sari is draped regally over her left arm.

'Oh, for God's sake—' I mutter under my breath.

'What do you think?' Rekha asks.'

'Lovely,' Lesley says. 'It's beautiful.'

Rekha picks up Lesley's straw hat and wafts herself with it.

'Hot, isn't it?' Lesley says.

'Too hot. I can scarcely bear it.'

'The kettle's just boiled. I'll get you some tea.' Lesley steps into the kitchen.

'Thank you. Tell me, Paul, my dear, was that Ian I just saw leaving the koothi with a slice of watermelon? He had a fabulous conch too.'

'It was, and he did. Would you like some? Watermelon, I mean?'

'I'd love some.'

Lesley and I almost bump into each other as she steps out of the kitchen with the tea.

'Oops!' I say. Lesley smiles but still doesn't look at me. She swerves and sits with Rekha. They talk while I slice what's left of the watermelon. After placing a portion in front of Rekha, I excuse myself and go outside. There's a sweeping brush lying up against the wall by the door. I pick it up and sweep the path in front of the koothi. I decide to do it until Rekha leaves because, as much as I want to ease this tension between Lesley and myself, I can't do it with an audience.

Waiting's difficult. Horrible. And seems to go on forever. It goes on for so long that the desire to heal begins to curdle as I hear Rekha and Lesley laughing about something. Why should I be the one to approach Lesley? I haven't done anything wrong. Lesley's been telling me about Swami Premananda for two years, so, above anyone, she should understand my reluctance to leave.

After brooding for half an hour, brushing the path, I'm bristling with anger as Rekha emerges from the koothi. She waves goodbye to me. I go into the relative gloom of the koothi, where Lesley's mood has improved. She approaches with a conciliatory look on her face and hugs me. The warmth of her embrace meets the cold rigour mortis of my anger, so she breaks away. She starts tidying the beds briskly, ripping a pillow out of the cover and then flapping it angrily. It cracks like a whip, and barely restrained outrage hangs in the air like static before a storm. Like two hedgehogs needing to be close but wary of the pain one wrong move could bring, we politely ignore each other with meticulous attention to detail.

I regret my behaviour profoundly, but I'm a hostage to my fears. I need to return the hug, but I'm holding back. She might reject it, and my ego can't let that happen. It will not allow that pain. So even though the urge to embrace Lesley grows more urgent, fear rises to meet it in equal measure. I'm paralysed, shocked at how powerful the feelings are. As they increase in intensity, I have what I'll describe as an 'out-of-drama' experience instead of an out-of-body experience.

I find I'm somehow outside of the drama. I see my mind, but I don't recognise it. I always assumed my mind, and I were the same entity. It was as much me as my skin and lungs, but I can see my mind *isn't* me. It's something that captivates me. It captures my attention, and I become lost in the tales it weaves. And when I try to escape and move beyond it, I am gripped by fear as I am now, standing before Lesley.

There's something else too.

Silence listens to the drama and remains untouched by the noise of it.

Stillness observes the drama but is pure and still, untouched by any emotional movement.

It's a moment of clarity before the slow, heavy undertow of sadness and sorrow drags me into the noise of thoughts which gnash and grind like old, worn teeth. For hours, this goes on as we studiously ignore each other. I have a curious, dark feeling of being held hostage by the mind as it stirs the simmering pot of thought and emotion. I'm pulled into their fall and swirl before briefly glimpsing the silence and stillness within, and then once more, I've been swept away into the drama of my ego.

Night sees us alone in our beds. Emotion has subsided. I look back through the miserable day we've just had and how the mind runs away with me. I've always assumed my thoughts and feelings to be part of the sum total of who I am. But how can that be when they seem to have a life of their own? At least, that's how it seems. They moved, and I followed in their wake like Captain Ahab pulled along by the whale Moby Dick. I struggled with them, but if they were mine, why do they seem to control me and not the other way around? They seem to be something which exerts control over me but

—
Wait —

Who is this *'me'* which is being controlled?

If I'm not what I'm thinking and feeling, who or what am I?

I roll over and look across the koothi to where Lesley is sleeping. Her breathing is deep. I'm ashamed of my weakness and how I spurned her attempt at reconciliation.

I turn back to look up at the ceiling. Now I'm not wondering who I am. Instead, I wonder what kind of insensitive shit I am? If I can't free myself from the grip of my ego/mind, then maybe I'm fooling myself. How can I even think about staying here and learning from Swami Premananda if I'm full of such bullshit? I was intent on staying just a few hours ago, and now I've dropped the idea because of a massive ego spasm.

But — isn't this the ideal place to learn how I step out of the ego?

Above us, the fan slowly turns, humming to itself, pirouetting like a squat, metallic ballerina.

Mesmerised by the dance, I sleep deeply

All of Creation rests within me.

There is no emotion.

No thought.

CHAPTER SEVEN

Banana Regret

Dark. I gasp. Night rushes into my mouth and fills my lungs.

My eyes are open —

'Hush!' Lesley whispers. She has a finger to her lips. Her hand is soft and warm on my arm.

'What — ?'

'Sshhh! Don't wake Mataji.'

I'm fully awake now. I sit up. I remember. Lesley is making a trip to the temples this morning.

'I thought Mataji was going with you?' I ask.

'No. And before you ask — it's nothing to do with what Swami said yesterday. Something she's got to do came up, so she decided it would be best if she stayed here.'

I shrug. I take this news as a confirmation of my decision to stay in the ashram, at least for today.

Lesley continues. 'I'm sorry I woke you, but I need the camera. I've no idea where you put it.'

'That's okay. What time is it?'

'Five-thirty.'

'Lord. Okay. Give me a second, and I'll find it.' I

rummage through my rucksack, find it and hand it over.

'Thanks,' she says. 'I'll see you later. Get some rest, and don't forget, there's a lingam blessing later.'

'I'll remember — and I'm sorry about the upset yesterday.'

'Don't worry about it.' She's polite but dismissive of the apology, still unhappy that I'm not going with her.

'Let me show you how to work the camera,' I say.

'I'll figure it out.'

I know she can. My offer was just a way to hold onto her a little longer. I don't want her to leave with this sadness.

'It's not rocket science,' she says, stuffing it into her bag. 'Anyway, I'd better make a move. The others are waiting outside for me.'

'Others? What others?'

'Adrienne and Naren and Rekha. Ian's coming along too. A few other devotees quite fancy it, so we've hired a mini-van.'

She hugs me. There's a feeling of flight in the lightness of her touch. And now she's gone. I slump back on my bed, heart heavy and dull. The day hasn't even begun, and already it feels like a burden. I turn over to face the moonlit wall. A shadow from the slowly rotating fan sweeps across it. I hear murmuring outside and footsteps on the path. An engine ticks over nearby. I want it to stop or to go away. It'll be the one taking Lesley on the temple tour. She'll be with other people, but I'm sure she will feel lonely. This makes me think of the greater loneliness she'll face if I stay in the ashram for good. The weight of this heavy thought depresses me. I burrow my face into the crook of my arm until the heat of my breath forces me out. The engine's still idling outside, almost tempting me to go.

But I'm not going to. Even though I ended the night full of doubt about staying in the ashram permanently, yesterday, I find myself drawn to this possible future again. It's an incredibly seductive idea. If it's possible to remove the veil from the mystery of my existence, why not take the chance? Just how much do I want to know the truth? If I'm serious about my search for God or myself, this has to be the best place to do it. If I don't take the opportunity, perhaps I'm not sincere in my need to know.

Should my relationship with Lesley — or anybody, for that matter, stand in the way of finding the answer?

Like walking out on the ice or inching along a tree limb that is beginning to buckle with my weight, an undercurrent of fear trembles beneath this inquiry, the internal drama becomes intense, and —

What's this —?

Suddenly, I'm acutely aware that part of me enjoys this drama. Maybe that's the wrong word. It's not enjoying it, but it's undoubtedly feeding off it. It sits on my shoulder like a vulture, picking over the bones. It's almost as if my present trouble is not about searching for the truth. Not anymore. It's become an exploration of the emotional wound this upheaval would inflict. And why? Because through this disturbance, my ego lives more intensely. The closer the cut comes to the wick, the more alive the ego is. My ego writes the drama, played out by my ego, all for my ego. It defines itself through confusion, complication, and conflict and takes power away from who?

Who am I?

Am *I* these things I'm thinking and feeling?

I push my sleeping bag away and slip into my sandals. I put on a Punjabi suit. The cotton is crisp and cold from the early morning air. Leaving the koothi and striding past the empty mini-bus, I head for the Prayer Hall. The smell of diesel obscures the incense until I'm almost at the open doors. The candlelight looks warm and welcoming. I step into the perfumed sanctuary and sit with my back against a wall.

So here I am.

Assuming Swami *does* want me to stay in the ashram today, I expect I'll find out why. Maybe I'll have visions. Or a sense of bliss. Something will happen, and I'll have some kind of revelation. I close my eyes to meditate —

— And fuck all happens.

Just the usual nonsense. Images slip through vague thoughts, which then hustle ideas into the half-light of my mind. Notions barter with musings. Themes unfold their fabric and wrap themselves in colour and absurdity. A dance of swirling and rushing, rising, falling and fading, faster, fasterfastafa —monkey mind.

I open my eyes, sigh and push myself to my feet. I can't describe how disappointed I am. I don't know how long has passed, but I know I can sit for months, and nothing will happen. I feel foolish, as if I'd had a date with God and God never showed up. Quietly I leave, padding down the warm steps to my sandals.

Lesley's boarding the mini-bus, which means I haven't been in the Prayer Hall very long. An impulse to go and hug her swells in my heart, but I dismiss it. Once again, I'm frightened she'll reject the gesture like I did yesterday. The driver bangs the doors shut. The engine of the bus coughs politely as if embarrassed by my timidity.

On the horizon, a blush of sunlight. Away they go. I hang my head.

***

Ma burst into the room and shouted, 'You've got no shame!'

I almost dropped the book I was reading as she thrust a crushed sheet of paper toward my face. I couldn't see what was written on it, but instantly, I knew what it said. Contrary to her claim, I was ashamed. Head down, I began mumbling an explanation, but she wasn't listening.

'How dare you do this in my house!' She threw the ball of paper at me. 'This! This — dirty filth!'

I'd hit puberty when my contact with the opposite sex was at an all-time low, and my interest was naturally at an all-time high. Thumbing through library books for titillation made me feel desperate and furtive. On the other hand, I was usually too self-conscious to take out any book that had any hanky-panky going on, which I could have thumbed through at home. So, I solved the dilemma by writing a book with sexy bits myself. To save time, I omitted all the boring bits, such as the plot, characters, conversations and clothes. Consequently, I ended up with little more than half a page.

Essentially, an attractive woman, who just happened to be a nymphomaniac, knocked on the door of our flat. She was doing a survey or something. Luckily, I opened the door just as her clothes fell off. For some reason, the appearance of a spotty bespectacled teenager caused her to drop her clipboard, morals and quite possibly her standards. She also bent to pick up a pencil she'd dropped, at which point we ran through the Kama Sutra, or at least the three pages I was familiar with, until the scene reached a climax. At this point, I lost interest in it and tore the sheet out of my typewriter. I shoved it under my pillow. Perhaps, subliminally, I was hoping the tooth fairy would turn up, and her clothes would drop off too. Unfortunately, it was a stupid place to have put the sheet. I had intended to move the evidence to a more secure location like Brazil, for example, so that Ma wouldn't find it. So, naturally, I forgot about it.

Ma threw the offending page on the floor, stooped, and picked it back up. She was in tears. She was furious too.

'What is this? My God! What have you been up to?'

'Nothing! It's nothing.'

'Jesus, Mary and Joseph! Is this a confession of some sort, Paul? Have you had a dirty woman in here?'

'What?'

'When did it happen!' she yelled.

'I made it up!' I yelled back.

'Made it up? Made it up?' She looked incredulous. 'You made this up?

'Yes. It's called fiction,' I said. 'people do it all the time.'

'This is too — too realistic. There's too much detail here for it to be made up.'

I couldn't help but take that as a compliment. Ma didn't mean it as such, obviously.

'Is this some sort of a cry for help?'

'No. It's more of a Christmas wish list if you want a name for it.'

Tony came into the room, a worried look on his face. We didn't do shouting in our house. Not very often. Jason appeared behind him, on the verge of tears. Ma took one look at him and said, 'Tony. Take poor Jason into your room. I don't want him hearing this.'

'You could try not shouting,' I muttered.

Tony looked at me quizzically as he took Jason's hand. I heard Jason ask what was happening as he was led away. Fortunately for me, the brief intermission brought some semblance of calm to Ma, who walked over to the television and turned it on so Jason couldn't hear our conversation. She sat on the edge of the sofa and opened the crushed sheet.

'My God,' she said, shaking her head and scrunching it again.

'Throw it away if it'll make you feel better,' I suggested.

'Sweet Jesus,' she said toward the heavens before turning back to me. 'I don't even know what half of this means. What the feck is fellatio?'

'It's a blowj — '

Ma gasped. She clapped one hand over her eyes in shock and threw the paper at me with all the power of Catholic guilt behind it. It bounced off my head, and she fled from the room in tears.

I sat with my head down and the sound of canned laughter on the television mocking me.

***

***

Is there a spiritual equivalent of canned laughter? I don't know, but I should be hearing it as the tail lights of the minibus speed off toward the ashram gates. My inability to sit and meditate has reminded me of how ordinary I am. It's not even my inability to meditate which is depressing me. It's the thought that I couldn't hug Lesley when she needed me to. If there's a minimum requirement for spiritual life, I imagine being able to hug someone you love might be it.

I also have the uncomfortable feeling I'd had earlier — that this is just a drama from which my ego will sustain itself. The emotional energy generated by the idea of leaving Lesley is just a way of producing 'food' for the same ego, *now* feeding off the relief I feel as I finally relinquish the idea of staying here.

I take my glasses off and rub the bridge of my nose.

This thought is too messed up for me to deal with. I put my glasses back on and go back to the koothi. Mataji's awake now and in the kitchen boiling the kettle for tea.

'They're serving breakfast in the Dharamsala,' she says. 'If you hurry, you'll just catch them.'

'I'm not hungry,' I reply, rubbing my arms. My skin is cold.

Mataji looks up at me momentarily and then back down to the kettle. I wonder if she knows how badly I've behaved, which makes me feel uncomfortable.

'You should eat,' she says.

'I think I'll fast for a while.'

'Did Lesley wake up on time this morning?'

'Yeah, but she's a bit upset with me.'

'Oh? It's not like you two to fall out.'

'I decided not to go on the trip to the temples.'

'Yes. Lesley mentioned it yesterday. She seemed alright about it, though.'

'She was quite upset when I first told her. But, to be honest, it was *really* annoying because I felt pressured into going. Obviously, I *didn't* go, but it made things very awkward.'

'That's quite odd. I've never known Lesley to be the possessive type. Did you discuss it with her?'

'No. I tried to, but things kept getting in the way.'

Mataji nods, but not to signify that she's agreeing. Instead, it's more an acknowledgement of what I just said, which, listening back, sounds pretty lame in my ears.

'I want to stay near Swami. Why go to the temples when anything I could find about spirituality is already here?' There's a hint of defensiveness in my voice. 'D'you think I should have gone with her?'

She drops a tea bag into her cup before replying. 'Swami often sends people off to see the temples. Culturally, he's a Hindu, so he respects that tradition. However, he could just as easily send people to a church, mosque, or Buddhist temple. He wouldn't have minded if you'd gone with Lesley.'

'So you *do* think I should have gone?'

'No. That's not what I'm saying. Stay here. Go there. It doesn't matter. Don't mistake proximity to Swami for the efficacy of his teaching. His physical presence may give you something to focus on, but that isn't what he is. Undoubtedly, it's better to be in his presence for some things, but if you want his guidance, it's not necessary. The ultimate truth is neither near nor far. Because if it depended on where you happened to be standing in relation to someone else, then it would just be an opinion, wouldn't it? It would just be a point of view. The Truth remains the same no matter where you are.'

'So how come you're here?'

'Because this is how *I'm* being taught, but that doesn't mean it's the only way. I also have a particular role here on the Ashram, but if he sent me away tomorrow, I'd go.'

'Does that mean you've learned what the truth is?'

'What truth would that be?'

'The Ultimate Truth, like you said a minute ago. Swami's your teacher, so has he taught you what it is?"

She's thinking. Gone away into the past for a few moments.

'He *is* my teacher. Yes, that's true. But it would be more accurate to say he's actually the embodiment of the teaching itself.'

'Which is?'

'Be yourself. Just — find out who or what you are and just be that. That's all.'

'But how do I do that?'

'Ask him.'

I nod, pleased that I've got something right because I *have* been asking Swami Premanada this question. Who am I? I've dropped my head into my heart and asked with all sincerity.

'I felt Swami wanted me to stay in the Ashram for the day. Is that possible?'

'Yes. It's possible. Anything's possible, but no matter where you were, if Swami wanted to find you, he would.'

'How?'

'Maybe he's everywhere and nowhere. Who knows?' Mataji smiles.

I'm none the wiser as she turns her attention back to the kettle, now coming to the boil. The gas jet sputters and spits as some of the water spills over. She turns it off and pours hot water into her cup. Something fragrant flowers the air.

'Make sure you get something to eat. And drink plenty

today. It's going to be very hot.'

'I will. But I'd like to have a good think about things beforehand.'

It might help to remember this. If you walk in someone else's footsteps, you'll find *them*, not yourself. Follow your own path. Always.'

I feel like I've been let off the hook in some way. A surge of humility softens me, and in that, there's a tenderness towards myself and everyone else.

'Thanks,' I say.

The brush with which I swept the path yesterday is waiting outside the front door. I pick it up on my way out and start to sweep the path which leads from the koothi to the water pump. This simple task is soothing, and I become engrossed with it, diligently gathering little stones and carrying them in an old rusty bucket to the outskirts of the ashram. I pour the detritus into the long dry grass and then trudge back for more. Sweat rolls down my back and stings my eyes. Yesterday I thought myself fit to walk the spiritual path. Yet, this morning I think I'm barely fit to sweep it. Where does the real me exist between these contradictions?

I measure my life out with the rhythmic rasp of the brush. Ordinary men like me, I think, with common concerns and frailties, can't have a life of *genuine* spirituality. To us is left religion, a mere husk of spirituality which we gnaw at for sustenance. As I resign myself to this, my heart begins to feel more cumbersome than the old bucket, at least for now.

A carnival of thought passes before me; the sacred, the mundane, the profane. I let them come. I let them go.

I slip into a meditative state.

I sense movement within stillness.

I hear noise within the silence.

***

***

Perhaps one of the worst things about living in Ireland was the lack of female company other than Ma, and she didn't count precisely for that reason. The usual routes through which a boy meets a girl were off-limits. Ballymun Comprehensive was an all-boys school, so that was a washout. There was a girl's school next to it, but I was too self-conscious in the rumbunctious school environment for that to be of anything other than an object of remote curiosity. It may as well have been on the other side of the world. I also didn't make friends with anyone outside the flat because the environment was too hostile for prolonged exposure. I found it best, through bitter experience, to limit myself to short trips. These were long enough to be hit by a root vegetable but not long enough to form a friendship with a girl.

They remained something mysterious and magical and out of reach. I was bemused at the stories on the television which spoke about the search for life on other planets. For me, there was nothing more mysterious than one-half of the population on this planet. Females were such an unknown element to me that I had doubts about whether they farted, despite the considerable evidence provided by some of my aunties.

The Religious Education Teacher in school had the onerous task of teaching us about the birds and the bees. This included talks about the male reproductive system, which was wasted on us. Most of us, if not all, were already researching that particular conundrum with the sort of enthusiasm that resembled a rendition of 'Flight of the Bumblebee', only without the violin. I've no idea why a man who believed the immaculate conception was a historical fact was considered the best person to give us the low down on sex. It was like having a man who believes in Batman speaking to us about law and order.

As someone who had resorted to writing his own smut, I think I knew more than he did, and that wasn't a lot. I believe Ma might have even agreed with me. When she eventually calmed down about what I wrote, she conceded I at least knew about the 'birds and the bees.' It was certainly more than she'd known when she was my age, and on the plus side, my spelling was excellent. However, she asked me to refrain from writing anything involving nudity or bodily fluids.

'God knows where it will end up,' she said.

Oddly enough, it would end up in my writing this book about how her son discovered he was nothing more than a work of fiction.

***

Dust rising
Heat on my back
Someone talking
'What?'
'The lingam blessing?' Mataji repeats.
'Lingam?'
'Lesley asked me to remind you.'

'Oh — right,' I say, caught mid-sweep. The path's now a duvet of sand snuggling warmly between my toes. Mataji's peering at me intently.

'Are you okay? You look a little hot.'

'I'm fine,' I say. We walk back toward the koothi. I leave my brush against the wall and go to the Prayer Hall. Inside, devotees queue before the doorway, screened by the curtain that hid me from Swami the day before yesterday. I have a lot of memories coming to the surface, times when I hurt other people, or they hurt me. I feel miserable because I feel miserable, and it's all quite pathetic —

But I can't seem to stop it. I baulk at the idea of joining the queue, but I'm too self-conscious and embarrassed to turn around and leave. More people are coming into the Hall, so I latch on to the end of the line. I cough as if I can startle this bruised lump of grief out of my throat. Instead, it bobs up and down as gravity tugs down the corners of my mouth, teasing it into a tremble.

But I will not cry

What the hell is wrong with me?

The queue rapidly shrinks as devotees pass through the curtain and exit another door. They're all smiling, which adds to my acute embarrassment. I feel like such an idiot as I pass through the curtain. I see one of Swami's disciples sitting with a lingam in the palm of her hand. Purity and sweetness light up her face, and forgiveness is in her smile. A sob lurches up from my abdomen, and I double up, falling to my knees. Bowing at her bare feet, I feel her warm hand press the lingam firmly upon the crown of my head where the fontanel had once pulsed. Where once I was soft as a newborn baby, the formless aspect of Shiva rests, just for a moment.

I leave the little room, snuffling snot and wiping my eyes. Mortified, I walk past a line of devotees waiting for a blessing. I'm trying to preserve my dignity, but my damned lip keeps quivering like a diving board from which my natural reserve has just bounced off and belly-flopped. I quicken my pace, desperate for privacy. My sodding sandals are slipping off, flapping and slapping my soles as I reach the door of the koothi.

Please don't let anyone be in — oh, shit! The door's locked! Why is it locked? It's been unlocked all the time we've been here! I rush to the back of the building and find *that* door is also locked. My clothes are on the washing line where Lesley hung them yesterday. My underpants are limp and dry, hung like a flag of surrender. The sun is peeking over them. I hunker down in the doorway and cry my bruised heart out. The desire to stay in the ashram slips away with my tears.

***
***

Ma prayed a lot in Ballymun. I would have told her she was wasting her breath, but I'd spoiled my credibility by writing my own porn. Or at least two paragraphs of it. She wouldn't have listened anyway. It was obvious how isolated her boys were in the tower, and she prayed for God to help us. The least God could do was give us some friends.

One day during our first summer, Ma must have thought God had answered her prayers. Teresa, her youngest sister, came up from her home in the centre of Dublin with a compelling piece of information.

'Did you know Delilah O'Reilly is living in Ballymun?' Aunt Teresa asked.

'Go'way!' Ma exclaimed, handing over a plate of Gingernut biscuits and a cup of strong tea.

'Yes. That's right. Her brother told me. He was outside the bookies when I was passing.'

'Imagine that. I've not seen Delilah in — it must be thirty years. Did she ever marry that fellah she was going out with?'

'She did, so I believe. He was a handsome one, wasn't he? What was his name?'

'Daniel — something?'

'O'Grady. Daniel O'Grady. Jaysus, but he was lovely.'

Thinking about this, Teresa dipped a biscuit into her tea but held it there a fraction too long. When she pulled it back from the brew, the bit which had been immersed was gone. She put the cup to one side along with her Gingernut stump.

'Shite,' she muttered. 'Yes. Daniel O'Grady was a fine figure of a man.'

'He was — Bighead of hair. Huge feet. Great dancer. And Delilah was only gorgeous.'

'She was.'

'I often wondered what happened to her after I went to England.'

'Well, if I bump into her brother again, I'll get her address for you if ye like?'

'I'm not sure. It's been so long — '

'Getaway out of that! Her brother said she'd not changed a bit. And she's got a family. So your boys can make friends with them.'

I heard this and felt a little flutter of optimism.

'And — ' Teresa paused for dramatic effect. 'She's got a young one about the same age as Paul.'

I blushed, held up the book I was reading and sank further into the armchair. This revelation that 'gorgeous' Delilah had a daughter sent my teenage hormones into overdrive. They batted aside every thought in my head in a rush to reach my heart and groin. My heart stuttered, and my stomach flipped. Then, like honey, one beautiful idea trickled along the grooves of my brain.

A friend — who was a girl. For me.

Her name was Mary, like the Virgin.

That night I was woken after midnight by sirens and flashing blue lights. I went out onto the balcony. Tony was already standing out there, smoking a cigarette. A stolen car had been abandoned in the car park below, doused in petrol and ignited—the air stank of carbonised rubber, scorched metal and black smoke. The Gardai had been summoned, and the scene reminded me of some primitive ritual where a fire crackled, surrounded by sinister, shadowy figures. Acrid belching smoke rose like another tower, writhing in its naked agony. The natives stood around in a rough circle on the edge of the darkness. Drunken teenagers jeered as the Gardai dispersed the onlookers. Then, finally, a fire engine pulled off the main road come to douse the drama.

Through it all, cupid trembled in the shadows. I was thinking about the unknown Mary. I imagined her to be a doe-eyed, kind-hearted colleen, coming into my life to soften the harsh light of my existence. I thought about her a lot, holding onto this feminine ideal like a drowning boy holding a strong hand.

Like a boy holding onto the mane of a scrofulous-looking pony as life gallops away from him.

***

* * *

I feel better now after having a good cry. I'm back in the Prayer Hall. The young woman who gave the Lingam Blessing is doing an abishekam. Earlier, she looked so pure and loving as I'd sobbed at her feet, but now, she seems quite ordinary. Sleepily I ponder this. Sweeping the path in the hot, baking sun earlier has wiped me out, and the unaccustomed emotional meltdown has also left me feeling empty. I'll be happy when the abishekam finishes so I can go and sleep. Then, when Lesley returns, we'll finally share an embrace that will not be awkward or begrudged. The tension between us will have gone, and everything will return to normal.

The Mataji now moves along the centre of the prayer hall, dipping her hand into a brass bucket. She scoops the water she's blessed and flings it out over the devotees. She comes down the aisle, a diminutive figure, blessing us all. She pauses beside me, sprinkling an old lady with blessed water across from where I sit. A tinkling of summer-scented rosewater on her upturned face brings a sweet smile to the thin lips of the wrinkled septuagenarian. She presses her palms together and bows gracefully.

Now it's my turn. I close my eyes and —

***

Here's how I remember it. Aunt Teresa arranged for Delilah and her family to visit us. Ma bought cake and biscuits and cleaned the flat forensically. She polished the coffee table so thoroughly the flies couldn't land on it without slipping and breaking a leg. The lavatory smelt like we had a solid diet of lavender and citrus. The scent of lavender, in particular, was overpowering. In concentrated form, lavender oil can make people drowsy. Ma had put so much in the bathroom it's a wonder one of us wasn't found face down in the toilet bowl, comatose.

This obsessive cleaning was meant to give Delilah a good impression of us. Ma was investing a lot of energy in this meeting, and so was I, though I sat in the lounge feigning disinterest. I sat on the sofa, doodling on a notepad, unable to focus on anything other than the possibility of having a female friend. The thought was so delightful I couldn't leave it alone. The rough edges of my world had softened with this catnip of the heart. Mary would be kind and soft and intelligent and demure and smell sweet and wear a floral dress. But, of course, I had no idea what she actually looked like. This was in the days before Facebook. Had I been born a few decades later, in the age of the selfie, not only would I have known what she looked like, but I'd have pictures of her friends, pets, family, her date of birth, favourite food, height without shoes, political affiliation and possibly the dimensions of her vagina.

Jason pressed his face against the window, trying to spot our approaching guests. He wasn't allowed to open the window and pop his head out for a better look. Not since we discovered the metal-framed windows sometimes slid shut with the finality of a guillotine. There had been at least one fatality in Ballymun because of the flawed design.

Tony was in his room smoking and painting with oil on canvas. He was becoming more reclusive. His ability to interact socially with people outside the family was withering away. His ability to do so within the family wasn't great either. Ma didn't have the heart to force her firstborn out of the house, even to have a walk to the shops. What was the point? He'd just come back more depressed than when he went out.

She didn't know how to make it better for him or us. She prayed, cooked, and cleaned, but making Ballymun accept us was beyond her. It never really occurred to me that she probably suffered more than we did. She was the one who had to watch her children struggle. She also had to deal with her own isolation.

She was trying to swat a fly in the bathroom when there was a knock. I dropped my notebook and pencil and nearly bowled Jason over in my haste to open the front door.

A fat woman with an oversized duffel coat over a meaty arm wheezed at me.

'How're ye,' she said.

Behind her, a mob of children were trying to push past. Her girth held them back like a massive thumb stuck in a Dutch dyke. To the rear of this rowdy bunch, a dishevelled, exhausted-looking man with a fag hanging from his bloodless lips waved at me.

I stood holding the door. Surely there had been a mistake?

This — is the gorgeous Delilah?

It can't be.

'Delilah?' I asked.

'That's me, love,' she replied wheezily. 'And I'm fuckin' sweatin'. Is your Mammy in?'

Peering out from behind me, Jason caught his first glimpse and gasped.

Ma nudged me to one side, scolding me in her poshest voice. 'Where are your manners, Paul? Delilah! I'm so glad you could make it! Come in. Our Paul will take your coats.'

Delilah came in first, dumping her duffel coat in my arms. It smelled of sweat and perfume and chip fat. The children behind followed along rowdily. Several looked at me and then at each other and smirked. They ranged from about seven to eighteen, and I bristled as they brushed by. With my now jaundiced view of the Irish, at least in Ballymun, they all looked like villainous simpletons.

Then I saw her.

Mary

The girl of my recent dreams

And she had all the soft femininity of Keith Richards. My heart fell like a mattress tumbling from the thirteenth floor — like a loveless root vegetable, it plunged and landed at my feet as Mary lobbed her coat into my arms. She didn't smell of flowers. She stank of damp tobacco, sour perfume and mouldy socks. If it were perfume, it would be 'Eau de Disappointment'.

I stood with my arms outstretched like Jesus as she and her siblings dumped their coats into my arms. I was all but buried by the time the last of them passed through the doorway. The father followed along behind. He was as thin as the mother was fat. I'd never seen anyone look that wasted before. It was as if each time he impregnated his wife, he had to donate a kidney or some other major organ to the embryo.

Consequently, he resembled a pale, emaciated corpse with a thinning thatch of ginger hair. As far as I could see, there wasn't enough blood in him to make a decent scab. Despite this, he was immensely cheerful.

Obviously demented, I thought to myself.

After he'd passed by and jammed himself into our living room with the rest of his unruly tribe, I let my arms fall. The coats fell on the floor at my feet. At that point, there was another knock. I opened the door to see a carbon copy of the father only this one was about my age and carrying a ghetto blaster on his shoulder. He was also wearing an all-white suit with a black shirt. He put his hand out and shook mine.

'How're ye?' he said enthusiastically. 'Is me Ma here? We couldn't all fit in the lift.'

'I'm not surprised — I mean, yeah. Yes. Come in.'

'I'm Alan. The handsome one,' he said deprecatingly. 'I'm here to get this fuckin' party rollin'.'

Raucous laughter came from the living room. Alan stepped over the coats and went to join the fun. I tagged along reluctantly. I was just in time to see Delilah lowering her humungous buttocks onto the sofa. I lunged forward to grab my notebook from underneath her. I whipped it out before she landed, but I heard my pencil snap as the cushions wheezed asthmatically.

'Here!' Mary exclaimed. 'Leave my mum's arse alone!.'

Her family fell about laughing.

'I was trying to get my notebook,' I said, hugely mortified.

Delilah's husband winked at me and said, 'It's alright, young fella. I was your age once. I couldn't keep my hands to myself either.'

'Notebook?' I said, holding up the evidence and waving it. I decided not to mention my pencil. The next time I saw it was when her

children hauled her to her feet so she could use the loo. It was wedged between her buttocks. I thought it best not to try and retrieve it.

The lavatory would soon smell of something with fewer syllables than lavender.

'Can you dance?' Delilah asked me when she returned. She'd made the toilet unusable for at least the next thirty minutes. The fly Ma had been trying to swat earlier was retching into the sink.

'No,' I replied, puzzled at the question.

'Here, Alan,' Delilah said, ' do your stuff, son.'

Alan punched the play button on his ghetto blaster. Disco music pumped out. He then waved his hands in the air like he didn't care. He moved his hips from side to side and pumped one knee up and down as his family clapped.

Beside me, Jason whispered, 'What's wrong with him?'

'He's got no shame.' I whispered back.

***

— I received a cold slap of water across my face, which made me gasp. The Mataji moves down the aisle, sprinkling devotees with the blessed water. I remove my glasses and dry them off with the hem of my dhoti. I can smell rosewater. I'm a bit self-conscious about how other people are sprinkled like flower petals, but I seem to have been deluged as if there was a particularly stubborn stain on my conscience, and she'd seen it.

Or maybe it just amused her.

***

Delilah and her family were still in our flat when the moon appeared — probably wondering what the bloody noise was. I'd had enough of our visitors after the first hour. So, several hours later, when Ma suggested Tony and I go for a walk with Alan, the disco dancer, I was more than ready to agree.

'You can get to know each other,' she said.

'Maybe Mary would like to go?' I suggested, hopefully. Even though Mary was something of a rough diamond — or possibly closer to being coal than a precious stone, I wanted her to come for a walk. I'd set my hopes so high before meeting her that disappointment had been inevitable. Perhaps if we got to know each other a little better, a little affection would blossom. I felt it was too raucous, rowdy and rude in the flat for this to happen. Having visitors who always appeared to be only minutes away from setting fire to their farts wasn't quite the atmosphere I had hoped for in which to cultivate a meaningful relationship with a girl.

Mary looked at me and exclaimed, 'Jaysus, no way! It's fuckin' freezin' out there.'

I was a little crushed. That left Alan, who was already on his feet and heading for the door. I felt like I knew him quite well already. Admittedly, what I thought about him was closer to a medical diagnosis than any affection, but — oh, well.

'I'll see if Tony wants to come,' I said. As usual, his room was pungent with cigarette smoke.

'Are they going?' he asked, hopefully, paintbrush poised over a portrait of himself.

''Fraid not. But Ma suggested we go for a walk with Alan.'

'Who?' Tony had still not met any of them other than two of the youngest.

'Alan is the dancer,' I replied.

'What dancer?' Tony had missed the performance, having remained in his room. 'Never mind. I'll join you. The noise is driving me mad.'

Out into the night, we went. There were five of us — Tony, myself, Alan and two of his younger brothers. We talked about music. Alan loved disco, obviously, and I hated it. He was passionate about *watching football, too. I'd much rather watch a dog chasing a stick than waste time watching a millionaire chase a bag of wind. He was having oodles of sex, or so he claimed. I'd written two paragraphs about a woman whose clothes fell off — but I thought it best not to mention this. Tony didn't say much. He was out of the habit of conversing with strangers. To encourage him, I made a point of laughing heartily at anything he said. For some reason, this laughter offended some lads sitting on swings that were barely visible in the darkness. I could see they were smoking. The glowing tips hovered like fireflies.*

'Hey, you!' an angry voice called.

Alan stopped and looked over, 'what?'

'Who said you could laugh near me?'

'Me? I wasn't laughing?'

'Not you. The one with the glasses.'

'Me?' I exclaimed, incredulous. I laughed out loud. The idea that I needed permission from a stranger to do so was so ludicrous I couldn't help myself. I guffawed.

'Stop fucking laughing!'

'That's ridiculous,' I shouted back.

'Who are you calling ridiculous, you four-eyed fuck.'

I turned to my companions to ask, 'Is he serious?'

It was serious enough for Alan. His earlier attitude of waving his arms like he just didn't care turned into pumping his legs like he didn't want to get beaten up. He and his brothers were running so fast that they were almost out of sight. Tony and I looked at each other for a moment of mutual alarm, and then the sound of many boots and angry voices coming toward us made us run too.

We never saw Alan or Delilah and her family again. When Tony and I got back to the flat, they were gone. My ability to laugh disappeared, too, shortly after. Perhaps it was running after Alan. Maybe it was because I'd realised I could never walk outside with a girl and let her see the shite I faced daily. I wouldn't want her pity or, even worse, contempt. I was going to be on my own for a very long time.

***

All is well. I'm walking across the ashram to the Admin building and enjoying the sun. The day has stretched out serenely, like a warm and lazy cat, and it's so lovely that I smile. I carry this smile into the small dwelling where the admin for the ashram is carried out. I pass an old typewriter. It's hunched on a desk, silent and black, brooding like a bird of prey. An old Bakelite phone, suitably sombre, sits beside it. A cream-coloured fridge with a chrome handle and rounded corners hums in the corner, minding its own business. I open the door. Bottles clink and rattle, toasting the world with soft drinks. I pluck a couple of bottles of Limka and go into the next room to peruse various ashram products. There aren't many, but selling them helps feed the hundreds of children clothed and educated by Swami Premananda. Ashram policy is to be as self-sufficient as possible in every respect.

The simple goods are laid out on a long countertop. I look among booklets and handwoven bags replete with the ashram logo. I want a gift for Lesley. I see a large piece of pale material about the size of a tablecloth with the smiling face of Swami Premananda, which will do nicely. I place the money for the drinks and cloth in an honesty box and then head back to the koothi. Along the way, the air is perfumed with the pleasant scent of the Ashram incense.

Mataji makes some tea, so we sit outside in the shade of the verandah with it.

'You know earlier when I said I didn't go out and see the temples because I wanted to stay in the Ashram to be around Swami?'

'Yes?'

'Well, I'd *actually* been thinking I should live in the

ashram for good and devote myself to spiritual practice. Because if I'm serious about searching for God or myself, this is the best place to do it.

'If you're sincere, then where you are doesn't matter.'

'Yeah. I sort of know that, but — surely there must be some advantage to being on the Ashram and in the presence of Swami?'

'For some things and some people, yes. But this isn't appropriate for everybody. Some of Swami Premananda's devotees might need a potent dose of spiritual medicine, you could say, and so they're near him in the ashram. Others are far away, but it could be that they're very susceptible to his medicine, so they don't need such a strong dose. Who can tell? Some life forms thrive on just a little light in deep, dark waters, while others struggle to survive on top of a mountain where they're closer to the source of the light.'

'Actually, the closer I get to Swami Premananda, the more uncomfortable I feel. It's a bit like walking into someone's house and suddenly realising you've got muddy shoes. I feel like that when I'm near him, but the mud is me. Or not me. I don't know who 'me' is. I just know that I thought being near him would end the pain of my being me.'

'A lot of people fixate on the *physical* presence of Swami Premananda. To do *that* is to miss the point. The body that you see isn't him any more than a picture of the sun is the sun itself.'

'But without the light, you wouldn't see the picture of the sun?'

'That's right. You could say the picture is necessary because at least you can see what the sun looks like. It's not something you can look at directly, but a picture allows you to see the sun in a way you can cope with.'

'So — are you saying I shouldn't focus on him as part of

my spiritual practice?

'No. There's nothing wrong with having an image or form on which to focus. What I mean is, if you simply have Swami in your heart, you're in his presence no matter where you are or where you think he isn't.'

'Would it not be better to have your teacher in your head? Having him in the heart sounds like blind faith.'

She finds this amusing. 'Swami says, 'Think, yes, but drop your head into your heart. This is the best way.'

'Okay.'

'I presume you've dropped the idea of staying in the ashram?'

'Yeah. I suppose I don't want to renounce the world when it comes down to it. I'd just like to drop the bits I don't like. I want the chocolate. I don't want the calories or the tooth cavities.'

This tickles Mataji. She sips her tea and sits quietly, watching the gardener I met yesterday pouring a bucket of water into the earth. His wife comes out and hands him what looks like a piece of fruit. She sees Mataji and says something in Tamil to her. Mataji replies in kind. The three of them have a good-natured chuckle.

'She reminded her husband that the flowers aren't the only ones who need water. She needs some to cook and wash with.'

I laugh because his one-pointed obsession with what he's doing and having to be reminded of the practicalities of life is an insight into the relationship between Lesley and myself.

Mataji says, 'This idea of renunciation means a lot of different things to different people. Giving up the attachment to *things* seems to be the general view, but I'd say it's more about not being attached to the habit of yourself.'

From the Prayer Hall, the sound of bhajans. We sit and listen for a while.

'Did you speak to Lesley about staying in the ashram? She probably picked up on how you were feeling.'

'You think so?'

'It might explain the way she reacted to you.'

Of course, it would. I should have thought of this myself. I feel like an idiot for not realising this, and I'm eager to see her now so I can put her mind at rest.

***

Here's what happens when Lesley steps down from the mini-bus. She sees me, and we smile and wave. Then, despite my eagerness to have her back, I suddenly disconnect. It's as if the line has gone dead. She's enthusiastically singing the praises of the temples she's seen, particularly at Madurai, but I feel nothing.

'I missed you,' she says. Her face is open and honest. Somewhere in the distance is the thought that I love this woman, but — it's almost as if I have to impersonate myself. I remain outside this comforting circle of tender warmth even when she embraces me. But now — thoughts and feelings move within. The residue of resentment. The fear of rejection. The desire for forgiveness. I feel like a voyeur, watching the drama of some other person begin to unfold. I'm looking out of my eyes like a ghost peering from an attic window.

She releases me, and I step back. I am the man in the Iron Mask, but the mask is my own face. I see the pain in Lesley's eyes. Can she see me drifting away? Does she feel the cold dead hand on the tiller? The expression on her face pulls me back to myself.

I reach out and cling to her until she eases into my heart.

We stay this way for a long time.

***

Is there such a thing as a fall from grace? Fall makes it sound like a sudden thing, like a catastrophic event. I don't think this is the case. I think it's a subtle shift. It's a quiet thing, like the turning of a page. A silent something, like a thought. A kiss on the cheek. A nick in your skin that's just enough for the poison to enter your blood. One day you look back, see how far you've gone, and wonder how it happened. How did you miss so much, get so old, or fall so far?

Our experience in Ireland gave me a quiet rage that grew and festered in my heart. It was sustained by the silent, bovine stares that followed me wherever I was. The weight of them remained on my skin for years. The salted cut of strangers sniggering at the names I was called poisoned my blood. A stranger had slashed at me with a knife and cut into the soft skin of my throat. It was just a small cut, deep enough to scar my mind. It was another scar to add to the others I accumulated through the years.

I went to a classmate's house one day. His name, for this story anyway, will be Sean. Most of the boys in our class didn't like Sean. He was the sort of boy who would rub his sweets along the crack of his arse rather than risk having to share. I only went to his house because he'd badgered me all day about accepting his invitation, and I felt sorry for him.

Sean had a massive forehead, like a house brick. His black hair jutted out from it like grass on a clifftop. He latched onto me in school, possibly because everyone else had told him to fuck off. His sense of humour either shot over the heads of most people or just flopped out like those times when you try to spit, and it just ends up drooling from your chin. He was also ferociously bright and collected knowledge the same way he collected sweets, hoarding it and only sharing begrudgingly. And just like his sweets, the other children often told him to shove this up his arse too. None of this seemed to bother him. He had that streak of superiority with which only the truly stupid could be gifted.

His main ambition was to leave school with good results to join the Gardai and be a bit of a bastard professionally rather than leave it to chance. Some children have a bit of a cruel streak. They pluck the legs off spiders. I think Sean would have pulled the legs of a giraffe, given a chance to do so.

We got to his house just before a storm broke. Rain pelted the pavement as soon as we stepped into the hallway, which smelled of greasy food and disinfectant.

'I'm going to let my parents know you're here,' he said, opening the door to the parlour. 'Wait here for me. I'll be back in a minute.'

A pungent bouquet of stale tobacco stink billowed up from a plump cushion as the sofa wheezily took my weight. A vase with cheap plastic flowers shoved down its throat sat on the coffee table before me. The ashtrays had been emptied but not cleaned. Rain drummed drearily on the window as I waited and waited — waited so long, I started to worry. Perhaps his parents didn't want a 'darkie' in the house. Finally, I got up and went to the door leading to the hallway. I heard Sean talking and some laughter. I took it to be a good sign. Then, feeling relieved, I sat back down. The sitting room door opened, and a scruffy, unshaven man with jowls like a bullfrog popped his head around it. He was an older version of his brick fore-headed son.

'Hello,' I said politely and smiled.

'How're ye?' he replied in a thick Dublin accent and then disappeared again.

I heard subdued laughter and voices.

When Sean opened the door a minute later, I got a brief glimpse of his whole family, who, oddly enough, were huddled together outside the door and giggling.

'My mum and dad thought you might be hungry,' Sean said. He handed me a banana and then walked out. I sat there with it in my hand, looking at it as his family sniggered and whispered in the hallway. I was

speechless. Chimp noises had been directed at me on buses, in shops and walking along the street. This was the first time I had been handed a banana. How could they be so thoughtless? — so cruel? How much of a stranger's self-respect are you willing to cut away for a cheap laugh?

What was I supposed to do? Storm off and let them see the hurt? Throw the banana at them? Peel it and try to slash my fucking wrists —?

I stood up, lips tightly compressed, breathing heavily through my nose. I wanted to pull the door open. Batter them with my hurt and anger. But, if I opened the door, I'd lose control of myself, and my loss would be even greater. It would be an admission of defeat to show how something so shallow had cut so deeply.

I was being pulled into their world because this was their game, not mine.

I sat back down. The sofa wheezed up at me again. Sean opened the door, and behind him, his family scattered like the cockroaches used to do when I switched the light on at night. The door closed. I wouldn't let them see I was wounded. To reveal my hurt would be like allowing a pack of hyenas to smell blood. I swallowed my pride and anger, closely followed by the banana. I smiled, and my face assumed a pleasant disposition as I dropped the skin on the ashtray.

Sean took the skin away and returned with his record collection. Every other child in Ballymun was listening to bands like Thin Lizzy, The Police, Blondie, Status Quo and UB40, to name but a few. However, Sean wasn't like other children. He carefully slid a Monty Python L.P. from its pristine sleeve with the sort of reverence that the Turin Shroud would have been unveiled with. I sat and listened to this tripe while hoping the rain would ease off. I was struggling to suppress surges of anger and worrying that some other insensitive prank would soon emerge from the sour bosom of his family.

Fortunately, the Monty Python album became so irritating that I could focus on it enough to distract myself from how I felt.

'Have you anything else we can listen to?' I eventually asked.

Sean looked shocked, as if he had, in fact, just shown me the shroud, and I'd blown my nose in it. A look of anger and then embarrassment came over him. He took the stylus off the record and lifted the album on the disc's rim with his fingers. Then, like a priest lifting the sacrament up to receive the body of Christ, Sean held it up toward the window inspecting it for dust. Finding some speck, he blew briskly before carefully putting the record back in the sleeve. Finally, Sean left the room to return it from wherever it came — hopefully the bin. He returned with an old acoustic guitar and a dog-eared songbook from which he extracted a Beatles songbook. He only knew one song. His rendition had all the sensitivity of a vet, ramming his hand up the arse of a bull in search of a tumour.

He sang 'All You Need Is Love.'

If all you need is love, what happens if all you get is a banana?

Yeah — maybe it was at that moment whatever humiliation I felt curdled into contempt for the 'Oirish.' It may even have filled the void where God had once been. Or maybe that void was where my sense of humour was last seen chuckling to itself before it was stabbed in the back.

That festering anger and the fall from Grace?

In my case, I may not have fallen. Instead, I might have just slipped on a banana skin.

***

Lesley and I are walking the grounds of the Ashram, wending our way along the long lanes of fruit trees. She's happily talking about what she saw on her journey to Madurai.

Even though I've already apologised for how cold I was toward her, I still feel bad. So, finally, I stop and take her arm, turning her toward me. She's looking out from beneath the shade of her straw hat.

'I'm *really* sorry,' I say.

'You've already apologised. I feel better now, so don't worry about it. Have you eaten?'

'No. Not really. I had no appetite.'

'Oh — well, I'm starving. Why don't you come with me to the *Dharamsala*? When you smell the food, it'll change your mind.'

We resume our walk, bound by silence as warm as the sun on our skin.

I tell her, 'I thought about staying.'

She gives me a sideways glance. 'I know.'

'Mataji said as much. I thought you were upset that I wouldn't go with you.'

'Of course not. It would have been nice. Lovely, in fact. But even before we left Manchester, it occurred to me you might decide to stay here with Swami. Going to Madurai on my own didn't bother me. It was the possibility of heading back to Manchester without you that was upsetting.'

'Why didn't you say something?'

'I didn't want to influence your decision. It's not for me to say what happens in your spiritual life. I have enough trouble with my own. Now — are we going to eat or not?'

I start to apologise again, but she holds her hand up. Waves away my regret. 'Forget it. Just make sure you are happy with whatever you decide to do.'

'I'm coming back to Manchester.'

'Good,' she says. 'I wasn't sure you would when I got off the bus. But after you hugged me for that second time, I felt a weight lift from my shoulders.'

With each step, the smell of food becomes more enticing. My appetite returns with a rumble as my empty stomach begins to churn with hunger as we enter the modest block where food is served. Swami Premananda sometimes takes a turn cooking in the kitchen but not today. We choose a selection of dishes from what has been labelled '**NON-SPICEY**' and sit on a bench at a nearby table. The food is delicious but hot. I break out in a sweat as soon as I start eating, scooping up mouthfuls of rice and rasam with my fingers.

'Wow,' I say, reaching with my clean hand for the water jug on the table.

A heavily perspiring devotee at the table says, 'You should try the spicey selection. It's the hottest thing I've ever tasted. Agony, but the locals love it.'

'That bad?'

'Yeah. Imagine grafting your tongue onto a comet. Then, as it enters the Earth's atmosphere and your tongue begins to burn up, that's how hot it is, and at the last minute, someone puts rice on top.'

***

After two years of living in Ballymun, I finally lost the ability to laugh. I didn't even know such a thing was possible, but I woke up one morning, and my sense of humour had left my belly. People would say something that I knew was funny, but I had to impersonate myself laughing. It sounds ridiculous now, but that's how it was.

My laughter was hollow. It was forced and malnourished. Nothing like the full-bellied laughter of which I was capable. The strain of going outside had become almost unbearable. Mixing with other people was an ordeal. People were like booby traps. Some would blow up in my face, like Sean. Others didn't, but I never knew which ones were ticking. So, all of them were a threat until they proved otherwise. This happened around the same time Sean and his family gave me the banana. Maybe I'd poisoned myself with it.

Even among my school friends, I felt anxious, anticipating slights. These friendships didn't flourish outside. I couldn't allow them to. The school was a controlled environment. To some degree, I could anticipate events. But to be with those same friends in a setting where a constant influx of strangers would introduce an unknown element was too much of a strain. So, I was on my own.

I was asked to accompany some of the lads into town once and made an excuse not to go.

'C'mon, for fuck's sake. It'll be great. We're going queer-bashing.'

'What?'

'Queer bashing. It's brilliant.'

'You mean — beating people up?'

'Yeah. Have you never tried it?'

'Why would I? That's just sick. It's immoral. And illegal.'

'So is being queer. Anyway, if you change your mind, we're meeting up after school on the green.'

I was appalled. Like me, these boys had reached puberty and were presumably discovering what a very entertaining thing a penis could be. Why would they want to go out and assault others because they extended their appreciation to someone else? I couldn't understand this at all. It was disconcerting, too, because the lad who asked me to go along with him had always accepted my noticeable difference without comment. It was a shock to find someone who could accept my colour, but the sexuality of a stranger drove them to violence.

I considered calling the Gardai to tell them, but homosexuality was actually a criminal offence back then. The Church and The State were the biggest 'queer bashers' of the lot, possibly because they'd lost the ability to laugh at themselves a long time before I did.

***

The light of day has long been drained from the sky to quench the thirst of the night. Lesley holds a small flame up to the tip of her cigarette. The light flickers and dies. The end of the cigarette fiercely glows as she draws the smoke in and lets it whistle out between her teeth. We're sitting outside the Ashram on the little wall.

'I'm going to ask Swami to kill my ego,' I say. 'I've been thinking about this for the past few hours — although, now I'm actually saying it, it seems a little melodramatic.'

'Yes, it does. Are you sure? He's got a habit of giving you what you want.'

'That a good thing. Isn't it?'

'Well. It depends on what you're asking for. It's not like seeing Santa Claus and asking for a train set.'

'I know. But it seems to me that the source of my pain over the past few days — over my life, is my ego.'

'Before you ask for it, are you sure you know what it means?'

'Yeah. I think so. My ego is the thing that defines me as a separate entity from you and everybody else. It's the sense of me. It's my I-ness. Or the stories my mind tells me about myself. It's what I think I am. I think.'

'Then why would you want to get rid of it?'

'Because whatever the feck it is, I feel like it's protected me and helped me grow, but it's also stopped me from growing in areas which require me to be vulnerable. Like an overprotective parent. Or even a jailer. It's wired with all these hypersensitive alarms which over-react to anything that could cause pain on an emotional level. So it shuts me down. So I somehow end up trapped in my own limited sense of what I think I am.'

'Like?'

'For example, you've been in relationships before me. My instinctive reaction is that it diminishes your love for me.

'Sweetheart, that's ridiculous.'

'I know, but my ego doesn't feel it is. It reacts as if there's only so much love, and the fact that you've already given some away means there's less for me. It can take the past and turn it into a threat here in the present moment. It's excruciating sometimes, even though I know it's utter nonsense. You gave away what wasn't mine before you even knew I existed, and I —'

'I didn't give anything away,' Lesley says a little testily. 'I shared my life with other people at some point through the years.'

'Well, there you go. There's a perfect example. Even though I'm only using this to illustrate my point, my ego, under the skin, is *still* outraged and considers the past a betrayal. This — insanity — is what I want to get rid of. This sense of 'I' that rubs against the world with all these raw edges isn't what I want to be.'

Lesley says, 'Trying to get rid of your ego is like trying to get rid of your own shadow.'

'So I just need more light?'

'More light means more shadows. Maybe? I don't know. Actually, what do you mean by light?'

'Enlightenment. I suppose. I'm not sure. I've got this idea that if I eliminate the negative emotions, I'd see my own divinity.'

'But wouldn't that be like getting rid of one half of life?'

'That's right. The crap half.'

Lesley pats me on the back of the hand. 'Good luck with that, sweetheart.' She looks thoughtful momentarily and then asks, 'Are you *sure* you wouldn't like a train set instead?'

We laugh and hug each other before slowly walking back to the koothi.

'I've already been asking Swami for what I want.'
'Oh?'
'Yes. Well, not in person. I've been asking in my head

and heart who or what I am?'

'Have you had a reply?'

'I don't think so because I've still no idea what the answer is. When I first came to the ashram, I'd have said I was my thoughts and feelings, but I'm not so sure now. I've been having this sense of separation from them sometimes as if they're something other than me, because I don't seem to have any control over them. They do their own thing. And I'm tossed about by my emotions while this thing which is supposed to be my mind — I'll say that again — *my* mind — runs away with an internal dialogue while I'm little more than a witness. Or maybe just a hostage. How's that even possible if I'm the mind and the emotions? Surely I should be in control of them at all times rather than being the thing *they* control?'

'I wonder — ' Lesley says, 'if asking Swami to kill your ego is like going to the doctor and telling him what medicine you need?'

She's right. I've gone from asking the saint a question to telling *him* what *he* needs to do to help *me*. The patient has stepped back, and the illness is talking. The open hand has turned into a pointing finger. My ego is masquerading as an internal guru who knows *precisely* what must be done to remove itself.

I cast a long, long shadow in the moonlight. It glides through the huddled darkness under the palm trees, following me. The shadow of Lesley reaches over and takes my hand.

***

Nighttime.
Bedtime.
A startled cry —
I sit up in bed, blind, fumbling for my glasses, frightened

of cockroaches.

Mataji asks 'what is it?'

Lesley exclaims, 'Something landed on my head!'

I swing my feet onto the floor, clutching the sleeping bag liner around my waist, adrenaline rushing. The light comes on. I cringe, imagining cockroaches — but it's only a frog. Thank God! Hang on—frog it might be, but it's a big one. It's about the size of my fist. It leaps from Lesley's pillow and plops onto the floor, so I hop after it, bounding along in the bag. It bounces left, and I stop abruptly. It leaps up and flops down closer to me. I jump back, alarmed. Jesus, look at the size of it!

I better get a grip on my nerves because I'll have to grab it. I take a deep breath and brace myself.

The frog croaks and jumps to the right, passing me. Come on, Paul, be brave. Clumsily I follow and jump toward it, scooping at the air as it bounds past my outstretched hand. A globulous eye meets mine as it goes by, and I think — Oh my God! Do I *really* want to catch this thing? What if I grab too hard? How tightly *can* you grip a frog before it shoots out of its skin like a ripe banana?

Lesley and Mataji are howling with laughter, which is no help. The frog looks exceptionally bored, which might be why it decides to end the farce by launching itself into my palm. Plop, Ribbet and Yuk! Cold and clammy, softly palpitating in the cupped cage of my fingers, the big googly eyes are looking into mine, waiting for a kiss, perhaps? Well, it's not getting one. Holding my sleeping bag liner up with my elbows, I shuffle toward the back door. Mataji opens it. I place *'Kermit'* under the palm tree where my shorts are still hanging. It sits, looking back at me.

I shudder, lock the door, wash my hands and imagine all sorts of tropical diseases spread by frog sweat.

I put the light out to modest applause and get back on my cot bed.   The night soon settles into soft snores.

I feel loved and content, but outside —

A small plaintive croak.

CHAPTER EIGHT
Tick. Tock. Boom.

Morning. Outside the ashram gates sitting on the wall and sipping our breakfast, a lukewarm cup of coffee, a pair of smiling sundials.

'I need tea and toast,' I say wistfully.

'There isn't any,' Lesley replies dreamily. She's lost, looking up into the blue sky, cigarette smouldering down to ash.

'I need sausages.' I mutter.

'There's rice and *rasam* in the *Dharamsala.*'

'I'm *not* having spicy soup for breakfast. Not this morning.'

'It's good for you. Make you sweat. Cool you down.'

'I'm already sweating. I want lashings of beans spilling over onto crispy fried bread and bacon. I want something salty and crunchy.'

She points to a small scab on her arm from an insect bite.

'That's disgusting. No thanks.'

'Don't say I didn't offer. Now can you stop complaining?

I'm enjoying the peace and quiet.'

'Sorry.'

We sit quietly a while longer. I don't even moan when something lands in my coffee. I put a finger in, lift it out and flick it away. It falls on Lesley's hand.

'Urgghh!' She shakes it off.

'Oops.'

'Damn!' she says irritably. 'It's gone.'

'What is?'

'The *Moment*'s gone. I was at peace with the world, and now I can't get the idea of toast out of my head. Thank you.'

'Bugger. Sorry. Can I get you another drink?'

She shakes her head. The long ash tip falls from her cigarette onto her trouser leg. She sighs and blows it off. 'No. It's okay. And I'm sorry for snapping at you. I didn't sleep well last night.'

'Too cold?'

'No. You were snoring.'

'Oh. Sorry.'

And I'm sick of spicy food myself. I need some bread or potatoes.'

'Great! Let's nip into Trichy.'

'Not so fast. I'm worried about missing the vibhuti when it comes.'

'Oh yeah. I'd forgotten all about it.'

'We'll have to find Mataji and ask. She'll know.'

I wonder if someone missed Jesus walking on water because they wandered off to the other end of the beach, hoping to buy an inflatable donkey.

***

Summer came to Ballymun once more. The long shadow cast by James

Connolly Tower tried to hide from the light, circling warily as the sun rose.

Life felt grim. We were all suffering from stress in different ways. Tony developed severe problems with his stomach. We presumed it was his nerves. Wondered if it was an ulcer. The doctor said it was wind. It turned out to be his appendix about to burst. Poor Tony, doubled up in agony, was rushed to the hospital. They cut him open and then cut it out.
*

Jason spent a lot of time jumping up and down on his bed. Later in life, he told me this was because he felt his heart would stop if he didn't. He thought the movement would keep it going. I wish he'd said this to me at the time. I could have explained that bouncy castles were rarely prescribed for cardiac problems. I could have told him that I was worried about my own heart. Afraid it would burst. I had pains in my chest, which frightened me terribly.

My abdomen was locked tight, a feeling of dread grasping my soft belly like a fist. It squeezed all the hope from me. Took my laughter and skinned it. Left it dry and tight, stretched to breaking point. I was a walking prison, locked in myself. Parole, or at least walking in the exercise yard, came in the form of music. The Beat and UB40 lured me away from my unhappiness. These multicultural bands were a great source of hope for me. I was also inspired and given some strength by Bob Marley and Steel Pulse.

I also became obsessed with the original Star Trek. The idea of humans and aliens coexisting was very appealing in a time when spit and insults and mattresses fell from the heavens. To think of the USS Enterprise up there, past the towers, lifted my heart up and away from Ballymun. I'd go to sleep imagining I had a berth on the ship. With my eyes closed, I could be anywhere. Many nights, I fell asleep on the other side of the galaxy.

***

* * *

On the other side of the world, warm life folds itself around us. A comforting blanket of sunlight, incense and the distant sound of devotional songs untangle our knots. We're talking about India and how lush, green and inviting the countryside is compared to my expectations.

The field by the little wall we sit on has a villager in it. He tends his goats and carries a long stick to shake the branches of the abundant trees. Nuts or maybe fruit rain down for the goats to nibble on. It's this movement that drew my eyes to him. The long narrow stick swishes through the air. Leaves and other morsels rain down.

Around the edge of the field, trees huddle together in whispering bunches. In the middle, a few trees stretch their limbs about them like dancers who have the floor to themselves.

Up high, a bird of prey, wing tips trembling.

I step closer, shielding my eyes from the glare. I want a picture, but my camera's cheap, and the bird is a long way off. I have no zoom function. The only way to bring it closer would be to dress as a succulent rabbit and then get hit by a truck.

I drain the last of my coffee. Shake the dregs onto the grass. Still watching the bird hover.

'I've got to get closer,' I mutter.

'Watch out for snakes and scorpions,' Lesley says.

So, I hesitate briefly. Squint-eyed and wary. I continue under the premise that bad things don't happen on lovely days when the grass is tickling your toes and the sun is watching your back. A slow smile lazily softens my lips.

Life occasionally lets hubris slip by without comment.

A child, partially hidden in a cluster of bushes, is picking red berries up from the ground. He drops them into an aluminium pot. I squat down before him and hold up my camera.

'Photo?'

He replies, but I've no idea what he's saying, so I take a photograph anyway. Click — and a pang of regret for having done so. Is it right for me to take his image like this? I feel embarrassed suddenly at having taken something intimate from a stranger without getting permission. I thank him.

He nods and returns his attention to the berries. His little fingers are stained with juice. I look up into the sky. The bird's gone. Whatever it was looking at, I think, is on the other side of the embankment ahead of me through a loose fringe of trees.

I climb up, loose soil burrowing into my sandals as I scramble forward. Seeing the child so at ease in the grass puts my mind at rest regarding snakes and scorpions. It can't be dangerous if the goat herder is comfortable with his boy being out here. At the top of the embankment, I look back at the child. He's throwing a glance or two in my direction like an old man occasionally throwing bread to the ducks. I wave again. He doesn't wave back.

I lean on a tree for balance atop the earthen barrier and slip my sandals off to shake the soil out. The scene before me looks ancient. A dark brown man toils behind two oxen pulling a rough wooden plough. It gouges the earth, which splits and furrows. The once-white flanks of each ox are discoloured with soil. The white vest the man wears is equally stained with the earthy colours of the field. They appear bound together in the furrow of life, hauling the long day behind them.

I'm looking at a dog sleeping in the shade of a tree. I've no qualms about taking a photograph of *this* scene. It will take a lot to convince me I've compromised the dignity of any creature that will sniff its bottom in public.

* * *

***

When I was sixteen, we got a puppy. I was the one who went to Dublin to pick it up from one of our aunties. The walk to where she lived was long and tiresome, especially on such a blisteringly hot summer day. I could've gone by bus, but I'd had enough of public transport by then. Sitting cheek to jowl with strangers was too uncomfortable. The effort to control my anxiety around them was a trial, and the underlying fear of embarrassment was too intense. I would much rather walk.

I told myself the people of Ballymun rejected us, so I rejected them too. I didn't want to sit with them. They couldn't even queue for the bus properly. When it turned up, there was always a rush for the door as people pushed in, barging each other out of the way. Refusing to join the melee, I usually ended up standing for the length of the journey. I'd then have people who couldn't understand the concept of passing through a narrow door one at a time, looking down their noses at me.

Yeah — fuck the lot of them. I'd walk.

When I arrived at our aunt's home, I was tired and footsore. The day had been scorching. The thoroughly baked pavement had been radiating heat up through my shoes for almost three hours, and the soles of my feet felt raw.

I knocked on the door. A small fair-haired boy about half my age opened it. He was one of our many Irish cousins. He presented me with a puppy in a box like I'd turned up at an illicit Korean Takeaway. A small bundle of soft, golden-haired 'puppiness' gazed up at me with big brown eyes. I was smitten. I stroked his blunt chin and loosened the red tartan dog collar, which looked a little tight.

'Me Mam's got the shits,' said the child. 'She said you've to come in, and she'll make you something to eat.'

'Oh?' I could smell excrement. It was awful. Not only did the hall smell of shit, but somehow it stank of shit that had passed its best-before date.

'She's on the toilet but won't take much longer. There can't be much

left now. Been in there for feckin ages.'

'Right. Um — I think I'd better be headin' back. I've got a bus to catch.'

The toilet flushed in the background.

'D'ye want a cold drink or anythin'?' *the child asked.*

'No,' *I replied, backing away.* 'Thanks. Say hello to your Ma for me. Hope she feels better soon.' *I turned and walked rapidly away, clutching the cardboard box to my chest. The puppy, looking over the lip of it, began yapping at all and sundry. His soft velvet ears flopped along as he bounced along in my arms.*

I had only mentioned the bus as an excuse not to be given my dinner by a woman with severe diarrhoea, but I soon realised getting home quickly was a priority. The heat would be too much for the puppy. It was panting and began to look utterly miserable. I bought a bottle of water and let it lap the warm liquid from the palm of my hand. Despite my concern, the little tongue tickled and made me chuckle.

A taxi was out of the question. I had enough money for a bus and nothing else. So, for the sake of my new best friend, I barged through the usual rabble, trying to squeeze themselves like human toothpaste through the narrow doorway of the bus. I even managed to get an aisle seat and felt a flood of relief. The worst was over.

When the bus lurched off, my elbows were pinned to my side. I was squashed up against a sizeable sweaty woman sitting on my right. On my left, a disagreeably large arse was within whispering distance of my ear. My legs were so tightly compressed that my recently descended balls were on the verge of being shoved back up. I felt faint. Intensely self-conscious, my embarrassment radiated waves of heat up through the neck of my T-shirt, burning my face and inducing a torrent of sweat. The puppy looked up at me as if fascinated by the beads of perspiration trickling down my face.

I gazed into the little brown eyes and smiled at the cuteness of the nose.

The floppy golden ears trembled a little as the bus hit a pothole. I felt a warm surge of simple happiness.

And then I felt a warm surge of something else. The smell of roasting shit rose like a miasma. Something warm and slow and heavy was spreading on my lap.

Oh — my — God!

It wasn't just my aunt who had diarrhoea. The puppy was voiding the liquidised contents of its intestinal tract all over me. In other circumstances, I'd have leapt to my feet, but I was hemmed in, a human sardine smelling of fish and now covered in hot sauce.

Please, God, don't do this to me.

God gave the puppy another little squeeze like a master baker icing a birthday cake for a very large, very lucky fly.

As the implications of my situation hit me, I was paralysed by an agony of embarrassment. I literally could not move, and then I realised — I didn't want to move. Why would I? What am I going to do? Get off the bus and walk miles in the sun covered in shite?

I'd go down in history as The Pied Piper of Flies.

Fuck that. Fuck this. And fuck you lot too.

I'd have to deal with the indignity, and so would everybody else. So, we bore the unbearable stench for the rest of that long journey. The excruciating embarrassment was mine alone. I heard people gagging and asking each other whence the awful stink was emanating. But, of course, those near me knew, especially when I stood for my stop, and the soggy bottom of the box slithered down my leg. As I squeezed through, I pushed between the people jammed into the aisle, mumbling regrets for anything I may inadvertently smear them with as I passed. My shame was beyond measure by the time I stepped off the bus. When it sped away, the passengers pointed at me out the windows. Some looked outraged. Others were confused. A lot of them were laughing.

I'd have been laughing, too, had I not been holding a sick puppy while wearing a very large, rapidly melting chocolate sporran.

Ma already had her hand over her mouth and nose when she opened the door. She'd been in the hall. I didn't even have to knock because the smell was that bad. Needless to say, I was in a very bad mood. In fact, I was, in a manner of speaking, quite literally steaming.

'My God,' she said through her fingers, 'What have you done to the dog?'

***

On my bed in the koothi, I drift among scattered thoughts. Death is here with them. It pulls and nudges the other thoughts, shaping them and reminding me of my mortality. I don't know why. Maybe it was seeing the bird of prey hovering above the fields, waiting. Perhaps it's because sleep has something of death about it when you slip away, falling backwards into yourself.

I don't fear death. Not here. Not on the Ashram with Swami Premananda nearby. I take great comfort from his presence in the world as I sink back into the emptiness from which I came. Beneath the driftwood of myself, I sleep the deepest of sleep.

I am unborn.

***

The looming grey edifice of James Connolly Tower, the Tombstone of God, had now been our home for two years. From the moment the old dry bones of the god I'd abandoned rattled down the chute, we were on our own. I lost hope that we would ever leave the tower. I somehow forgot that everything changes. Everything comes and goes.

Even puppies.

Ours went with indecent haste.

The flat in Ballymun was the only refuge we had. The dog disturbed this by barking continuously, emptying its bladder prodigiously, eating like a horse and then blowing the food out the other end. None of us wanted to walk the poor thing. I know. It was something we should have considered beforehand, but we didn't. Ma didn't want to do it. Jason was too young. I could barely cope with the stress of going outside, so I baulked at the idea. We didn't even consider the idea of Tony walking the dog. He hardly ever left the building anymore, especially in daylight.

The solution was simple. Everyone loves puppies, so the dog wasn't the problem. Instead, we were the problem, my brothers and me.

I took the puppy to the lift and pushed the grimy button to make the greasy gears grind it up to our floor. When it arrived, I stepped in, and the puppy followed. It wagged its tail, enthusiastically sniffing the stains. I pressed every button for all thirteen floors except the ground. As the doors began to close, I stepped out. The yapping of the puppy faded as the lift ascended, and my heart fell through my boots as I walked away. Someone would take it in, of that I was sure. It was cute. It was a puppy — it wasn't black. Knowing all this didn't make it any easier.

A few days later, I saw the dog on a loose leash, loping along after a small boy. It was still wearing the red tartan collar. My guilt dumped me there and ran after the happy duo, wagging its tail. I couldn't blame it because I was poor company, even for guilt.

Everything comes and goes away again. Puppies, people, dogs and dirty great concrete monuments to dead Irish men — all pass away. Look at the history books. Most of the authors are dead and forgotten. All they've done is compile a list of things for us to forget soon enough.

I love history, but perhaps remembrance is best reserved for ourselves.

Who were you before you were born?
Before you had a name, who did you know yourself as?
Who am —

***

I lay on my travel cot in the koothi. Peace permeates the Ashram. It's in the air like the fragrance of a flower. I'm warm. Safe. A holy man nearby, somewhere, somehow.

Motes of dust drift lazily on shafts of sunlight. I feel the lightest of touches and a soft breath as the air slowly stirs.

Such peace.
Stillness.
The rise and fall of breath.
Dust settling.

***

Ma met one of our neighbours in the lift and discovered this woman had a son called Kevin, who was teaching himself how to play the guitar. Tony was a good guitarist, adding that to his hobbies, so the two started a little band in Kevin's bedroom. We were delighted because Tony could leave the flat without leaving the building. I felt a great deal of relief that he'd made a friend. I was never really worried about Jason, our younger brother. He wasn't exposed to Ballymun other than when he was in school, and I wasn't aware of any of the difficulties he encountered. But, on the other hand, Tony was obviously struggling, which pained me.

Tony always looked out for us when we were younger. He was my protector. The big brother who once broke the jaw of another boy with one punch. The other boy, a tough nut, had started the fight. Tony finished it. In my eyes, he was strong and brave with a good heart. We were beyond his protection in Ballymun, and I think this ate away at him. It gnawed at his self-esteem like a hungry dog given a bone. He couldn't save us from what lay outside. He couldn't even save himself.

Outside was too hostile and caustic to his dignity for him to survive out there for too long. So, as the tips of his fingers hardened with the steel rasp of guitar strings, he became more remote. Locked within himself within a concrete tower, he was withering on the vine emotionally, intellectually and physically.

Tony bought a bass guitar, asked me to play it, and said he'd teach me. Despite having no particular desire to do so, I agreed to help out. This act started me off on a musical journey which led to me, years later, standing in the flat of another musician, looking at a picture of Swami Premananda. That picture would lead to a dark night when all my pain and sorrow would be smashed like a clay pot before my eyes.

By giving me that bass, Tony gave me the thing which would lead me away from my troubles and unlock the door, which led to peace in my heart.

The shape of a guitar always reminds me of a large key.

Around this time, I also acquired several friends, the most important being Ciaran. Unless you're laughing at yourself, life requires you to forget yourself to have a belly laugh. I did both with my friend Ciaran and laughed at him, too, for good measure. He joined my class at the end of the second year.

It had become increasingly easy to dismiss the Irish with broad brushstrokes of contempt. Ciaran and his family were the antidotes to this. His friendship provided fine detail to the canvas and the subtle colours of a real human being. He was also walking down the street with me when I had a most peculiar thought.

I'll tell you about that in a bit.

Let me just say it was probably the closest I had ever come to waking up from this dream of life on that day when —

***

I open my eyes. I'm alone, but the palm of an unseen hand is on my face. Warm and comforting, it remains on my cheek, and long moments pass before it's taken away.

'Swami?' I say in a questioning tone.

I look around, sitting up, already knowing I'm alone. Nobody came. Nobody went. My mind can't cope with an invisible hand, but my heart feels blessed. I sit up and try to make sense of what just happened. The 'mind' is playing tricks, says the same 'mind.' But the heart remains silent about what it knows.

I go for a shower. Gasp at the cold cascade of water and then spout water from my mouth like a fountain. It feels great. I feel invigorated, which is just as well because the water has to be replenished. Three showers a day, cooking, washing clothes, and drinking tea rapidly empties the large water barrel.

I take two plastic urns to the pump. Working the handle to fill them up feels like hard work and weakens me. Then, when I lug the urns back, I'm exhausted and have to sit on my bed.

Lesley and Mataji come through the door.

I tell them, 'I just woke up with a hand on my face.'

'Don't worry,' Mataji replies. 'It's just Swami.'

'Oh,' I say, disappointed at how *blasé* this reaction is. But then I remember Mataji has known Swami to be in two places simultaneously. She's seen him heal people and produce golden statues out of thin air. So, I guess *blasé* is fine.

'Well —,' I mutter, 'it certainly beats an alarm clock.'

Lesley yawns, stretches, and then says, 'The next time you start snoring, I wonder if Swami can wake you up with a slap?'

We're laughing when a young man appears at the door. His silhouette, framed by bright sunlight, obscures his identity. I don't recognise the voice, but he's been running.

Is the vibhuti coming? I wonder.

'We need men to carry rocks,' he says breathlessly. I'm momentarily alarmed, thinking there's some emergency, but he says, 'It's for a drainage ditch.' His haste comes from enthusiasm and not panic.

'Sorry, mate. I'd love to come and help. But I'm not feeling well.'

The silhouette shrugs and leaves with as much eagerness as he had arrived.

'Are you okay?' Lesley asks.

'I feel very weak. I couldn't carry a tune, never mind a boulder. So I'm going to lay back down for a bit.'

She comes over and feels my forehead. 'Hmmm,' she says, taking her hand back. 'I'll get you some water. You might be dehydrated.'

Mataji's already got a glass of water for me.

'Thanks.' I drink it down. Mataji now puts her hand on my head.

'Feverish?' I ask.

'Empty,' she replies with mock seriousness. 'I'll get some more water for you.' She goes out into the kitchen. Lesley sits beside me on the bed.

'We're going for a walk with Adrienne and Rekha. Probably best you stay here if your feeling poorly.'

'What about Trichy? We said this morning we might go and get some food?'

'I don't think you're up to it, so we'll leave it until tomorrow.'

'Yeah. I think you're right. What about the vibhuti? Any word?'

'Swami says not today.'

Mataji returns with a jug of water and refills the glass in my hand before putting the pitcher on the ground. They leave. I lay back. Close my eyes. Fall into a deep sleep. The Bible says God took seven days to make the world. I made it disappear by nodding off.

'Oops' barely seems sufficient by way of an apology.

***

The end of our time in Ballymun came quite unexpectedly. One day I returned from a long walk into Dublin, a brace of dog-eared, second-hand books under my arm. I found my family loading our furniture into a van.

'What's happening? Where are you taking our stuff?'

'We're moving,' Ma said, handing a bin liner full of clothes up to Jason, who was in the back of the vehicle. Tony and our uncle Val came round the corner of the building, holding our sofa between them.

'But — I was in town!' I exclaimed. 'What if I hadn't come back now? How would I have known where you'd gone?'

'Stop fussing. Go and give Tony and Val a hand with that sofa. I'm going back up to check we've got everything.'

'I don't understand! Where the hell are we going?'

'We've got a flat in Dublin.'

I stood there, open-mouthed. It was over. We'd survived Ballymun.

'Thank fuck for that.' I said with considerable feeling.

Ma stopped in her tracks and turned to me. She points a finger heavenward.

'Thank God,' she said. 'I've been praying for this since we got here. You should say a little prayer in the back of that van when we start the journey back into Dublin.'

She turned on her heels and entered James Connolly Tower for the last time. I looked up at the long, cold and grey concrete length of it with loathing. It pointed to the blue sky, God's last known address. Pointed into the heavens above, in which Ma still had faith.

'Go fuck yourself,' I said to God, even though I knew from bitter

experience He rarely did requests.

Tony knew this of God too.

A few weeks earlier, in a desperate, courageous effort to do something, he'd gone to a recruiting office and joined the Irish Army. We were still waiting for him to be called up.

Sitting on our sofa in the back of the van, holding a standard lamp in one hand, I watched Ballymun recede. At the time, I felt like I was leaving Ballymun, but the truth is Ballymun came with me. It existed in me, not the other way round. It was my experience. I was not the experience of it. Both it and I were a dream passing before the eyes of — who?

Who was the dreamer?
Well —
Nobody.

***

Years ago, Adrienne had a dream in which Swami Premananda pointed at Lesley and said, 'Lesley has something wrong there.' When Adrienne woke, she rang Lesley and told her what Swami had said, which prompted Lesley to seek medical advice. X-rays showed she did indeed have *something* 'there', and an operation was rapidly arranged to remove it. After the surgical procedure, it took some time for her to recover from the anaesthetic. When she finally came to her senses in the hospital bed, the surgeon came to see her.

'How are you, my dear?' he asked.

She nodded, unable to reply for a moment. Her mouth was dry, and her tongue felt as if it was glued to her palette. The doctor stood by her bed, an inquisitive expression on his face. When she could finally speak, she said, 'I'm okay. It's a bit sore, but I'm glad the operation's over.'

The doctor tilted his head, not looking convinced, which worried Lesley, prompting her to ask, 'How did it go? Did you manage to get it out?'

The surgeon looked a little embarrassed as he explained what had happened.

'Well — you see — the thing is. It seems to have disappeared.'

Lesley was pleased with this news, naturally, but the peculiar expression on his face worried her.

'That *is* good, isn't it?' she asked.

'Yes. Yes, Indeed. We're just a little bit — curious, shall we say, as to *where* it went.'

'I don't understand. Didn't you —?'

'Take it out? No, my dear, we didn't. We made the incision and had a look round, but — it was gone.'

'Gone?'

'Yes. Gone. Most peculiar. All I can do is apologise. There's been some mistake somewhere along the way. I don't know how because it's quite clear on your X-ray. And the tests we did — ?' He looked down at his notes and shook his head. The doctor looked back at her. 'We can run more tests, but quite frankly, it would be a waste of your time and mine.'

Lesley held her hand up, wincing at the effort, and waved away his words. 'It's alright. These things happen.'

'In your case, it would appear they do.' He nodded, still looking befuddled and left the room.

The Indian anaesthetist then popped his head around the door, pointed to a photograph of Swami Premananda by her bed and said laughing, 'Friends in high places, Lesley?'

'Something like that,' she replied.

Funny things, dreams.

***

* * *

I'm awake now and looking up at the ceiling. Something small rustles in the rafters. Sunlight, bright and sharp as a surgeon's knife, cuts the air. Specks of dust are drifting like shoals of tiny fish, drawing my eyes toward the open door. I sit up and go out onto the veranda, pulled like a moth to the light. I yawn like a lion. Stretch like a cat. Sit on the wall. Idly wonder what the rest of the day will bring.

I shut my eyes, enjoying the warmth, feeling loved and blessed. A large grasshopper lands on the ground before me when I open them. Insect eyes observe me, an unseen fuse slowly burning away. I feel apprehensive. Worried about moving. It might panic. Jump. Ricochet off my eyeball. Leave a wing under my eyelid.

So, we sit here.
We look at each other.
Two of God's creations.
Tick.
Tock.
Boom.

***

Thwock!

I heard the impact above me, looked up and saw a pigeon falling. It landed at my feet, dead, neck broken. I stepped over it. Somewhere inside the walls of Guinness's Brewery, there was at least one dark, intensely pungent puddle of grog where pigeons presumably congregated for a drink. They must quench their thirst, become inebriated and fly under the influence of the black stuff, which I assume explained the feathered corpse I had stepped over. Pigeons who were too pissed to fly took to staggering down the street, possibly looking for a phone box in which to urinate.

I had been on the way back from the shop when this happened.

Our new home was in the heart of Dublin, unlike Ballymun, which, as I've said before, was in the arse end of the city. We had a flat in an old four-storey apartment block. The occupants were mainly pensioners or mature working-age couples. They quickly got used to the sight of us, so we had almost no trouble within the vicinity of our new flat, which consisted of one room.

It had a kitchen in a nook slightly bigger than an upright coffin. Dracula would have felt right at home, peeling his potatoes in the ceramic sink where we had to wash. There was no bathroom. Once a week, we dragged a tin bath in from the yard, boiled up pans of water and had a bath. It was cramped but not as cramped as the bed.

We had just one, a double, which took up two-thirds of the room. We all slept in it. Four of us. Head to toe like sardines. I've no idea how we managed, but at least we were warm at night, which was just as well. There was no central heating, and once the coal fire died away, the room grew cold — but not as cold as the toilet, which was outside. The loo was cold, draughty, and full of spiders who ate each other and then sat in a corner watching you. Sitting in a toilet without imagining a tarantula on my back remains a delight to this day.

It doesn't sound ideal, but it was much better than living in a tower block. Our street was opposite a church and bookended by pubs, one of them was called the 'Old Harbour Pub.' Brendan Behan, one of many Irishmen to grace the world stage, collapsed there on March 20th 1964. He famously described himself as 'a drinker with a writing problem.' Unfortunately, he died shortly after collapsing. His gravestone bore a bronze image of his face until someone stole it, leaving a hole that is perhaps more appropriate to commemorate a death.

***

The grasshopper jumped into the grass, and now the moon has jumped into the sky. We're sitting on the veranda. The fragrance of flowers and incense is in the air. I feel a gentle wind stirring itself, warm and comforting like God sighing with contentment. The night sky is a wishing well, old coins glittering in the depths. Time sleeps beneath the dark water.

Adrienne gently snores in the koothi.

Quietly, Lesley and Mataji are talking as I make notes. I can just about see with the light of the moon and the candlelight coming out of the koothi.

Mataji yawns mightily and says, 'That's me done for the night. I'm off to bed. Sleep tight, you two.'

Lesley wants a cigarette before turning in, so we walk down toward the Ashram gates. Before getting there, we stop in the middle of the path and stare up into the sky. The night sky above any city is utterly impoverished compared to what we can see. Without artificial light to mask them, the sky is glittering with countless stars.

I shake my head in awe and wonder if the night sky looks into us as deeply as we look into it.

Beautiful isn't it,' Lesley says.

'Yeah,' I say wistfully. 'It is. But it's not God, is it?'

She shrugs. 'Some would say it is.'

'No. That's God's handiwork. I want to see God, not his calling card.'

We stand in silence for a few minutes, looking up. A meteor streaks across the sky as if someone up there is trying to light a match. Perhaps what preceded the Big Bang was a strong smell of gas. I feel so small, standing like a child, looking up and longing for the universe to hold my hand.

'Why can't I have a vision of God? I've read about it happening to other people, so why not me?'

'Like Paul on the road to Damascus?'

'Yeah. That sort of thing.'

Lesley shrugs. 'There's no reason why you shouldn't. But there's also no reason why you should. I used to see all sorts of stuff, but it stopped after I met Swami.'

'Oh?

'Yes. It was just a distraction. Or so I was told. It can give you the impression you're making progress on the spiritual path, but having a vision doesn't make you a spiritual person.'

'True. Maybe vision is the wrong word. I want some sign that whatever there is, which is pure and divine and full of love — actually sees *me*. I guess that's it. Yeah. I don't know why I didn't think of it before. I don't want proof of God. I want proof that God sees *me*.'

'You want preferential treatment by the creator of all things bright and beautiful? Isn't that a little bit egotistical?'

'No. I don't want it all the time. All I want is a second, just an instant of realisation. It's not a lot to ask for out of eternity.

'It can take many lifetimes according to the Buddhists — '

'Balls to that. The only life I have is now. Here. This one. This moment. If not now, then when?'

Overhead another meteor. Another match is being struck.

Lesley resumes the slow walk toward the Ashram gate for her cigarette. I follow her, along with my train of thought. I catch up, and she slips her hand into mine.

She says, 'Maybe it's a matter of faith?'

'Faith instead of proof is ridiculous. Faith is just proof that you have no evidence, that's all.

'Faith has to come into it to some degree, even if it's only faith enough to sustain you until you find the proof you're looking for?'

Lesley sits on the little wall by the gate while I stand and look back at the stars. The pungent stink of tobacco smoke fouls the pleasant scent of incense for a few seconds. Lesley wafts the air in front of her and says, almost to herself, 'I'll have to stop this soon.'

'Why not now? I say, teasing her.

She ignores my suggestion. Blows smoke into the heavens. Continues to talk. She says, 'I can't tell you the countless nights of study, prayer, and meditation I've put in over the years. And I'm still waiting.'

She falls into silence, thinking about that as the light of galaxies and suns slip in and lay upon my eyes.

Wistful, she continues. 'One time, my heart opened to such a degree I had complete empathy with everybody. Love poured in. Love poured out. Day after day. It was beautiful until — it disappeared.

I remember Lesley telling me this not long after I met her.

'I fell into a lonely, depressing place when it left. I was bereft. I didn't know what to do with myself. Eventually, I spoke to one of Swamis' disciples about it. He told me I was back in the state I'd been in before my heart opened. Compared to what I'd experienced, my ordinary perception was so narrow, it was as if the light in my life had gone — ' She looks at me and shrugs, almost apologetically. 'I've seen it. I've been there. I need to find my way back.'

I find this a little frustrating. 'But that's the thing. Why do we have to spend loads of time looking? It doesn't make sense that whatever it is should be playing hide and seek. I want to know what God is *now*. I want to know what *I am* now. I want to know what all this means.'

I kick a small stone off the path.

'Sit down, sweetheart. You're starting to pace.'

She pats the wall beside her. I sit. I sigh. The stars are still above, glittering and twinkling as if something's amusing them.

I say, 'Remember when you were a child, playing hide and seek, and you saw the curtain moving? You knew somebody was hiding behind it. You could see the shoes sticking out or something. For me, Swami Premananda is the movement of that curtain. I know it. God is here. I don't mean actually on the ashram. I mean *here* at this moment. So why doesn't God come out from behind the veil?'

'Do you know what God looks like?'

'No.'

So how do you know you haven't seen God?'

'Because I wouldn't be such a monumental arse if I had, would I? Everything would be different. Better. Somehow. I wouldn't be filled with pride, lust, anger, and insecurity.'

'You missed out on gluttony.'

'I'm saving that one for pudding.'

Lesley laughs and takes hold of my hand. She yawns. We head back into the Ashram. Some night bird or maybe a bat flutters across our path into the trees on our left.

'Maybe *that's* God?' I suggest, and then something occurs to me. I stop for a moment. 'Could it be I'm looking for the wrong thing?'

'I'm not with you?' Lesley says, looking back at me.

'We're supposed to be made in the image of God,' I say. 'But what if I'm looking for a God made in *my* image?'

'You mean short-sighted?'

'No, I mean — someone or something I can relate to. Maybe that's where I'm going wrong. I should be looking for the unknowable.'

'That sort of makes a search for God redundant before it starts, doesn't it? Because why would we continue?'

'The desire to know?'

'The unknowable?'

'Hmm. When you put it like that, it sounds a bit pointless.

'Huge nose,' Lesley says as we approach the koothi.

'Yeah,' I say, thinking about it for a second before realising it makes no sense. 'Pardon?'

'Sssshhhh!' She puts her finger to her lips, about to place the palm of her hand on the door to ease it open. 'Don't wake Mataji and Adrienne up.'

'I don't understand. Whose got a huge nose?' I whisper.

She pauses. 'What?'

'I said — '

She hushes me again and, leaning closer to my ear, whispers, 'Not huge nose. Why would I say — never mind. I said, *who* knows.'

Oh

Right

Huge nose, indeed.

***

I'm lying on my bed. Slipping away. Unseen fingers are undoing the knot of my being. The rope unravels. The end of my travels. Asleep in the consciousness of God, sustained by the consciousness of God, known only unto God.

All this so I can rise in the morning to look for God.

Anything this ludicrous has to be a dream. Enlightenment may be nothing more than falling out of bed. Those things which trouble us so much and make us look for the meaning of it all could just be life itself snoring.

Disturbing the peace.

CHAPTER NINE

Along The Moon-Drenched Streets Of Dublin, My Shame Burns Brightly

It's cold in here. It's dark, but I still see someone moving about in the gloom. It's not Lesley because I can see she's sitting in bed, rubbing her eyes, so it must be Mataji. Or maybe Adrienne.

Lesley asks, 'What day is it?'

I can't reply, being in the middle of a humungous yawn.

The figure in the dark lights a candle on the altar. It's Adrienne. She whispers, 'It's Thursday.'

Lesley slides her hand along the edge of her bed until her fingers locate her watch. She peers at the little round face before turning to Adrienne and saying, 'Good lord, you're up early.'

'Mataji woke me when she opened the door. She's gone to the Prayer Hall. I'm going to follow her over for the morning Puja if anyone wants to join me?'

'Later. I need a cup of tea first.'

Adrienne quietly closes the door behind her. Lesley pushes herself from the snug pocket of her sleeping bag and sits on the edge of her travel cot. I do the reverse, snuggling down deeper.

'Would you like tea?' Lesley asks.

'No. Thanks. I'm going back to sleep. I didn't sleep too well.'

'Oh?'

'I kept waking up, utterly frozen. Why is it so hot in the day and so cold at night? It makes no sense.'

'Something to do with the lack of cloud cover.'

'It's ridiculous. I'm not getting up until the sun warms the continent up like it's supposed to do.'

'We're going to Trichy today, remember?'

'Oh — crap. Yeah. I forgot.' Reluctantly I emerge from the depths of my sleeping bag.

'We've run out of rupees, so we'll have to find a bank. And I'll have to find the office for Saudi Airlines to confirm our reservation for the flight home.'

'What about the vibhuti?'

'I'll speak to Mataji. If it's not coming today, we'll grab a taxi into town this morning before it gets too hot.'

***

Compared to the flat in Ballymun, our new home was tiny but so were the lifeboats compared to the Titanic, and I know which one I'd prefer. We were also living in an area that was familiar to us. We were close to St. Brendan's Mental Institution and my old Basin Street Christian Brothers school. I was too old to attend now and was still going to school in Ballymun, but Jason, on the other hand, was just the right age. By now, the teachers weren't allowed to hit the pupils, so he didn't have to face that.

I returned to the Comprehensive for two months leading up to my final exam, the Intermediate Certificate. As much as I didn't want to go back to Ballymun, I decided to enrol in the college there. The alternative was to leave the educational system for good, which worried the bejesus out of me. It was a time of high unemployment, and I couldn't imagine anyone giving me a job. Not someone of my colour. It was a very defeating idea, but I believed it to be true then. I'd become a racist in a way, looking at myself through the eyes of an imaginary potential employer and dismissing myself out of hand because of my colour. True, this was due to my experience in Ireland, but not everybody had rejected me.

Fear of rejection made me reject myself before anyone else could do it. I projected negative reactions to my presence in the past into the future, which ruined the present. Even though we'd left Ballymun, I was still sitting on the back of the lorry that had taken us there. The boy I was could still hear the voices of those men telling me to go back to where I'd come from.

Yeah — I was still stuck there as if they'd nailed my feet to the ground.

***

Lesley, Naren and I are sitting in a taxi parked outside the Prayer Pall, waiting for Rekha. Earlier, Mataji told us the vibhuti would happen tomorrow or the day after. A young man approaches and speaks to Naren up front beside the driver.

'Are you going to Trichy?' he asks.

'Yes,' Naren replies.

'Could you buy a towel for me? I left in a hurry and don't seem to have packed one. I'll pay you, of course.' He holds out a handful of rupees.

'No problem. Where can we find you?'

He points toward his koothi but says, 'I'll find you when you return. I'm really grateful for this. Thank you.' He hands the rupees to Naren and then steps back as the car starts. Rekha arrives, gets in and off we go onto the road leading out of the Ashram.

'Wasn't he gorgeous,' Lesley says.

Gorgeous —

The word smirks and slinks around my head. It's mocking me. Jabbing a finger at my inadequacies. My insecurities are coiling and uncoiling in my belly, taking strength from my sudden weakness. Hurt circles my heart, seeking entry. I'm thinking back to all the lonely years in Ireland. Hollow years, of which I remember the isolation and the fingers pointing, the gormless bastards gawping, and the sniggering. Unable to be invisible except when it came to the possibility of being known and loved intimately. To that possibility, I was utterly anonymous.

Invisible.

A ghost of the heart.

The taxi passes the ashram gates and eats the road, spitting out the grit and bitter dust.

I feel so sad.

The car is dragging my past along behind us.

***

The mark I got for The Intermediate Certificate was, I think, below average. Nevertheless, it was enough to achieve a pass mark. I'd done some study for the mock exam, which preceded it and failed dismally. So, resigned to failure, I didn't bother to study for the actual exam. How I managed to pass, I've no idea.

I enrolled in the College for Higher Education in Ballymun. My decision was greatly influenced by how unprepared I felt for the outside world. Ciaran had also entered the college, which was another reason for staying. It had also occurred to me that college was possibly the only place I would mix with girls my age. The prospect of female friends was thrilling but also seemed too good to be true.

The first day was a disappointment. All the boys sat on one side of the class, and the girls sat on the other. I sat in the middle, unable to relax with either group. Ciaran was the only person I was comfortable with, but I'd only see him in passing. Being more academically disciplined than I was and very clever, he was put into a higher class.

I felt alone among strangers, but it didn't bother me much. I'd done this before and knew things would get better. It would just take a little time, that is, if I lasted long enough. The college was a long way from Echlin Street, and I struggled to get there on time. I had great difficulty sleeping during the night and walked for miles when the sun went down, trying to unwind. It was as if the stress of living in the tower had yet to leave me. I'd wake in the morning, footsore and exhausted. Often I turned my face to the wall, listening to the clock tick until I went back to sleep.

During one of these absences, I missed some necessary work for some subject or the other. One of the girls was kind enough to suggest I borrow her workbook for the weekend. I accepted gratefully, blushing hotly.

I was a lonely eighteen-year-old with a fiercely creative streak and surging hormones. When puberty hit me, I'd written erotica for myself or, to be more honest, unsophisticated smut. One story. Not even that. It was half a page to channel my sexual energy and release it. I've told you what a great idea that turned out to be. But, as if to show that I hadn't learned from that particular debacle, I decided to draw my erotica/smut instead of writing it.

Short of drawing paper, I had to rummage in my school bag for an exercise book. Finding a blank page, I began to draw a naked woman. In theory, it seemed like a good idea, but it was more complicated than I imagined in practice. Drawing the mysterious area between her legs took great concentration and even more imagination because I only had a vague idea of what 'down there' looked like. I was reasonably sure it involved a lot of hair and lips, but then again, so did Karl Marx. In Ireland at that time, it was easier to get water blessed by the Virgin Mary than it was to get a picture of anywhere remotely near the region from which baby Jesus may have emerged. And by that, I don't mean

Bethlehem.

God knows what my drawing of 'down there' must have resembled. Excruciating embarrassment has erased it from my mind, but I suspect it may have looked like a woman giving birth to a small grizzly bear. It was a crude drawing and showed my immaturity in every sense of the word. I should have torn it out of my copybook and ripped it up. I didn't. Instead, I forgot about it and had another extended absence from college, unable to face the journey.

When I returned after a few weeks, the headmaster called me over before I went into class. He was concerned about my commitment to education and wanted me to use the opportunity to improve my prospects like the other students. I agreed it was the right thing to do, and I felt buoyed by his encouraging words. As a result, I went into class feeling good about myself and sat in the neutral zone between the two genders.

The girl who'd been kind enough to lend me her book approached and asked for it back.

'Only if you've finished with it?' she said.

'Yeah. It — it was very helpful.' I stammered.

'You're welcome,' she replied, taking it back with a friendly smile. As she returned to her desk, I put my head down to concentrate on the work before me. I happened to glance her way after a few minutes. At that moment, she opened the workbook — and the shock on her face — and the disgust — she got up and dropped it in the bin.

Oh — God.

Shame burned in my heart so fiercely that it incinerated the nerves in my legs, feet, arms and fingers. I was paralysed. Pressed between the sheets of those clean white pages had been the picture I'd drawn and forgotten. I'd somehow used her book instead of my own. I couldn't even apologise because what I had done was so unforgivable. There was no going back from this shame. I could not endure it.

So I never went back.

***

* * *

I'm in the taxi, talking to Lesley like my heart isn't dragging along the dusty road behind us. She's holding my hand. I roll the window down with the other and taste grit from the road on my lips. Feel it on the fold of my eyelids. Sweat trickles down my back and tickles the back of my knees. Naren, upfront, is talking to the driver. Rekha's got the other back window rolled down a little. Lesley gives my hand a little squeeze before letting it go. Discreetly she wipes her palm on her pants leg. I dry mine on my dhoti. It's hotter than hell, even with the windows down, and the journey is long and uncomfortable, but it gives me time to return, and here I sit in the present moment. I lean my head out the window, closing my eyes while the meter of my happiness rises. I smell the freshly roasted suburbs of Trichy seasoned with diesel. Other scents adrift in the air go about their business, and I inhale their otherness, remembering where I am but not who.

My lips melt into the rubber of a slow smile.

There's a Sri Lankan saint less than half an hour away who knows my name. God has come back from the dead. I'm with a woman I love, on my way to buy fresh crusty bread and crisp, warm buttery biscuits in India. So what is there to be sad about?

When we arrive, the bank looks like it fell from a hole in the pocket of the Empire as it was backing out of India, thanking the owners for lending their continent. Mumbling an apology about the mess. Large wrought iron gates stand stiffly to either side of us as the taxi enters the courtyard. The gates are quietly rusting away, possibly contemplating the weathered grimy building they guard. Millions of rupees have passed through them, but very little seemed to have lingered long enough to pay for a coat of paint. As a result, the bank walls are filthy, like the hands of a money-lender in an alley.

Among the pillars leading up broad steps to the entrance, hunched men are sorting small bundles of rupees into little piles, pausing only to jot incantations on scraps of paper.

I get out of the taxi with our Travellers Cheques hidden in my dhoti and enter the bank, finding myself in a large room partitioned into cubicles, each delineated by a low, polished, wooden wall. There's a wooden slab of a desk in each of these little fiefdoms. Each desk is slightly elevated to let the supplicants know precisely where they stand in relation to the teller. The tellers have severe brown faces atop white shirts. Neat rows of pens, the campaign ribbons of officialdom, peer from pockets, watching the world pass by. Overhead fans are whirring while sharp minds tick over with the implications of Mammon. Voices are whispering, and papers are shuffled. Eager brown fingers ruffle through notes, like snouts looking for truffles. Mutely counting lips, mouth mantras of numbers.

Naturally enough, this place takes itself very seriously.

My last encounter with Indian officialdom and Travellers Cheques was at the airport. I don't hold out any hope that this transaction will be any smoother, so I take the bull by the horns, wanting to get the unpleasantness over with. I pick the nearest cubicle in which a teller is sitting. He's surrounded by a *'humble'* of supplicants and regards them with an expression that is hard to read. It's a cross between contempt and wanting to know who just farted. They meekly wave bits of paper at him. Or perhaps they're just wafting the smell away.

Feeling that a confident demeanour will serve me best, I stride over to his desk and hold up my Travellers Cheques for him to behold. He looks at me up and down as if he's not sure which end to start loathing first. Another man pushes himself forward to stand beside me. None of what the teller sees makes any impression other than to give him what looks like indigestion, or perhaps he's sitting on one of his testicles and can no longer ignore the discomfort. Whatever the look on his face means, whatever's going on behind those dark eyes, it isn't anything helpful. Not yet. No. He looks down at a pink form on his desk. He looks at it for a long time. Even longer.

I *'harrumph'*, noisily clearing my throat.

This also is ignored. As the seconds tick by, I'm ignored so intently, so completely, *so utterly* that I even begin to doubt my existence. Unsure of myself, I look at the other nonentities gathered before this desk. They're waving passports, papers, pictures of their children and flowers for his mother in the vain hope of getting his attention. I do as they do, thrusting my cheques forward.

Is it possible to bleat and maintain one's dignity?

He looks up, disappointment on his face, as if there's an incantation on the pink piece of paper he's been studying, some spell meant to make us disappear, but — here we are, still standing in front of his desk. Inconsiderate bastards. With weary bitterness, he sighs, stamps the pink paper, and hands it to the man beside me. The man hurries off. At least it made *him* disappear.

I catch the teller's eye and feel a brief glimmer of hope, but he ignores me again.

I think, therefore, I am.

I queue, therefore, I am not.

Finally, he lets his gaze settle on my traveller's cheques. He waves them away, places a form in front of me and taps a cracked nail on the sheet I need to sign and — you know those dreams in which you suddenly realise you're not wearing any trousers?

Well — I suddenly realise I'm without a pen in the land of Officialdanistan. Patting myself all over as if I've mislaid the treasured fountain pen of my grandfather, my eyes rove over the desktop, hoping one will appear. Nope. I can see a row of biros in his shirt pocket, but I don't want to ask for one. It's like falling into the ocean and seeing the message *Please ring this number if you need assistance'* written on the tonsils of a shark.

'May I borrow your pen?' I ask.

Obviously, he's misheard me. The disgust on his face implies I've asked to borrow his penis.

'You've got loads,' I say.

He's hesitating. Eyes flick over me in the hope of a skin disease or two. Anything to justify not handing over a precious biro. Finding nothing, he takes one from his pocket. He's testing it on a blotter. Or is he doing this to show me how it works, presuming I'm an idiot?

Apparently, you write with the pointy end.

He slaps it on the desk for me to retrieve. I sign my name, feeling his eyes bore into me, but when I try to return the biro, he refuses with an impatient shake of his hand. He's tapping the wooden handle of his teller's stamp on my traveller's cheques.

'Sign,' he snaps.

I point at my signature and tell him I have.

'Sign here! And h — ' I think he may have gasped. His previous resentful expression morphs into one of bewilderment — then outrage. His mouth opens and closes like a fish out of water.

'But — you are only supposed to sign *this* box in front of a supervisor!' he blusters. 'O*ther* box! You should have signed other box!'

'Oops!' I say, smiling apologetically, hoping he'll assume I'm a bit dim and not a pen-borrowing international fraudster. Unfortunately, he picks option number two, snatches his pen back and raises it like Excalibur. This act summons his supervisor, who looks down at me over the heavy black frame of his spectacles. His gaze is majestic. His pens are magnificent. The weight of his imperious gaze drops onto the cheque. The bank teller lives up to his job description by telling his superior something in Tamil. I expect it ended with the words, '— *and* the swine borrowed my pen to do it with.'

In his wisdom, the supervisor picks up the cheque with thumb and forefinger and gives it a little shake.

'You must *not* do this,' he says. 'It is *most* incorrect.'

I feel vaguely ashamed, as if I've been caught trying to sharpen a pencil using the wrong end of a cat.

'I'm sorry. I didn't realise.'

This contrition provokes a witheringly stern look from the Teller and sympathy from the Supervisor. He places the cheque before me and asks me to sign now.

'Right,' I say, relieved. Once again, I'm patting myself down in search of a pen.

'May I borrow —?'

With a grimace, the teller hands the pen to me once more.

I sign. Junior refuses the pen when I try to return it. Instead, he points me to another queue.

For fuck sake.

In the new queue, I stand behind a young white woman. It turns out she comes from Manchester too. We chat for a couple of minutes, pleasantries, and so on. Then she asks where we're staying.

'On an ashram,' I say.

'Really?' She sounds surprised. 'We're in a hotel for a few days. The Femina.'

'I know it. We've had ice cream there.'

'Cool. We thought we'd chill out for a few days, then head down to Goa.'

'If you're in Trichy for a few days, you should come to the ashram.'

'No, thanks. I'm not religious.'

I chuckle. 'Neither am I. Not really. But there's a saint — have you heard of Swami Premananda? — no? — Well, not to worry. You'd be welcome anyway. He's doing a miracle in a few days.'

The look on her face says it all. She thinks I'm a nutter. Some silly arse caught up in a cult. She laughs.

'A miracle? What, like turning water into wine? Is it a piss-up?

'No. Nothing like that. He's going to manifest some vibhuti,'

'Vibhuti? What the fuck's that? Is it like vindaloo or something?'

'It's a — sort of — sacred ash. It comes out of his skin and — '

I sound utterly insane. It's as if I'm suddenly hearing myself for the first time. So, now I'm backing away from my words, shrugging and adding a *non sequitur*. 'I've not seen the vibhuti thing being done myself yet, but I have it on very good authority that it's — '

What?

Not ridiculous?

' — very interesting.'

She's looking uncomfortable. I can't blame her. She turns away to see how the queue is doing, but really, she just doesn't want to talk to me anymore. I can see this. I understand. I sound like I've lost my mind or at least relinquished it until something better comes along.

***

* * *

When I told Ma I wasn't returning to school, she was peeling potatoes at the sink. She didn't stop scraping away with the knife. Instead, she shrugged and said, 'I can't make you go back.'

'You're old enough to decide for yourself. I left school when I was fifteen. So at least you're a couple of years older than I was.'

'I've given it a lot of thought,' I said. I couldn't tell her I was too ashamed to go back. And that was how I left school. I joined the ranks of the unemployed, which turned out to be not as bad as I thought. I was unemployed and too young to sign on the dole, but we were much better off because Tony had been sworn into the Army and had started his basic training. It was very hard for him after nearly three years of virtually being a recluse, but he stuck with the training and endured whatever racism he encountered. He earned enough money to put bread on the table, keep a roof over our heads and give me some pocket money.

We also had more space because Ma had somehow got another flat down the end of the road. Looking back, I remember it as having no windows, which can't be right. I also recall that it stank of rat piss, which probably it was. So after the Pied Piper had finished luring the rodents out of Hamlyn, they settled in Dublin.

***

I've come out of the bank feeling deflated because the young woman from Manchester had looked at me as if I was a poor deluded soul. That pitying look makes me wonder how much of this experience I can share with my family. The knowledge that holy men and women walk among us is such a profound and lovely thing to know, but it does sound peculiar.

I wouldn't say this knowledge has turned my world upside down. If anything, the world has been placed the right way up. I feel the way I did when I was younger and purer of heart. Some would say more gullible. But, I feel as if I've stumbled upon the knowledge that *Santa Claus* actually does exist. I have these little moments of wonder, rediscovering that mystery in my heart. Oh, how I'd love to tell my family that Father Christmas *did* leave the presents we found beside our beds on Christmas morning.

And this brings to mind the day when I blew Father Christmas up.

It was a giant inflatable one, and it was tall as me when I was seven. I was playing with a set of darts, throwing them across the room at a dartboard. One bounced off the board and — to my horror — headed for Santa. The dart hit and — bounced off his head.

I was amazed and utterly delighted at the discovery that Father Christmas was indestructible.

'Ma! Tony! Come quick! Look at this!'

Alarmed, they ran into the room.

'Watch this!' I shouted joyously and launched a dart through the air.

Big blow-up Santa blew up with a big bang.

The same thing had happened to God when I'd hit him with a prayer of longing and despair.

Bang.

A shocked silence.

And now here I am, and God's here too.

No sign of Santa yet, but anything, it seems, is possible.

But I can't share this with my brothers and make them see what I've seen because my experience is mine alone. That's why, as I'm passing these men on the steps who are still counting their money, I feel like a rich man who can't give any of his newly found wealth to the people he loves.

***

The other flat down the end of the road was half the size of the one we'd lived in for a couple of months. It had a living room and a bedroom, not much bigger than the cheap single bed wedged up against a wall. It was dark and stank of hops from the Guinness Brewery and rat piss from the rodents under the floorboards. Before entering, I knocked loudly and waited a few seconds to give them time to scurry out of sight. Despite their droppings and the possibility of contracting a disease from their urine or even being bitten, I preferred their company to that of the denizens of Ballymun.

Most of the time, I had the place to myself. Tony was still doing his recruit training and only slept in the flat when he had a weekend pass. He was so exhausted that it was usually time to return to his unit when he woke. I'd ask him how things were in the barracks, but he didn't say much about it. I knew it wasn't easy for him from the few things he did say.

The first night he returned on leave, the rodents had a rat punch up, tumbling around with tooth and claw and squealing. Tony was snoring in the other room on a sofa bed. I couldn't sleep with all the noise, so I got dressed and went walking along the moon-drenched back streets behind Guinness's Brewery. It had started to rain, but I kept going. I loved walking in the night. Cobblestones, when wet, mirrored the moon. The rain also kept people off the streets, so I could relax while walking around.

I wandered along like a ghost, haunting my own past. Down the road by the Christian Brothers School. Up past the insane asylum, which was still hunched behind its massive walls. Down the cul-de-sac of Kennedy's Villas. Along the grooves in history where once we'd lived. Mind-wandering down the ruts of the recent past. There were many good memories there, too. Playing football with other lads. Listening to Elvis on the record player. When we lived in Kennedy's Villas, Jason was an infant, and Tony was a teenager. Ma was a young woman. Father Christmas still came to see us. God wasn't yet dead though Elvis soon would be.

I went down the end of the cul de sac, Kennedy's Villas, to where a rusted fence was meant to stop people from wandering into a patch of undergrowth bordering a polluted river. I used to think it was the Liffey, but I'm unsure now. It was dark and stank of neglect and ignorance. The water flowed around abandoned bodies of rubbish caught in the rusted ribs of discarded prams and bicycle wheels. From where I stood, leaning on the fence, the water was swallowed by the black mouth of a tunnel. The older boys frightened the younger ones by telling us the ghost of a monk emerged from that dark emptiness to walk on water like Jesus had gone wrong. This monk abducted children. That's what they told us, and I believed them.

I was terrified.

The past, emerging out of a dark grave.

I stood there like a dog licking at a sore, unable to leave the past alone because it hurt.

We lived in Kennedy's Villas when Ma had tried to enrol Tony in school. The school rejected him with racist slurs. I thought back to him in the flat where he was sleeping, exhausted beyond words. Poor Tony. Poor Jason. Poor Ma.

My belly was tight with anger, as if I was going to punch myself in the gut. But, instead, I grasped the metal mesh of the fence, wrapping my fingers painfully in the lattice and shook it with a furious burst of rage. Shook it as if I could loosen the anger and sadness. Shook it as if that chain held me to those emotions. I didn't realise that any chain that binds you to the past is a chain that you hold. It's not holding you. You're holding it.

The key to the lock is the simple act of letting go.

All you have to do is exhale.

I returned to the flat where Tony was still sleeping. I held my breath and tip-toed past.

***

Just look at all this. I'm standing outside Vincent's, the bread shop. Behind a display window, hot as an oven to the touch, fresh loaves of bread with crisply crackling crusts are laid out like cobblestones. The warm smell of sweet things is wafting seductively down the road. All the other odours of Trichy, the heavy spices, the dust and the gasoline, tug their forelocks and step aside.

You know those moments when the face of the one you love suddenly appears in a crowd, and all other faces disappear?

My nose is presently doing that with the smell of jam.

Lesley goes inside with Naren and Rekha and orders five doughnuts, a sliced loaf and six packets of biscuits. I'm staying outside because of the heat, like a dragon's breath coming out of the open door.

By the time we return to the taxi, I've already eaten two doughnuts. As the car pulls away, I'm licking icing sugar off my sticky fingers. It's *soooo* good. I *have* to have one more. Reaching into the greaseproof bag, I'm having a momentary impulse toward moderation because surely two doughnuts are enough for anyone?

If I didn't have this third doughnut in my mouth right now, this moist, chewy, jammy-gushy deliciousness in my mouth — I could probably answer that question. Vaguely I register the fact that Lesley's only had one, but I've now devoured three. She's probably full, I tell myself. Besides, this last one isn't as fresh as the other two. In fact, eating it might not have been a good idea because it was possibly a little stale.

Oh well.

It's gone now.

***

When I woke in the morning, Tony was gone. I got up, went to the sink, and filled a pan with water to make tea. There were some digestive biscuits in the cupboard. The sight of rodent droppings, where I kept the sugar and tea bags, shrivelled my appetite for breakfast. How I never caught a nasty bug, I don't know. I was particularly at risk from Weil's Disease, spread through water contaminated by rat urine. I must have inadvertently drunk gallons of it in the time I spent in my flat. Who knows? Maybe the rats caught something off me because I used to piss in the sink when it was freezing outside.

I'd already picked up an infection. I had hatred running through my veins. Most of the time, it was dormant. My friend Ciaran and other good people I haven't named kept it from consuming me. I knew it for its emotional and intellectual laziness, but nonetheless, hatred of those I thought hated us was there under the floorboards.

It gnawed away like the rodents.

Waiting to piss on my chips.

The only antidote to this poison in my system was forgiveness and understanding. I had the example of Martin Luther King to sustain my non-violent stance, but really, I was fooling myself. I wasn't a true advocate of Non-Violence. Hate is violence. It's a parasite clutched tightly and drawn deeply inward. My emotional intelligence knew how toxic this hate was, but sometimes it felt like hate was all I had to sustain me.

***

We left the taxi outside the Femina Hotel. Rekha's gone shopping for more suitings with Naren patiently trailing behind. Lesley and I need to confirm our travel arrangements with Saudi Airlines, so we've come to their office, which is humming with quiet efficiency. It wears its modernity with pride. Plastic plants stand in the corners, enjoying the frigid air pouring out of the air conditioning. Posters on the pale blue walls advertise destinations with a lot of sand.

Behind a highly polished counter, a young,

immaculately dressed man sits. I detect his aftershave even as I approach. If a fly attempted to land on his head, his hair is so slick it would most likely skid off and break a leg. He's looking down as I stride to the counter and place our documents before him.

'Hiya,' I say. 'I've come to confirm our tickets.'

'If sir would take a seat, I'll be with you in one moment.' He follows this up with a pleasant smile.

'Ok,' I say, impressed with the service thus far. I've been fobbed off without having to wait, which is a great time-saver. I sit with Lesley and smile at her.

'I hope we don't get the same pilot,' I say.

'Sshhh!' she says, with a warning look.

I shrug, not pressing the point. On our flight to India, back in Heathrow, London, as the plane was taxing along the runway, the pleasant voice of the pilot had come over the intercom. He gave the usual speech, thanking us for flying with Saudi Airlines, and told us of our expected arrival time and the weather. He then commenced wailing, 'Alllaaahhhh Akhbaaaaaar!'

'Jesus Christ!' I exclaimed. 'What's wrong with the pilot?'

Lesley had patted my hand and said, 'Calm down. It means God is Great.'

'I know what it means. So why is he shouting it now?'

'It's traditional to thank the almighty at times like this.'

'Does he *have* to sound so eager to meet him?'

'Never mind. Just hold my hand. You know how I hate the take-off and landing.'

I mutter, 'he could have at least turned the bloody volume down.'

'Well, he's unlikely to do it again until we land, so you can relax for now.'

'Relax? How would he feel if *I* were the pilot and I shouted, 'Jesus is feckin' marvellous?'

I'm thinking about this when Lesley interrupts my thoughts by saying, 'I think he's ready for you.'

The young man behind the counter nods at me. I go over, and he listens intently as I explain that we must confirm our flights back to England.

'Can you make sure everything is okay for us?'

'Certainly, sir,' he says. 'May I see your tickets and other relevant papers?'

I hand them over. He taps away on the keyboard briskly, filling me with confidence. We're in good hands here. He's examining our paperwork with admirable diligence. I'm struck again by how lustrous and slick his hair is. It's probably got the same radar signature as a stealth bomber. He's humming away to himself, evidently quite happy with his work. I take this to be a good sign.

I'm most grateful when he hands our papers back to me with a polite nod.

'Is there anything else I can help you with?' he asks.

This excellent efficiency is only spoiled because, several days later, when we got to Madras airport, Saudi Airlines had never heard of us.

***

Outside, so much is happening. Bicycle bells ring and mingle with horns that honk their indignation like geese. We're standing at a roundabout. On the other side, there's a shop we'll go to, but first, Lesley's having a cigarette. I'm happy to wait, taking in my surroundings.

I close my eyes. Make myself the centre of this little universe. The sound of some big smoke-belching bus swells and rolls over me. Lorries growl, pulling their guts out in mechanical grunts of gear grinding. Old wheels crush the ancient earth, and countless souls rise in the dust. Diesel fumes thicken and taint the air. Cigarette smoke curdles. Sweat trickles. Tickles. Distracts me from the sweet stink of rotting fruit, but now I hear voices, soft unintelligible murmurings, sandals flapping, and hot soles slapping the pavement. Desire and hunger rush around the roundabout, and life pulls at me — life is friction, and the sun is hot.

I raise my hand. Touch the delicate fold of skin over my eyes. I'm keeping them closed. Holding back the intricate movement of metal and flesh and dust and sound. Tiny grains of dirt rest on the warm damp, fluttering lid. My eyes begin to roll. Around me, the universe whirls and grinds out another day of blistering heat.

Dizzy, I step back and open my eyes.

Before me, the curious stare of a child. He's squinting because of the sun. His head is cocked to the side. A bashful smile. A hesitant wave.

I wave back.

We move on.

The shop is a gift shop. Guitars hang from the ceiling. Glass-eyed dolls ignore us. Transistor radios stand mute on ironing boards. Toy trucks are parked beside harmoniums. All sorts of everything are all over the place, and all of it is for sale.

As soon as we enter, Lesley grabs my arm. 'I don't feel too good,' she says.

'Do you need to sit?'

'No, I'll be alright. You carry on,' she says. I stay within arm's reach. Despite this restriction, I find a present for Jason. A pair of boxing gloves. We can spar together in the backyard.

Two days from now, I'm going to punch myself in the face with one of them. I'll tell you about that later. For now, let me say this. A lot of people have tried to punch me over the years. I happen to be one of the few who succeeded.

***

We're in the Prayer Hall, listening to the devotees singing. Soothed by the sound, I'm smiling contentedly. The unity of voices is beautiful. Not for the first time, I feel the music as a living thing, its heart pulsing in my palms as I clap.

Swami appears. Up ahead. Steps out from behind a curtain.

The only heart I hear now is my own.

My eyes adore him.

The centre of my chest whirls with instinctive delight.

This is all very nice, but there's another emotion in here. I'm feeling a little fear. Seeing his purity, knowing the bad things I've done in the past, makes me squirm. I'm so uncomfortable, I want to leave, but I won't. I won't let this sense of unworthiness keep me away from being in the presence of this saint. To do so would be like not having a bath because I felt like I wasn't clean enough.

Is this feeling of unworthiness, which I intuitively recognise as my false self, what stands between me and my spiritual nature? If the spiritual path is a journey in which this false self withers away, I need a lift. This desire for help might reduce the act of prayer on the road to salvation to the equivalent of hitch-hiking, putting a thumb out and trying not to look like a criminal, but I don't care. I can't live in peace with myself as I am — whatever I am.

Swami's walking down the centre of the prayer hall. His eyes are scanning the crowd. The merest look settling on me for a moment is devastating. Inside I'm cringing, as though every vice, misdeed or harsh word I've ever uttered is here for him to see. I burn with shame. It exudes through the molten pores of my skin. My perverseness, my cravenness, the secret thoughts scurry beneath the rock of my desire to be good. All of it is written on my face.

Swami walks past.

I hold my breath.

***

— awake!

Thunder rumbling.

I sit bolt upright.

Rumble —

There it is again.   Rumble gurgle —

I look down. The ominous, mutinous grumbles are coming from my abdomen. Something akin to a cannonball rolling across a wooden deck emanates deep within.

Oh lord!

I leap out of bed, desperate for the toilet. My bowels blow the emergency escape hatch one nano-second after I squat over the ceramic hole. Oh, my God. So violent and forceful is the excremental evacuation I instinctively clutch the walls. It feels like an earthquake.

I'm so utterly miserable. Humiliated. I've got the same expression as my dog when I woke up and found it shitting into one of my shoes.

I'm thinking, '*Please* don't let the others wake up.'

The kitchen door creaks.

'Are you okay, Paul?' Lesley asks.

'I'm fine. Go back to bed!'

Mataji pipes up with, 'he doesn't sound fine.'

Oh, this is just fantastic. Now *everybody's* awake. All I need is for the family next door to knock and ask if we need a plumber.

Lesley whispers, 'I know. Did you hear him rumble?'

'I did. It woke me up. Is he okay?'

'No idea. It sounded to me like the poor thing just exploded. I'd be astonished if there's anything left of him other than his sandals — '

Louder this time, I say, 'I'm fine. Please! Just go back to bed.'

'You're sure?' Lesley asks, sounding dubious.

I hear the back door being opened, and no — that isn't a euphemism. The smell is awful. It's so bad we could also do with taking the roof off. Lesley quietly closes the kitchen door behind her and pads back to bed.

I'm shivering now, squatting, with the chill night air creeping under the door, and I stay this way until the initial rush of events, so to speak, calms down. At this point, I ruefully recall the last doughnut I'd so selfishly wolfed down.

Quite a while passes with only mild spasms and then none at all. I have a quick wash and general refurbishment of the area. Gingerly I step from the loo into the kitchen — Rumble-grumble-gurgle-bloop!

Less gingerly, I leap back inside. My intestines go through their entire back catalogue of spasms, gripes, twinges and farts. And now I'm worried. If this keeps up, I'll spend the night looking at the back of the toilet door. Another attempt to leave is thwarted, but I manage to grab the Imodium. A quick scan of the dosage. Add the sachet to water. Gulp it down, hoping it'll work. I take another on the principle if one sachet is good, two must be even better. If this doesn't work, I'll have to use the box as a cork.

***

In Ireland, I knew I was ill. I knew our experiences had poisoned me.

Symptoms varied. A certain numbness of feeling with bouts of seething anger. I dragged hopelessness around with me like a corpse. These were the lows. Then there were almost feverish periods of creative energy. Writing lyrics and songs and thinking and thinking and thinking. What does it all mean? Why does life hurt so so much?

***

I'm exhausted. The cramps have stopped. So long as I don't sneeze, I'll be able to lie down without soiling myself. So I return to my bed, where peace soon comes. Settles on me like the shadow of a Mother Hen lowering herself upon the earth.

I plummet into oblivion.

Mother Hen opens an eye, and the moon shines upon us all without favour.

All are loved equally.

CHAPTER TEN
Singing The Song Of The Unloved

The sun beats the earth with heat like a housekeeper pounding dust from an old carpet.

Considering how bad I felt last night, I feel surprisingly well now. Sure, I'm weighed down by fatigue after my toilet trauma, but that appears to have settled itself. My intestines have been stunned into inactivity by an unhealthy dose of Imodium. I may not have a bowel movement for the next six months, but — all in all, I feel good. To be on the safe side, I'm not going to stray too far from the loo or sneeze, which is why, on this lovely morning, I'm slowly sweeping the path.

I'm thinking about Swami Premananda and how being near is overwhelming when he exudes love. There are other times, though, when my shadows are all the more apparent to me in his presence because of the light which comes off him. I laugh mirthlessly at myself. I came all this way to see Swami Premanada only to look away from him. I'm like a man who breaks out of a dark dungeon only to find the light hurts his eyes, and sometimes it's too much.

You can imagine how I feel when Mataji suggests Lesley

and I wash the feet of Swami Premananda. I'm appalled. The ritual is a mark of respect known as a Pada Puja. It's also an act of humility by those who do the washing.

I refuse. Such close contact is too much for me, and the very idea sends me into a panic.

'There's no way I can touch his feet,' I say.

Lesley points out I already have.

'When?' I ask.

'On the night of Shivaratri. We both did. You remember?'

'Oh. Yeah. That's right,' I reply, surprised I'd already forgotten.

But surely, you need to have clean hands to wash someone's feet?

***

I found it hard to sleep in Ireland without the soporific of a nightly orgasm. The tension of the day left me. Guilty pleasure lulled me to sleep. The world fell away from me and —

Nothing

Nothing was all that lay on the other side of that exhalation.

Each orgasm shrugs off the past. Closes its eyes blissfully on the future. Exhales into the now of nowhere and nothing and nobody.

Mine released me from me and helped make life bearable.

Not that life was so terrible in Echlin Street. I could walk to the shops and probably not have anyone call me a nigger. This was so much better than life in Ballymun. Of course, the longer one stayed out, like a blind proctologist, the more likely one was to find an asshole.

***

Lesley and I are in Babakka's, the café at the end of the ashram road. It stands near the main gate as an afterthought, almost as if the devout, leaving the presence of the Saint from Sri Lanka, will most certainly be thinking, 'What have I forgotten? Oh, yes. Something to make me anxious on the way home. Strong coffee.'

We've ordered a coffee, but it's not here yet. Maybe the lid's stuck on the jar. Perhaps it's real coffee and needs time to percolate. I'm too much of a peasant to tell the difference between fresh and instant, but the fact that I've asked for such a potent beverage this afternoon is a good sign. It means I'm confident my tummy troubles are behind me.

I'm still banging on about not washing Swami's feet.

'No way,' I insist.

Lesley's not looking at me. Her attention's on the doorway through which our coffee will be carried.

She says, 'Mataji thinks we should.'

'I don't care. I'm not doing it.'

'Where's this coffee?' she mutters. 'I'm gasping. And I need a cigarette.'

We sit in silence for a while until Lesley sighs and turns her attention to me. 'Oh, well. I guess it'll be here soon. Sorry — you were talking about feet?'

'Yes. I'm not washing Swamis' feet.'

'Why not?'

'Because I couldn't clean my hands enough to touch someone so pure? I just can't do it.'

'Have you heard of soap?' she asks, smiling. 'I could point it out if you want?'

'Hilarious, but no thanks. I need more than soap.'

'My God,' she says with mock horror. 'Where've you had your hands?'

'Well — nowhere unhygienic. Not since I took that Imodium. I'm completely bunged up.'

'Oh, dear.'

'Yes, I know. But it's better than the alternative.'

She laughs and reaches out toward the coffee, which is now being carried out of the kitchen.

'Thank you,' she says to the young boy carrying it. He waggles his head and smiles. She puts the cups on the table and adds two sugar lumps to mine, plopping them in singly.

'Lovely,' I say.

'All jokes aside, I know how you feel. I love Swami to death and beyond, and I've hung on to him as my spiritual guide for all these years, but the thought of washing his feet — makes me want to run a mile. Like you, I don't feel worthy, but it's silly to feel this way. He's the last person on earth to look down on anyone and judge them.'

'I know.'

'You're — *we* — are being too hard on ourselves.'

'I suppose. Yeah.' I take a sip of my coffee, which tastes bitter, and ask for two more sugar lumps.

Lesley picks up another two and drops them in my cup. She smiles her best, bright-eyed smile. The sugar between us swirls and dissolves.

***

Yeah. Echlin Street was far better than Ballymun. I was almost relaxed when I left home, but I knew better than to let down my guard. Now and then, though, on days when something good was happening, I forgot.

The day Tony stood with other soldiers on the parade ground in Collins Barracks was one of those days. He looked very handsome. Proud. So he should be. He'd dragged himself out of the pit he was in, and now he stood at ease with a rifle by his side, the equal of any man out there.

Our Aunt Teresa and her daughter, young Teresa, came along.

Young Teresa was the same age as Jason, and they quite happily held hands. Ciaran had come from Ballymun to share the event. He was a good friend. On the other end of the scale, I was surprised to see Ken, the fuckwit with the doorstep forehead from Ballymun, whose family had offered me a banana. Over the years, he'd been in the same class as Ciaran and myself. No matter how often I distanced myself from Ken, he kept inveigling his way back into my company.

He'd met Ciaran on the bus and invited himself along. Despite the banana incident, I still felt sorry for him because he had no other friends. Now I'm older, I realise there's sometimes a good reason for this, but at the time, I assumed people were mean to him just because he was a dick. Still, I thought it was one more person to support and applaud my big brother's achievement, so I refused to let it piss me off.

The ceremony in which a hundred recruits became newly qualified soldiers went well. When it was over, Tony returned his rifle to the armoury and then met up with us. He wanted to change out of his uniform for the walk back to the house, but Ma persuaded him to wear it.

'You've sweated blood for that uniform, Tony. I want you to wear it with pride because if anyone deserves it, you do.'

The walk back home to Echlin Street was an agony of expectation. I walked on a tightrope of acute tension, watching the reaction strangers had to Tony in his uniform. I couldn't help but recall the day Tony was brought to school, and the school told him to fuck off and laughed at us. I thought of the day I sat on the back of a lorry in Ballymun, and those men told me to return from whence I came. These memories and many more sniggered in the background, waiting to happen again.

I felt sick to my stomach, but we got as far as James Street without incident. I was almost giddy with relief as the anxiety subsided. We passed St. James Catholic Church, where two elderly men were standing on the steps, having just come out of the building. We turned at the Parochial Hall onto Echlin Street, and a great weight lifted off me.

Ma asked Tony to stand outside the flat while she took a photograph of him. We all stood aside. Ken was chuckling away to himself.

'What's so funny?' I asked. I was relaxed and smiling, enjoying the moment in this place of safety.

He leaned closer to me and said, 'Did you see the two ol'fellahs on the church's steps?'

'Yeah.'

'One of them said to the other when you all walked by, "Jaysus, would ye look at dat? Dere letting feckin' niggers into de army now.'

***

We're back in the Prayer Hall. Swami Premananda's sitting in his chair while a devotee washes his feet. This ancient ritual of humility and respect honours both of them, but I'm stressing about touching his feet.

And once again, I'm feeling very uncomfortable in my skin. I'm not usually like this in my 'normal' life back in England. Life has had too many difficulties for me not to be sympathetic towards myself, so what was this feeling? I'd dropped most of my Catholic guilt after noticing the blood dripping from the hands of various Popes, so it wasn't that.

What is this uncomfortable, almost physically painful feeling as Swami looks at me?

It's the feeling of being an imposter. So much of me is a lie because, within the noise and colour and sound and movement of my personality and life story, I have no idea who I am. It's almost as if I have to impersonate myself until I can define who I am. 'Who am I?' 'What am I?' 'What am I to you?' What am I to myself?' 'What am I to all of this?

My discomfort is caused by the feeling that I'm not genuine, whereas Swami is.

I feel he is what he is, whereas I appear to be what I'm not.

Yeah.

It doesn't make a lot of sense.

But this is how I feel.

***

Those two old men on the steps of the church —

God forgive me, but I wanted to rip the tongue out of one and ram it down the throat of the other.

I wanted to tell them what they'd just done, but I was too angry for words and too considerate for violence, so the violence of the words not spoken ground me to dust.

Why can't all these bastards just leave us alone?
Why can't they just
Fuck —

***

— Off

I can't believe this. The ceremony's over. I've not had to wash the feet of the saint. The devotees are standing up and heading for the exit. I escaped the discomfort of coming into contact with Swami Premananda — ha-ha — what a relief — hang on — what's this?

A young man with a camera calls me to where Swami stands with Lesley and two others.

Quickly, I get to my feet and walk the other way, hoping to lose myself amid the devotees as they leave.

And now Lesley is calling me. 'Paul! Come back. Swami wants us to have a photo taken with him.'

My relief at *not* coming into physical contact is now turning into panic. I'm even getting angry because other people are also saying I should go back. I don't want to, but I have to stop and turn as if I've just heard.

'Come!' Swami says. 'Come!'

Burning with embarrassment, I make what seems like an awfully long walk to join them. I stand behind Swami, off to one side. Swami puts his arms around the others while a young man with a camera urges me to get closer. I incline my head toward Swami. It feels like he's the edge of a precipice, and I'm frightened about getting too close.

Then a flash of light

***

I had a moment of insight.

It happened many months after the two old men had said what they said on the steps of the church.

If this insight had come to me in a temple or church, perhaps I would have known it for what it was, but it didn't. Instead, it came to me in the most ordinary of places on a cold day, walking down Echlin Street with my good friend, Ciaran.

A silent voice in my head told me I was nobody and this life was not mine.

It was ridiculous because, of course, I was somebody. I was walking with my friend. I had a flat. I was almost within throwing distance of it so long as what I threw was a rat, and it ran the rest of the way home. I existed in space and time. Above me, drunken pigeons flew. Around me were stone-cold sober walls where bird necks snapped like dry twigs when they flew into them. I knew this because I witnessed it.

Because I'm somebody.

The idea that this life was not mine was just silly.

After all, I was with my friend, passing beneath the window of an elderly woman, Mrs O'Grady. She was tossing pieces of bread out for the birds. She liked to watch them eat. One day soon, she'd lose her mind and then her bra. She'll lean out her window with her massive bosoms like baby seals on her plump, folded arms. Across the road from her, a priest will say goodbye to his flock, leaving the church after Mass. He'll notice his parishioners tittering. He'll look up and see Mrs O'Grady.

He'll shout 'for the love of God, woman. Put a brassiere on!'

Mrs O'Grady will respond by throwing a bible at him out of her window. I'd see all of this because I would be there. I was somebody. Liturgy and dead pigeons would fall from the sky. Pages would flutter like wings. A book with a broken spine would be crushed by passing cars, and I would see it all because that was my life, and I was there.

I was.

The idea that I was nobody was absurd, but something about it deeply unsettled me. St Brendan's Mental Hospital, hunched in shame behind high walls, was down the road away. In there, sane people ran spasms of electricity through the bodies of the insane. If I had told a doctor about the words of the silent voice, which did not appear to be mine, I might have been considered crazy myself.

Of course, this life was mine. I've got photographs to prove I was there. You can see me —

***

Smile for the photograph.

Swami smiles. So does everyone else. Not me. I'm dying of shame. I'm exposed. Every impure thought and deed I've ever had is exuding through the pores of my skin. I'm a comet in the gravitational pull of the sun. The closer I get, the more it hurts as my shell burns away.

Tell me, what remains when the ash blows away from the pyre?

***

Ciaran and I went to Ma's flat, where she lived with Jason, and I lit the fire. We slumped into the armchairs on either side of the hearth. Jason was in school, and Ma was out working. She'd got a job taking pre-heated meals around to various pensioners in the area.

I told Ciaran about the weird thought that had popped into my head.

He was flipping peanuts into the air, letting them fall into his mouth.

'What's new?' he said. 'You always have weird ideas.'

'Not like this. This was different.'

'Oh?'

'Yeah. It came out of nowhere.'

'As ideas do,' he said, balancing another peanut on his thumbnail.

'I know, but not like this. It was like — imagine air trapped in a bottle beneath the ocean, and the glass suddenly shatters. A bubble of air rises to the surface, and then there you have it.'

'Have what?'

'The idea.

'What idea?'

'I'm not who I think I am. I'm not even what I think I am.'

Ciaran looked at me for a long moment and asked, 'So, if you're not who you think you are, then who are you?'

'I thought I was the one who owned this life, but — this thought I had said something different.'

Ciaran looked dubious.

'A voice in your head told you this?'

'Yeah. No. Not a voice. It was just a thought. An instant thing. Like dropping a stone in water and — this feeling that I'm not what I thought I was are — sort of like the ripples.'

'I don't understand.'

'This life doesn't belong to me. I'm like a hood ornament on the front of a car. I assume the journey's mine only because I can't see the driver. Does that make sense?'

'No. Not at all.'

'Oh — I suppose it doesn't. Well — it's like this. I think I'm *deciding which way to turn. I think I'm deciding where to stop, but I'm not. Nothing in this life belongs to me. It belongs to whatever is behind me.'*

Ciaran looked even more confused and said, 'It still sounds crazy.' But then, he leaned forward and looked concerned for me.

'You don't actually believe this, though, do you? Because if you believe you don't exist, then who the fuck is it that believes you don't exist other than you? Which means — Jaysus — you're givin' me a headache.'

'No,' I said, ' I don't believe it. I'm telling you because it was such an odd thing to pop into my head.'

'Good. Because if you did believe it, you'd be in the madhouse down the road the next time I see you.'

He flipped a peanut into the air. It came down, bounced off his chin and landed on the floor. Picking it up, he examined it and then flicked it into the fire.

'If you're not you, then who am I supposed to be?' he asked. ''Because if I'm not me and you're not you, we're in the wrong house.'

'You're the one who's eating all the peanuts,' I replied, holding out my hand. He passed the bag to me and rubbed his hands together to remove the salt. We sat staring into the fire. I felt a little unsettled, as if wherever the silent voice had come from was watching me, like the eyes of a vaguely familiar stranger in a crowd. I looked away, but that gaze was on me every time I looked back. Over the days and weeks, I looked over less and less until I forgot about it. Then, quietly and humbly, it melted into my heart, forgotten by —?

By whom?

Who forgot I was nobody and this life was not mine, according to that silent voice?

***

My legs are shaking. I'm walking out of the Prayer Hall

with Lesley and Mataji. Whatever the truth of me is, that truth adores Swami Premananda. But everything false within me lives in fear of him because it fears being dragged into the light.

***

My Irish Grandfather had died not far from the flat where Ciaran and I had sat. Ma was about nine years old. She'd sat in the room with him as he lay on his sickbed, dying from emphysema. He beckoned his child over and whispered.

'If I stop breathing — don't be frightened — just cover my face — with the sheet — then get your mother.'

Time passed, pulsing through his heart. She stayed with him until it became 'obvious.' The unnatural stillness —

She did as she was told. Covered him up. Ran for her mother. Good girl.

Dust on the wind,
   The journey is not yours.
   Colours,
   Wet on canvas,
   You are not the artist.
   Word on this page,
   I am the author,
   Not you,
   But I too, am written,
   By that which is not spoken,
   Nor sung.
   Wave on the ocean,
   Not knowing of the tide,
   Or the turning of the Cosmos

There is nothing of this,
That you can hold.

***

Lesley and I've been given a room to ourselves. Even though my bowels are still stunned by all the Imodium I took yesterday, the first thing I do is check out the toilet. It's a gleaming porcelain hole in the ground with a bucket and receptacle for sluicing water down it. It's also out in the backyard rather than part of the dwelling. I'm not sure when my bowels will move again, but I'm sure when they do, I'll be in there for a very, *very* long time. It also holds everything we need for a shower, a bucket and a large barrel of clean water.

I pat the white wall, which feels warm and reassuring. I'm grateful for all of this, but gratitude is not why I'm here. Lesley's asked me to bring her a bucket of water, so that's what I'm doing. As far as I can see, our new accommodation looks immaculate, but she wants to give it a quick frisk with a damp cloth. So when I walk back into our new room with a bucket of water, she rolls her sleeves up.

'Have you seen the dust in here?' she asks.

'Eh — no?'

She opens the fridge and reaches into the back of it.

'How about I go and get some cold drinks?' I suggest.

'Good idea. I'm boiling.'

'Is that why you've got your head in the fridge?'

'No. I want to make sure it's clean. It's easy to get food poisoning in this climate, as you found out with that doughnut.'

'I know. What a night that was.'

'Well — it could have been worse.'

'It *would* have been if I'd coughed on the way to the toilet.'

'That's true, but that's not what I meant.'

'Oh?'

'If it'd been up to me, I would've *shared* the doughnut, which means we would've both been ill. But, you being such a glutton saved me from having an upset tummy.'

'Don't thank me,' I say, backing out the door. 'I'll go and get those drinks.'

It took ten minutes to return with an armful of cold *Limka* and *Cola*. They rattle each time the fridge door opens, toasting anybody who looks inside. It does this a lot because the day is unbearably hot. Soon we're on our beds, wilting like lettuce, unable to go out into the furnace.

'I wonder if this heat is why India has so many saints.' I say, fanning my face with a Bhajan booklet.

'Hmm?' Lesley mumbles. The heat has made her drowsy.

'It's too hot to move outside, making it more advisable to move within yourself. And if the Kingdom of Heaven *is* to be found within then, maybe you have a better chance of finding it in a hot climate.'

'What?' Lesley raises her head from her pillow and looks at me, possibly checking for heatstroke.

'I mean — if — never mind. Would you like another cold drink?'

'No, thank you. It'll just make me thirstier.'

'Okay. Where's the bottle opener?'

'No idea. You had it.'

In which case, it's lost, but not to worry. I've opened many a bottle of beer in the past using the nearest convenient edge. I go out to the yard and place the lip of the lid on the edge of the wall enclosing the loo. With a swift smack of the bottle cap with my palm, the cap pops off with a chunk of the wall. Oops. That's not supposed to happen. I better find the bottle opener, or the wall will be a pile of rubble by the time we leave.

Adam's apple bobbing like a rubber ball, I chug the pop down. I taste brick dust, and my throat is burning, but I enjoy it. Satiated, I go back into the room, where Lesley is now softly snoring. She's partially clothed and perspiring, contoured by her cotton dress. I stop in the doorway, lust making my breath shallow. Damn. I go to my bed and lay with my back to her. We respect the rules of celibacy in the ashram. Mind you, there's no harm in looking, is there? I turn back to face her until I feel like an alcoholic looking at the contours of a bottle of whiskey.

A few days ago, I intended to renounce the world and become celibate. My spiritual development was *the* essential thing in life.

But now —?

As with many decisions in life, it's incredible what a difference an erection makes. I roll back over and bury my face in the hot crook of my sweaty arm. Then, when my dhoti has relaxed, I get up and sit on Lesley's bed.

'Lesley,' I whisper.

She opens her eyes. 'What is it?'

'Let's go to the Femina.'

'What? Why?'

'Because — '

She's looking quite confused and sits up. 'Are you okay?'

I point downwards in the direction of my groin.

'Oh,' she says sympathetically. 'Has the Imodium worn off?'

'The Imodium? No! Not that. I've been thinking. Maybe this celibacy thing isn't a good idea.'

'Poor thing,' she says, patting the back of my hand. 'Don't

worry. It's good to be celibate for a while.'

'We have. It's been great. Now let's go and celebrate.'

'Sweetheart, it's only been a few days.'

'Christ. It feels like a month.'

'I was celibate for nearly ten years at one point.'

'Yes, well, we don't want to encourage that sort of thing, do we? I'll order a taxi.'

'Paul, I'm not leaving the ashram. What about the vibhuti? Surely you don't want to miss that.'

Oh — balls. I've forgotten all about the vibhuti. Gloomily, I nod.

'Good boy,' she says. She yawns and stretches. Lies down. Turns her back on me.

I'm back on my bed, restless and clammy. Sensual thoughts are nibbling my ear.

'Sweetheart —?' Lesley whispers.

I sit up at the speed of a rake being stepped on. She's had a change of heart! Sod the taxi. I'll wheel her bed to the hotel and —

'Any chance of a cup of tea?' she asks.

Oh — feck

***

My desire wilted and waned with the falling temperature, so I'm not struggling with it anymore. Instead, I'm enjoying the cool air outside the ashram gates. Lesley's sitting on the little wall contemplating the world through a cloud of cigarette smoke. I'm on my own, crossing the field where I'd seen the young boy and the bird of prey. Unlike the last time I walked here, what might lurk in the grass isn't bothering me. The things that hide in the mind and trouble the heart are far more unsettling. I was okay with Lesley not reciprocating my desire, but I remembered something she said yesterday. It's been bothering me ever since. When we were going to Trichy, a young man asked us to buy a towel for him. I remembered Lesley saying how 'gorgeous' he was, which set off a long monotonous round of insecurity chasing its tail. The mind plays with it like a cat with a mouse, and I can't help but wonder if she'd have been so reluctant to leave the ashram if I looked like him. My heart has been sinking ever since. Even now, as I wander over this field, it's falling through the soles of my feet, deep down into the earth.

I know how toxic the thought is, but I can't help myself. Like a starving beggar reaching for rotten fruit, my mind continues to feast on it. In the grass where snakes may lurk, jealousy and insecurity pull me this way and that. I fear the joyless place these feelings will lead to, so I'm trying to push them away, but the struggle just saps my strength. Trying to push a shadow away is exhausting.

More natural shadows approach as the evening draws in. The scent of food moves on the cooling air, and soon a solid brass bell, rung over by the dharmasala, calls the hungry to eat. We stroll toward the sound of pots and plates, my skin feeling the chill of the rising moon.

I feel myself slipping into a deep depression. I tell Lesley, not because she has anything to answer for, but because she's the person standing on the riverbank while I'm about to be swept away. She tries to reassure me, but her words aren't helping. There's no reason they should because this isn't about what she said. It's about some unloved part of myself finding a discarded bone with which to beat itself. I go as far as the entrance to the Dharamshala and stop.

'You go in,' I say.

'Aren't you hungry?' she asks.

'No,' I reply in a voice which is so flat I want to slap myself for sounding so pathetic, but — I can't help it.

She puts her warm hands on either side of my face, but all I can do is look down and step back.

'Come and eat. You'll feel better.'

'I can't. I'm sorry. I keep falling into these dark holes inside myself, but I can't seem to avoid them. I'm just —'

I'm lost for words.

'Just what, sweetheart? I can see you're struggling, but I don't know what else I can say.'

'It's okay. There's nothing you *can* say. How I'm feeling has very little to do with how things are. I *know* it. But my feelings are running riot, and I can't seem to control them.'

'At least have some food —'

'I can't eat,' I say.

'Eat for me?' Lesley says. 'Please? I'm worried about you.'

I wave her concern away. I'm walking backwards. She's standing in the light of the Dharamsala, watching, and I'm being swallowed up by the shadows of the night.

'Paul —?'

'Go and eat. I need to walk until this bullshit drama wears off.'

I turn around and walk faster. My heavy legs feel like they're turning the world on a treadmill, drawing the large rocks beyond the far side of the ashram toward me. The light of the ashram falls behind me. I want to hide out here, to take this darkness and wrap it around me, so nobody will see the state I'm in. Beneath my sandals, dry grass rustles. Small things are crushed while above the distant stars glitter coldly. The roof has been ripped off the world, and there's the night for all to see. The moon is curved like a cradle. The rocks around me are cold with silver light. A huge boulder which fell hard a million years ago is lying on its side. I slump heavily onto it. Bury my face in my clammy hands and rock slowly back and forth.

Emotions and thoughts run wildly through me. Like half-mad mongrels, they whirl.

What the fuck is wrong with me?

***

Not long after we moved to Echlin Street, I joined the F.C.A, the Irish part-time army. Ciaran joined as well. I loved it. Considering my experience thus far, you'd think racism would rear its head, but it rarely did. I remember one incident in the armoury when we were waiting to be issued our rifles. One of the lads made a joke about my colour. I'll call him Murphy. Just like in school, I wouldn't be bullied. I went up to this lad and got in his face, striking his forehead with mine. It was like butting into a wall.

'Fucking hell,' I said, rubbing my forehead. 'What have you got in your head? A rock?'

He looked red-faced and startled.

'Sorry,' he said.' I didn't mean to offend. I was just joking.'

'If I'd known your head was made of concrete, I'd have kicked you in the balls.'

'It's a good job you didn't. These boys actually are made of concrete.' He cupped his crotch in his hand and grinned.

Murphy proved his head did indeed contain a large proportion of concrete. We were on the firing range a few months later, shooting targets up to 300 yards away. When the cease-fire order came, I fired off the round in the breech, applied the safety catch and then pulled back the bolt to eject the cartridge. With the breech open, I took the magazine off and stood, rifle across my chest, muzzle pointing up the range towards the sky. At the word of command, 'Ease springs!' I worked the bolt back and forward to eject any rounds which might have been stuck in the breech. Finally, still pointing the rifle into the air and up the range, I thumbed the safety off and squeezed the trigger. The idea was to fire off any round still in the breech if my previous efforts to render the rifle safe had not worked.

On this particular morning, when we were given the order to 'ease springs', I saw Private Murphy look down the barrel of his rifle and reach for the trigger. Luckily the weapon wasn't loaded because the bullet would have just ricocheted off that big ol' stupid head of his and maybe hit me.

***

Sitting on a boulder, looking down the barrel of my life, I'm utterly wretched. All I have to do to stop this turmoil is stop pulling the trigger, but I can't.

I'm lost, being mauled by a mind running wild with misery, dragging me through the wreckage of my life.

Here's what's happening.

Thoughts trigger emotions that agitate thoughts that provoke emotional reactions that pull thinking down into the depths where feelings arise, and on it goes. On and on— I'm helpless. Tossed about upon waves of self-lacerating emotions, I despair. Have I travelled thousands of miles for *this* bullshit? Have I come all this way just to be surrounded by these destructive thoughts and feelings, to witness myself being pulled apart?

But wait a minute.

Just hold the fuck up.

Who is this *me* who's being torn? Surely this chaos can't be me, can it? There must be some stillness against which this movement is seen. Some silence in which these voices are heard.

Who am I?

Am I this idiot sobbing and snuffling snot?

Raising my head, rising from the claustrophobic shelter of my arms, I check to see nobody around to witness my becoming undone. I'm looking around, mortified at the thought of being seen like this, gripped by an ego spasm, but I can't stop crying. The light of the Ashram attracts my gaze across the dark fields of wild grass and scrub. The moon traces the sturdy outline of the Prayer Hall. The doors are closed, but the lights are on, warm and inviting, and I wonder if Swami is in there.

I have a deep longing for him to lift me out of this confusion. An unspoken prayer for these waters to be still. Wipe the tears from my eyes and let me see who or what I am within creation because surely I can't be this inconsistent mess. Can I? Just look at the state I'm in? I've dribbled spittle onto my knee. I wipe it off and wonder if maybe this is it. Perhaps this pathetic mess *is* what I am?

Maybe this unhappy collision of past and present *is* all there is.

And maybe I'm wrong about Swami Premananda. He's full of light. Of that, I'm sure, but can that light illuminate me? If it's down to me to illuminate myself, I'm well and truly fucked. How can I answer the question of who I am when I'm the one asking the question? It's — it's — like picking up my phone and trying to ring myself on it. No matter how often I dial the number, the line will always be busy. The act of asking myself the question will forever obscure the answer, but I can't help but ask it.

Maybe it's the spiritual equivalent of a salmon swimming upstream.

Whatever the answer, if there is one, I feel sure it must come through my heart and not my head. Without a higher spiritual intelligence to guide it, the mind's a movie playing out to an impressionable chimp.

I'm breathing deeply now, each breath shuddering as I start to feel better. Finally, I get off the boulder and pat it like an old friend. I return to the ashram, weary of myself.

***

Neither Lesley nor Mataji mentions my tear-sodden eyes when I enter the koothi. I'm grateful for this, as I don't want to talk about what I had just gone through, and besides, sitting on my bed, I realise the experience had been very cathartic. I feel none of the earlier distress, but my longing to see the peace beyond all this nonsense is as intense as ever.

With all the humility I can muster, I close my eyes and silently ask Swami Premananda to show me what I am. What is behind this form? What is the truth of this? Who am I?

'One oxo cube.'

I open my eyes and see a young woman in the doorway. She's barefoot, holding something small, square, and silvery between her finger and thumb. She looks very pleased as she steps into the room.

'Hello!' she says, adding the warmth of her smile to those I've already had from Lesley and Mataji.

Mataji says, 'Paul, this is Agatha. Lesley mentioned you weren't eating, and she ran off to get an Oxo cube for you. She's going to make you a drink from it.'

'Oh — thank you.'

Bless her. It's delicious. I'm sipping its restorative beefiness and listening to the soothing murmur of female voices. I lie down facing the wall. Mataji asks Agatha to sing a bhajan. She's singing a soft and sweet song for Swami. The melody lulls and pulls the last of the sorrow from me. I close my eyes. I'm listening to the world around me. I hear bare feet pad across the floor as Agatha leaves. A teaspoon stirs in a chipped mug. The fridge hums an electric song to itself. Occasionally it shudders a chill down its spine. Children laugh someplace near.

Sleep is coming.
It comes from within, not from without.
Full of forgiveness, it absolves me.
I become silence
Love is infinite.
No beginning.
No ending.
Nothing between.

CHAPTER ELEVEN

Dust Falls From The Wings Of Angels

The stock cube, bold and beefy, has chugged its way through me. The mosquitoes must have been pleasantly surprised. Not only did I fall asleep with my arms exposed, but my perspiration had basted me in a delicious gravy. Still, despite the itch from the bites, I feel good. I'm thinking about last night. Seen from the calm place my mind rests in now, lying on my bed, I feel like it happened to someone else.

'How are you this morning?' Lesley asks, sitting up in her bed. She kicks off her sleeping bag liner and plants her feet on the floor.

'Good,' I say, sitting up. The floor feels cold underfoot, and I clench my toes in a minor protest. 'Sorry about last night. I was in a mess. I hope I didn't make you feel bad?'

'No. Well, maybe a little. I was just worried about you, mainly.'

'I'm fine now.'

'You're sure?'

I smile and feel the warmth in my heart flood into it. I know she sees it. She smiles back.

'What's the plan for today?' I ask.

'We'll have to go back into town.'

'Not to the doughnut shop.'

Lesley laughs. 'Not unless we get you some more Imodium. No. We need to get some food in. We've just about run out of everything. Not that we had much in the first place. I'll ask Mataji if it's okay to leave the ashram. And stop scratching your bites.'

I hadn't even realised I was. I stop scratching. 'I'm starting to think the vibhuti will never turn up. How long is it since the night of Shivaratri?'

'Five days, maybe. Six? I've lost count.' She gets up off her bed. 'I'll pop the kettle on.'

I yawn and scratch. Let myself fall back onto my bed. I've lost count of the days too. Despite my occasional crisis, the days have been long and sweet, like bubblegum stretching in the sun.

'Bugger,' Lesley mutters. 'There's no electricity.' She clicks the switch on the kettle a few times. It remains inert.

'You're joking?'

'I'm not.' She looks in the fridge for something to replace tea.

'Damn. I'm starving.'

The vibhuti now seems less important than my breakfast. I barely ate anything yesterday.

Lesley holds up a bottle of warm pop and the last of the Rich Tea Biscuits. 'We'll have to make do with this until it comes back on. Or we could go to Babakas and — they won't have any power either, will they?'

She hands me the bottle.

'Bottle opener?' I ask.

'Nope. Still not found it.'

'Not to worry. I can get the top off by smacking it on a

corner.'

'I'd rather you didn't. Not if it means taking another chunk off the wall out there.'

'It's only a small chunk.'

'True. But that's how the Sphinx lost his nose. Some thirsty Egyptian worker stops for a drink. Knocks the lid of his beer off with a quick tap on the nostril. Probably seemed like a good idea at the time.'

***

Water falls, cascading down my chest. Swirls in my open mouth. Gushes in rushing rapids down my shivering spine. Oh, — Joy. This is wonderful. My eyes are closed as the bucket above my head rapidly empties. Showering like this has grown on me since my first attempt. Spluttering, I open my eyes and see a massive bee hovering before me.

Oh shit! I jump back. It's big and black and menacing, like a flying bear with a hangover and what looks like a dagger sticking out of its bottom. Suddenly it bucks and veers into the yard. I grab a towel and follow to keep an eye on it. Drying myself as it bumbles around, I notice the bites on my arms. Of course, being bitten on the arms during the night isn't as bad as being stung on the balls in the morning, so I keep my distance.

Lesley calls out to me from inside the koothi. 'I've been over to see Mataji. She asked Swami if we could go to town. It'll be fine, but we need to go now. I'll need a quick shower before we go. Will you be much longer?'

'I'm just drying myself, but there's a huge bee out here.'

'A what -— ?' She pops her head around the door, ' — oh dear! What the hell is that!'

'Shhhh. Don't make it angry.'

'My God. Don't tell me that's a bee?'

'If it is, it doesn't need pollen. It could just go into the shop and take a jar of honey. Who's going to stop it?'

The bee suddenly lurches to the left and then up over the wall. Maybe I've just given it an idea.

***

Our funds are limited, so we're going to catch a bus. We set off at a comfortable pace, out of the ashram gates and to the left. The road to the village of Fatimanagar stretches untidily along the road as if not too sure which way to go. Our slow sun-drenched progress is attracting the attention of many locals here and there. They sit outside their houses or stroll along the thin strip of baked buildings. There's no pavement here. It would look out of place if there were like wearing a cravat with a pair of overalls. There isn't even a bus stop. You put your hand out when the bus appears in the distance. Hopefully, it will stop. Ideally, it doesn't just keep going with your arm attached to the wing mirror while the rest of your body now waits for an ambulance.

A young boy, squinting in the sun, is watching us pass. His hand's above his eyes to shade them as he swivels to keep us within sight. I feel self-conscious with all the attention. Like the unblinking gaze of portraits hung in galleries, the eyes follow us. We keep walking until we come to a little shack which appears to be the local tobacconist. Lesley buys some cigarettes called *bidis* and lights up, drawing the smoke in. I can hear the glowing tip crackle faintly for a moment. A slight cough from her as she wafts noxious fumes out of her face and says, 'These are a lot stronger than what I'd usually smoke. I think they've got more tobacco in them than normal.'

'More hair, leather and toenails, too, if the smell is

anything to go by.'

She sniffs the air and then says, with mock surprise, 'I thought that was you?'

We walk along the road again in the shade of single-story buildings that look to be held together by pastel paints and vivid posters. Dust follows a massive lumbering lorry which rumbles by, forcing me to close my eyes to protect them. I feel the heat of the earth passing over us. Diesel stinks up my nostrils. I open my eyes and feel the imposition of grit on my right eyelid. Wipe it with the back of my hand. Here comes a wooden cart pulled by a bullock slowly overtaking us. No sign of the driver. Presumably, he's asleep in the cart. The bullock lets rip with an unforgivably generous fart as it passes.

'Charming,' Lesley says, blowing smoke after it.

A goat comes along and is about to walk by us. It stops abruptly, looking at me. Then, startled by something, it turns and trots back the other way. I have a ridiculous urge to call it back. I want to explain I'm not the one who farted, but I don't because — well, because it's a goat. Once we get beyond the odour of the bullock flatulence, we stop to wait on the bus. It's as good a place as any. We smile at each other. This moment feels so good and right. I look around, still smiling and notice nobody is looking at me. Instead, brown eyes, full of curiosity, are looking at Lesley.

'I'm — invisible,' I say, with a little awe.

Lesley looks at me, which proves I'm not.

'All the people we've passed who were looking at us are actually looking at you. Not me.'

Lesley nods. 'The same thing happened in Sri Lanka. White females get more attention because we stand out. You never noticed it when we were in Trichy?'

'No. A bit. But not like this. It feels great.'

'It does?'

'Yeah. For me, anyway. Remember I told you how people in Ireland stared at me and how it made me so self-conscious that sometimes I couldn't handle being around people. I still can't, sometimes, even now.'

'I know. I remember you getting out of my car at traffic lights once and running off. We were on our way for a meal with my friends.'

'Yeah. I panicked. I couldn't bear the pain of it. Part of me is still stuck in Ireland, and *that part* broke and ran.'

'It certainly did. I had no idea it was so bad at that time. But you don't feel like that now, do you?'

'It's in here. Yeah. But not today. Not now.'

'Because I'm the one they're staring at.'

'That's right. Nobody's looking at me. It's beautiful.'

***

I can hear the bus. I look down the road, squinting in the sun and shielding my eyes. Even from this distance, I can see it's packed. Not packed in the way buses in Ballymun were packed. This is different. As the bus approaches, I can see people packed in like sardines. No — not even like that. Sardines can all fit in the can. This bus has *actually* got passengers sitting on the roof. Not upstairs, you understand, because this is a single-deck bus. Passengers are sitting on top, on the roof, clutching whatever is at hand to stop them from falling off. Hand-rails. Luggage. Each other.

'What the hell is this?' I ask.

'It's a bus, darling,' Lesley says. She's seen this sort of thing before. I, too, have seen something similar. It was on the news. A young man in America was standing on the roof of a moving bus for the rush of adrenaline it gave him. He called it '*urban surfing*'. In India, it's called '*no room downstairs.*' I wonder how daring the young man would feel if his granny was up there with him and she was holding a chicken.

The bus passes, absolutely crammed with people. They're not just standing in the aisles; some may even be wedged into the luggage racks. The bus honks in passing as if apologising for not stopping, but I'm relieved it kept moving.

'Good God.' I say, standing in a toxic cloud of diesel the bus has left in its wake. 'That looked like the last helicopter out of Saigon. I am *not* getting on anything that crowded unless it's a lifeboat and Fatimanagar has just hit an iceberg.' I can feel a slight panic rising at the prospect of sitting cheek to jowl with all those strangers. I remember children with sticky fingers putting their hands in my hair while their mothers looked on.

'Yes. That one *was a* bit crowded.' Lesley blows her own noxious cloud after it, then stubs her cigarette out on a low wall.

'Crowded?' I say, my voice increasing in volume. 'The rivets were popping off! The only way to get anyone else on that bus would be to stick them in a blender and spray them through the window!'

'If the next one's like that, we'll go back to the Ashram and get a taxi.'

'Okay.' Relief floods through me like a sigh.

The following bus is a much better prospect when it comes into view. No people on top. Good. Hmmm. A couple of passengers are hanging off the near-side, and the bus is tilting that way, but it looks like there's room inside, which means those hanging on *outside* are doing so through choice rather than necessity. The bus is rattling toward us at an unhealthy speed. The closer it gets, the more I think it isn't going to stop, but at the last minute, it does. The driver's smiling at us through the open door. A little wiggle of his head invites us on board. We step up and wedge ourselves into the aisle with the other sardines.

The bus conductor's sitting down at the far end of the bus. I can see the top of his head upon which a battered hat is perched at a jaunty angle. The man's brain *must* be gently simmering. The *heat* — my god. A slim brown arm reaches for a little bell. The muted ring is wholly inappropriate for how the bus now takes off. A starter pistol would have been far more suitable because the driver slapped the laws of physics in the face, rammed the accelerator through the floor, and took off with the sort of velocity usually associated with a getaway car. We're rattling along the road, and a cloud of dust worthy of a stampede runs after us. The driver's grinding his way through the gears as if he holds a grudge against them. From the crunching, it sounds like something under the bonnet is eating the bus. We sway to his steering, jerk to his gear changing, and we become the world's first synchronised Heimlich manoeuvre when he applies the brake.

***

There's a reception committee waiting for us at the Trichy State Bus Stand. It consists of hot fuel fumes, the smell of urine and old fruit. They welcome us with a soft punch in the nostrils and a bouquet of unsavoury odours. My eyes are stinging and watering a little, but I can still see a man pissing by the side of the road. Whistling. Sloshing in a large puddle of his own making. Nobody but me appears to think this is, perhaps, being a little too relaxed in the company of strangers. So we move on, eager to get away from air so polluted that it might yet coagulate into steel wool.

A building site to our left is a hive of activity, which, in this heat, is an unusual sight. I'm fascinated by the number of female labourers. I've never seen such a thing. They're walking up a ramp with stacks of bricks balanced on their heads. Somehow, burdened as they are, they move gracefully. I can barely take my eyes off these women as we pass. The slope they walk up with building materials has become a catwalk in my eyes. But now I see the tiredness in these women. Now I see compressed vertebrae. This is no catwalk. It's a conveyer belt, and these women are the products it churns out.

'Do you want some bread?' Lesley asks. 'we're near the shop where we got some.'

'No. I'm still bunged up from all the Imodium.'

'If that bus ride didn't shift the blockage, I don't know what will.'

'Another doughnut,' I mutter.

We're in what seems like an upmarket residential area. It feels unnaturally quiet after the noise of the bus station, and suddenly we're quite alone. The world may not be ours, but the pavement certainly is, and that's just as good. You can only ever walk where your feet are. On either side of the street, houses look out demurely from behind painted walls on which the blush of colour is faded. The walls have an abundance of fading posters that were once vibrant and gaudy. All of them are advertising epic films. The plots all seem to involve laughing heartily, dancing gaily, singing joyfully and shooting people in the face.

In the Bread Shop, we avoid doughnuts. Instead, we get a loaf, biscuits and directions to a place which sells bottle openers. This nugget of information leads us to a wide road, thickly fringed with shops and full of people. At a busy roundabout, we ask for directions again and are sent to Junction Road, so-called because one end of it meets up with Trichy Junction Railway Station. If all the roads were given such descriptive names, our journey so far would have been thus: We arrived at Man Pissing in Road Square, proceeded down Doggie Droppings Avenue and then took a left onto Man Scratching Balls Boulevard.

We find ourselves in a market area where stalls and open-fronted emporiums noisily mingle. Shiny things glint and beckon while colour blushes in self-conscious radiance. A bead of sweat rolls and tickles my forehead. I wipe it away with my arm, leaving the skin slick and uncomfortable. My shirt is stuck to my back. My knees are sweating, and it trickles and tickles my calves as we stand before a stall with stainless steel goods. Pots, pans, woks, grilles and knives hang from every inch. The man behind the counter has stopped short of shoving a couple of spoons up each nostril and wearing a frying pan on his head, but only just.

Lesley asks, 'Do you sell bottle openers?'

The man looks blank. We've possibly picked the only man in Trichy who doesn't have a smattering of English. He proves this by presenting her with a ladle big enough to fit on the front of a small tractor.

I take over the negotiations.

'Psst!' I say, making a 'bottle opening' motion with my hand.

He points down the street.

Lesley stops me before I confuse the issue any further.

'He thinks you need the toilet,' she says.

'No chance of that,' I mutter, thinking of my chronic constipation.

'Let me have another go,' she says. 'I'll mime it for him.'

'No. Wait. I'm good at this sort of thing. Watch this.'

So, I hold an invisible bottle in front of myself. After a suitable pause for dramatic effect, I now reach for the bottle with my other hand, pull something off it and make a hissing noise which is meant to be effervescence. I then toss the invisible cap toward the man, who steps backwards and looks alarmed.

'Why's he looking worried?' I ask.

'You just mimed priming a grenade and then threw it at him.'

Oops

'Let me try,' Lesley says, stepping forward. She does what I did without the added hint of a grenade, which works for some reason. Light dawns on the man's face, and he rummages in a drawer. Then, smilingly modestly, as if expecting a round of applause, he holds up a bottle opener for our inspection. I notice a studious-looking gentleman in his middle years observing this drama. Tufts of grey hair peek from behind his large ears as if they think hiding from his receding hairline will preserve them from falling out as the rest of their brethren have done over the years.

'Oh, look!' Lesley exclaims, pointing to a stainless steel cup with a lid.

'What is it?'

'It's a tiffin tin. If I get that, Babakka can fill it with tea. Then, we'll take it back to the koothi. It'll stay hot for ages.'

'Good thinking.'

The stallholder passes it to Lesley, who smiles with delight at her discovery. Anything which enables the smooth flow of tea into her bloodstream is always of interest to her.

'Lovely,' she says. 'We'll have this and the bottle opener.'

The stallholder takes them back to wrap them rapidly, rustling the brown paper with enthusiasm and a ball of string.

'Stop!'

The onlooking gentleman has raised his hand. He speaks to the stallholder in a language I don't understand, resulting in the wrapping paper being torn from our goods. The gentleman says, 'That tin is *not* good quality. Your tea will leak from that item.'

A different tin is held up for our inspection. We look to our unexpected guardian for approval. He nods sagely.

'This will protect your tea. It will keep it warm, and you will delight in its freshness.'

'Thank you.' Lesley says. 'You've been very helpful.'

He holds a hand up to deflect the praise. The gesture is almost an act of holiness in the depth of its sincere humility. His work here is done. He turns and walks away into the crowd.

Little did we know at the time, but the recommended tiffin tin will also leak. However, its memory stayed warm and delightful in its freshness, so we can't complain.

On we go. We thread our way through the warp and weave of Trichy. A man on a black bone-rattling bike waves us down. His limbs are long and also clad in black. He'd been travelling in the opposite direction, ringing his bell, which rattled rather than rung when he saw me. His bell may be choked with rust, but his brakes are excellent if how abruptly he stopped is anything to go by. He becomes a rock in the stream of life, and the market flows around him.

'Young sir,' he says. 'Have you ever thought about becoming a Christian?

'No,' I reply, even though I was baptised a Catholic. Of course, I don't point out that many other Catholics I've met didn't seem to have given it a moment's thought either.

'That is okay,' he says sympathetically.

'Why do you ask?'

'I'm a Christian Pastor.'

'Oh?'

He's reaching into his pocket and withdrawing a card. He

places it in my hand. The card is disturbingly damp.

'This is my calling card. If you change your mind, you can ring me.' He climbs back on his bike. Cycles off again. The market swallows him, and I look at his calling card. The writing is blurred beyond comprehension.

***

Some things are hard to understand. Ma got a job taking meals to the elderly in their houses. The meals were pre-heated, and Ma collected them from a van. She also reminded the pensioners to take their medication. Sometimes she'd put the tablets out for them. On Thursdays, she went to see a pensioner called 'Moira', who usually sat in her armchair waiting for the food. She'd be cosy by the fire, holding a polished spoon. On some days, Moira would be in bed, which was also in the living room, because she could no longer manage the stairs. This day, however, she was nowhere to be seen. Ma was puzzled and increasingly concerned. She looked in every room. Called her name. Looked in the yard too, but Moira was nowhere in sight. Finally, back in the living room, Ma stood, baffled and wondering what to do next. An urge to look under the bed saw her on hands and knees.

'Hello,' Moira said. 'Sure, isn't it lovely weather we're having?'

'Moira, what are you doing under your bed?'

Moira wouldn't say. Or she had no idea. With the help of a neighbour, Ma got her out from underneath and settled her in the chair.

The following day, Moira was again missing. Ma looked under the bed first of all.

Moira was dead.

Outside, the sun was shining.

***

'Hello? Anybody there?'
'Wh – what?' I mumble.

'It's me. Adrienne. Can I come in?'

I sit up. Confused. The sun's gone down. I'm on my bed. When we returned from Trichy, we were so tired that we had to lie down. Forty winks turned into a deep, peaceful sleep.

The door creaks. Adrienne enters, holding two cups.

'I came round earlier, but you were both sleeping deeply. That was two hours ago, and I thought you'd like some tea?'

'Thanks. That's lovely. Lesley, wake up. Adrienne's brought some tea.'

Lesley yawns. Her bed creaks. She sits up.

'Tea? Lovely. God, it's dark. What time is it?'

'We've slept for ages,' I say.

Adrienne tells us the generator's offline, so there's still no electricity. I take the cup she offers.

'Do you have any candles?' she asks.

'No,' I say. 'Damn. We should have picked some up in Trichy because the electricity was off this morning.'

'Torch?'

'Nope.'

Lesley says, 'Paul, be a love and go to the shop, will you? Just in case the generator doesn't come back on.'

The walk from Mataji's koothi, where Adrienne made the tea, had cooled the beverage enough for me to down it in one.

Off I go. Looking for the light in the darkness.

***

Where did you go, Moira?

You went under the bed, but nobody came out.

Even before the light left your eyes, inside you, there was darkness. The human heart is not illuminated. The sun can't penetrate the deep darkness our ribs are wrapped around. Being tightly wound around the journey of our trachea and intestines, our physical self is too dense. And yet, we are hollow. Life passes through us. It ripens into tears which fall in joy or sorrow. It flows through us and around us. The tide swells and brings us into our mothers' arms and, in time, carries them away into the arms of their mothers.

Life is a mystery.

As I walk, I begin to feel a rising tide of anticipation. It rushes in whispers among the devotees. I see them walking toward the prayer Hall.

'What's happening?' I ask.

'Tonight. The vibhuti! Swami will manifest the vibhuti tonight!'

Sacred ash will pour from the skin of a small Sri Lankan saint.

Life.
Death.
All in-between.
I understand nothing.

***

Between the hours of ten and twelve this evening, the villagers who live nearby shuffled through the double doors of the Prayer Hall. Everyone who could make it came along. Coconut vendors, goat herders, leathery grandfathers, wide-eyed daughters, peppery-haired grandmothers and all in-between came to see Swami Premananda.

Years ago, reactions varied when they first heard of the Swami from Sri Lanka. Some good. Some bad. But over time, even the cynical and wary saw this man was blessed. The steadfastness of his goodwill slowly drew the indifferent into respect and appreciation of his presence in the community.

The pious sought his blessings and the wise his counsel. Tonight, they sit in the fragrant heart of the Prayer Hall. I can't see much of what's happening because I'm outside, pressed against a window. With so many people out here doing the same thing and so many people inside, it's hard to see much other than the occasional glimpse of Swami as he bestows his blessings on the locals. I step back from the knot of devotees at the window.

'What can you see?' Lesley asks.

'Not much,' I say.

She's craning her neck to see over the crowd. A gentleman, possibly Indian, maybe Sri Lankan, steps forward for a better look, pushing his arms between the people by the window. At first, I think he's rather rudely pushing his way in, but he lifts a young boy up and away from the window. Places the boy on his broad shoulders and gestures for Lesley to step into the gap. She thanks him and steps forward to peer through the lattice of the window. The hot, clammy bulk of other people pressing in makes it too uncomfortable for her to stay too long. She pulls away and returns to my side. Mataji appears out of the night.

'It'll be a long time before you see him,' she says. 'This'll go on 'til the early hours of the morning, so we should go and rest. Maybe have a little to eat as well.'

Before we leave, Lesley again thanks the kind man and his boy. Then, we three fall into step and head toward Mataji's koothi. Under cover of long moon shadows, Lesley slips her warm, soft hand into mine and squeezes. The night has settled onto the woven roof of the hut, like the plump shadow of an owl sitting on its nest. Inside, the candles beside Meenakshi flicker and glow. The skin of the Goddess is golden and warm, like summer honey. Fresh flower petals lay at her feet.

Mataji points to a little golden figure of Ganesh on the

small table, which serves as an altar. Then, almost wistfully, she tells us, 'That was the first statue Swami ever gave me.'

'I remember,' Lesley says. 'I was there. It came up out of the palm of his hand. Literally. It just appeared, and he handed it to you.'

Mataji laughs, remembering, 'You remember how hot it was? I couldn't hold it.'

'That's right. You lobbed it in my direction. I caught it, but it felt like it'd come out of an oven.'

'You were throwing it from hand to hand like a hot chestnut until it cooled down.'

Mataji and Lesley chuckle over the memory.

All of this was before my time. I ask, 'Was Swami manifesting vibhuti at that time?'

'Yeah. But I'd seen Swami do it before. The first time was in — let me think — nineteen eighty-four. Swami had gone to England. Wales, too, I think. He was manifesting all sorts of things back then.'

'That's when he gave you the *rudraksha mala*?'

'No. Not then.' Her fingers go to the necklace she's wearing out of sight beneath her Punjabi suit. She draws it out so we can see a large rudraksha berry linked by lotus beads on a string. 'Swami gave this to me when I was in Sri Lanka. I was with Gina, and it was the oddest thing to watch because he pulled it out of a hole in the air quite slowly, link by link. It was like something on the other end was holding it, but there was nothing that I could see. He was standing at arm's length right before me as he did it.'

She looks very distant. She returns to the past momentarily and then says one quiet word.

'Weird.'

***

***

I'm sitting on my bed while Lesley has a nap. A candle on top of the fridge gives off a muted glow. I've got a bunch of grapes in my hand. I pluck a plump one. Pop it in my mouth. Massage it gently with my tongue. The skin bursts. The sweet juice is so lovely it makes me want to hug myself.

I'm not actually hungry. I'm just trying to pass the time. Maybe I should meditate or do something spiritual.

I have another warm grape.

I can't concentrate enough to do anything. I'm too wound up with anticipation. Swami producing the Vibhuti has been described as miraculous, and he's doing it at this very minute in the Prayer Hall. I must wait my turn to see this marvellous thing like hundreds of others, but the wait is almost physically painful.

I burst another grape.

***

I could've cried, but I didn't. I wouldn't. But, Jesus Christ — I was in so much pain. The big toenail on my right foot had been surgically removed. Because of my age, the hospital had been obliged to keep me in a ward for a few days. I was, I think, fourteen. I'd already had the procedure done on the other foot a year ago, but it had been nothing like this. I was feverish with the agony of it. Remorseless pain throbbed through me, squeezing through the painkillers. Concentrated, prolonged, it pulled me from the mercy of sleep. Gnawed me back to consciousness like a rat under the floorboards.

Ma came to see me. She brought comics and chocolate, biscuits and books. I could hardly talk to her. The pain was electric, a live wire searing my nerves.

I saw it reflected in her eyes. The pain of a mother for her child. I tried to sit and talk with her, but I had to lie back down. It was too much for me. Seeing Ma made it harder for me to hide the agony.

She took my hand.
The pain faded away.
Oh — thank God — thank God — thank God —
Ma stood to leave.
I was drifting off to sleep.
She put some grapes on the cupboard beside me.

***

Feck —

All the grapes are gone. I'm holding a thoroughly denuded stalk and Lesley's stirring. I hope she doesn't want one. The candle's gone out, but I can still see her rubbing her eyes.

'Is anything happening?' she asks.

'No. Swami's still in the Prayer Hall with the locals. I popped out earlier to have a look. Couldn't see anything. Too many people over there.'

'How long have I been asleep?'

'Not sure. An hour maybe?'

'It feels like minutes. I'm exhausted.'

'Sod that. It feels like hours from this end of the equation, and I'm bored.'

'You're bored?'

'Well — not bored — sick of waiting. I hate waiting.'

'More than you hate queuing?'

'At least with a queue, you can see the end of it. We could be waiting all night to see Swami producing the vibhuti.'

'We could be, right enough. Where'd you put the other candles?'

'In your bag.' I have a sudden worrying thought. 'What if there's no vibhuti left when we see him?'

'I wouldn't worry about that, sweetheart. It'll still be

coming when we see him. Now, be a love and pop the kettle on while I get a candle.'

'The electricity's off. That's why we're sitting in the dark.'

'Oh, yes. Silly me.'

'Let's go for a walk. I'm going stir crazy in here.' I grab my camera. 'I'll get some pictures of you sitting on the wall.'

Walking past the Prayer Hall with its multitude of devotees outside, it suddenly occurs to me that there isn't the same degree of anticipation, song and electricity in the air as there was on Shivaratri night. In fact, by comparison, they look pretty muted. So my earlier sense of anticipation falls rapidly. I feel as if maybe this part of Shivaratri's not as impressive as when the lingams appeared. Oh well. I'm still glad to be here to see it.

We sit on the little wall outside the ashram gates, a pair of smiling moon-dials with a moth flitting around us.

'Moths always look as if they're panicking,' she says.

'I expect they are. Probably can't breathe with your cigarette smoke in their lungs.'

She tuts and waves a hand to waft the smoke away.

'I don't think it's that,' she says. 'To you and me, it's a moth, but to a bat, for example, it's probably the equivalent of a breath freshener. An after-dinner mint with wings.'

My tummy rumbles.

'Hungry?' Lesley asks.

'Not particularly. I think it's all those grapes I ate.'

'All?' I hope you saved me some?'

'Of course.'

'You didn't, did you?'

'It depends. Do you like the stalk?'

'No. Obviously.'

'Oh. In that case, no. Sorry.'

'Thanks,' she says.

More to change the subject than anything else, I remind Lesley about an incident in Sri Lanka.

'Didn't Swami materialise some biscuits for you and Gina?'

'Yes. And a good job too. There were food shortages because of the civil war, and we were hungry. Going out to look for supplies was extremely dangerous, so we tried to avoid it. We talked about Jacobs Lemon Puff biscuits one night in our room. The next day, Swami smiled at us and suddenly twisted both his hands in the air, and two packets of Jacobs Lemon Puff biscuits appeared out of nowhere. Remember, we were in Sri Lanka, and probably no one even knew what those biscuits were, let alone stock them in their shop.'

'Lemon Puffs?'

'That's right. Lemon Puff biscuits. Like the little Ganesh statue, they just appeared in his hands.'

'Were they hot like the statue?'

'Oh no,' said Lesley. 'Just as well because they would have melted. Or maybe not. They stayed fresh for a year.'

'You didn't eat them?'

'No. It felt sacrilegious to eat something miraculously pulled out of thin air. Not everyone was convinced this *was* something miraculous, of course. Someone told us that once, Swami asked *him* what he wanted. He asked for a Toblerone. If I recall correctly, this was outside at goodness knows what temperature. Swami clapped his hands together, and one appeared.'

'It's a bit like the story of Jesus feeding the multitude with loaves and fishes.'

'I'm not sure a packet of Lemon Puffs and a Toblerone has the same sort of biblical cache about it. But, nonetheless, they did appear out of thin air.'

'What did you do with the biscuits?'

'I kept them for about twelve months. Probably had them with a cup of tea. Not sure about Gina. Probably longer. And speaking of tea, I could do with one now — she nods toward the ashram. Some of the lights have come on. The electricity's back.

'Ok. You can stay here if you want. I'll bring it to you in the tiffin tin.' 'Lovely,' she says, smiling.

And that's why I'm walking along the long path from the gate alone. The crowds outside the Prayer Hall have dispersed. That's odd. I wonder where they've all gone?

I walk over. Peer in the window.

Over the heads of those sitting inside, I see —

Swami —

There goes my heart fluttering like a moth.

He's in the red silk waterfall of his robes, his arms are raised, and from his lips, a thin stream of powder is blowing like a fountain into the air.

I gasp.

Step back.

Fu – Fu - Fumble for my camera.

It's tucked into the folds of my dhoti. I take a picture. I know where everyone has gone now. They're inside. I've got to get Lesley. I'm running. My sandals slap my heels, urging me on while slowing me down simultaneously. I want to shout for her, but it feels sacrilegious. I can see her. Blowing smoke out like Swami's blowing vibhuti.

With a whispered shout, I call, 'Lesley!' She's standing now. Coming toward me.

'What is it?' she asks.

'The vibhuti!'

'It's coming!?'

'Yes!'

She stoops, extinguishes her cigarette in the sand and pops the fag-end in her packet.

Now we're both running. Four sandals are slapping. Something unbelievable is happening up there. Lesley quickly goes to our koothi and has a wash and change of clothes, and then we enter the Prayer Hall.

***

Mataji's at the door. She's waving us into the Prayer Hall. Into the noise. Into the heat. Into the densely packed space filled with devotees. She urges us on. We move forward, picking our way through the hundreds sitting on the floor. Halfway along the hall, we squeeze in as politely as possible in the crush and sudden rush. Apologetic smiles and nods of gratitude as people budge up to make space. There's no sign of Swami, and I fear we've missed it all.

But here he is again, stepping through the doorway at the far end of the hall. He's in his red robe and wearing a yellow dhoti beneath it. Vibhuti billows from his lips and drifts in the stifling heat like a perfumed veil. From his palms, powder falls, sprinkling into the hands of the devotees. Upturned faces touched by his fingers are left with a fragrant dusty smear of pale grey ash. He touches the face of a young man. Tears slip a wet trail darkly through the dust on the man's cheeks. A bald head bows before the saint, and Swami settles his hand on it. When he lifts his hand, vibhuti is on the dome. Wherever his hand touches, the sacred ash remains.

He's moving through the crowd, coming closer to me. My mouth may be agape. I don't know. I'm stunned at the sight of his lips covered in dust, his eyelids half-closed.

How can he breathe?

It's spilling from his nostrils, trickling over his lips.

But how can —

It's poring through his skin. Exuding from his pores. Down his arms and legs. He's exhaling it into the air. His breath is visible and fragrant and composed of powder and — what?

I don't know.

What does this mean?

What *is* this?

My entire life seems to have rushed to this moment, but the moment is moving so fast that my mind can't grasp it. Wait. Wait. Wait. What does this mean? The fingers of my mind are clutching the edges of the void, trying desperately not to let go.

I'm utterly mesmerised as Swami blesses each person he passes. Vibhuti falls like dust from the wings of an angel. The scent is heavenly. It remains as he steps through the door at the top of the Prayer Hall and out of sight. There's a commotion outside the door he stepped through. The non-indigenous men are being called forward. I stand slowly so as not to topple over. We're so tightly pressed together it isn't easy, but I manage it. Carefully, I pick my way forward until I'm at the front with other men who have done the same. We're led into the little room where I'd sat a few days ago, wondering if Swami could see me through the veil.

He's in here. Waiting for us. Big smile embracing us all. He's beckoning us in. Closer and closer. Come closer. And now we're all pressed into the small room. He stands with us, a fragrant, bushy-haired Island of goodwill. I hear the door behind, closing. It mutes some of the noise from the bhajans. We're asked to sit down so everyone can see. I remain standing because I'm at the back.

So, here we are. Swami is before us, smiling. His chest is bare, shoulders covered by his silken robe.

One of his helpers explains, 'Swami wishes you to see the vibhuti issuing from all over and every place on his body.'

Swami opened his arms.

I take a photograph.

Someone to the side snaps, 'No photographs!'

I look at Swami, but he just smiles and turns in a circle. He keeps his arms open so we can see the fine coating of dust on them. We can see the vibhuti falling in powdery streams over his stomach and chest. It ripples slowly down his skin as he speaks. A picture cannot capture this. It's like trying to catch a bird in flight. One image is not enough to convey the rising of a wing, the manifestation of vibhuti, or how it falls.

'The vibhuti comes from everywhere,' Swami says as he turns and turns again.

His back is covered. The vibhuti has started to gather on the waistband of his yellow dhoti, a sacred snowdrift. He turns to face us again, smiling his big smile, saying, 'You must see for yourself how it comes from all over.'

Modestly he lifts the dhoti to show the vibhuti on his upper thighs. His shins are grey with the dust. His feet are planted firmly on the floor amidst a layer of vibhuti as it steadily gathers in drifts by his toes. He moves his foot and leaves an imprint. Still, the vibhuti keeps falling. Men in robes are scooping it up with the palms of their hands and putting it into small sacks. Swami is showing us as much of his body as decency allows.

'This is why I let only men see.' Swami says. 'Swami is gentleman.'

A man, presumably as baffled as I am, reaches to touch one of Swami's legs.

Swami says, 'Be careful of my banana.'

Saint or sinner, there isn't a man on the planet who doesn't enjoy a banana joke, and we all laugh.

The man touches Swami's leg, and his hand comes away, covered in vibhuti. Ash slowly exudes to cover the area uncovered by the devotee's palm. He prostrates himself before Swami, who places a hand on the man's forehead when he rises, leaving a streak of vibhuti above the devotee's wide-open eyes. The gathering of men presses forward for a blessing. He holds his hands out, and vibhuti slips along the creases of each palm onto the floor. I'm one of the last to prostrate myself before him because I had wanted to observe, and this gesture of humility and respect does not come naturally or quickly to me.

Swami's helpers ask us to leave. Then, they gather up the vibhuti on the floor as the devotees return to the Prayer Hall.

I don't care what the others are doing.

I'm *not* leaving.

I'm staying where I am. The compulsion to witness this uncommon miracle is too powerful to be brushed aside just to comply with good manners. I expect someone to ask me to leave, but nobody says anything. Swami ignores me. His helpers ignore me too. They're carefully scooping the vibhuti off the ground where it has fallen from his body. They pour it into large bags, and I'm shocked at how much there is.

I'm wondering how this is possible, but it's like trying to describe one hand clapping. I remember noticing tiny bits of grit in some of the vibhuti I'd been given back in England. This is why. It had been here on this floor.

Silent — almost frightened to breathe in case I'm sent away, I recall watching Swami Premananda through the veil in this little room. He *knew* I was there then and knows it now, though I may as well be invisible for all the attention anyone gives me. Swami adjusts his robes and looks over at me. I feel terribly exposed. Self-conscious and humble but firm in my conviction that I'm not leaving this room. I smile at Swami. He acknowledges nothing other than letting his eyes rest on me, and now his gaze moves elsewhere. He's exchanging a few words with his helpers. Now he steps out through the curtain once more to give his blessing to the devotees in the hall.

I'm standing in the doorway, looking at the hundreds as they clap and sing bhajans. I can see Lesley clapping and singing, probably out of tune, but her heart will perfectly harmonise with this devotion as Swami moves through the crowd smearing vibhuti on foreheads. Palms open like flowers to the sun, and he sprinkles hot ash on them.

Vibhuti still spills out of his skin and mouth, and nose. I see Rekha clapping. Adrienne's sitting nearby, her face smudged with vibhuti. She presses her hands together, eyes raised, looking at him as he passes. It goes on like this for a long time as he walks among the devotees, sacred ash billowing from his mouth and trickling from his nostrils. He's only a few feet away from me, and I see all this clearly. He strides to where I stand, and his hands are white from the vibhuti, his chest and belly covered in ash. I see it on his arms and legs. He's reaching out. Touches the bowed head of a man. Steps closer to me. I step back, and he's striding past through the doorway, red robe a soft rustle. Bushy hair is almost in my face. The heavenly scent of sacred ash is in his wake. He keeps going out through the back door, out into the night. His helpers follow after him.

I go to the doorway, peering into the night, trying to see him. Where is he? My eyes take a moment to adjust. Where's he gone? Moonlight illuminates the banana leaf roofs. Cuts into shadows. Reveals a cluster of people standing around a figure. They seem to lurch in the direction Swami lives, and then they stop again. Voices are raised, almost in a panic.

What's going on?

I step out of the small room and down the steps. Moving forward, tentatively —

There he is!

Those people surround Swami. They're fussing around him. It's hard to see what's going on. I think he's producing more vibhuti. A torch shines through the dark. A bright beam. A concerned face. Grass. A multitude of bare feet. Bushy hair.

Swami's talking in Tamil.

It looks like —

— those people are half-carrying him.

And this is more shocking than anything I've seen. I'm falling into a quiet place where all this noise is swallowed. Falling into the sound of one hand clapping.

Swami collapses. The little knot of people gasps and cries out.

'Get back!'

'Give Swamiji some room!'

'Quickly! Water!'

I'm scared. I'm walking toward the saint, but I'm frightened.

I mumble, ' — Swami?'

He's back on his feet, walking like an old man wracked with pain. His helpers brush the ground before him as if to sweep the small stones away.

But why —?

I don't understand.

I'm close enough to witness this. I neither help nor hinder. I follow. We pass beneath dark, whispering leaves over the dry grass and the stone-pitted path.

Swami stops again. I hear water. I see a pool gather at his feet. For a moment, I think he's urinating.

I circle, paler than the moon. Mute.

Now I see the water being poured over his legs, and I

remember that when the vibhuti passes through Swami Premananda's skin, it burns like fire. Of course, it does.

Ash comes from fire.

Oh, my God.

Poor Swami.

No wonder the stones were being brushed off the path before him. The pain must be excruciating.

I want to reach out and hold him.

But now, here's something else. A powerful instant of self-reflection in this drama. I see myself as I'm looking at Swami and his suffering. I feel compassion for him but can also see how rigidly I control its expression in case I embarrass myself. Compassion is endless. It's like water, below the surface in abundance, but the walls of my well are narrow.

That narrowness is me.

Poor, poor Swami Premananda. He's walked for hours among us. He's given us the vibhuti and allowed this mystery to pour through him. All we had to do was hold out our hands for him to give his blessing.

And all of that time, he was walking through fire.

Swami reaches his humble koothi and sits heavily in a chair on the porch.

A concerned voice is asking, 'Swami? Are you okay?'

I think this voice may have been mine.

Swami waves the concern off.

'This is normal,' he says reassuringly.

The man with fire under his skin takes my concern and returns it with a blessing.

With visible effort, he gets to his feet. He opens the door of his koothi. Slowly, he steps inside. The door closed behind him.

Silence.

I'm shaken.

I walk back to where water was poured onto Swami's Premananda's legs. I'm on my knees. I bow down to where the water has soaked the earth. I press my forehead into the warm, damp soil.

My pride blushes.

My scepticism sneers at me.

My fear looks over my shoulder.

But my heart knows what I saw.

***

That's right.

I know what I saw, but now I'm back in the koothi with Lesley, and my mind cannot cope with the night's events. It keeps running back with wide eyes and then in circles asking, 'What the fuck was that?'

Naturally, Lesley's got the kettle on.

Unnaturally, I've just spent a couple of hours watching a man breathing fragrant, sacred ash through his nose and mouth and the pores of his skin.

Wha —?

I'm sitting on my bed, utterly baffled.

How —?

Lesley drinks her tea, brushes her teeth and lays down to sleep. She's utterly unperturbed at having seen a human being breathing dry powder and exuding bags of fragrant dust.

Did I mention the size of the bags? They were as big as a bag of sugar, and there were loads of them.

It's utter madness.

***

Not sure how long has passed, but I find it hard to sleep.

My mind is still running along the grooves in my brain, looking for an answer to what happened tonight.

I don't know.

But what if I did?

What use would the knowledge be if you don't know the knower?

I'm a mystery to myself. My very existence is an answer, but from where did the question arise? Who asked it? The manifestation of the vibhuti is a mystery, yes, but no more of a mystery than I am. How did I come into being?

Why?

Why am I here?

Who am I?

The unknown is a silent witness to the unknowable, and somewhere between them, I turn over in my bed and tangle my legs in the liner as my mind ties itself into a Gordian knot. Moving before the eye of the mind, Swami Premananda is exhaling powder.

All things are possible through the Will of God. I say this to myself to explain the night, but it's a cop-out. It's just a way of saying I don't know. Saying this is the Will of some unknown force is just life looking at itself and shrugging because it hasn't the foggiest idea what the fuck is going on. Why even try to figure it out, I think to myself. Swami isn't like an ordinary human being. Swami isn't bound by the physical laws the rest of us live by — but then the memory of him staggering and falling comes to me. I see his door closing behind him and the quiet dignity of his silent suffering.

He feels pain as I do.

I'm shocked by the realisation that he's *more* human than I am. He completely understands what it is to be human because that's what he is. It's the acceptance and transcendence of that perceived limitation which is the mark of a saint. It isn't the miracle. It's not the vibhuti or the Lingams. Or walking through walls. It's the act of selfless service. It's walking through fire to bless those who ask it of you.

    A tear slips onto my pillow.
    Breath softens.
    Something without name
    Without form
    Silent

CHAPTER TWELVE
God Forgive Me

I'd fallen asleep with the radio on. The sound kept me company and masked the noise of the rats scrabbling under the floor. Tony was away in the barracks, so it was just me, the rodents and the radio. It was February 14^{th,} 1981. Valentines Day. I remember the date because the news came on the radio. There'd been a fire in a nightclub called the Stardust, and forty-eight people had been killed. Most of them were in their late teens, but every one of the deceased was the beloved of some mother or father or brother or sister. I've looked at the autopsy report to understand what those poor children endured. I did this because my reaction at the time was possibly the worst thing ever to pass through my mind.

After the initial impulse of sorrow, I lay listening to Dire Straits 'Romeo and Juliet' being played as a tribute to the deceased. I can't remember what happened that day or that week, but it doesn't matter. I was feeling particularly bitter toward Ireland and the Irish. Of this tragedy, what it meant to me, was that there were fewer Irish in the world who would grow up to be racists.

Until then, I thought my exposure to racism was the worst thing ever, but I was wrong. What was so terrible about Ireland was that it peeled away the layers of my assumed civility and exposed a capacity for hatred. The Irish didn't hate me. God bless them. Most of them didn't even know I existed. To most of the people who saw me, I was nothing. A face passing by. One amongst many. A nothing they would not remember. Some of them laughed at me. The majority did not. Occasionally they spat. The majority did not. Frequently they called me a nigger, but once again, the majority did not.

In the same way that strangers looked at me and saw a colour, I looked at strangers and saw a racist. We were the blind looking back at the blind. I'd been treated with contempt, and now I was utterly contemptible, without empathy for the suffering of others. Bitter. Angry. Callous toward the agony of all those involved. My troubles erroneously allowed me to think I had an excuse to turn my back on the unbearable suffering of others. Heart clenched like a fist, ego condensed and as unfeeling as a walnut, I turned my face to the wall and listened to the dying strains of Dire Straits 'Rome and Juliet.'

All over Dublin that night, lives were being torn asunder.
Beneath me, the rats bickered.
My heart was a stone.
God forgive me.

***

Blue sky above me. Birds circle and swoop. I woke up feeling something profoundly spiritual happened last night. I don't understand what that was or what it means, but I'm sure it means something. At least, I think so. I know it hasn't made me a better person. I feel the same as I did yesterday. Does witnessing something spiritual make a person any more spiritual than someone who hasn't? No. I don't think so. I saw India from the plane's window as it landed, and I'm no closer to being a bird, so I guess the answer is no.

Lesley's sitting on another wall across from me. She's

talking to a woman she met on the road to the main gate yesterday. This woman walks everywhere with her bare feet. She says it brings her closer to nature. I think it brings you closer to stepping into something nature dropped out of the back of a cow. I observe the two of them for a while as they send smoke signals into the sky. Lesley's wearing her straw hat, and the other woman has her hair in braids. Her style is strongly reminiscent of a Native American woman. I think of the Lone Ranger and Tonto, only the Lone Ranger didn't smoke, and Tonto wouldn't go anywhere without his moccasins. It's hard to get buffalo shit from under your toenails.

Yeah.

I'm *definitely* no more spiritual than I was yesterday.

I lay my head back down on the wall. Their voices recede to a murmur at the back of my mind, and then I withdraw too. The world is lapping on my shores as I nod off.

Paul!

I wake up and see the blue sky once more.

'Are you coming for a walk? You'll fall off that wall if you stay there any longer.'

I sit up. Lesley's companion has gone. Back to the reservation, I presume. Lesley and I wander off to where some huge rocks are standing in the fields. I take a few photographs of her atop one of the smaller ones. She takes the camera and captures my left ear, a leg and what will eventually turn out to be one of her nostrils, but only after much speculation.

She hands the camera back to me and sits on one of the rocks, which must have nodded off and fallen over at some point in the distant past. Or maybe it was so in awe, looking up at the stars for a million years, it toppled over. This sort of thing embarrasses other rocks, so they ignore it.

I sit beside her as she lights a cigarette. She takes a pull and exhales, sighing.

'I wish I'd gone to the morning abishekam,' she says.

'I'm not,' I reply. 'My mind would have been out here anyway.'

'It's such a lovely day, isn't it.'

I reach down and pull some dry grass out of the earth.

'Why do you do that?' Lesley asks.

'Hmm?'

'Pull the grass out of the soil. How would you like a big hand to come out of the sky and pull you up?'

'After last night, I don't think I'd be all that surprised.'

'Oh, I know. I've seen Swami materialise things in the past, but I've never seen anything like what happened in the Prayer Hall.'

'Oh? I thought you'd seen that sort of thing before?'

'No. Not like that. Not that amount of vibhuti. It was extraordinary.'

'You didn't seem to be affected by it last night?'

'I was stunned. I had to lie down and be quiet. Besides, I was exhausted.'

We're both silent for a minute or so, thinking about it. Just Lesley, myself, the rocks and the infinite sky having a quiet moment.

I break the silence by saying, ''I don't think I'll ever be able to convey just how odd the experience was. But what happened afterwards is the thing I'm most affected by.'

'When Swami collapsed?'

'Yeah. And the fact that he was in pain.'

Lesley wafts a hornet away with her straw hat. 'I don't know *why* that should surprise you. The fact that he felt pain. I told you about that time in Sri Lanka when I had a dreadful headache. Or did I? Maybe I didn't. Anyway, he appeared behind me, placed his hands over my eyes, and the pain disappeared.

She clicks her fingers.

'Just like that. I was so relieved. It never occurred to me to think where the pain had gone, but later on, I saw him sitting down, holding his head in both hands.'

'I asked one of his helpers what was wrong with him. He said poor Swami has a bad headache.'

'Oh yeah. I forgot. You did tell me that.'

'It's all very well having someone tell you the Kingdom of Heaven is within, and the way to it is through being selfless, but if that person doesn't know what it's like *to be* you, what value is there in what they say?'

'I guess. Yeah. If your child falls into a deep dark place, you can shout down from the top about climbing back into the light, but the best way is to go in after them. Lead them back up. Show them it can be done.'

'That's right,' Lesley says. She takes her hat off and takes a swipe at another hornet. Maybe it's the same one. If so, it might be addicted to nicotine because it had to fly through a cloud of smoke to reach her. She puts her straw hat back on and looks out beneath the rim, smiling at me. Her eyes are twinkling. 'Remember, I told you about the statue appearing in his hand and how he passed it to Mataji, and she tossed it to me. I had to keep tossing it from hand to hand so it didn't burn the palms of my hands. Cosmic fire, dear. *Spiritual* fire. From where else would sacred ash come? Of *course*, it hurts, but it doesn't stop him.'

'It'd stop me,' I mutter.

'Yes, that's why you're *you*, and he isn't.'

'I hadn't thought about what making vibhuti would feel like for him. If I had, I would have presumed it felt like some sort of bliss. I don't know. Cosmic indigestion, perhaps? A disturbance in the force like Obi-Wan Kenobi. But pain? No.'

'It's not quite like that, as far as I know. I don't think Swami's walking around making the vibhuti as such. It happens spontaneously through him. I'd say he's like a conduit for these miraculous events, so wholly surrendered to the Will of God there's nobody there to decide if he'll do it or not. Maybe like a weather vane with no unchanging direction of its own, though it exists as a thing in itself.'

I stand up. The rock has soaked up enough of the sun to begin burning the back of my legs.

'Part of me has given up questioning what Swami's capable of because it feels right, but then I think, hang on a minute, *that in itself* can't be right. Nobody can do what he does. There has to be something else going on. So I go from swallowing it whole to regurgitating what I've seen.'

'I was like that when I first met him,' Lesley says. 'But he proved himself so many times in so many ways that now, I accept him wholeheartedly. I think some things are taken and understood deep within, like when a baby drinks its mother's milk. The milk nourishes where it will and passes through where it won't. The body knows what it needs and accepts it. So maybe what's pure and good in us recognises the pure and the good in someone else.

'Simple as that, eh?'

'Maybe it is, though I think being sceptical isn't a bad thing either, considering what's at stake. But, on the other hand, being cynical refuses to allow for the possibility of the truth being found.'

'I guess.'

'Mataji told me Swami points to the sign which points to Trichy. He says you must follow the signs if you want to get there. Don't just point at them and be content with that. You must get up and go. It's the same with God. Or your spiritual nature. The *real* you if you like. There're signs all around, so you must follow them. Without the journey, a sign is nothing but a sign. It's not the thing itself. You have to follow those signs which lead to the truth, and then one day, your journey lead's you back to yourself.'

'Sounds like a lot of hard work,' I said. 'If the journey leads me back to myself, I think I'd much rather just wait here until I turn back up.'

We both laugh heartily.

Lesley jumps up as a wasp comes a little too close. She's waving her arms to ward it off, ducking, diving, and turning circles as it dances with her for a few seconds. It suddenly finds itself flying in the opposite direction as the concept of concussion is introduced by her straw hat. She regains her dignity by placing it back on her head and smoothing her Punjabi suit.

'I think this might not be the best place to wait until we turn up,' she says, looking a little flushed.

We leave the standing stones where hornets hum.

***

Nigger
Coon
Wog
Darkie
Nig-nog
Black bastard

These words stung and circled and stung and circled and stung and circled until I was poisoned. That poison expressed itself in my lack of empathy for the victims of the fire. It might seem like that poison was why I behaved in such a callous manner, but life would teach me that this wasn't the case. This poison gave my ego a reason for not showing empathy. It gave my ego power because it gave it an excuse to say my suffering was more significant than that of others.

I had a choice at that moment, and I took it.
I mattered.
They did not.
God forgive me

***

Swami Premananda's going to give individual blessings later on today. The entrance fee into the cubicle is three limes and one coconut, although if you don't have these, you can have the blessing anyway.

I'm surprised to see men and women queuing up in the same line.

'There goes the neighbourhood,' I say.

'Pardon?' says Lesley.

'Bi-queuing. It's the beginning of the end.'

'Oh,' she says.

Mataji's at the rear of the queue, which I guess is the end of the beginning. She's smiling at us. So we leave our place and go to join her.

'Why do we have to give coconuts?' I ask.

'It's a sacred fruit,' she replies, holding hers up appraisingly. The notepad under her arm starts to slip a little, but she clamps her elbow down to stop it. 'In Northern India particularly, it's considered one of *the* most sacred fruits. They call it -' she closes her eyes, thinking of the word - '*Sriphala*. It means the fruit of Sri. She's the Goddess of Prosperity.'

I hold mine up and shake the water inside. 'Well, who would have guessed the humble coconut was so well connected?'

'Yes. It's a symbol of fertility too.'

Having grown up watching the Benny Hill Show, I'm

not surprised.

'It's quite a good symbol of the human condition.'

I pointed at myself and said, 'You mean quite brown and hairy?'

'You're not hairy,' Lesley pointed out.

'True, but I am brown.'

'And nicely so.' Mataji said.

'Thank you.'

'You're welcome. Now, with a coconut, the hard shell represents man's ego. Only when it's broken can you see the purity of the soul within.'

'The ego of men? What about the ego of women?'

Lesley holds up the lime. ''the ego of women? That'll be what this is for, then.'

Mataji and Lesley chuckle. I roll my eyes. The line moves forward. Despite having avoided Swami several times over the past few days, I'm looking forward to seeing him now. The door up ahead leads to the room where I watched the vibhuti fall away from him. Even though I've been incredibly uncomfortable at the idea of being in his presence, I don't feel intimidated at all. Not now. No idea why. I pass through the door when my turn comes, smiling like a child. The scent of vibhuti is still in the air.

Swami is sitting in a little cubicle.

What is this I feel now? Bashful. Like the young boy, I was when Ma took me to see Father Christmas.

'Hi, Swami', I say. I offer the offering, which he takes, still smiling at me.

Great.

What do I do now? Damn. I've not thought this bit through.

'Eh—.' It was easier with Santa Claus. All I had to do was ask him for some toy soldiers, but somehow that doesn't seem appropriate at this moment.

I'm bowing, feeling awkward. As I lower my head, Swami reaches over and places his warm hand on it. I go down on my knees and feel the grit on the floor. Swami's hand is still on my head, and he speaks with his voice of honey and gravel.

'You no worry. I take care of.'

And then I'm up and out the other door, holding a sachet of vibhuti. I feel deeply blessed and highly amused. Lesley gives a smile which mirrors Swami's as I pass her. Then, she goes through the door.

***

I told myself 'the Oirish,' who treated my brothers and I with such disdain, were a shower of bog trotting, drunken, uncouth left-footed, fucked-up bigoted bastards.

On the other hand —

The Irish people I knew personally were kind and humorous, and they kept alive my faith in the kindness of human nature.

Two voices told me two different stories, pulling me this way and that.

Love and hate, truth and lies.

Two powerful emotions pulled me apart one minute and ground me together the next.

I had days when I'd see a gang of youths looking at me. I'd cross the road to walk through them, wanting them to say something. I was so keyed up with the expectation that they would I could scarcely breathe. I needed the release for the sake of my sanity but —

Nobody ever said anything when I was like this.

Nobody

Not ever

The stress of it, hour after hour, wore me down. Only when I'd weaken and begin to think not today. Just leave me in peace. Then I'd hear it:

Nigger.

Love is the only way. I always knew this, but hate was so seductive. It was an immediate source of energy. It burned brightly, not like the sun, but with the feverish light of phosphorus. It gave power to me in my powerlessness. I could look at some bastard and know if I let this anger go, that person would regret what they'd done. My power was not how I could change people but how I could hold back myself from hurting them. I held onto my anger as tightly as a rope over a chasm.

***

Lesley comes out crying. She's blowing her nose as she descends the steps of the Prayer Hall.

'What's wrong?' I ask, concerned.

She can't talk but takes my hand. We walk past Swamis koothi while big fat tears roll down her cheekbones. Splashing onto the dry earth.

'What is it?' I ask again.

'Swami said - ' she chokes back a sob.

'What? What did he say?'

I'm worried now. Swami once told Lesley she had a growth by sending a message through Adrienne in a dream. What's he told her now that can be this upsetting?

'He said — he — said,' Lesley breaks into a big sob.

We're passing a boulder. I sit her down and squat down on my haunches before her.

'Lesley, what did he say?' I'm squeezing her hand. 'Tell me.'

She takes a deep, shuddering breath.

'Swami said I have a very good heart and not to worry. He'll take care of me and never forget me.'

'Pardon?'

She sniffed. 'He said —'

'Yes. I heard. I'm just not sure which bit you're upset about. Is it the bit where he says he'll take care of you or the bit where he tells you you're a good person?'

Hearing it like this, she laughs, snuffles and blows her nose on a tissue, then takes another deep breath.

'That's just it,' she says. 'I'm not a good person.'

'Of course you are,' I say.

'I'm *not*! I get angry and petty and—'

'*Everyone* gets angry. *Everyone* can be petty. Don't concern yourself with that. You're the nicest person I know.'

'There's a difference between being nice and being good.'

'But you *are* a good person.'

'I don't *feel* like a good person!'

I'm relieved that's all she's worried about. I get up off my haunches and sit beside her. 'Well, maybe that's what *makes* you a good person. You don't take your own inherent goodness for granted. You keep trying to do the right thing. And anyway, it's a matter of degrees. Compared to some people, you're a saint. And to others, you're a complete sinner.'

She blasts her nose into the tissue again and stuffs it up her sleeve. 'I guess you're right.'

'Of course I am.' I hug her. She seems frail, taking shelter with her damp nose in the crook of my neck until she's ready to walk again. We continue along the path, following the smell of food wafting from the Dharamsala.

***

Having a faceless, amorphous mass to hate, like 'the Irish', helped direct my anger into the ether. Love the individual. Hate the herd. At least, that's what I told myself. But, like a secret alcoholic sipping the brandy out of a liqueur, I was fooling myself. Hatred of 'them' is an incubator in which hatred of the individual grows.

Eventually, something in me would break. Hatred of 'them' will pour out and coldly rush toward one young man. All I wanted was to be left alone, but he couldn't do that one simple thing. He couldn't leave me and my fragile dignity in peace because he wanted a cheap laugh. I say cheap, but that was only from his point of view because he assumed he wasn't the one who would be paying for it.

Where would he have been, I wonder, on the night all those people died in the fire on Valentine's night? Perhaps he was praying for the mothers and fathers who lost their children while I turned my face to the wall.

Who knows?

He won't know he's drawn the short straw when our paths cross. The barrel had turned on my patience for years, and the hammer had fallen on an empty chamber. But, when this lad calls me nigger, the chamber would not be empty.

There would be no click.

There would just be a —

***

Bang!

A sandal smashes an insect onto the tabletop.

Wait. Let's go back for a minute.

Lesley's sitting beside me, dabbing her mouth with a napkin. Our food this evening has been delicious. A little bit on the incendiary side, true, but still very satisfying. I notice something crawling across her back. It's got more legs than any creature could possibly need. It's horrific. The sort of thing only its mother could love and probably eat if my limited knowledge of insects is anything to go by.

I have several options. Get it off her, ignore it or hide under the table. Considering the meal I've just eaten, I can probably incinerate it by belching, but manners forbid this. I reach over. Flick it off Lesley's back. She doesn't even notice. If it hadn't landed on the arm of a woman further along the bench who screams and leaps up, shaking her arms to get it off, the incident would have passed without comment. The insect spins through the air and lands with the grace and precision of Nureyev, although the sudden smack of a sandal makes the insect less likely to consider top marks for style a bonus.

***

We take a pleasant stroll to where we caught the bus yesterday. Scrubby fields on either side kept us company along the way. Birds sing, and butterflies do whatever it is they do. A squat building just off the road is being painted canary yellow. It's a new local business hoping to open in a few days and will include a workshop for local gem cutters who can sell the products there. They've invited Swami to the official opening as the guest of honour. He's done a lot for the locals, providing free education and food when times were hard. He's also addressed some of their health concerns and given spiritual guidance.

We pass some horned cows that make guttural announcements from one end or the other along the road. Then, with bony knees rising and falling on either side of rickety wheels, people on bikes cycle by. Pistons of flesh and bone work up and down and carry them away.

Lesley wants to buy more cigarettes from the little shack, hence the visit. She takes more time today to look at the different brands. I stand and watch the slow flow of village life. Not much appears to happen, at least not on the surface. A few villagers are sitting in the shade, chatting. Raucous Tamil music rattles out of a radio somewhere down the road. I hear laughter and the clatters of pans and pans. The smell of cooking makes my tummy rumble.

Life feels good.

Little do I know that I'll shatter like a clay pot a few days from now.

***

The total of all the suffering in my life thus far was nothing compared to a single moment of grief the people involved in the Stardust fire had to endure. The moment I decided my suffering was more important than theirs, the moment I turned away from the natural empathy we have for each other, was when my ego licked its lips and looked in the mirror.

It liked what it saw.
And in the background, the sound of others weeping.
God forgive me.

***

I'm in a taxi, and I'm irritated. I wanted to be wide awake for the next abishekam. Swami Premananda was going to perform the ritual, but I took a nap to refresh myself and missed it. Of course, nobody was to blame but myself, but I felt irritated with Lesley for not reading my mind and waking me up in time. Unreasonable, I know.

So, I went for a walk to take the edge off my irritability, which is how I ended up in this taxi. It was parked outside the Prayer Hall, and I suddenly wanted to get in.

'How much to Trichy?' I asked the driver.

'Twenty rupees. Trichy,' he said, squinting up at me. The sun was at my back.

'Okay. Let's go.'

He leapt out of his car. Virtually jumped over the bonnet to open the passenger door before I could do it myself. He was pretty small, even for a Tamil and looked fortyish, with grey chin stubble and a neat little moustache. He invited me to enter the back of the taxi with a bit of head waggling. On his way back to the driver's side, I could see his shirt was stuck to his back with sweat.

We speed through the countryside. He's obviously a graduate of the Bonnie and Clyde School of Driving, but the speed suits my mood. I roll the window down, luxuriating in the rushing air and the green swathes of land we cut through. We only slow down to pass an oxen cart. The cowbell clunks beneath the loosely-skinned neck of the beast, whose only burden appears to be the driver having a nap on the back of the wagon.

I've got a small book called Vivekananda's *Pearls of Wisdom* tucked away into the folds of my dhoti. I was going to look at it during my walk, not knowing I'd end up in a taxi. It's digging into my hip, so I take it out and put it on the seat beside me. Soon we're in traffic and slicing through streets of low roofs and crumbling walls held together with the cliché of faded film posters. The car's gently swerving. I'm swaying gently. My seat is a warm harbour. A hammock in the sun. My eyelids are heavy with heat. The driver's talking. Something in English. No idea what he's going on about. I open one eye. He's looking at me expectantly in the rearview mirror.

What did he ask me?

No idea. It doesn't matter, whatever it is. Lazily, I nod and close my eyes.

The car lurches, abruptly turning off the main road.

What the — I sit up. This isn't the way to Trichy. Or is it? It's not the way the other drivers have taken us. In fact, I think this is the wrong way altogether.

'Trichy?' I say, jerking my thumb over my left shoulder.

He nods and flashes his teeth in a grin that would have been pleasant under other circumstances. Unfortunately, at this particular moment, it looks a little deranged. The paranoia I had at the airport concerning taxi drivers now returns with a vengeance. Am I being kidnapped?

No, wait.

That makes no sense. Why me? Catholic guilt aside, I *am* actually worthless. I don't work for the government unless you count my taxes. I can't divulge any national secrets. Most people already know our government are a bunch of corrupt, self-serving cunts, some of whom are war criminals. Still, there's always a good old-fashioned mugging to consider.

The driver turns to look at me. He's still smiling. Talking too. Something in Tamil? No idea. What on earth is he banging on about? Oh, — wait. I *think* he's trying to reassure me.

'That's very nice,' I say, 'but I'd rather you kept your eyes on the road, mate.' I'm pointing to the windscreen and jabbing. He turns his attention back to the driving, but he's waggling his head as if to say, 'Don't worry, I crash here all the time, and nobody's ever made a complaint.'

I sit up. My adrenaline is surging. What's going on here?

Oh, wait —

I suddenly understand some of his words. I presumed he spoke in Tamil with the odd English word thrown in, but he isn't. Instead, he's talking in *very* broken English. By broken, I mean pretty much smashed. Held together with nothing more than spit, gesticulations and teeth.

'Your buns?' I ask. Did he just say buns? Surely not.

He's chuckling. Nodding and blethering as if we're old

friends. His eyes meet mine in the mirror, and I *think* I detect a hint of anxiety. What on earth is he saying? Slowly, my ears are tuning in to his accent. If this continues, we can discuss various spiritual topics, such as 'slow down for the love of God' to 'Jesus Christ, please keep your eyes on the road.'

'Hospital?' I ask

'Yes, yes.'

'You need a hospital?' I say, hoping he doesn't mean a psychiatric one. 'Something about your — son?'

'Yes! Yes!' he says, and now he's babbling about his sons' eggs? I'm onto something here because he's getting quite excited. I stop him talking by waving my hands. 'Wait. You've got a son with a broken egg?'

From the way he's looking at me, that's very obviously wrong

'Broken — legs?'

'Yes! Son! Yes! Yes! Five minute. One trips. Two jobs.'

I sigh with relief and slump back into my seat. I smile at him and nod.

'Fair enough. Two jobs. One trip.'

On we go, deeper into the ragged fringes of Trichy. We're travelling a lot slower. I'm not sure if having the windows down is helping. The walls of the houses passing on either side of us seem to be bouncing the sun into the car. Washing hangs like white flags, surrendering to the heat. Children, barefoot and unafraid, watch us pass.

I think the conversation has exhausted us both. The driver puts on the radio. Up north, there's some trouble between Hindus and Muslims around Ayodhya. Traditionally, Ayodhya's regarded as the birthplace of Tama, a Hindu deity. Some Hindus claim the Muslim mosque, which stands on the site, was created from the original Hindu temple. Outbreaks of violence are reported.

We're blessed in England because religious dissent has mainly disappeared. There may be controversy over which biscuits the vicar likes with his tea, but for the most part, relations are usually harmonious between the various faiths. Of course, there are frequent querulous outbursts by people who think God would object to women being priests, but at least these people are no longer burning them as witches. They're not even allowed to toast them lightly, so it's all very civilised nowadays.

We stop in front of a small stone building. The windows, without glass, are little square pools of black set in a crumbling façade of yellow paint. Bits of rusty bikes have been neatly placed along one wall. A buckled wheel casts a web of shadow. A boy emerges from an open doorway with a dazzlingly white plaster cast on his left arm.

So much for the broken leg, then.

The driver is out of the car and opening my door for me. He's calling the boy over and introducing us.

'Hello,' the boy says. 'You are English?'

'Yes,' I reply, 'but I want to be an Indian.'

He laughs. He tells his father what I said, and his father is laughing too. He gestures toward a gate at the side of his house.

'Please,' he says. 'Please, come.'

I'm following him. Feeling wary again but smiling. I look around as if interested in my surroundings, which I am — but I'm also watching my back. The house backs onto a small rocky knoll where the air feels nice and cool. I see a little altar which the driver points at, speaking to the boy, who nods and then turns to me.

'This is the shrine of our family.'

Incense smoulders on the altar. Fresh flower petals are scattered on the top. I bow from the waist, my hands in an attitude of prayer. The driver looks on approvingly. He points to the top of the knoll. I look, shading my eyes from the sun.

'Muslim shrine,' he says.

Beyond some bushes, a cluster of small rocks has been neatly arranged.

The driver points again to his shrine.

'Hindu shrine,' he says. 'Muslims. Hindus. One God. No problem.'

We stand in silence. The incense from one place of veneration perfumes the air of the other.

On the hill, a goat bleats mournfully.

***

The boy's in the taxi with us. He sits in the front with his dad. When we get to Trichy, I buy some bread and biscuits. I also get three coconuts we drink sitting in the shade of a tree, comfortably silent, sucking the liquid through flimsy green straws.

We drop the boy off near the hospital. As the car pulls away, he turns to wave goodbye with his good arm. On the road back to the ashram, I remember the book I brought, so I give Vivekananda's *Pearls of Wisdom* to the man for his son.

Surrounded by fields, speeding through the furnace of the day, I see a plume of smoke rising in the distance. It gathers like a fist and grows enormous. Then, like the ghost of Babel, it reaches up into the sky. Black, malevolent, gathering brute strength.

***

The older I get, the more I think about that fire in Dublin.

The light of that funeral pyre was the light by which I saw my darkness.

God.

Forgive me.

***

'Sorry,' I say.

Lesley's a bit miffed.

'I spent ages looking for you,' she says. 'Why didn't you let me know? I would've come along.'

'It was on the spur of the moment. I saw the taxi and jumped in.'

The truth is, I'd gone because I'd missed the puja and was pissed off like a proper goon. I stand in the doorway of the koothi with biscuits in one hand and bread in the other as a peace offering.

'I got some bread,' I say, holding up the loaf.

'Any fruit?'

'Nope.'

'Shower gel?'

'Any of the other stuff we might've needed?'

'Eh — Biscuits?'

'I can't wash my hair with biscuits.'

Damn. I feel deflated. I toss the biscuits onto my camp bed. They roll off and land on the floor.

For fuck sake.

'I thought I was being kidnapped,' I say to change the subject.

'Oh? Well, you've come back, so what went wrong? I certainly wouldn't — I mean — didn't pay any ransom.'

'The driver wanted to give his son a lift to the hospital.

He took me to see his family shrine too. It was beside one for a Muslim family.'

'Have you heard about the trouble in Ayodhya?'

'A little. On the news in the car.'

'Around two thousand dead and injured.'

'Christ,' I mutter.

'Yeah. Awful.' Lesley sighs and comes and hugs me. 'I'm glad you're back.'

'Me too. I'll make you a brew.'

'Bring some biscuits, and we'll walk down to Babakka's. Then, I'll treat you to a coffee.'

Our walk to the café is interrupted by the sight of a man sitting in the bushes. He's got a pair of crutches which lay by his side. A small brown dog is snuffling in the grass a few feet away.

'Is he okay?' Lesley asks.

'Looks like he's just having a rest,' I say.

She observes him for a few seconds. When she's sure he's okay, we walk on, get a coffee, and sit on the wall.

A stick insect is sitting on Lesley's foot. I watch it, fascinated.

Nothing is as it seems.

She moves her foot.

The twig crawls away.

We're upside down.

The sun is below us.

Above us, the world sits on the soles of our sandals.

***

I've taken the time to shower in the yard to cool myself down. I've returned to the koothi, and Lesley's sleeping on her bed. Perspiration makes her dress cling to her body. I lie on my bed and imagine I'm back in the cold shower until I fall asleep.

***

The sun falls from the sky. The moon, like a messiah, pale and bloodless, has risen.

We've been asleep for ages. The sound of bhajans woke me up. Or maybe it was Lesley. She's padding across the floor barefoot, asking what time it is. She flicks the light switch, but no light comes on. Parts of Tamil Nadu are prone to power cuts. Or maybe the Ashram generator has packed in. In either case, we're left with the light of the moon.

I look at the time on my watch and whistle. 'We've slept for about four hours. The world's longest nap.'

'You're not kidding. We should go over and join in the bhajans. It'll wake us up.'

Over we go. We sit in the candlelight and sing devotional songs. We clap along until our palms are hot and sing until our throats dry. My belly feels empty. My heart feels full. We walk down the path to Babakka's, hoping for some noodle soup, but we're too late. By the light of a candle, we eat a bowl of rice and rasam in the quiet hubbub of the hut.

Now, here we are, sitting on the little wall outside the Ashram. Our small talk falls into silence. Some silences are awkward. They need to be covered like a hasty grave. This silence, though — this is one of the precious ones. Like the space between two thoughts, it's empty yet peaceful.

Lesley stands up. She hugs herself, smiling, gently rocking herself like a child. The gesture is natural and spontaneous, like smiling when the scent of a rose envelops you. She begins to turn slowly and opens her arms. Beneath the vast moon, she swirls like the Milky Way. The motion swells in my heart, catching me in this pure joy.

A harsh cough followed by the sound of a globulous gout of phlegm disturbs the moment. A man walks out of the darkness and spits again. One of his lungs — at least, that's what it sounds like — lands wetly on the road. He passes by without noticing us. He doesn't enter the Ashram. Instead, he continues walking past, off back into the night.

We laugh, bemused at having our moment stolen.

The lights on the Ashram come back on.

***

Sitting with the devotees in the Prayer Hall, we listen to Swami Premananda. No matter how profound this talk is, it can't hold my attention. I don't speak Tamil, for one thing. Even though we've been told it'll be repeated in English, I can't see the point in sitting and listening to what I don't understand. Of course, this assumes I'd understand what he was saying if he spoke English. I consider getting up and walking out, but this might be considered rude.

Eventually, I feel agitated, my impatience fizzing away like a fuse. The mind wanders off, sheep-like, grazing on the day's events. Then my body wanders off too. I get up and walk nonchalantly out of the door. I stroll beyond the sound of his peculiarly, roughly-smooth voice. I say to myself, Swami is above being insulted. Insult implies ego, and he has no ego. Therefore, I'm free to wander off and do my own thing.

'Uncle?'

I turn toward the voice of a child. Two small girls are standing, looking up at me.

'Uncle,' they say, pointing toward the Prayer Hall. 'Swami is speaking.'

They're looking at me as if, in my foolishness, I've just walked past a pot of gold.

My face colours. I feel somewhat chastised by these children as if I've been caught playing truant.

'Yes, I know. I'm - uh - I'll be back in a bit.'

So — now I'm walking as if I have some *very, very* important meeting to attend. I do this for the benefit of the children, who I'm sure are watching me with great disappointment in their big brown eyes. I would turn around and go straight back to the Satsang, but I don't want to look like an idiot. So, like an idiot, I circle the block, rapidly walking, sandals slapping my hot heels. I think that perhaps I *should* have stayed. Maybe Swami sent these children to send me back? W*as* it insulting to have walked out? No, of course not. As I've already said, Swami's above being offended, so I don't have to worry about hurting him. I can come and go as I please.

I walk back into the Prayer Hall. As soon as I sit down, Swami stands up and walks out.

I feel personally insulted.

***

Lesley thinks it's hilarious. We're walking back to the koothi, and I've just told her what happened. She's delightfully tickled. When I tell her how offended I am that he should walk out on me, she laughs so hard that it's no longer ladylike. She's doubled over, clutching her side and holding my arm.

'Oh, stop. I can't breathe,' she gasps.

'I'm glad it amuses you,' I say, waiting for her to regain her breath. I'm not sure why she finds it so funny. Finally, she dabs her eyes with a tissue to blot away the tears, and we resume our walk back to the koothi. After a minute or two, I see a vaguely familiar figure sitting off to the left in the grass. It's the man we saw earlier with crutches and a little dog. He's resting with his back up against a tree.

'Hey,' I say. 'Look. There's that man again.'

'Where?' Lesley asks, peering into the dark along the pathway. 'Oh, yes. I see him.'

His crutches are to one side of him, and his dog is on the other.

'We'll bring him some food,' Lesley says. 'I'll make something up in the koothi for him. You can bring it over.'

There isn't much in the koothi due to my ineffectual shopping spree earlier. I'd returned with biscuits, bread and an anecdote about a Muslim shrine.

Bon Appetit!

Lesley sends me back to the man with half a loaf and some biscuits, which he takes silently, nodding his acceptance. He seems content.

'What did he say?' Lesley asks when I return. She's tucked up in her bed.

'He didn't say anything. He just nodded.'

'Did he seem okay?'

'He's better off than me by half a packet of biscuits, so, on the whole, I'd say yes.'

'Good. Right. I'm going to read my book in bed. Are you going to sleep now?'

'No. I'm going to fill in my diary.'

'You're sure?'

'Yes. Why?'

'Well, if you *are* going to go to sleep, I won't read. So you can turn the light off now.'

'No. I'm going to write for a bit. I'll turn the light off before I go to sleep.'

'You're sure?'

'Yes.'

'Okay. It's just that I'm *really* comfy, and I don't want to have to get out to switch it off later.'

'Don't worry about it. I'll turn it off whenever you want.'

'Ok. Thank you.'

'No problem.'

I stretch out on my bed. I only wake when Lesley flicks the light switch. She's walking barefoot in the dark and chill air back to her warm bed. Before I drift off back to sleep, I hear her muttering.

Such language.

And from a lady, too.

It's enough to make a saint blush.

CHAPTER THIRTEEN
Howling At The Moon

The morning hasn't started particularly well. My hands are covered in mosquito bites. The cotton liner from my sleeping bag protects my body, hood, and face, but I have to hold it in place by gripping it with my hands. Hence, all these bites on my fingers and damnably itchy thumbs.

'Stop scratching,' Lesley says. 'You'll just make it worse.'
'It's hard not to.'
'I know, but try to ignore them. Take the rubbish bag down to the tip. It'll give you something else to think about. I'll have a cup of tea waiting for you when you return.'

I get dressed quickly and remember that I didn't turn the light off last night after saying I would.

Oops.

She doesn't seem to have remembered, so I won't mention it. I get the bin, a black plastic bag hanging from a nail in the yard. I tie it off and go back through the house.

Lesley's holding up her lighter.
'You'll need this.'
'For the tip?'

'Yes. Don't just dump the rubbish. Burn it. It keeps the scavengers and vermin down. I went with Mataji yesterday. There'll be paraffin or some other combustible there, but be careful.'

'Don't worry. I'll stand well back from the fire.'

'I didn't mean for *you* to be careful. I meant to be careful with my lighter. It's the only one I've got left.'

'Oh. Well — thank you for your concern.'

'It's nothing personal, sweetheart, but I can't have a cigarette with my tea if you lose the lighter.' She lobs it to me. I catch it and head for the door.

'Wait!' she says. I turn. She's looking thoughtful with a finger on her lips.

'I've just had a thought. If you go up in a puff of smoke, I can at least use your smouldering carcass to light my cigarette. So — I can stop worrying.'

A sweet smile brightens her face as she picks up the book she was reading last night, licks the tip of an elegant finger and uses it to turn a page.

'Oh — and thanks for switching the light off last night.'

'But I didn't — ahh. Right. Sorry.'

***

Humankind puts a lot of effort into activities by which it can avoid the void. The void had politely tapped me on the shoulder on Echlin Street and told me I was nothing and nobody. If the eyes are windows to the soul, what I knew as 'Paul' wasn't even a speck of dust on the glass. Not even a twitch of the curtains.

It was ridiculous.

Had I paid more attention to the thought than it took to digest a digestive, I'd have lost my mind.

All the more reason for burying it beneath the —

***

— Rubbish. Loads of it. Tons of the stuff. Standing by a large pit filled with smouldering piles of refuse, I marvel at how much there is. I dump my bundle onto the rubbish and look for the paraffin. Finding a rusty container nearby, I lift it and hear the contents sloshing around. I take a deep lungful — not a good idea because it makes me feel woozy. It certainly smells inflammable. If rust could talk, I'm sure it would tell me it ate the writing on the can years ago, but I'm pretty sure this will do the job.

Excitement quickens my blood. Fire fascinates. I kneel and pour some paraffin onto my bundle of rubbish. I'm a bit worried, to be honest. What if the fire I'm about to light gets out of control? My excitement turns to horror briefly as I imagine myself accidentally burning down the ashram.

I see the story unfold in my mind's eye. I see flames devouring the dry grass, the air shuddering with the heat.

I came to the ashram looking for God.

Now, God's looking for me, and he's rather annoyed.

And his beard is singed.

Yeah, I better be careful here. I put the can safely to one side. A piece of paper picked up from the scrubby grass and twisted tightly serves as a taper. I ignite this with Lesley's lighter and drop the taper on the rubbish bag. Nothing happens. Feck. I lean closer to pick it up —

'Whoosh'

I leap back from the flames.

My passport photo looks nothing like me as it is, even with my eyebrows intact. Losing them in a puff of smoke won't improve matters. I'd have to turn up at the airport with a pair of brown caterpillars glued to my forehead, hoping nobody notices the difference.

Fortunately, I'm unhurt from the smell of charred hair in my nostrils. I watch the fire, feeling immensely satisfied. Little tongues of flame lick their lips with relish as they devour the bag in which I'd brought the bread and buns back. A mongrel comes along, wagging his tail but not for me. Instead, he's following his nostrils, hoovering up the smells, savouring the sour, the sweet, the pungent and the acrid. Tracking his progress, my eyes discover a line of ants marching across my sandalled feet. They're tickling my toes with their movement by way of an apology. They carry all sorts of detritus aloft, away from the pit. There they go, past the warm and dry nose of the dog rooting in the grass, still sniffing and snorting.

I step back from the pit and take my sandals off. Shake them to get rid of the ants. The earth beneath my feet feels good. I walk towards our koothi until stones and bits of grit bite my tender soles. I put my sandals back on.

In my mind, images of Swami Premananda.

Ash billowed from his lips.

Falling from his hands

***

Some sweetness.

An aching bitterness.

The sourness of further disillusionment with the Irish.

These were the flavours of our experience on Echlin Street in the pungent embrace of the Brewery.

I remember sitting with Ma, Tony and Jason, watching the Late Late Show, hosted by Gay Byrne. Terry Wogan was the special guest, charming as ever with his paddy-whackery. He told a story, the punch line of which was ' —just don't come home with a black.'

The audience was in hysterics, but I was cut to the quick. It may have been they were laughing at the small-mindedness of people who were appalled at the idea of bringing a black person into the family, but to me, it was another slap in the face. I remembered sitting in Ken's house and being given a banana. I remembered the story of my dad being introduced to my granny and her speaking to him in pigeon English. Sprinkling him with holy water behind his back. I remembered monkey noises coming from the window of that school that we took Tony to. I remembered two old men on the church's steps laughing at my brother in his uniform. I remembered a lot of stuff while the audience laughed and wiped tears of laughter from their eyes.

It wasn't all bad, though, as I say. There was sweetness. We were a lot better off now. Tony was bringing in a wage. I even had pocket money with which I could buy books. I frequently had the company of my friend Ciaran. We'd walk the length and breadth of Phoenix Park, talking and finding much to laugh over.

Another friend from Ballymun came back into our lives. Kevin, who'd lived with his mother in the flat next door, turned up and asked Tony if he wanted to form a band. They asked me to sing and play bass, and the three of us subsequently did a lot of jammin' and battering the bejaysus out of other people's songs.

It felt good to be part of something, like being in the F.C.A. Even though I was by now excruciatingly self-conscious, I'd learned to live with it. The excoriating embarrassment of my existence was as close to me as my skin. I shed it whenever I forgot myself, but the claustrophobic chrysalis never enabled me to be born again. When I remembered myself, I was locked back inside the walls of myself. Something foreign in the middle of the Irish. Something not quite right in the middle of the herd.

Music became a way of losing myself. Listening was viscerally pleasurable, and I'd lose myself between the pulsing of the bass and the crack of a snare drum. There was space between the notes. Where many other people heard a wall of sound, I could slip between two violin strings as they vibrated in the ether. Even within my limited capacity, playing would sometimes fill me with a rush of explosive joy I could scarcely contain myself.

Becoming so thoroughly absorbed in whatever I was doing kept me intact, psychologically and emotionally. It was, perhaps, life's way of teaching me the troubles I thought I had, belonged to who I thought I was.

If there was nobody here, then to whom did these troubles belong?

They belonged to me, of course.
But who is this 'me?'
Well — now, there's a question.

***

Sitting on my bed, dabbing calamine lotion onto my mosquito bites, an excited young man appears in the doorway.

'Quickly!' he urges, 'Swami is performing a fire yagam. You must go now to the Prayer Hall if you want to see it.'

'What's a — ' I begin to say, but he's already dashed off. I can hear him relaying the same message to our neighbours.

Lesley, on her bed, has been fired up by this news. She drops the book she was reading and gets to her feet.

'What's a fire yagam?' I ask.

'It's wonderful,' she replies. 'I saw one years ago when Swami was in Wales. He sits around a huge fire, reciting prayers and chanting mantras. Then, he'll throw flower petals and incense into the flames, maybe even precious stones. It's been a long time, but I remember the atmosphere was electrified. You could feel this raw energy rising, and it went on and on through the night for hours.'

'It sounds amazing. What happens at the end?'

Lesley claps her hand together like a child in delight. 'At the end of the one I saw, he pulled a large golden statue from the ashes!'

I whistle and dump the calamine lotion on the bed. Considering how impressed I was with the bit of fire that burned up my empty bun bags, I'll be ecstatic during the fire yagam.

'Do you think my dhoti's clean enough to wear in the Prayer Hall?' I ask.

'No,' Lesley says. 'You smell like an arsonist. I can smell the paraffin over here.'

'Damn,' I mutter. 'Where's my clean stuff?'

'Try the washing line.'

I run out to the yard and grab a dhoti.

'Lesley, where's my — .'

A wadge of clean t-shirt softly smacks me in the face as I re-enter the koothi.

'Thanks,' I reply, gratefully if somewhat muffled.

'Please be quick. I'd like us to be near the front.'

'Maybe he'll materialise another statue!' I say, quite excited by the idea. I want Swami to reach into the ashes of my old self and pull the *real* me from the wreckage.

I'm ready.

We dash through the doorway, happily surfing on a warm surge of anticipation.

***

Picture this, if you will. An old carriage-style pram with a large, old mattress on top of that. Get someone to walk beside you while you push this contraption along a busy road. Next, add a hill with exposed cobbles and the occasional clunky drain cover. Now, make sure one of the wheels is slightly buckled. Just enough to disturb the delicate equilibrium so that the ends of the mattress on either side of the pram bounce up and down. From a distance, it looks like you're pushing a large, fat duck trying to fly in a fit of deranged optimism. Unfortunately, the hill is making it hard to control. It's getting faster, the wings are flobadobbing along, but the thing still isn't flying.

Swear a lot.

This was what it felt like trying to get our band off the ground. It's not surprising that Tony left, but it is a pity. He may have benefited from the experience. I met some of the most influential people in my life through Tony, who introduced me to playing an instrument. Music would eventually lead to the Ashram through my being introduced to Lesley through a musical connection.

Kevin and I carried on after Tony left. We tried to recruit a drummer. One lad seemed promising at first. He sat down at the kit and did a great drum solo. Kevin and I looked at each other with big smiles and plugged in our guitars. Unfortunately, the lad played the same drum solo no matter what Kevin and I played, so we had to sack him.

A few weeks later, we tried another drummer. On the rare occasion, he managed to start a song at the same time as we did, he'd usually end up finishing before us. It was as if he liked the end of some songs and wanted to listen to them without being distracted by actually playing the drums.

We concluded that all the good ones were already in bands, and we didn't have enough pulling power musically to get the one we needed. So we used a drum box that I programmed, thinking drummers would knock on our door once we were established. Of course, we'd only accept drummers who could knock in time and not injure themselves in the process.

Now, if you go back to the image of the mattress on the pram.

That was how we left Echlin Street. Ma had somehow managed to be allocated a house across the other side of the Liffey in a place called Montpelier Hill. I think our Aunt Teresa had something to do with it. Ma and I took the last of our furniture across Dublin on the pram. We didn't have enough furniture to warrant the hiring of a van. Tony was in the barracks, and Jason was in school, so it was down to Ma and me to do the moving. Ma balanced the stuff on the pram while I pushed. We looked like a cross between a circus act and a pair of refugees.

I remember the Gardai stopped us. I can't remember what the officer of the law said. Probably checking for a pilot's license.

Flobadoba

The sound of my future musical career

Oh — let me add a dog to the picture of the mattress on the pram. Not long before leaving Echlin Street, we got another puppy. I can't remember where we got him, but I do recall he didn't shit all over me, so he was already a vast improvement on the last one. Kim, we called him. He had beautiful eyes and long lashes. Ma didn't want to leave him in the new house alone in case he started pissing all over the place. So, he had to come with us while we moved the mattress. I had to tie his lead to the pram so he didn't run away. I wouldn't have blamed him if he had. One car, instead of honking at us, slowed down. The passenger called Ma over.

'Missus,' he said. 'I don't know what you paid for your camper van, but you were ripped off. Go and get your money back.'

***

We've been sitting in the Prayer Hall for ages, maybe two hundred devotees hoping to see a fire yagam. The surge of anticipation that brought me here has soured into irritation. I *hate* waiting – especially after being told to hurry up.

One of Swami's helpers appears and informs us, 'Guruji will be along later to perform the yagam.' So, I feel a little bit cheated. Devotees get to their feet, some stiffly after the long wait. They make their way over to the exit while Lesley and I look at some elaborate and colourful symbols drawn on the floor. These are part of the ritual. I have no idea what they mean, but I'm impressed with the detail and care lavished on them. When I look up, tiny swirls of light are moving like small shoals of fish before my eyes. These rapid pinpricks of brilliant light are not something new to me. I've seen them many times, but they're unusually vivid now. People describe these circles of light as *prana*, the vital force permeating everything. I don't know myself. Maybe it's my blood pressure.

With light rushing around my eyes, we're politely ushered out of the hall, and the doors are locked.

***

Ma opened the door of the new house. She let me in and then hurried off again toward Echlin Street. Jason was in school and too young to walk all this way on his own, so Ma had to pick him up. I dragged the mattress through the doorway and up the stairs. I put it in the back bedroom, pulling, pushing and punching it just for fun until it flopped onto the clean bare floorboards. I dropped down onto it, knackered after pushing the pram all the way from Echin Street. I lay for a while contemplating this move. It felt like an immense turn of the wheel to have started in Ballymun and ended up in a three-bedroom semi-detached house. We had a garden at the front and the makings of one at the back. We had central heating and, joy upon joy, an indoor toilet. No more sitting down in the loo with the uncomfortable feeling that I had a tarantula on my back. We even had a bath! So, no more washing in the sink or a tin tub in front of the fire.

Life felt great at that moment. I could scarcely believe how lucky we'd been. If anyone had told me that, within twelve months, I'd be laying there high on acid, I would have been shocked. But, on the other hand, if they said Tony and I would be climbing over our back wall in the middle of the night, intent on kicking the considerable crap out of a neighbouring family that was harassing us, I would have been disappointed but not that surprised.

Within a fortnight, I'd be within millimetres of having my throat cut in the middle of the street by a passing stranger.

***

Back to the Prayer Hall. Quick! Hurry! We get ourselves seated near the front. The symbols are still on the floor. I'm even more excited than before, but the longer we wait, the more agitated I get.

>The seconds grind away on the face of the clock.
>I get angrier.
>Fuse smouldering
>Oh dear

***

I left the house one morning to take Jason to school. A man in an oversized black grim reaper coat called us niggers. I put Jason behind me and rebuked the man, calling him a stupid bastard, making him angrier than he already was. He went for me, and in the ungainly scuffle, he pulled a knife. If a young man on a bicycle hadn't called out a warning, the blade would have punched through my jugular as the angry man swung at me.

Now that I'm thinking about this event, it occurs to me that the stranger didn't just save my life but also that of the nutcase with the knife. Maybe even Jason, too. The grim reaper walked off rapidly down the road, no harm done physically other than the little trickle of blood on my neck.

'Jaysus,' the stranger said, 'are y'all roight?'

'Yeah. Thanks for stopping.'

'Dat was fuckin' disgraceful.'

I shrugged. 'We get that kind of crap all the time. The verbal abuse, I mean. Not the knife. That was something new.'

The young man looked disgusted.

'Anyway,' I said. ' Thanks for stopping. You're the only person

ever to stop and help in any way. It means a lot.'

'Anytime,' he said. We shook hands, and he cycled off. I could feel myself shaking. I patted Jason on the shoulder to reassure him.

'Come on,' I said. 'We're going to be late.'

'I don't want to go,' he said.

'You have to,' I said. 'And anyway, we've come this far.'

Jason was quiet as we walked, but I talked a lot because my adrenaline was pumping. I was also trying to distract him, but it didn't work because when he finally did speak again, he asked, 'Why did that man do that?'

'He's mad,' I said. 'Don't worry about it. He's gone. And it was good that the other man stopped to help, wasn't it?.'

Sadly, he nodded.

Bitterly, I wondered, what does it take for us just to be left alone?

***

There'll be no yagam today. After all the waiting, it's been cancelled. After being extremely annoyed for a while, I've calmed down. These things happen, and who am I that the world has to move according to my timetable and not the other way around? Waiting with patience and grace is a trait I admire in people. The quiet acceptance of how things are is, I think, at the root of spiritual growth.

I'd like to think if ever I was in front of a firing squad, I'd have the presence of mind to forgive the executioners and fill my heart with love for one and all. But, given my vehement dislike of waiting, I suspect my last thought would be this.

For God's sake, pull the f—

I've got my camera with me so I can take some photographs for my diary. Having eaten at the dharmasala earlier, Lesley's having a nap, so I walk around the Ashram alone. Slowly meandering, happily wandering, enjoying the peace, I feel blessed. Over there — there's a bird in silhouette beneath the banana leaf roof of an open-sided hut. It's perched on the handlebars of an old motorbike. I take this picture, drawn to the sharp contrast between light and dark.

Like a man with a hidden knife and a stranger on a bike.

Life and death.

Back in the koothi, I lay on my bed, the blades from the fan turning. Warm air wafts onto our hot, clammy foreheads.

***

We wake at much the same time, a little bit dizzy, saturated with sleep. The room is pleasantly cool, and it feels like a pleasant evening. We step out onto the veranda and find an old man perched on the wooden rail. He's got a well-worn walking stick propped against his left leg. We've seen him before in the ashram. I don't know his real name, but he's known as Tata. Tata renounced worldly life to concentrate on his spiritual unfoldment. He walks around the Ashram, tapping the ground beside his feet with the walking stick. It sounds like a slow metronome. If you hear the metronome stop outside your door, he's probably hungry. So, devotees offer him a little food out of respect and hospitality.

Lesley greets him with the warmth and deference to which he's accustomed.

'Paul, would you go and get some food for Tata?' Lesley asks.

I root around in the fridge. There's bugger all in it. Some fruit and the few biscuits left after Lesley gave away a load to the last old man with a walking stick she came across. I've hardly had any, so I'm *not* giving away the last of my biscuits. Besides, he doesn't appear to have any teeth. I take up a small, sweet banana and some grapes. I hand them over to him and back away with what I feel is a show of deference. It probably looks like I'm being obsequious and hoping for a tip.

Tata's peeling the banana, popping the top of it into his mouth, gums working on it. A second or two passes before — he stops chewing — he frowns and —

Ptooey!

He spits the banana into the bushes and looks at the rest as if the poor thing had bitten *him*. It, too, is tossed into the bushes. How very rude. He puts a grape in his mouth and —

Ptoo!

It lands on the banana mush.

I'm not sure what etiquette demands by this point. I'm looking from Tata to Lesley and back again, hoping for a clue. Perhaps it's some tradition, like throwing salt over one's shoulder? Should I get a banana and drop-kick it over the Prayer Hall?

Lesley whispers, 'I think it's too cold for his gums.' She goes inside and comes out with my biscuits — for crying out loud! Why don't I just drop-kick *them* into the bushes so *everyone* can have some?

Tata accepts the offering with a nod and tucks them into a fold of his dhoti. He's not even bloody eating them! Tatu reaches out to Lesley, who takes his hand to steady him. Strong, sinewy muscles flex on his thin arms as he pushes himself up with his walking stick. I still have my camera, so I hold it up to take a picture. He nods. Lesley smiles at him as if he's the one being blessed. His stick stands like another thin leg by his side.

He waves a casual blessing and slowly sets off down the path.

Tock — Tock — Tock — goes his stick
Bare brown feet pad quietly along beside it.

***

***

The back garden of our home in Montpelier Hill abutted against the others on our block. All the yards had a clear view of all the others. The neighbours on either side of us were very nice people. There was, however, a family who moved in behind us and off to the side. For some reason, they threw their rubbish into our garden. Small stones randomly smacked against the window. We suspected it was them but had no proof until Ma spotted the kids throwing bottles into the garden. She went around and had a word with the woman of the house. Can't remember what happened when she did, but the harassment continued. Tony built a wall to discourage them, but this just seemed to encourage them. My solution to the problem was relatively simple.

'Let's go round and batter the fuck out of them,' I urged.

Ma wouldn't hear of it. She said, 'I don't want you and Tony getting into fights, d'ye hear me? I won't be having the police at my door.'

That was that. We did what Ma said. Until one evening, a bag of rubbish, rank with nappies and rotting food, came over the wall. We heard laughing on the other side. I said to Tony, 'We have to stop this, or it'll just get worse.'

Tony, not much for talking, said, 'Okay. We'll go later.'

It got late. Past midnight I think. I know there was no moon. It was black as sin.

We wanted all the people in that house to be asleep. They were drinkers and possibly druggies and very often had a lot of people inside, so I figured the best thing to do was go through the house violently and quickly. There were children in the house too, which was a complication, but in my anger, I dismissed them. The people in that house were trying to bully us, so fuck them. I wasn't going to put up with being harassed.

Tony and I didn't tell Ma what we were going to do. We just got up, opened the back door and stepped out.

'Where're you going?' Ma asked, suspicious.

'To sort the neighbours out,' I said.

Ma leapt up and barged through the door, and stood before us.

'No, you're not!' she said fiercely. 'You're not getting into trouble —'

We walked past her, heading for the wall.

Ma started praying, 'Holy Mary, mudder of Jaysus.'

Tony leapt over the wall, which was head height. I landed beside him an instant later and ran for the back door, which we knew was always left open, but — the damned thing was shut and locked. I was stumped. I'd not thought this bit through. Then, like a sack of potatoes being lobbed off a wall, a heavy thud behind us made us jump. Ma had somehow managed to get over the fence. She was too small and too heavy, but there she was.

'What are you doing? I whispered harshly. 'Get back over the wall.'

She ignored me, picking herself up from the ground and dusting the dirt off her cardigan.

'What's happening?' she asked.

'Shhhh!' I urged. 'We want the advantage of surprise.' I then pound on the door with my fists, contradicting myself in the loudest manner possible short of setting off a foghorn. Not to be outdone, Tony smashed his fist through the window, and the house erupted in shouts, screams, and curses.

Oh — Shite!

We turned and grabbed Ma, bundling her over the wall. She landed with a thud on the other side.

***

From where we stand, we can see Swami in the distance. He walks the ashram grounds every day, ensuring things are running smoothly. He gives advice here and there or perhaps even a rebuke when necessary. We're on our way back to the koothi.

I stop.

'You go back,' I say. 'I want to watch Swami for a while.'

'Okay,' she says. 'You should go over and say hello.'

'Nah. I'd rather keep my distance.'

I follow discreetly. He's easy to see with his red robe and bushy hair. Saying that — he also disappears easily too. He goes behind a building and doesn't reappear. Damn it. I increase my pace a little. He'll come out the other side in a second. Or will he? Maybe not. Where's he gone? I'm fearful of losing him, but at the same time, I'm wary of getting too close. Ah — there he is, examining the ground where foundations have been laid for more building work. He's about thirty feet away from me, which is as close as I want to get. I stand by a series of square pillars, each about waist height, with a fragrant froth of wildflowers spilling from the top. I lean back on one of these to observe.

A desperate need to speak to him rises. But, though it's compelling, I can't move. All I can do is stare.

My heart is pounding.

A fist on the door in the dead of night.

Go to him.

But — no.

Ego demures.

Let *him* come to me.

Why should *I* risk rejection?

Swami looks up at me, impassive, observing. My face pulls itself into a smile, but it's hollow. Empty. No wonder Swami doesn't return this smile that isn't a smile. He stands watching me.

My feet are nailed to the ground. Fear of rejection. Fear of looking foolish. I am mute and immobile.

All I want now from him is a smile. Just something to say, he thinks I'm a nice person. Trying to do my best.

Swami walks away.

It's utterly devastating.

***

We dropped down beside Ma and picked her up.

'Jaysus Christ and all the saints! Get in the house!' she urged. Kim was barking. Other dogs were barking too, and lights were coming on in the back windows of the other houses. Standing in the doorway and looking bewildered, Jason asked us 'what's going on?'

Ma bundled him and us back into the house.

'Turn the lights off,' she said. 'Jaysus. I can't believe we just did that. What's the world coming to?'

Tony and I are buzzing off the adrenaline and laughing at Ma getting over the wall.

'Put the kettle on,' she said. 'Tony, give me one of your cigarettes, will you? My poor heart is in my mouth. God almighty.' She sat down on the sofa and put her hand to her head.

I went to the back door to see if the bastards had followed us over the wall. They hadn't, but we'd stirred up a hornet's nest. I could hear them swearing, and all the lights were on.

'Tony, keep an eye on the back here for us.'

'Where are you going?' he asked.

'To make sure they're not coming round the front. No idea how many were in that house.'

Tony reached behind the sofa and pulled out a golf club someone had passed on to him. I went to the front of the house and, to my horror, saw flashing blue lights pull up outside. Oh — shit! Ma must have seen them too because she shouted for us all to get into our beds. We ran upstairs and dived under the covers. The knock on the door, when it came, sounded ominous. We heard a Gardai talking to Ma. It was hard to understand, but the sound of a man's boots on the stair wasn't. They were coming up to check — or arrest us. Christ. I rolled onto my side in my bed and covered most of my face. When the light came on, I turned, squinting and asked, 'What's going on?' I'm sure there was some alarm in my voice because I certainly felt it.

'Well, now,' the Garda said. He was a big fellah. Middle-aged. Old for a policeman. 'One of your neighbours reported a disturbance, and we're just checking it wasn't anything to do with yourself, was it?'

'No,' I said, blushing.

'That's good,' he said. 'D'ye see the t'ing is. We're swamped tonight, and if someone was to report an incident, shall we say, in which a family of alleged scumbags, who are known to the Gardai, were to be given a bit of a batterin' —well then — I have to say, with regret, mind you — that there'd be a considerable delay in our responding to the call to render assistance to said scumbags in their hour of need. D'ye follow me?'

'Ehh, yes. I think so. Yes.'

'Good. I'll bid ye goodnight then. I can only apologise for interrupting your beauty sleep.' He turned to go, reaching for the light switch, but he paused and turned to me.

'One last t'ing,' he said. 'next time — if there is a next time — and I'm not sayin' there should be, take your shoes off before ye get into bed.'

I looked down to where my shoes were poking out of the end of the sheets.

He switched off the light. I let my head fall back on the pillow and listened to him descend and leave. I gave it a few minutes, then got up and went to the landing. Tony and Jason were up too.

'Did you hear what he said?'

Tony nodded.

'Let's get them,' I said, launching myself back down the stairs.

Ma was waiting at the bottom, blocking us.

'Where d'ye think you're going?' she asked, arms folded across her chest.

'To finish the job,' I said.

'You're not. That's enough. I'll sort this out tomorrow. You leave it to me. There's no need for all this unpleasantness.'

'Ma,' I said. 'Move out of the way.'

She looked me up and down and shook her head as if she couldn't believe what she saw. She addressed Tony and Jason over my shoulder. 'Would you listen to him? Just because he's up past twelve, he thinks he's Batman.'

I felt somewhat deflated.

'Ma, the Gardai more or less said they wouldn't be in a hurry to get here if we went around and sorted them out.'

Ma sneered. She actually sneered at me.

'Don't be such a gobshite. If that family's known to the Gardai and the Gardai can't sort them out, what makes you think you can?'

She had a point.

'Now come down, all of you. Tony, go and make sure the back door's locked. I'll put the kettle on.'

That was that. The night was over. I went into the front room and looked out the window, feeling drained. Jason came in, exasperated and almost shouted, 'What's going on? Why did you jump over that wall? Why were the police here?'

As I turned to answer him, I caught a glimpse of something outside. I leaned in closer to the window and saw one of the 'scumbags' to use the semi-official police vernacular, standing outside the front door with what looked like a weapon in his hand. His hand was raised above his head, waiting on one of us to appear. Of course, that would have been me if I'd gone out.

'Get Tony,' I whispered, putting my finger to my lips. 'Be quiet.'

Tony came through. I pointed at the lad hiding by the door with his back to the window and quietly spoke.

'Open the window when I say. Okay?'

He nodded. I went to the front door, took a deep breath and said, 'Now.'

Tony turned the latch and began opening the window, shouting.

I pulled the door open and ran out to get the bastard, but the lad was already running off out the gate. He turned for a second and made a wild throw in my direction. I ducked down as a bottle smashed off the wall behind me.

I didn't catch up with him. Just how serious all this was suddenly hit me. I felt weary, and the idea of fighting in the dark now struck me as a bad idea. I was, after all, wearing glasses, and without them, I'd be at a severe disadvantage. I walked back to the house and stooped to pick up the neck of the bottle. The jagged edges were wickedly sharp.

Tomorrow, that bastard would be mine.

***

I'm alone.

Sitting on a rock crying.

I'm so upset that I couldn't walk over to Swami and that he, in turn, walked away from me.

But something silent and still and peaceful is observing this drama.

It sees my ego and how it sets the terms for how I give or receive love. If the terms and conditions aren't met, my ego will have me do without the love I need and deny it to others. Even though this love given or taken under a condition is more of a commodity, a poor imitation of love, my mind uses it to weave stories about my worth.

Homeless tears roll down my face and fall on the rock.

Ego stands at the door.

I look up into the darkening sky. The fallen sun, a saffron hue on the horizon, blushes. Lifetimes away, other suns are long dead. The memory of them is just a flickering light. Yet, fool that I am, I speak to them.

I ask, 'How much longer must I live like this?'

My back curves over my soft belly. My shoulders are

shaking. I'm broken and folded over and sobbing. My dignity dissolves into snot and dribble. I feel wretched. I'm *so* sick of being scared. I could howl at the moon in my misery. Looking up through my veil of tears, I see it behind a cloud shaped like a wolf's head with its muzzle raised.

Silently it howls above me.

Oh great — a cloud is mocking me. Life is *actually* taking the piss out of me while I'm having a breakdown. It's not even doing it behind my back. It's up there in the fucking sky. I must be a mess if even God is mocking me.

I burst out laughing at how ridiculous this feels and try to get myself together enough, so I can take a photo. A long, deep shuddering breath does it. I wipe my rheumy eyes, blow my nose and take the shot.

I sit awhile, breathing deeply. My sense of isolation is intense despite the distant sound of devotional songs. Like the other night, warm light from the windows of the Prayer Hall is beckoning. The steps leading to the open doors are suffused with it. I get up from the rock. God knows how long I've been sitting, but my throat, heart and arse ache.

I walk over toward the light, drawn like a moth. The ashram flag with love, truth, wisdom, purity and devotion catches the wind. The words flutter above the Prayer Hall in the fragrant air. I see it and turn away because I'm none of those things. I can't enter the Prayer Hall. I walk by and find I'm standing on the ground where Swami Premananda collapsed on the night when the vibhuti poured from his skin.

So, I'm sobbing my heart out.

Again.

Voices come out of the night. I feel ashamed. I cover my face, quickly wiping my eyes. Shadows move past. Other shadows shifted within me, half-remembered, hurtful things forgotten until now. The act of being remorselessly ground down by life in Ireland. Enduring my particular purgatory. Each day a compromise. Each night another nail in the lid. Self-respect slipping and then ripping away like a fingernail. I recall the dread of stepping outside in a place where I wasn't wanted. I was desperate to join the game of life, but like a counterfeit coin, I rolled back out of the slot each time.

Remembering —

So many things I thought I'd forgotten.

A better man would pray to God, but I'm not that man.

I accuse God with bitter words that ache in my throat as I spit them out.

'All you *ever* seem to do is break me. When are you going to put me back together again?'

I feel so wounded in the depths of myself that I don't know what to do with this pain. Up into the sky, through my tears, I whimper. A whipped dog whining to the infinite emptiness of nothing and nobody.

'What the fuck is wrong with you?' I ask God. 'Can't you see I'm *already* broken? Ireland got there before you ever did, you son of a bitch.'

Thunder rumbles like a freight train in the distance.

Moving away from me

Desolate

CHAPTER FOURTEEN

On The Other Side Of The Glass Where There Is No Me

'**Oh** shit!'

I sit up in bed, hands over my throbbing nose.

'What! What is it?' Lesley jumps from her bed, her sleeping bag slipping down her legs. She grabs it. 'What's the matter?'

I'm looking at her over the two red orbs where my hands should be. Her eyes are wide as saucers.

'Sorry, but I just punched myself in the face.'

She's looking back at me, her mouth open, not knowing what to say for a moment. Then, finally, her befuddled, sleep-sodden brain deciphers what I've said, and she slumps back on her bed, hand on her chest.

'You frightened the life out of me. I thought — actually, never mind what I thought. I've got two questions. First, *why* are you wearing boxing gloves in bed?'

'I put them on to protect my hands. I had all those bites when I woke up yesterday. I thought these would save me from the mosquitoes, but I forgot I was wearing them. So I tried rubbing my nose.'

Tucking the gloves under my arms, I pull them off. My hands are hot and itchy. They smell musty.

Lesley shakes her head slowly, tutting.

'How have you managed to get this far in life without losing at least one limb?' she asks.

'It could have been worse. Normally when I wake, I scratch my balls.'

After a long exasperated sigh, she rolls over and pulls her pillow over her head.

'You had a second question?' I ask.

Her voice is muffled, weary. 'I *was* going to ask why you punched yourself, but after hearing your explanation, I feel like punching you myself. Now, *please* be quiet. I'm going back to sleep. And you should too. It's too early to get up.'

***

The morning after our troublesome neighbours had called the police on us, I lay awake on my bed for the longest time. Too tired to get up, too tense to sleep, I recalled the night as if it were a bad dream. I felt sick as if what had happened had gone cold and curled in the pit of my stomach. Half expecting an attack of some sort in the night, I'd slept in my clothes. I needed a shower to wash the night away, but taking my clothes off was out of the question. It would have left me feeling too vulnerable.

I'd already decided that the only way to end this bullshit was to bring the violence to their door, hoping it would keep it from ours. Ma had tried to stop them from hassling us by having a polite word with the head of the household, but they took this as a sign of weakness. So now the situation was escalating, turning violent. I was going to go and lay into whoever was in that house. I wasn't the type to stand in the street shouting, and besides, the last time I tried yelling at someone to make them back off, I nearly had my throat cut. Our neighbours also seemed too stupid to understand that just because a dog won't bark doesn't mean it won't bite.

I heard the latch being taken off the front door, and I tensed, breath held and heart rushing. It was Aunt Teresa coming to support Ma. Their low intense whispers filtered up the stairwell. I looked at my watch, holding it close to my face to see. It was just past eight o'clock. Reaching under the bed, I retrieved my glasses and stood up. Undid the strap of my wristwatch. Put it on the windowsill and wished I could dispense with my spectacles just as easily. But, glasses or not, I was going to sort this thing out on this day. All I needed was for Ma and Teresa to move away from the bottom of the stairs.

I didn't want to talk to them. Didn't want to speak to anyone who would be kind and civil. The last thing I needed in my heart was kindness and civility because such simple decency would weaken my resolve. I wasn't violent by nature, but there seemed to be no other way to neutralise the hostility toward us that morning.

Ma raised her voice just a little, enough to reveal the ragged edges of her agitation. She was wound up tighter than I was.

I heard her say, 'Teresa, get out of the way. I'm going round there now while the boys are still asleep.'

Aunt Teresa was saying, 'Calm down. I'm sure it'll be fine —.'

'Teresa. Move, or I'll go through you.'

I pulled my shoes on, remembering the glass outside the door, and took the stairs two at a time, but Ma was gone. The front door was open. Teresa was standing in the hall, blessing herself.

'Mother of Jaysus!' she cried. 'Paul, she's going round to that house. She'll feckin batter that bitch —.'

I was past Teresa before she could finish.

'What're you doing, Ma?' I said, getting in front so I could speak to her. She moved me aside without breaking her stride.

'I'm going to have a word. Don't get involved.'

I walked beside her, trying to talk sense. 'You go back. I'll sort this out.'

She ignored me. We turned the corner. The matriarch of the other family was standing in their unkempt garden.

'Come here you, ye' dirty whores mouth of a —.'

The hard-faced, hard-drinking woman came toward Ma, foul language spilling from the gaps between her teeth. She was expecting a slanging match, but Ma grabbed her by the hair and started swinging her around. The other woman started howling. Fear, pain and outrage. The door of her house opened. I leapt over the garden rail and ran at it. The lads inside saw me and slammed it shut. So much for blood being thicker than water. Behind me, their mother was screaming.

I turned and saw Aunt Teresa hopping on one foot. She was trying to take one of her shoes off and was shouting.

'Dolores! Let her go! Jaysus!'

But Ma was in no mood for clemency. She was dragging the other woman out of the garden by two fistfuls of hair. Seeing it was awful, but it turned farcical when Teresa threw a shoe. It bounced off Ma's head, making her yowl. One hand went to where she'd been hit. The other held onto the woman who had so enraged her. Ma was pulling her out into the road.

I pulled her away from Ma and threw the wretch back into the garden her family used for empty beer bottles and rubbish. She was wailing and banging frantically at her door. It opened. She fell in, and the door was slammed shut.

Hysterical laughter. Teresa was doubled over at what she'd done with her shoe. I picked it up and took Ma by the arm, leading her away.

'Who hit me with that feckin' shoe?'

'Oh God, I'm sorry,' Teresa said, ' I was aiming for that cow.'

Ma yanked her arm out of my grasp. 'And why did you grab that bitch away from me?'

'Because I think you made your point,' I said.

Tony and Jason were walking toward us, still in pyjamas and barefoot. I winced, remembering the broken glass from last night. Ma had been out on her hands and knees early that morning, sweeping the broken glass away from our door. It turned out she'd been awake all night, determined her boys wouldn't be involved in any more unpleasantness.

Bless her

***

Lesley's in the backyard, sloshing buckets of water over herself in place of a shower. I've just put the kettle on to boil. By the time she returns, I'll have two mugs of tea ready. In the meantime, I sit on my bed, thinking how much better I feel. I see myself sitting on that rock last night on the outskirts of the Ashram. It's almost like the emotional upheaval belongs to somebody else in a place far from here.

Lesley comes into the room. Her damp hair looks black against the pale Punjabi suit.

'Good morning,' she says, smiling.

'Morning,' I say.

She sits on her bed, facing me.

'You were very upset last night when you came in,' she says. 'Are you feeling — what's wrong with your nose? It looks very red.'

'I punched myself with the boxing glove this morning.'

'Oh yeah. That's right. I forgot. Sorry, I was a bit grumpy with you.'

'That's alright.'

'Are you feeling any better?'

'Yeah. Loads.'

'You want to talk about it?"

'No. I'm done with it now.'

The kettle politely bubbles to a boil in the background. I get up, make the tea and put Lesley's cup on a little table beside her.

'I didn't ask why you were so upset last night,' she says. 'I thought it best not to intrude.'

I sit down beside her.

'Thanks. It would have been like trying to talk about falling into a hole while plummeting past.'

She nods and pats me on the knee. 'Poor you. I was surprised when you came back and looked so forlorn because I thought you were going to speak to Swami.'

'No. I didn't speak to him. I followed from a distance.'

'His presence intimidates you?'

'Yeah. It's confusing because I'm drawn to Swami, but at the same time, I'm too scared to approach him.'

'Did he say something to upset you?'

I snorted. 'No, he didn't say anything. He just looked at me. That's all. He looked at me, and I fell to pieces.'

'But why? Why didn't you go to him? I'm sure he would have made you feel better.'

'I couldn't. I wanted to but —'

I can see myself, stuck at that moment yesterday, staring at Swami Premananda. Held hostage by the fear of rejection. Unwilling to pay the ransom of humility. But who, I wonder, was holding who hostage? I couldn't have been doing that to myself, could I? Was I two people at that moment pulling in two different directions? How can that be? Am I that which pulls to the left or the right? Am I that which moves toward or away? Which of these contradictions am I?

There has to be some point within this movement, emotion or madness when I can say *this is me*.

Surely I can't be this divided thing?

Lesley breaks into my thinking, pulling me away from those thoughts.

'But what —?' she asks.

'I stood and stared at him, unable to move.'

She doesn't say anything. Instead, she watches me, searching my face with her kind eyes.

I sip my tea.

Eventually, she says, 'Maybe he's mirroring you. You didn't go to him, so he didn't go to you. He might be showing you something about yourself.'

'You might be right. He was looking at me the way I was looking at him.'

'And how was that?'

'From a distance. That incredible Love he sometimes emanates wasn't there. At least, I didn't feel it. He was quite cold. Just looked back at me without a smile or anything.'

'You've still not explained why you didn't just go over and speak to him?'

'I couldn't risk him rejecting me. I couldn't allow myself to feel that vulnerable. I was afraid, which is, in itself, very disturbing. It means something, which I guess is my ego, had more control over me than I do. The ego isn't always present because it comes and goes, so it can't be me, can it? If the ego isn't me, I'm presumably the owner of the ego. In which case, why has it got more control over me than I have over it? If the tail is wagging the dog, power lies with the arse and not the head. That can't be right, can it? Who am I in all this? Am I the head or —?'

'—the arse,' Lesley says. ' Definitely.'

We laugh, and it feels good.

'I tell you, Lesley, all I wanted from Swami yesterday was a smile. A wave. Something to let me know I'm not a bad person, but what did I get? Nothing.'

'If you ask me, you got more than a smile. You got to see and be acutely aware of how you and your ego have different agendas.'

My ego?

Who is this *me* who supposedly owns this ego?
I still don't know.
'You'll have to go,' I say to my ego.
'Sure,' it says, holding the door open.
'After you —'

***

After Ma demonstrated why throwing bottles at her family was a bad idea, we had no more trouble with the people at the back of our house.

Things began looking up in many respects. We seemed to have less hassle when walking around the streets in Dublin. Of course, it was around this period when I almost had my throat sliced open, but that didn't happen every day, and on the plus side, someone had stopped to lend assistance. That was the only time anyone ever did, but the fact that someone had, meant a lot.

I even got a job working with Ciaran, who was working in a factory by then. He put my name forward when they needed another employee, and I got the job. I'd given up on the idea of anyone seeing past my skin far enough to employ me, so I was taken aback at this turn of events. Even though I was excited by the prospect of bringing a wage into the house, the idea of having to get a bus every day during rush hour filled me with anxiety. Ciaran, the good friend he was, solved the problem by offering me his bicycle.

I was immensely proud and felt like I was following in Tony's footsteps. He'd worked in a factory when he was younger because Ma wouldn't put him into a school where the children shouted 'nigger' as soon as we entered the gate. He was thirteen and a valued employee. I was eighteen and would have been valuable, too, had anyone been able to find something I was good at.

On my first morning, a lanky lad called Dermot, who scowled at everyone from beneath a mop of blonde hair, was asked to show me the ropes. He took me to his workbench and pointed to a selection of tools.

'Roight,' he said, 'have yever used a drill?'

I had, but only as a doorstop to stop it from slamming.

'Yes,' I replied confidently. How hard could this be? Dermot put a plank of wood on the worktop.

'Hold that with one hand and drill a hole in it.'

I did what he asked, and to be fair, the hole was very neat. If the hole hadn't been in my hand, I would have been asked to drill another one. The blood didn't start flowing immediately, as if even my blood was amazed at my incompetence. However, it soon remembered what it was supposed to do and began to well up out of the wound.

'Jaysus. I meant for ye put a hole in the wood.'

He took the drill off me and sent me to the office. Luckily all it required was a plaster. The hole was between the thumb and forefinger and hadn't gone too deep. The foreman, known to everyone as Jimbo looked worried. I'd only been in the building ten minutes, and already I had a new hole in my body. He had good reason to be concerned. Whenever I picked up a drill, it became potential evidence in a coroner's court. Jimbo kept trying me at different jobs during the day, but ultimately, he decided it wasn't worth the effort. He gave me a sweeping brush and told me not to break it. Then he stormed off, muttering something about my having read 'How To Be A Labourer by Hari Kari.'

Midway through my first day, Jimbo came out of the office and beckoned me over. He wanted me to get something from the storeroom. I listened with the intensity of a lip reader, not wanting to make a mess of this new task.

He paused mid-sentence before asking, 'What're ye' doin'?'

'Eh?'

'Your nose. It keeps twitching,'

'It does?'

'What are ye? Some kind of feckin' rabbit?'

I hadn't been aware of the twitching until it was pointed out. My nostrils were twitching. I broke out into a cold sweat.

'Sorry,' I said. 'Itchy nose.'

'Well, scratch it then.'

I scratched, and he resumed talking. I barely took any of it in because my nose was still twitching. Oh, God. I'd been worried for days that my skin would make me an object of ridicule. It never occurred to me my nostrils would want to get in on the act. As soon as Jimbo finished talking, I ducked out into the corridor and went to the Men's Room, where I stood before the cracked mirror, hands grasping the lip of the sink, looking at my nostrils in despair. They were perfectly still, but who knew when they'd resume their dance again? I let my head sink onto the mirror, closed my eyes and spoke to the universe.

'God. You utter dick. What next, you fuckwit?'.

'Do you mind? Less of the fuckin' blasphemy. I'm trying to have a wank in here.'

It turned out that Dermot was obsessed with the singer Tina Turner and regularly popped into the cubicle behind me for a spot of autoeroticism. Her picture was sellotaped to the back of the door. He did this without embarrassment, whereas I blushed and stuttered, stumbling over my words as if they were loose teeth if anyone even spoke to me.

I apologised and left him to it.

***

I'm almost finished with this cup of tea. Lesley's in the backyard, where the sun is drying her hair. You'd think it would have more important things to do, but it doesn't seem to mind.

She calls out various suggestions for what we can do this morning.

'We'll get some supplies and eat out for a change.'

'Sounds good,' I say.

'I'll make a list of the things we need. Can you bring those rolls of film that are on the table? Mataji asked if we'd get them developed?'

'On the Ashram?'

'No. In Trichy. She also told me about a shop called Poompuhar.'

'Pumpa-who?'

'Poompuhar. It's a state-sponsored shop. The prices are regulated, so we don't have to worry about paying over the odds. We also need to buy some little presents to take back to England.'

'You're sure about the name?'

'Yes. Why?'

'I don't know. It sounds wrong.'

'I wrote it down. Mataji spelt it out for me. It's on my list. On the table with the rolls of film.'

I pick the note up, and there it is in black and white. Poompuhar. I burst out laughing. The word runs around my head, tickling me.

Lesley comes back in, her hair dry.

'What's so funny?'

'Poompahar.' Just saying the word chuckles the dignity out of me, and I become almost hysterical with laughter.

'It's just a name.'

'No—' I gasp. 'It's not. Sainsbury's is just a name. Poompuhar sounds like a verb used to describe farting through velvet.'

Lesley rolls her eyes, leaves me to my hysteria and begins adding things to her list. Tears run down my face, and I can hardly breathe. It takes a minute or so, but I calm down.

'If you've quite finished, can we go?'

I nod. If I speak, I'll probably start laughing again. I have to remove my glasses to wipe the tears off the lens. Then, after a long deep breath, I put them back on. Lesley hands me a roll of limp bedraggled rupees and the rolls of film, which I tuck into the fold of my dhoti.

Out into the sunshine. My mind is clear and sharp—my heart full of reverence for the warmth and light. I'm speaking to Swami in my head and feeling the breath of each word deep in my heart.

Free me from my ego.

Remove from me that which is not real.

'Shall we get a bus?' Lesley asks.

'I think I'd prefer a taxi.

'We need to be a bit frugal. We're running out of funds.'

I'm not keen on the bus.

'Come on,' she says. 'I'll buy some currant buns for you?'

'Ok. It's a deal. We get the bus.'

So, we walk to the local village where the bus stops. How will I spend my time during the journey? Will I contemplate the nature of my existence or think about sticky buns?

Am I meditating on my true nature?

Not *currantly*.

***

I enjoyed the journey to work and back. I listened to music on a Sony Walkman I'd bought with a little of my first paycheck. I gave Ma the rest of the money, just like Tony did. Like millions of others, I listened to Michael Jackson. Once the Thriller album kicked open the door and Michael Jackson moon-walked onto the world stage, there was a definite change in how the Irish viewed me. People who would have been shouting 'Nigger go home!' were now moon-walking backwards down the street. Being pointed at and called 'Michael Jackson' was better than being called 'Kunti Kinta!' Both were considerably better than nigger.

As much as I enjoyed the journey to work, being there became more problematic. The ten-minute breaks and lunchtime were very stressful. Having nothing to do but sit around and talk sent my anxiety levels through the roof. I was so anxious about anyone speaking to me that I could barely swallow my food. Trying to eat the prodigiously stuffed sandwiches Ma handed me each morning was like eating a mattress.

I'd also acquired the habit of obsessively touching my nose when talking to people. I don't know if, subconsciously, I was trying to hide or if I was trying to disguise the twitching of my nose, but the loss of control bothered me. I don't recall anyone being particularly unkind about any of this. My colour also didn't seem to have been an issue for them. If anyone, it was I who had the problem because I was hypersensitive to any kind of attention. Subconsciously, I associated being the centre of attention with the hostility I'd encountered in Ballymun.

After a few days, I stopped bringing food with me, which gave me an excuse to leave the building. It also took my mind away from the 'me' who was stressed. It let me settle back into the 'other' me. The other me was a musician. Music was my country, and other musicians my fellow citizens. My ability was modest, but it gave me self-worth and belonging. Without my bass guitar, I was an outsider. With it, I was an insider. Music changed the emphasis from what I looked like to what I could do. It gave me a currency and a language to buy passage into this other land where people accepted me. It opened doors internally and externally.

After a day of stress, sweeping, twitching and touching my nose, I was almost home when I heard singing and an acoustic guitar being played. The music came from a garden down the road from where we lived. I stopped the bike at a green wooden gate, and there stood a young man, elegantly dressed in a fedora, waistcoat, shirt, tight jeans and a pair of winkle-pickers. In those days, it wasn't exactly typical attire in Dublin. He may as well just have worn a big sign saying, 'I don't care what you think.' He was lost in his groove, singing 'Psycho Killer.' Even when he opened his eyes and saw me there, he didn't stop. Instead, he nodded and smiled, closed his eyes and sang on.

When he finished, I said, 'That was great.'

'Yeah,' he drawled. 'Thanks, man. You play?'

'Yeah. Bass.'

'Fuuuuck! Great! You done?'

'I'm not sure. I might be. Done what, exactly?'

'No, man. My name. It's Eudone.'

'Oh. Right. I'm Paul.'

'Alriiight. Get your shit and come over. We'll get a little bit of a jam goin'.

'I've not got an amp,' I said.

'Don't worry. We can use mine. I'll go set it up.'

When I got back, he was in his kitchen. It smelt like burnt toast and nappies. He plugged his guitar into a battered amp covered with cigarette burns. Old beer labels were stuck all over the casing like grimy but colourful plasters.

Eudone's girlfriend, Lisa, entered, drifting by on a fragrant cloud of marijuana. She waved at me with the tips of her fingers and gave me a sweet, elfin smile. I decided, there and then, they were the coolest couple I'd ever met.

'I've got houmous,' Lisa said, almost as an after-thought which confused me for a moment. I'd never heard of houmous and wasn't sure if I should appear sympathetic.

'Would you like some? I made it myself.'

Eudone answered for me.

'Lisa. You can't jam on houmous. Get him a beer.'

Lisa pointed at the fridge and smiled sweetly.

'Beer's in there. Help yourself.' She walked by, heading dreamily toward the door. The scent of patchouli oil, crushed grass, and fresh sweat tugged at my heart, and it followed like a puppy.

Eudone broke into a rendition of something by Dylan. No idea what it was. The works of Dylan were as much of a mystery to me as this 'houmous' thing. Of course, I'd heard some of his songs, but I was one of the few people who thought Dylan was over-rated compared to sitting down and not listening to a nasal drone set to music. Still, I knew *enough that voicing this opinion would have been considered heresy, so I played along. Halfway through, another man walked in. He was wearing a colourful jacket reminiscent of something a shaman would have worn. It made everything around it look grey. Beneath dark hair, which was in danger of being a mullet, his brown eyes were no stranger to laughter. He waved to us and put the kettle on. By the time we'd finished the song, he'd made himself a cup of herbal tea.*

'You want one?' he asked.

'Sure,' I said.

'The name's Joe. No point in waiting on this reprobate to introduce us. Most of the time, he's not sure who he is.'

Eudone paused in the act of raising his beer bottle to his lips as if he was about to object, but then he shrugged.

'Yeah. That's true. This here's Paul. Another gangsta of the groove.'

I held my hand out to shake hands, adding, 'I'm more of a petty pilferer of the groove, to be fair.'

Joe laughed and sat down on the sofa to listen. Eudone gulped down the last of his beer, belched loudly and then sang 'Homeward Bound' with a sensitivity that was at odds with the eructation that had preceded it. Joe and I clapped in appreciation. Eudone held out his guitar to Joe. 'I need a shit. Help yourself to the guitar, man.'

Joe winced and said, 'I'll pass, thanks. You probably didn't wash your hands after the last one.'

'Suit yourself.'

Joe was older than I was by almost ten years. He looked at me for a moment or two with an expression of mild bemusement.

'So, where do you belong in all of this?' he asked.

'I was just passing by earlier. I heard Eudone playing his guitar in the garden. We started talking, and here I am.'

'Oh. So you've just met? That makes sense.'

'It does?'

'Yeah. You don't strike me as the sort who hangs around with the

Eudones of this world.'

'Really?'

'Yeah. Really.' Joe chuckled to himself. 'Anyway. I'm glad I called by. I was going to ask Eudone if he knew any good bass players. I'm recording a demo and want someone to lay down some tracks. Would you be interested?'

'I've not been playing long,'

'Well — maybe I can borrow your bass? I can pay you, and you can come along if you're worried about getting it back?'

'I said I'd not been playing long. I didn't say I was crap.' I laughed, and so did he. '

'Great. I'll get a tape to you so you can work something out.'

'So, how do you and Eudone know each other?'

'Lisa and Eudone used to be my lodgers. I went to India for a while and let them stay in the house to look after it for me.'

'India? Wow. I'd love to go there one day. How long were you there?'

'About six months. I went to Goa. I got back and found Eudone had sold all my furniture to fund his heroin habit.'

My mouth was agape. I was aghast. Joe just laughed and waved Eudone's larceny away. Joe was like that. Unable to hold a grudge. And now I knew why Eudone and Lisa were so laid back. They were stoned. My infatuated heart almost fell over its own feet as it backed away from Lisa to jump back into my chest where it belonged.

They were — JUNKIES.

A gaggle of paranoid voices made urgent demands in my head. Of course, respectable society had been warning me about drugs and junkies in one way or another for most of my life thus far. But, Jesus — if Ma had known I was sitting in the same room as a heroin addict, she'd have dragged me out while smacking Eudone with a broom handle.

I tried to act as if being offered homemade houmous by a smackhead was nothing unusual.

'Do you do drugs?' I asked Joe.

'Heroin? No. I tried it. Didn't like it. Same with coke. Nasty stuff. I do a little acid now and then. How about you?'

'Sugar in my tea. Too much chocolate. That's about it.'

The year was 1984. By the end of 1985, I'd have £2000 worth of lysergic acid diethylamide pressed between the pages of a comic tucked under my bed. The L.S.D. would belong to Joe. The comic was also his. I was looking after his stash as a favour because he very much changed my life in a good way.

We had a lot in common. He did many things that I did but did them so much better. I wrote a lot, but he was a writer. I liked to draw, but he was an artist. I read a little, but he read a lot and passed on books I would never have read if not for him—everything from farce to philosophy.

Joe was a very complex character, ferociously intelligent, generous and loyal. The first person I ever met who swam against the tide by choice. Whereas I struggled to fit into my environment, he struggled to break out of it. Then he ran back and kicked it in the arse to ensure it didn't let him back in. When he felt hemmed in by what other people thought of him, he'd consciously break out of it. Not all the time, but enough to let his ego know it had a fight on its hands. Sometimes we'd be walking down the street — or at least I'd be doing that, but he'd be walking on his hands or dancing. As someone who didn't like having anyone look in my direction, I was very uncomfortable with this. I'd be hotly embarrassed — for both of us — but I felt it was my embarrassment rather than his courageous silliness that was wrong, so I refused to let myself hide away from situations in which this happened.

Joe was the first person I knew who consciously wrestled with his ego.

Man — I'd forgotten all about that.

I was going to tell you Joe was the person who taught me how to fight but looking back, maybe I learned more than how to use my fists —?

I don't know.

God bless him wherever he is now.

***

We're on the bus to Trichy, sitting at the back. Unlike the last bus we'd been on, this isn't packed like an overstuffed suitcase. It's turning out to be an enjoyable journey. The wind is blowing through gaps where windows once sat. The smells and sounds the refreshing breeze brings are making me smile. The colours, the reds, greens, blues and yellows and all in-between blend with the spices and sounds. Each frame of the movie is new and fresh to my eyes. I can but smile contentedly.

As with our previous ride on a bus, I'm being ignored while Lesley is *the* person of interest. She isn't bothered by this. I can see wide-eyed toddlers peering over the shoulders of their mums. One young lad is staring in such an unconscious manner that I'm reminded of a cow chewing the cud and watching the world pass through bovine eyes, warm but devoid of curiosity.

After my experience on the buses in Ballymun, I was never comfortable on public transport, but now I feel invisible.

It's such a liberating state in which to be.

It's so lovely to be nobody.

***

Three weeks into my job, I was as useless as the first day I arrived. My nostrils had stopped twitching, but I had replaced this with an unconscious habit of continually touching my nose. A psychologist would point to this as an indicator of possibly lying. The only lie I was telling, if that particular theory is correct, would be the lie that I was somehow doing okay and not drowning in my own life.

I tried to make the best of it. The way I coped with lunchtimes was to disappear. When the lunch bell rang, I left. I hopped on the bike Ciaran had lent me and cycled away. Despite everything, I was soon full of smiles on this particular day. The summer sun's heat was on my face, and the warm breeze was flowing over my skin. I had a surge of happiness. It flooded my chest and rose into a beaming smile. I couldn't resist closing my eyes for a second and lifting my face to the blue —

Blam!

I landed on a car bonnet. My face was against the windscreen. I rolled onto the pavement and leapt to my feet, propelled by fear and embarrassment. For that instant, I was sure I'd collided with a moving vehicle, but fool that I was, I'd somehow hit a parked car. Fortunately, the car and I were both uninjured, but the bike — the front wheel looked like an elephant had sat on it.

It wasn't even my bike! It belonged to Ciaran. Oh — God. I picked it up and went to a secluded spot behind an abandoned factory, where I tried to push and pull it back into shape. I just couldn't face going back and telling Ciaran I'd buckled his wheel by riding around with my eyes closed. I rolled back into the factory car park, late back from lunch, sweating like a wrestler and looking very embarrassed. Later that day, Ciaran caught sight of his bike and asked me what had happened to the wheel.

'Nothing,' I lied.

I probably didn't even touch my nose when I said it.

A few days after this, I was politely asked not to return to the factory.

***

Two minutes walking in the burning heat of Trichy is enough to convince us we need a taxi. We find one outside the Femina Hotel and jump in. We've dropped Mataji's rolls of film off at a shop called Chitra's, and now we're being driven to Poompuhar.

Ha-ha.

Sitting beside me in the back, Lesley's speaking to the driver.

'We need a cold drink before we get to Poompuhar. Can we stop somewhere?'

The driver nods and yanks the steering wheel like an old quack pulling out a molar, bumping us up onto the kerb. We stop beside a stall selling juice. Lesley and I approach the proprietor, who's got a generous supply of teeth. Most of them seem to be vying for a seat up the front where the view's better. He's stuffing ripe oranges down the throat of a large trembling juicer. It's whirring, grinding, and gushing a copious flood of juice into a bucket. Unfortunately, the bucket's got a halo of flies. Lesley, not wanting to offend the man, leans closer to me and whispers, 'It looks a bit unhygienic.'

'Unhygienic? Lesley, I can *actually* see a blue bottle washing shit off his feet with the juice.'

The man and his teeth turn to us. He's wiping his hands on a towel, possibly the only thing more virulent than the juice bucket for miles around. I point to the fridge. He points to the bucket. I shake my head in a way which is only slightly less demonstrative than sticking my fingers down my throat. We'll not be drinking anything from that bucket unless it's at gunpoint.

Two minutes later, we sit on a sturdy wooden box by the roadside, drinking cold bottled pop from the fridge. The driver stays in his car eating something. Between us and the traffic, there's a rusting rail. It gives some feeling of security, but not much. The busy road is pulling grime-laden chaos into itself. It's a whirlpool of rust and chrome.

***

* * *

Being unemployed meant I had more time to play music with the band. I also spent more time with my newfound friend, Joe, playing bass on his demo. A friend of his, Henrik, who had hearing so acute he could almost hear a bat blink, was the sound engineer. Henrik lived with his wife, Sonya and their seven-year-old daughter, Milly, in suburban Dublin, and we recorded the demo in his living room amongst toys, cups of herbal tea, and cans of beer. Henrik had the sort of beard grown by castaways. It was long, unkempt and probably full of crumbs if his prodigious appetite for Hobnobs was anything to go by.

We worked through the day and into the evening using a TEAC 4-track reel-to-reel. On the second night, while Joe and Henrik bounced three of the tracks onto one, I went into the kitchen to get myself a beer. Sonya was about to make a hot chocolate for herself and offered to make one for me.

'Yeah,' I said. 'That'd be great.'

I sat at the kitchen table while she stood by the cooker, waiting for the milk to boil.

'How long have you two been friends? She asked, meaning Joe and myself.

'A couple of months.'

'Oh? You don't seem like the sort of person he usually hangs out with.'

I laughed. 'That's what Joe said when he first saw me in Eudone's house.'

She laughed along. 'Yeah. I can see that. Eudone would probably steal the steam off your piss if he could sell it to get drugs.'

'My current social life, believe it or not, is a big improvement on how it was a few months back. Most of my friends were imaginary.'

'Don't get me started on imaginary friends. Milly's had one for years.'

She didn't laugh when I did, making me feel a little uncomfortable.

'Seriously?' I asked

'Yes. It's a pain in the arse, to be honest.'

'What makes you think it's not in her imagination?'

'Because if it is — it's in mine too. And Henrik's.'

'You've seen it?'

'Yeah. Well —no. Not directly. But I've seen things move on their own, and Milly giggles when it happens. She thinks it's great fun.'

The hot milk started to rise in the pan. Sonya lifted it and turned the gas off.

'You want sugar?'

'Two, please.'

She placed two mugs on the worktop, poured the milk in and dropped two small sugar cubes in mine.

'Are you being serious? About the imaginary friend?'

'I am,' she said, putting the mug on the table in front of me. As an afterthought, she slid a coaster underneath.

'How long's she had this friend then?'

'How long? Christ, let me think. She was four when it first turned up. Or maybe it was always there, and I never noticed.'

'What made you notice in the first place?'

'I was living in London at the time. Just me and Milly. Her biological dad turned into an arsehole, so I left him. Milly and I had to live in a small, single-roomed flat until I could get sorted. A couple of days after moving in, I was looking for my hairdryer. Before heading off to work, I washed my hair in the sink. I used to drop Milly at my mum's in the mornings. The hairdryer — I kept it in a drawer —it was missing. So, I looked everywhere for it. Milly pointed to the top of the wardrobe and said it's up there.'

Sonya took a sip of her chocolate. The top of the wardrobe was almost up to the ceiling. Now — I knew there was no way the hairdryer was up there. Milly was too small, and I had to stand on a chair myself to reach the gap between it and the ceiling. She's small for a seven-year-old, but she was tiny back then. Anyway, I carried on looking. I was so frustrated. And worried about losing my job. And my relationship was *over. And Milly kept saying it's up there. I snapped at her. Told her to stop being silly because it wouldn't be up there. But then Milly was getting upset, so I apologised, pulled over a chair, and stood on it just to show her it wasn't up on the wardrobe. I put my hand into the gap — and there it was. My legs went weak. I pulled it out and asked Milly how it got there. She said I told you, Mummy. It was my friend.'*

I wasn't sure what to say. It brought to mind something Ma had told me.

'When my Ma was pregnant, carrying my younger brother, Jason, she was huge. Jason was a big baby. Her back ached all the time, and she struggled with moving, especially near the end.'

'Poor thing,' Sonya said.

'One night, Ma sat on the edge of her bed, struggling to get her legs onto the mattress because of the back pain, when something took hold of her feet.'

'No?'

'Yes. It lifted her legs onto the bed. Gently, you know? Like it cared. No idea what it was. Some friendly spirit?'

Sonya said, 'That's nice. I could use something like that around here to help in the house. Henrik's bloody useless.'

'You'll have to show Milly's friend where the mop is.'

'It's as useless as Henrik is. I love him, but God knows why. Anyway, we best not go through our back catalogue of spooky stuff. I have trouble sleeping as it is. I'm off to bed. Just leave the mug in the sink when you've finished. I'll wash up in the morning.'

'Okay. Thanks. Sleep tight.'

I forced myself to stay in the kitchen until my drink was gone. I was freaked out but didn't want Sonya to know. After she left, the kitchen seemed unnaturally quiet.

***

Our taxi pulled up outside Poompuhar. A young boy comes

over to us as soon as we get out. He speaks to us with great enthusiasm as if we're long-lost relatives.

'Hello, Uncle! Hello Auntie.'

We scarcely have time to reply before he launches into what seems like every word of English in his repertoire.

'I am studying standard English. Do you think my English is good? Do you like cricket? Yes? I am *very* good at cricket. You are English, I know. Yes? My friends also like cricket. And my father? My father, he said I should study standard English. I can get good job. Do you have good job, Uncle?'

What can I say? I work in a dry-cleaners. Before coming to India, I was steaming piss stains from the trousers of strangers.

'I— ' don't get time to say anything. The boy rushes headlong into his monologue.

'My uncle works for government positions. He is the very essential man in office. He is working for Mister Mucurtiyrakkaventharantarumtytum, and Mr Mucurtiyrakkaventharantarumtytum is insisting I write letters to him for the practising of the standard English. I always and often — '

I'm not listening. I can't. My brain is trying to process how a man with approximately sixteen syllables in his name can fill out a job application and have enough room to put anything else on it. That name was like listening to a wooden ruler placed between the spokes of a bicycle.

The boy's miming something. Hitting something with a stick?

'— with cricket!' he exclaims, and now he's laughing.

Behind us, religious music blasts from the cab of a passing lorry. Other drivers honk their horns in a sort of metallic amen. The noise drowns out the noise from the boy.

Lesley holds up a hand to silence him.

'Very nice,' she says. 'but we must go now. We've got a hectic day ahead of us. So you run along and play.'

'But where are you doing the going, Auntie? Are you having the Poompuhar!'

I guffaw, and Lesley gives me the look women reserve for silly boys. The *actual* boy points to the shop behind him.

'Poompuhar is excellent shop. I show you *everything*, Auntie. I will be your guide. Best guide ever! Uncle. You come! Come!'

I'm waving him off, but his departure isn't in the offing. Instead, he's backpedalling to the door and opening it for us. He bows as we enter and then reappears in front. He lights the fuse on a long, enthusiastic monologue about his sister and casually tosses it to us.

'My sister, she will marry very excellent boy, but it is great shame for me. I cannot afford present, Auntie. A great shame for my family. And poor father, too. What can I do, Auntie? Uncle, can you help me?'

Lesley looks bemused. She says, 'Why don't *we* get a present for your sister?'

The boy gasps. He claps his hands together. 'Auntie! Uncle! You will be having the blessed!' He grabs a bracelet and points out other, more expensive jewellery glimmering like honey behind glass. We'll have to limit his generosity toward his sister because our funds are running low. Maybe there *is* a wedding. Perhaps there isn't. Lesley's enjoying his happiness. While the boy isn't looking, she catches my eye and winks.

***

By the time Henrik had finished recording my bass line on the last track, I was ready for bed. He bid me good night and called Joe in to record another vocal. Joe would sleep on the couch, so I had the spare room to myself. Earlier in the evening, I'd considered this a good thing, but that was before Sonya told me about Milly's imaginary friend. In the light of day, I wouldn't have worried about being alone. My scepticism would have dismissed the story, but the middle of the night was different altogether. When I needed it, I found my scepticism was unavailable for comment. Every time I tried to connect with it, it hung up.

So, I undressed with the bedside lamp on and jumped under the covers. Only with effort did I turn off the light. I kept imagining myself waking up on top of the damned wardrobe. I lay awake for ages in complete darkness. Alone. Just me, my imagination and Milly's imaginary friend.

I slept uneasily until the early hours. The door to the room had creaked. A shadowy figure was creeping into my room.

'Who's that?' I whispered, sitting up.

'It's me. Joe. Sorry. Didn't mean to wake you.' He stepped further into the room, sleeping bag under his arm. 'I'm going to crash on the floor here. Go back to sleep.'

I lay down, snuggling my head into the warm nook of my pillow. I was relieved to have company. The reassuring sound of Joe making himself comfortable on the floor put me at ease. Then it suddenly occurred to me — why was he in my room? He said he was going to sleep on the couch. I stopped worrying about poltergeists and started worrying about homosexuals. All the warnings Ma had given through the years about wandering off with strangers gathered in my head for an impromptu panic. So, while Joe soon began snoring like an old faithful heterosexual Labrador, I lay awake watching the light of dawn slowly prise open the window curtains.

***

I gasp for air, a bucket of warm water pouring over my head, the sweat and grime of Trichy being washed away. It feels so good to be back in the Ashram. So good to be clean.

Lesley's taken Mataji's photographs, the ones we developed for her, over to Mataji's koothi. I'm thinking about finding Swami as soon as I've finished showering. I feel bad for having followed him around without saying anything. Apart from being bloody stupid, it was also very discourteous. I should go and apologise, if only for that reason. The thought of it has me holding the bucket up, shaking my head disapprovingly before tipping the water over myself. I followed Swami around like he was an exhibit in some zoo, staring at him like — well, I guess the way people used to stare at me in Dublin.

The water pummels my head and cascades noisily around my ears. Spluttering, I drop the bucket and grab my towel. I need to speak to Swami and prove I'm not just an idiot who can only stand and stare. Soon as I get dried and dressed. I know where Swami lives. I saw him go into his koothi on the night of Shivaratri.

I saw him standing with the water around his feet.

Saw him collapse.

Poor Swami —

***

Before Sonya had shared her story about Milly's imaginary friend, the child had sort of faded into the background for me, but from then on, I was keenly aware of her presence. She was sitting at the breakfast table when I went into the kitchen. Sonya was pouring milk on some cereal for her.

'Good morning, Paul,' Milly said, carefully pronouncing each word in the way children sometimes do when they've been told to remember their manners.

'Morning, Milly,' I replied, sliding along the bench on the other

side of the table. I sat facing Sonya, leaving room for Henrik, who came in and sat beside me. He reached across and took one of Milly's cornflakes. The two of them giggled. Sonya told the two of them to stop playing with their food. She rolled her eyes at me.

'I've only just got Milly to stop playing with her food, then Henrik starts. It's like having two children instead of one.'

Henrik plucked a piece of dry toast from the rack and started crunching.

'We got a lot done last night,' He said, pausing to brush crusty crumbs from his beard. 'Should finish today if we make an early start, though it depends on Joe. He was finishing the last of the backing vocals last night.'

'He's still asleep,'

'Oh? I saw the lounge was empty. I thought he'd gone for a run. Crazy man likes to jog.'

'He's in my room.'

'I thought he was crashing on the couch?'

'He came in last night and crashed on the floor. He's still asleep.'

Milly flicked a fallen cornflake from the table. She looked up and saw I'd witnessed her naughtiness. Her eyes were big and blue, like Sonya's, but they seemed a little too large for her sockets. She smiled and returned to her bowl. I returned my attention to breakfast. There was a teapot on the table and cups, a toast rack, a sugar bowl, butter, marmalade and a jug of milk — the usual suspects. There was also a green plastic frog on the worktop beside me. Sonya poured my tea, and I put the milk in and stirred.

The plastic frog started to slide slowly across the worktop.

I stopped stirring. The tea kept swirling. The frog kept moving. Then it stopped too.

Sonya was staring at it.

'Did that —,' I began.

'Yes,' Sonya snapped. She looked at Milly, who was engrossed in pouring more milk on her cornflakes, before returning her attention to me.

393

'Sorry. I barked at you. We don't talk about that sort of thing in front of —.' She made a slight incline of her head toward Milly.

'Oh. Sorry,' I said.

'That's okay,' she said. 'You weren't to know. We just don't want to encourage it, that's all.'

Milly slurped the excess milk from the side of her bowl. Henrik tapped the table in front of her.

'Milly, are we a Labrador or a person?'

'A person,' she said.

'Do we drink out of the bowl or use a spoon?'

Milly rolled her eyes and took up her spoon.

'Toast?' Sonya asked, shoving the toast rack toward me.

'Thanks.' I scraped the butter knife onto a cold slice, smearing it with marmalade. I wasn't sure where to go with the conversation, so I remained quiet, trying to crunch quietly.

'How's the recording going?' Sonya asked. 'Oh — Henrik, you said when you came in, didn't you?'

'I did. It's going well,' Henrik replied. 'I'm going to compress it later. Cut and splice it. Lovely stuff. Should be finished today.'

'That's good. I can get my living room back.'

Joe came into the kitchen, rubbing his unshaven chin.

'Morning all,' he said, pulling up a chair and sitting at the end of the table between Milly and Henrik. He lifted the teapot and poured half a cup before it dribbled to a halt.

'I'll make a fresh pot,' Sonya said. She pushed herself away from the table and got up. 'I've got some herbal tea in here if you'd prefer?'

She opened the kitchen cupboard above the microwave.

A box of cereal flew over her shoulder.

'Milly!' She shouted, making Milly jump. For an instant, I thought Milly would burst into tears, but she didn't. Her little face looked indignant for a moment, and then she calmly returned to her cereal. Sonya took a deep breath — sighed — and calmly spoke.

'Milly, can you stop that?'

'It wasn't me, mommy. It was my friend. I told you before.'
Joe picked up the cereal box from the floor.
'Can whatever that was, throw out a fried egg?' he said.

***

So here I am, striding down shrub-lined paths, feeling like I'm the prodigal son. I'm wondering how Swami will react when I knock on the door. Will he greet me with a great big smile? He might even usher me into his koothi.

Or —

He might shoo me away from his door.

Oh crap. I'm slowing down a little. What am I doing? This could be excruciatingly embarrassing. My resolve trickles away. A bead of sweat tickles as it slips down my cheek. I can see the koothi where Swami lives. My heart thumps as if it ran ahead and is already hammering on the door.

I step onto the verandah and into the shade, unsure if this is the right thing to do, but I'm going to knock anyway.

Here goes nothing.

'Can I help you?'

That voice came from behind me. I turn. A middle-aged woman regards me with an expression not usually associated with that of a welcome committee.

'I was hoping I could see Swami?'

'Swami's not on the ashram until later.'

My heart falls through the soles of my feet. I think she sees my disappointment because her face softens.

'Can *I* help you?' she asks.

'No, thank you, but no.'

Feeling foolish, I step out from the shade and start a slow rambling walk around the edges of the Ashram. The mind nibbles on what just happened, gnawing away like blunt teeth at a fingernail. I suddenly realise I haven't come to see Swami hoping to pay my respects to him. What I was trying to do was patch up my bruised ego. I wasn't calling as a devotee, but as a travelling salesman, come to sell my ego back to myself. I wanted to show Swami I wasn't that fool who stood still to stare at him. Instead, I was this other fool, the one confidently knocking at the door.

I feel silly.

My ego stopped me from approaching Swami yesterday. Today, it has me knocking on his door.

What am I?

A piece of wood carried on the tide? A dog chasing a bone? A mouse running from a cat?

This life is supposed to be mine, so why do I feel like something that's swept along by it? Am I this whirling carnival of thought and feeling, none of which remains long enough for me to hold onto? Am I a bystander witnessing the accident of my birth?

Or am I a ghost wandering through the rooms of my life?

***

Joe wanted to show me what he had recorded during the night, so we left the others in the kitchen.

'Listen to this,' he said, handing me the headphones. 'This is the last vocal I did on track three.'

I put them on and pressed play. The reels on the 4-Track turned, rolling out the muted hiss of tape before the sound of music came through. I nodded my approval, but Joe waved that away.

'Just listen,' he said.

'I waited for the vocal to start. It did, but it faded into the background after a few seconds. I heard some breathing.

Joe asked, 'hear anything?'

'It faded away.' I manipulated the headphone wire. 'Something's

going on with the volume. Rewind it a bit. You've got three of the channels muted too. Am I listening to the right one?'

'Yeah. I bounced everything onto that track. Listen again.'

Joe returned the reel to the start point, and I listened again. The same thing happened. The music faded once the singing started. The sound of breathing dominated the track. I shrugged and told Joe there was something wrong with the recording.

'You heard the breathing?'

'Yeah.'

'That isn't me.'

'What?'

'It's not me. I was singing. I checked the level each time, and the signal was good. But each time I listened back, the music faded away, and that breathing had appeared.'

'Some glitch on the tape?'

'No. That's a new reel because the same fucking thing happened on the other one.'

'That's crazy. It's got to be you breathing.'

'I know, but that isn't my breath. And even if it was, why is it picking up my breath and not my voice?'

I put the headphones back on and listened again, examining the microphone, a new SM-58 held on a vertical stand. I tried to find a reasonable explanation for the anomaly but couldn't find one. The hairs on my skin prickled as I pictured the scene. If that was breathing, then whatever or whoever it belonged to must have been only inches away from where Joe had his face close to the mic.

'This —,' I said and then had no words with which to continue.

'I don't scare easily, but it freaked me out.'

'That's why you slept in my room?'

'Yeah. I'm surprised I got to sleep. I was wired.'

We finished the recording that afternoon, as Henrik had said. I was more than a little relieved. When I got home, I ran myself a bath. Before getting in it, I brushed my teeth. Looking at my face in the mirror, I moved closer to the glass, imagining how close that invisible face would have been. I looked into my eyes, and it occurred to me there was no me on the other side of the glass. The face in the mirror wasn't looking back at me. There was nobody there.

If there's nobody on that side of the mirror, could it possibly be there's nobody —

***

Here.

Right now.

Swami's in front of me. In front of us, actually. He's singing devotional songs in the Prayer Hall. Two hundred or more devotees are listening to the honeyed gravel of his voice. Perhaps my ear isn't accustomed to the subtleties of the melody, but Swami can't carry a tune in a bucket, not if this is anything to go by. He's got soul, that's for sure. This impromptu performance has all the informality and poignancy of an immigrant down in the belly of a ship, singing of home. It's the song of someone smuggling the memory of love deep in his heart, carrying it over the border between spirit and matter.

The song of devotion has ended. People are asking questions about spirituality. As far as I'm concerned, they're wasting their time. What's the point in asking complex spiritual questions if you don't know who, what or from where you come? Or maybe they do? Perhaps it's just me who is clueless. I look around. Nope. They seem clueless too —

I wince at my unkindness.

How can I think I'm more enlightened than they are just because my ignorance has led me to ask a question?

I'm *almost* in *awe* of what an arse I am.

A thought appears, full and conscious and pure, as if

someone had just blown it into my head.

It says —

*Your body takes in food. It keeps what is nutritious to stay healthy and lets go of what it doesn't need. If the body holds onto anything, it will eventually corrupt and poison you. Good things happen. Bad things, too. Let them come and go. They all produce waste. If you take hold of these things and say these are mine, and this is me, you will become ill. Let these things come and go as they will. They pass **through** you, but they are **not** you. They cause you no pain. Only your attachment to them brings pain. They are nothing without you to sustain them.*

You know your wrong thought, but the wrong thought does not know you, so where is the power?

Does it lie with the thought or feeling?

Let them all go.

I was pleasantly taken aback. All of this — came fully formed. An instant hit of understanding. Something sprouted in my brain's furrows like a seed planted and instantly grown. It was like I'd nodded off and was sleepwalking down the path of self-criticism, exploring the underbelly of narcissism, and something woke me up.

Satsang is over. People are getting up and leaving. Swami's moving like a farmer in his field, sowing a word here and there. I'm glad he's not walking this way. Despite wanting to introduce myself earlier when it suited me, now I want to keep out of the way. So I'll just take a photograph, which will be more than enough for me.

I raise my camera to focus — a hand grabs it. I turn and see Brian. I don't think I've mentioned him before. He's tall, brown, handsome and German. He's got *the* most perfect afro this side of the 1970s and is pointing toward Swami.

'Go,' he urges. 'I'll take a picture of you and Swami.'

'What? No —, ' I splutter.

'Quickly!'

Brian takes hold of my arm and pulls me toward Swami. This young man may have the perfect afro, but his grasp on body language leaves much to be desired. I'm virtually ploughing up the floor of the Prayer Hall, trying to backpedal, but he's *still* dragging me toward the diminutive saint.

He says, 'I'll take a picture of you together.'

I say, 'Eh, no— thanks.'

It makes no difference.

Brian calls out, 'Swami? Swamiji!'

Oh, God, shut up!

Swami turns. For the sake of what little dignity I've got left, I stop backpedalling. I am *so* absolutely mortified I can barely speak, but I manage to mumble, 'Is it okay to have a photo taken beside you, Swami?'

'Yes, yes, yes,' he says.

And so, now I'm standing beside him. I'm so excruciatingly self-conscious that it's physically painful. I can hardly bear this moment.

Take the bloody picture, Brian!

The camera flashes. Swami walks off, and Brian hands my camera back to me. His smile is broad and perfect and generous, just like his hair.

'Thanks,' I say, without meaning it. Weeks later, when I pick the photos up from the chemist, Swami isn't smiling. The expression on his face mirrored how I felt on the inside. My heart was cold and clutched in the fist of my ego.

Face lies.

Heart tells the Truth.

I should have let my head drop into my heart, like a coin into a jukebox machine. Let it fall and listen.

That picture is old now. Everything that was not true

has changed, but what was true then is true now. The more photographs I take, the more time slips away—no point in hanging on to any of it.

You blink, and it's gone.

Just like Joe. And Ciaran. And me. And you.

All that remains is what witnessed their passing.

***

Mataji was in the koothi earlier this evening, but now she's gone. She popped in for a chat and a cup of tea. She's been busy with Swami over the past few days, so we haven't seen much of her, but I wrote down some of the things she said about Swami.

When Swami goes into a deep spiritual state, vibhuti sometimes manifests in his hands while in Samadhi.

How weird is that? Sacred ash comes through the pores of his skin when he goes into a state of prayer.

Lesley comes in from the yard, which is lit up by moonlight. She's just washed her Punjabi suit for the morning. I was about to tell her what happens when Swami goes into Samadhi, but I change my mind. She's seen Swami levitating backwards down a motorway. Mataji's seen him walking in two different places at the same time. I'm surrounded by people who've seen him do all sorts of things, making the rational mind stop and slap itself.

I don't want to see any miracles.

All I want is to know *who I am*.

'Do you want a cup of tea before you sleep?' Lesley asks.

'No, thanks,' I say, closing the book and putting it on the floor. I pull the boxing gloves I bought for Jason out from under my bed and pull them on. It's not easy to get comfortable like this, but soon enough, my thoughts are scattered.

Breath breathes itself into my nostrils.
Slowly, my abdomen rises.
I am humbled.
I leave the way I came.
From nothing to nowhere.

CHAPTER FIFTEEN
Kicked In The Toffees

It's so hot this morning. I have to alter my position every few minutes because of the intense heat radiating from the stones of the wall beneath me. Lesley and I are, once again, sitting outside the ashram gates. We're watching two people in the distance who are walking along the parched and dusty road from Fatimanagar. They look weary. Lesley can make out the details better than I can. She doesn't have to squint like me. She's got her sunglasses on and the shade of her straw hat.
'Looks like two women. One large. One small. Backpacks on, so probably not locals.'

She's right, though I've had to wait until they're much closer to see them clearly. One of the women is solidly built with a rucksack that reflects her chunkiness and strong shoulders. The straps are snug. Her thumbs are under them to ease the weight. Her face is red with sunburn.

The other woman is equally burdened, but without the muscles of her companion, she's leaning forward as if the pack is riding her bareback and goading her on. She's also more petite and pale. As she gets closer, she straightens up, appearing to shrug off her fatigue. Tin utensils clunk quietly with each footstep.

Standing before us, sweat running down the dimpled knees, the older one barks out a question.

'Is dis der ashram!?'

'Yes,' Lesley replies. 'It's right through these gates.'

The big one turns and marches into the Ashram. The smaller one follows, like a pale moon caught in the gravitational pull of the more significant body.

***

Around the time I was having breakfast with poltergeists and being offered houmous by heroin addicts, Tony left the army. It had taken him a great deal of courage and endurance to have done something he had loathed so much for so long. He put a crowbar through the car bonnet of one contemptible scumbag, which says something about what he had to put up with while he served out his enlistment. He never spoke about it.

When Tony left, the army lost a good soldier, but Ciaran joined as if to take up the slack. His departure would have left a considerable gap in my life had Joe not been around. He came up with more songs for me to play bass on but decided not to return to Henrik. I can't remember why but it may have been down to the poltergeist fucking up the recording. Either that or Sonya, who I also had a crush on, wanted her living room back.

We did the recording in Blanchardstown, in a house belonging to someone else Joe knew. I don't remember who they were, possibly because I was busy laying down some bass on the 4-Track in the front room. Oh — and I was also tripping my tits off, as they say. After a few months of observing people on heroin and cocaine and a lot of research, I had finally decided drugs weren't for me — unless they were called Lysergic Acid Diethylamide.

Acid, as it's more commonly known, appealed because it opened up the possibility of expanding my consciousness. Just exactly what that meant was a bit vague, but I was eager to clarify it by exploring the options. I did worry a little, wondering if I'd get to the edge of my knowledge and find I was unable to get back to where I'd started. On the other hand, there were stories of feeling at one with the universe, which sounded like it would be well worth the trip.

Joe cautioned against taking a whole tab for my first foray into the unknown. I'd grown to trust him implicitly, and so took his advice. The acid was impregnated into a card sheet with hundreds of squares printed on it. Each square had a little picture of the pink panther, and each square was one tab. Joe tore one away from the strip, tore it again and handed the half to me.

Within the hour, I was lost in the music so thoroughly that it was as if I'd been painted into it by Rembrandt. The song was a pastoral scene. Joe's acoustic guitar sounded like a rickety cart being pulled along by a donkey. We strolled along a country lane, warm summer air scented with sage and lush summer grass delighting my senses. Each note I played on my bass was like having a 'wadge' of soft, warm fudge gently shoved in my ears. The fudge melted in the middle of my head and became a smile so big and full and soft that it slowly, delightfully, oozed like honey into my chest.

The music wasn't just the best thing since sliced bread. It also toasted the loaf and slapped on a big smile of strawberry jam. I went to sleep with that expression on my face, secure in the knowledge that I'd be acclaimed as a musical genius by no less than the entire world. My bass lines were the concentrated essence of all that was good in music, at least they were until I woke up.

My mind had fooled me into thinking each note I played was sublime when they were so very ordinary, and on hearing the playback, my disappointment was heavy. I was also disturbed by how the mind filtered and interpreted everything. Nothing is allowed just to be what it is. The world is understood through Chinese whispers, with the mind being the whisperer. No wonder life was so confusing and hard to fathom. Through this process of 'whispering', the walls of perception move constantly, and I had no 'pure seeing'. All I had was whatever story the mind told me about whatever I was experiencing, so how could I know what was true if the only tool I had was the mind itself? The mind cannot dig down into the truth because it would have to remove the layer of mystery upon which it stands, and the mind will not destroy itself.

What is there, then, which is beyond the mind?

No idea —

***

What is Swami Premananda talking about? Something about the nature of the divine?

Hundreds of people are listening, and I should be too, but I'm not. So instead, I'm smiling and relaxed, sitting on this borrowed cushion. The wall supporting my back is warm, and I feel at peace.

On he goes. Swami. Talking. Love. Truth. Purity. Divine Love.

Blah-blah

That's what he may as well be saying because my sleepy mind is quietly wandering through sensual thoughts. Languid and lustful in the heat of the afternoon sun, I feel love and desire. I could just stretch out here and lay down to sleep —

Oh, wait. Swami's just got up from his chair, and he's walking in this direction. I'm not so relaxed now. Like a naughty boy jumping back from hot buns left to cool on a windowsill, my mind jumps back from the erotic and leaps into the neurotic.

Turning my head to follow his progress and wondering why some devotees are chuckling, I see Swami stopping in front of a small boy standing alone in the middle of the aisle, who has just discovered a rather interesting thing like an acorn. The boy is oblivious to everything around him except what he's discovered below his belly button. The boy holds himself in his chubby fingers.

Swami kindly asks him, 'What you do?'

The boy looks up. Realises he's being watched. Drops his acorn.

I cringe. Moments earlier, I'd been preoccupied with my acorn.

Swami has a mock-solemn expression on his face.

He says,' You not do this.'

To the sound of chuckling from the devotees, he goes back to his chair and starts talking again.

So, now — I'm listening.

***

I discovered my 'acorn' at a similar age. We were living in the house which was infested with cockroaches. I was in bed reading a comic, absent-mindedly fiddling with myself, when a peculiar but not unpleasant feeling slowly made itself known to me. It was so subtle it didn't even pull my attention away from my comic, but suddenly, I curled up, a bundle of unexpected bliss.

Oh — God —
I thought I was dying.
I couldn't have cared less.

***

The delicious smell of food in the air and the sound of cutlery and cups add to the convivial atmosphere in the dharmasala. Lesley's laughing because I told her where my mind had been when Swami Premananda spoke to the child in the Prayer Hall.

'I felt sure he was talking to me.'

'I expect you weren't the only one whose mind was

wandering.'

'Not if it's true that men think about sex every seven seconds.'

'That can't be true, can it?'

'Well, sex *has* been quite popular for some time now.'

'No. Not that. I meant the part about men thinking. Can I have your rice if you're not going to finish it?'

'Very funny,' I say, scraping it onto her plate. 'It could just be a coincidence, of course, like when I wondered if Swami could see me behind that veil, and he turned and looked at me through it.'

'You think it was a coincidence?'

I shrug. 'No. Maybe. Who knows?'

'There's a lot of people here who can tell you about times when he's read their mind. For example, answering a question before you ask it isn't unusual for him. He can read the devotee's letters by just holding the envelope. So maybe reading a mind isn't much of a leap. Sometimes, to illustrate a point, he might use somebody or something else to get it across. It's a very gentle form of teaching. Maybe a lot of people's minds were wandering this afternoon. Celibacy isn't something people are used to.'

'Why not address the person you want to teach directly and remove ambiguity?'

'You *wanted* him to throw a bucket of water over you?'

'Hmmm. Yeah, maybe the indirect approach is better.'

'Anyway, the teaching wouldn't have been just for you. *You've* made it personal, not him. That's your ego at work. The fruit on a tree doesn't have individual names on it. You take what you need and leave the rest. And I guess there's always a chance it could be a coincidence though if that *is* the case, then he's *very good* at them.'

'Good at what?'

'Coincidences.'

I laugh, and suddenly my laughter seems very loud because the room has become hushed without my noticing until now. I look around. On the other side of our table, further along, the oldest and largest of the two women we met this morning at the ashram entrance has got enough food on her tray to fill a small bucket. She's eating with such gusto, such one-pointed enthusiasm, noisily snuffling air through her nostrils that she's also sucked in the pleasant murmurings of conversation. She isn't speaking to her companion, whose gustatory exertions are far more modest. Large portions have left no room for small talk.

Lesley pats me on the arm.

'Can you pass me the jug of water? And stop staring. It's rude.'

I look along the table to where the jug sits opposite the large woman. I turn to Lesley and shake my head, whispering, 'I'm *not* reaching down there. She'll have my arm off.'

'Don't be so judgemental.'

I reach for the water and drag it across the table. I shouldn't criticise or mock, but I do feel antagonistic toward the woman whose eyes follow the jug as it slides away from her. Of course, I know for each finger pointing at someone else, there are three pointing back at you, but these other fingers aren't usually being licked clean at the time.

***

Back in our koothi, waiting for the kettle to boil. Mataji's here with a bundle of letters tucked under her arm. She places them neatly on her lap after sitting down with a grateful sigh.

'Busy morning?' I ask.

'Yes. I've been working on some of Swami's correspondence.'

'He must get a lot. Where does he find time to read them all?'

Mataji laughs. 'He doesn't. He just holds a letter in his hand, and he'll know what's in the envelope. So it's labour intensive for me, but not for him.'

Lesley asks if Mataji's had time to eat.

'Not yet. I'll pop over to the dharamsala and get something later.'

'You better hurry, ' I say. 'There's a visitor on the ashram hoovering food into her face like she's expecting a famine.'

'I heard about her. I believe she ate well.'

'Ate well? No. Lesley and I ate well. She just ate.'

Mataji smiles with gratitude as Lesley hands her a cup of tea.

I feel outraged at the behaviour of the big backpacker and can't help but pile on the criticism. 'Being hungry enough to eat a horse is one thing, but that woman wouldn't even pause to let the jockey get off first.'

Lesley hands me a cup of tea.

'Thanks.'

'You're welcome. I do hope,' she says, sitting down, 'that they left a contribution for the food they ate?'

'They did, actually,' Mataji replies. 'They left some culinary advice. They said the food left something to be desired.'

We gasp at this and laugh.

'After the way she shovelled it in, I'm surprised there's any food *left* to be desired.'

Mataji laughs too. She says, 'Swami never turns away a hungry mouth. And who knows what their story is? Most people who visit know we feed and clothe hundreds of children, so they show some restraint. Of course, we wouldn't take food meant for one mouth to put into another. We'd sooner starve ourselves. The children always come first and never go hungry. Contributions are welcome, as you know, but not compulsory.'

I lean forward as if sharing a secret and ask, 'What would Swami say about the fat woman?'

Lesley says, 'She wasn't fat, Paul. She was large.'

'Largely fat.' I insist, uncharitably.

'Swami would say don't criticise other people. Look at yourself. See your own shortcomings and work to correct them.'

I feel like I've just been told off. But, in my defence, I say, 'That's because he's a saint. I'd have handed her a bucket and said, make a donation or put the food back.'

'A bucket of regurgitated rice isn't going to be much help, is it?' Lesley says.

'Very funny. The bucket would be for a cash donation.'

Mataji changes the subject, leading me away from criticising the visitor. I feel cheated. Part of me wants to keep on about her. I want to keep picking over the bones because I feel righteous, and it feels good. The taste of righteousness is far too delicious to stop, so I want to keep returning to the table for more.

While Mataji and Lesley are finishing their tea, I wonder who has the more unsavoury appetite.

The hungry woman or me?

***

Things aren't always as they seem. Life occasionally kicks you in the crutch to prove the point. For example, Shiva, the destroyer of illusions, once danced with me in a garden in Ballyfermot.

If you hold your hand up before your eyes and sweep it across your field of vision, you'll catch a brief glimpse of a series of afterimages.

They follow in the wake of your actual hand. On acid, this echo of the physical object was intensified. I used to find this particularly fascinating. This fluidity in the movement of objects made me wonder what was real. Was everything beyond the now an illusion, like the afterimages chasing my fingers as I waved them before my eyes?

My friend Joe taught me how to defend myself while I was on acid. His arms blurred and multiplied like those of Lord Shiva. With many arms and legs, he came at me, smiling. Weaving and bobbing and ducking and jabbing.

Shiva wore boxing gloves.

Punched me in the face.

While I was on acid.

The drug acted as an analgesic, allowing me to endure the pain barrier. I trained intensively, mind concentrated and will focused for hours on end. Joe gave me enough of what he knew to keep me in one piece through the years. He also tried to teach me not to underestimate an opponent. He brought me to a club where he sometimes sparred with other martial artists. I saw how people like them, and him could quickly demolish an enthusiastic amateur like me without raising a sweat. They put my meagre ability into context. If I tangled with the wrong person, they would take me apart with the minimal effort it takes for a cartoon lion to pick a bone out of its teeth.

I was more Bruce Forsyth than Bruce Lee, but it was enough.

Early on, Joe taught me a lesson in not underestimating one's adversary that I still remember. A young man called around for a sparring session. I pulled the gloves on and sized him up. He was smaller than me, with quite a short reach. Not an ounce of fat on him at all. He looked like a strong wind would pick him up and blow him over.

Joe said, 'This is Liam. He's a ballet dancer.'

'A what?'

'A ballet dancer.'

Liam was doing a series of stretches. 'I'm not actually a ballet dancer. I'm studying dance. Ballet's just one of the arts we practice.'

I decided to go easy on him. Probably a bit of a mummy's boy.

We circled each other warily. A couple of tasty jabs from me stung him. Nice, I thought. He swung at me, missing. And again. I feinted with a jab and tried sweeping his legs from underneath, but he stepped over this. He had some fancy footwork going on. The acid danced in my veins, and I smiled at this young man's many arms and legs. I wasn't bothered. Dance all you like, I thought. That was just before my balls shot up into the back of my throat. I fell like a sack of coal.

Joe stood over me and tutted.

'I did say he was a dancer. He can't punch for toffee, but those feet are fast.'

'Yes,' I croaked. 'He just kicked me in the toffees.'

***

Nothing much happened during the day, so the evening pushed it aside. Hunger rose with the moon. We ate roti and spicy potatoes and are now waiting on coffee. Lesley's dabbing vibhuti on her right foot between the big toe and ankle. Something bit her earlier in the day, and a perfectly round blister came up.

'It's not sore,' she says, ' I just don't want it to burst.

''Yeah. We've got plasters back in the koothi.'

She looks up and sees a familiar face. I turn in my seat and take a moment to recognise the distinguished gentleman who translates for Swami during satsang. Lesley stands and introduces herself.

'Hello,' she says, pressing her hands together in a *namaste.*

The Doctor returns the namaste with a smile.

'This is Paul, and I'm Lesley. I just wanted to compliment you on how well you translate for Swami.' I wave from where I'm sitting but then decide it's impolite to do, so I stand with them. The Doctor nods with a modest acknowledgement of the compliment.

He says, 'I'm very blessed to speak for Swami during satsang.' His voice is warm but also carries a sombre sincerity. 'May I ask how long you have known Swami?'

I reply first, mainly to get my answer out of the way. Lesley's experience with Swami through the years would have been much more interesting than mine. 'I've known about Swami for a year and a half. I read a book about an Indian saint, and halfway through, I thought, if there *are* saints, I don't want to read about them. I want to meet one.'

The Doctor nods, encouraging me to continue.

'A few weeks later, I met Lesley. You can imagine my surprise to find out she not only knew about an Indian saint but had met him in person.'

The Doctor turns his attention to Lesley.

'And where did you learn of Swamiji?'

'I met him in 1984 when he was in Britain for a few weeks. I went with a friend.'

'And her name was?'

'Gina. We were fortunate to have seen him at that time. There were so many people who wanted a blessing or advice from him.'

'It was meant to be,' The Doctor said, confident that such things aren't merely fortuitous. I could hear it in his voice.

'Yes, I agree. I don't think we could've avoided meeting Swami even if we wanted to. On one occasion, when we turned up, hoping to see him, we found the venue was packed. Couldn't get anywhere near him. After a long wait, we eventually decided it made no sense to wait any longer. You see, we had to travel back to Manchester through the night for work in the morning. So, we turned to leave. At that moment, something — like an invisible finger —nudged me in my right eye and Mataji in the ear. We both cried out, turned around and what did we see? One of Swami's disciples was looking at us, wagging a finger. It was pretty clear we weren't meant to leave. The man told us that Swamiji would see us later and we should wait, which is what we did.'

Listening to Lesley, I'm reminded of laying on my bed and being woken by a gentle hand on my face. That was a few days ago. It seems like a lifetime. There was also the incident when someone, or something, woke me with what felt like a breath blowing out a candle.

'Did you see Swami when he returned to Sri Lanka?'

'Yes,' Lesley says. 'That same year.'

'You were there in 1984?' The Doctor looks a little surprised.

'Yes. It was November of that year.'

'A time of great difficulty for Sri Lanka.'

'The civil war had started, but we had no idea about all of that. Not at the time. We just thought it would be marvellous. Swami had said it would be his birthday, and he'd treat us like queens, so we leapt at the chance. After all, it isn't every day you get invited to celebrate the birthday of a saint *by* the saint himself.'

'That is quite true. Did you enjoy your visit?'

'We slept on stone floors, nearly drowned in a tropical storm on a mangrove swamp and ate a lot of rancid rice in the middle of a civil war, but — yes, it was enjoyable. Sort of.'

It sounds so ludicrous we all laugh.

The Doctor asks, 'Had you not heard about the civil war before you went?'

'No. We were just two simple English girls off on a quest for enlightenment. As you can see, I'm still waiting for the enlightenment, and now I think about it, I'm not sure I got a slice of birthday cake either.'

'Life is never dull around Swami Premananda.' The Doctor takes a glass of water from a young man passing with a tray. 'Did you go to Matale?' he asks after a sip. 'Swami founded his first Ashram there.'

'We went, but not at first. It was too dangerous, and besides, Swamiji was staying in Colombo, so that's where we went at first. Then, about a week later, he took seven of us into the mountains to see it.'

The Doctor looks genuinely saddened, saying, 'It's such a pity it was burnt down. Swami was there for ten years, looking after the orphans. He fed them, educated and clothed them. Teaching them how to live a correct life, Swami kept his devotees and the orphans they cared for safe for as long as he could. But, the time came when it was wise to leave Sri Lanka. So, he brought everyone to the safety of the Tamil Nadu.'

***

The first Ashram founded by Swami Premananda was called *The Abode of Peace for all Religions.* That didn't stop it from being destroyed. People whose egos are enflamed by religious and political differences will potentially set fire to anything, including themselves. By the time Lesley and Gina got to Swamiji's old ashram in Matale, Sri Lanka, they found it hard to imagine the broken buildings had known children's laughter or that the Ashram had been imbued with the scent of incense and the sound of prayer.

All that remained were many shells of destroyed buildings and one humble building that still had a roof, which housed a family who offered a simple meal to the visitors, which was eaten off freshly cut banana leaves. Before the last grains of rice were taken up, the monsoon began to pour its heart out into what remained of Matale. Swami Premananda stepped out into the relentless rain with a big smile and called for Lesley and Gina to join him. The torrential rain bounced off the earth, dancing ecstatically at his feet as he walked around the grounds holding an umbrella over his head, giving them a tour. Water streamed down their faces as they peered through sodden fringes, blinking rain away from dripping eyelashes. Swami Premananda, under his umbrella, seemed to be walking around in the warmth of his inner sunbeam.

Finally, he pointed to them and then at the monsoon rains and said, with delight.

'You see. I baptise you.'

The heavens flowed like a river into the earth as he chuckled.

Water is very much associated with the Divine Mother. Lesley first spoke to me about this idea of the Divine Mother not long after we met. Despite my Catholic upbringing, God the *Mother* made more sense to me than God the Father. I saw the nature of the Divine Mother in *my* mother. Through the principle of male and female union, my physical being was manifested. Ma had often gone hungry to feed us, and the contentment she found in us being warm, safe, and happy was easy to project upwards onto a Divine source.

As above, so below.

Ma was a limited source of sustenance and love, but the Divine Mother was a limitless source of infinite love and sustenance. This seemed to be not a matter of faith but logic. The mothering instinct was a manifestation of the Great Mother of all creation, working through that creation itself. But, as with our parents, sometimes we don't recognise what is done for us out of love.

***

Six months before I met Lesley, I was attacked in a pub in England. I was standing amid a crowd of strangers with a lad called Finley chatting away while we were waiting to be served. Someone tapped Finlay on the shoulder and asked for the time. He looked at his watch. 'Nine o'clock,' he said. The lad who asked him walked off. A couple of minutes later, Finlay was tapped on the shoulder again. When he turned, a stranger headbutted him. He flew back against the bar. A fist flew out at me, connected with my face. Luckily, by this time in my life, I'd ditched my glasses in favour of contact lenses.

In front of me was a wall of angry faces. I punched the nearest one. And another. Lots of shouting. Cursing. Men. Women. Then someone jumped me from behind. I found myself bent over with my head tucked tightly under some sweaty stranger's arm. Oddly, I felt very calm. Joe had taught me well. I could have taken down whoever was holding me there, but I could see shards of broken glass on the floor. I was also aware that while my assailant was holding me so close, nobody could get to me because the bar was so tightly packed. I could see the door from the corner of my eye, so I surged with all my strength toward it, barging the two of us through the crowd, through the doorway and out into the street.

Once outside, I took a firm grip on the stranger's left hip. My leg was already behind his, so all I had to do was pull his hip backwards and twist, and he began falling back. The way Joe had taught me to do this was to let the attacker fall. They instinctively loosen their grip. You're on them as they hit the ground, jabbing in the eyes.

But what did I do?

When my assailant began falling backwards, I saw the back of his head was heading for the kerb. I broke his fall with my hand. Despite everything, I didn't want to hurt anyone. The feeling wasn't mutual because as I stood up, another stranger grabbed the front of my jacket and started to swing me around. His hands twisted into the material. His face contorted with aggression. I put my arms over his and my thumbs on his eyes and —

I found I didn't want to hurt this person either. So rather than gouge his eyes, I just rubbed. He cursed and let me go.

I had a brief, somewhat detached moment of savage joy, aware of the ominous thumping of footsteps. Vague shapes were approaching rapidly. My heart sank as I realised my contact lenses had come out. Then the world fell on top of me. I was knocked down by a dozen men who had run at me all at once. Kicks and punches from everywhere, slamming into me all over. I rolled up into a ball, covering my front, head, and sides as much as possible. I kept moving while I was down, spinning around, trying to make myself a moving target. Even this, Joe had taught me.

He'd told me about fear, and I was frightened.

I was outraged.

I was going to get kicked to death, and I had no idea why this should be. It was just mindless, senseless violence by strangers. Ma flashed through my mind as the boots hit me, pounding me like rain on the pavement.

Where was the mercy I had shown to those who had attacked me earlier?

I heard Joe say, 'Let them think they've hurt you if you go down.'

I heard my voice, shrill and mortifying, as I howled with the fucking injustice, fear, and frustration of being so helpless.

Where was the Divine Mother come to rescue her child?

***

Night has settled on the Ashram. I want sleep to wash away the sins of the world and to hold me tenderly. So, lying on my bed, on the edge of the emptiness from which all things come and go, I listen to my breathing and wait. That state which exists before I am given a name and, after that name fades, remains unchanged, comes for me. That which remains when I go and is unchanged when I emerge takes everything and reveals it to be nothing. Between the exhalation which dissolves creation and the inhalation of delight and surprise that births it —

In that state where dreams come and go.
I am —

***

And I was — saved by women. They launched themselves at the pack of men who had surrounded me. I heard women screaming above the thud and scrape of boots connecting with my flesh. I saw them swinging their handbags. Finally, high-heeled shoes were raised like pickaxes, and the men ran off. Women pushed and pulled me to my feet and shoved me into an ambulance which had suddenly appeared.

Does the Divine Mother have matching shoes and handbags?

The doors slammed, the siren wailed, and I saw a bright light before my eyes.

'Follow the light,' a man said, moving his little torch in front of me.
I felt so tired.
My eyelids were heavy.
Sleep embraced me.

CHAPTER SIXTEEN
The Light Shone In The Darkness

The sun has been waiting for us, lying across the doorstep to fill us with warm smiles as we emerge from our koothi. How lovely it is to be strolling along the path, looking forward to a coffee in this place of prayer and peace. We sit outside the ashram gates, feeling blessed and drinking a latte. Cigarette smoke is rising. A bird of prey flutters and then becomes stillness — as still as the pause between two breaths. It waits -— now drops like a stone.

Life eats life.

Lesley fans herself with her straw hat.

The grass tickles my ankles.

This world, clean and connected, bright and precise like the unwinding of a clock, feels like all the proof of divinity one could ever need. I put my head back to drink my fill of the blue sky, feeling the artery in my neck pulse. Life fills my lungs, my eyes, and my heart.

Lesley puts her hat back on and then takes my hand in hers.

We say nothing.

It's perfect as it is.

Eventually, I drop a sentence into the silence.

'This is just so timeless. I can hardly imagine we'll be leaving in a couple of days.'

Lesley smiles wistfully. 'I think part of us will always be here, with Swami.'

'Yeah. I think you're right.'

'Did I tell you there's a special abhishekam for us?'

'There is? For us?'

'Yes, I mean no. Not just us. It's for the devotees who'll be leaving soon, including us. So, you'll need a clean dhoti.'

'I'm not sure I've got one.'

'I'll wash one for you if you need it. It'll be dry in no time with this heat.'

'Okay. Thanks.'

'And you've got a mosquito on your leg.'

Slap!

I lift my hand. Look at the remains. Revulsion mingles with grim fascination. I wipe my palm on the dry, crackling grass. Another mosquito lands on my arm and bites me. I slap hard and kill it. This is all it takes to sour my mood. The bite irritates me, and I feel annoyed at being irritable.

Stupid, I know, but —

Here I am in India, on a beautiful day, with someone I love, having witnessed something sacred, and I'm still — what's the word?

Oh, yes — I'm still me.

Smoke rises.

Ash falls.

Lesley blows more smoke into the air.

And like that, my good mood has soured. I have a growing sense of disappointment. I felt so much at peace, close to God, just a moment ago. How can something so small distract me from something so huge? Shouldn't I now be more tolerant, rooted in my newly found appreciation of the goodness in God's creation?

Apparently not.

How about the love Swami exuded, which felt like nothing I'd ever known?

Surely that should make me a better person. I should feel something different in myself. Something purer. Kinder. More at ease. Because not too far away, there's a holy man, and I've been blessed enough to know there is goodness in the world. If I'm drawn to it, there must be goodness within me too.

But I'm looking at my palm. It's itchy. There's a trace of blood from the insect on my hand. I wipe it off on the hot, rough surface of the wall. It's abrasive like me, irritated to be so easily pulled away from the peace moments ago.

Maybe I'm expecting too much of being here?

Why would proximity to a saint increase or decrease my own 'saintliness?'

The bus drivers who pass by the Ashram are no holier than those who work in Delhi.

If anything, I'm feeling far from saintly at this moment — quite the opposite.

Shit.

Just look at me. I feel more resentment at being bitten than Swami does toward the people who burned down his Ashram.

I'm so disappointed in myself.

I want to feel more like him and less like me. Something profoundly spiritual is here, blossoming in the sun, but it's not flowering for me, and we're almost at the end of our time with Swami. I'm like a man who's walked through a field of roses, expecting to be a little more fragrant, who just realised his feet are covered in manure.

Lesley distracts me from these darkening thoughts by wafting an insect away. She's peering up into the sky, and I look up too. It's so blue. So beautiful. Blue like the robe of the Virgin Mary. I remember statues of her, sculpted stone cloth falling from her open arms.

I ask Mary, why am I still like this?

Knowing what I know now and having seen a living saint, why am I, not a better person?

There is no answer for me to hear.

Nothing.

Silence.

The sound of my breathing. A bead of sweat trickled down my face, splashing into the dust at my feet.

Why am I still so — me?

Yeah, I know. Back in Ballymun, I threw God and the bible down the rubbish chute. I know that. But look at me now. I'm on first-name terms with Shiva and Jesus. It hasn't been easy getting to this point. You'd think the journey would have made me a better person, but it doesn't seem to have done so. I'm just the same old me.

My mood curdles like the milk of human kindness left in the sun for too long.

What good is this spiritual journey if it doesn't make you a better person?

'Fuck all,' I think to myself and sigh deeply.

'You okay?' Lesley asks.

'Yeah,' I say. 'I'm too hot. Think I'll go back to the koothi.'

***

Where was I up to with my backstory?
 Sparring
 Poltergeists

Sacked
Kicked in the balls
Experimenting with acid
Dancing with Shiva
Right.

The band I was in played its first gig between the above. We still had no drummer, but this didn't stop us. I programmed a drum machine to propel the three of us through our set. There was more room to move about on stage without an actual drummer. And this I did with much enthusiasm. The adrenaline rush was such that I couldn't have stood still to save my life. I slid back and forth between fear and ecstatic excitement, trembling like a tuning fork and — oh my — how I loved that applause. It felt like acceptance over rejection and forgiveness for all my sins.

We gigged as often as we could, usually as the support band. Sometimes other bands would wipe the floor with us, but that was fine. I was determined that we would get better. The signs were encouraging. Someone even tried to poach me from the band. The minion of the manager of a signed artist approached me with an offer. I declined out of loyalty to my bandmates. A few weeks later, a management company showed interest in signing us. They promised to launch our careers with a gig on the roof of a building on O'Connell Street. Pure bullshit, but it sounded great. They didn't sign us in the end because we weren't good enough on the night. Another band made us look like the rank amateurs we were, but the initial interest boded well. A few small write-ups in the music press were good omens, and our demo was played and praised on the radio. In my heart, these tiny seeds were the start of something big.

Life was as good as it had ever been in Dublin.

Ma had somehow got us out of Ballymun. We were living in a place I liked. I could go a whole fortnight sometimes and not hear the word nigger. I had friends. I had a purpose. I had an identity. I had hope.

'I had hoped you would be pleased,' Ma said.

I was too shocked to be pleased. I had just returned from

rehearsing with the band when Ma said, 'We're going back to England.'

***

Lesley points to a group of devotees walking across a field between the Ashram and the road leading to Fatimanagar.

'I wonder where they're going?' she asks. Then, shading her eyes, she spots Mataji leading a loose line of about thirty people. 'That's odd, isn't it? Are we missing something?'

I shrug. I've got no idea. At this moment, I don't even know why *I'm* here.

'Let's go find out.' Lesley takes my hand and draws me toward the others. We catch up with Mataji and join her little expedition. She tells us Swami is the guest of honour at a celebration. The locals are opening up a workshop for local gem cutters. I remember seeing them painting the building a few days ago when Lesley and I went to get the bus into Trichy.

Across the bone-dry grass we go. Snakes, scorpions, and other creatures will be sheltering from the unbearable heat, so I'm mindful of where I put my feet. I see butterflies flutter into the air as we pass. I don't know how they can survive this temperature, flitting giddily through the air like a game one can't quite grasp.

When we reach the road leading to the outskirts of Fatimanagar, it's just a short walk to the gem cutter's building, which smells of fresh paint and sits smugly like a squat yellow canary. A large awning provides shade and shelter to locals and devotees alike, many of whom are both. There is a marquee outside, which is fat with mums and sticky-fingered children. Devotees stand at the edges of the marquee with the men and older boys of the village. There's a long table at one end of the awning, where assorted local dignitaries are waiting on Swami before taking their seats.

Great. More waiting. Just what I want. I stand, feeling the urge to put my hands in pockets my dhoti doesn't have.

Big ol' speakers hanging from the awning corners begin blasting Indian pop music at us. I assume it's called 'pop' because, at this volume, that's precisely what my eardrums will do if it doesn't stop. God Almighty! Does it have to be this loud? I see other people wincing at the musical equivalent of a slightly deaf, mildly xenophobic tourist speaking to a foreign waiter, replacing comprehension with volume.

Abruptly, the music stops.

***

Ma told me, 'I've been in touch with your dad back in Manchester. He's helping me find a house to rent. So we should be back in England by the end of this month. I thought we'd be okay here, eventually, but we're not. Tony's very unhappy. You can see that. And I don't want Jason to go through any of the trouble you and Tony have had.'

So there it was.

The end of all the crap we'd endured for years.

Up to and beyond the death of God in Ballymun, I'd longed for this day, and now the gates of the prison were opening —

And I'm staying in it.

'I'm not going,' I said.

Ma was shocked. She actually flinched. 'But — why?' she asked.

'I'll go when I'm ready.'

'Oh?' Ma said. She shook her head and sat down on the sofa. 'I'm absolutely flabbergasted. You, above anyone, wanted to go back. I thought you'd be over the moon.'

'I am,' I said. 'I'm happy for Jason and Tony, but I'm not done with Ireland yet. I've got my band. I want to see if I can get someplace with it. Besides, I like living here in this house.'

Ma's face took on the sort of expression usually followed by the word, 'Oops.'

'What? I asked

'You can't stay here.'

It took a moment for that to sink in.

'Why?'

'I've given this house up to your uncle Joe. So he'll be coming here to live with his family.'

'You're joking?'

She shook her head.

'But this is my home! Where the hell will I live if this goes?'

'You can live in their old house.'

'In their house? And where's that?'

'Clondalkin.'

'Where the bloody hell is Clon-bloody-dalkin? I've never even heard of the place.'

***

The awful noise has started again, blasting out without regard for eardrums or pacemakers. Balefully, I look up at the speakers and the thick wire loops from which they hang. If this damn awful noise is anything to go by, hanging's too good for them.

Under my breath, I mutter a curse and see Lesley peering at me from the shadow of her straw hat. She leans in close. Shouts in my ear, 'Stop swearing. We don't want to offend anyone now, do we?'

I shout back, 'If I wanted to offend anyone, I'd have to write it down and ask them to read it. That bloody music is drowning out everything.'

A particularly shrill note drills into my skull as I speak, making me grimace. Lesley's trying not to look as if she's sucking a lemon.

Mataji appears, pleasantly smiling, as if trying to hear the faint musical lilt of Vivaldi in the background. She's about to say something, but a crescendo of tremulous wailing cuts her off. The noise condenses into a white-hot wall of feedback which stops just before my head pops like a watermelon.

'Oh, for f —'

Lesley elbows me in the ribs.

People are pointing down the road. We turn and see the old car Swami uses as a runaround.

A child is shouting excitedly.

'Swami's here!'

Her mum hushes her as the car pulls off the road, crunching gravel and back-firing. The back door of the vehicle opens. The big afro, a significant bushy presence of scented hair, appears, and then beneath that, the main event. Swami smiling his big smile and waving. He sits in the place of honour at the long table, and all the dignitaries sit with him. The gem cutters, looking both proud and bashful, gather behind Swami.

Sheltered from the sun, we listen to many speeches.

I'm so bored I almost wish the music would come back. I watch an elderly villager self-consciously stand up from the relative anonymity of the table to hold forth in Tamil about — I have no idea. It's all in Tamil. He's got his speech on bits of paper that flap as he tries to put them in order.

I feel like my head is being basted in sweat. I'm so uncomfortable and don't know why I'm here. Why am I two thousand miles from home listening to a dull monologue in a language I don't understand about something which doesn't interest me, delivered by someone I don't know?

What am I doing here?

I'm looking at Swami Premananda.

He's smiling as if today is his birthday and the villagers have just given him what he *always* wanted.

And what he wanted, so it seems, are exceedingly monotonous and very long-winded speeches.

***

They've gone.
> *Gone*
> *Back to England.*
> *Jason*
> *Tony*
> *Ma*
> *I'm all alone.*
> *Not me myself, and I*
> *No.*
> *Just me.*

Soon I would be gone, too. Compared to everywhere else we had lived, Montpelier Hill felt like a safe harbour. The thought of leaving it for someplace I'd never even heard of filled me with dread. My abdomen was a balled-up fist of anxiety. It gnawed away at me like the rodents beneath Echlin Street's floorboards. I felt disfigured by the past and was frightened of the future as if it were a mirror that would throw my reflection back at me. Sometimes I struggled to breathe as if I were drawing each breath up out of a deep well, and even then, all I could do was sip. Because of this, one night, I lay down on my bed, driven by a strong desire to slow my breath and breathe consciously.

I mentioned this incident earlier in the book. It was the time when I noticed the clock on the wall slowing down. Each spasm of the minute hand lurching forward seemed to take longer and longer until time stopped. From the ever-widening gap between each inhalation, I saw my body wasn't breathing. I thought I was dying. I sat up, grasping at life, panicked by this peculiar state.

The clock was ticking again.

Time kept ticking, and I found myself standing in the back of a battered, blacked-out van. I was wedged into a corner, my guitar clutched in one hand, mop in the other. My foot was braced against a sofa bed where I'd placed the Teac 4-Track, which Joe had been good enough to lend me. It was buried beneath my bedclothes. My records were on an overstuffed armchair with the record player. Books in boxes. Clothes in bin bags. I didn't have much. Ma had sold most of our furniture to fund the move back to England. She left what she couldn't sell to her younger brother and his wife, the new tenants in Montpelier Hill. The van had already made a few trips to bring the contents of their old home to what had been mine. On the last trip, the back of the van swallowed me and my few possessions. When the doors slammed, I felt like a hostage.

The long journey in the gloom saw me shaken and rocked like dice in a cup. I felt numb, uprooted and rolled out before the eyes of the unknown. I could have been back home in England with my family, but instead, I was in the back of a van, not knowing where I was going or what the future held.

Even as she waved goodbye a few weeks ago, Ma had been mystified about why I wouldn't leave. I knew why, but I couldn't explain it to her. If I had left Ireland, it would have been a defeat. A fucking rout. Like it had just chewed us up and spat us out. I wasn't having that. It just wasn't right. I wanted to find meaning in what had happened to us because if I didn't, it would have just been for nothing.

If I could come out of Ireland with something worthwhile, it wouldn't have been a waste of time. On the contrary, it would exalt the sacrifice if I could succeed as a musician or songwriter. Recognition of something other than the colour of my skin would turn this water into wine.

And it would be a great way to say fuck you to the Irish.

***

* * *

Bored, hot and thirsty, I move to the outskirts of the gathering. For the sake of good manners, I smile and clap after each speech, but it's a real effort. I feel resentful and don't want to be doing this. I want to go back to the Ashram. Dreadfully bored, sweating, and impatient to leave, I look at Swami.

He's still smiling.

He *must* be bored with this, but look at him, for God's sake. Just look at that smile. His heart seems to be overflowing with joy, lighting his face up, and I can't help but stare at him as I did a few days ago, but this time I'm not intimidated by his presence. If anything, I'm annoyed by it. Why couldn't he have smiled at me like this when I'd followed him around? He just stood and watched me as I watched him. No smile for me. Nothing. Not a flicker. Not a damned thing, and then he walked away, and I felt crushed beneath his footsteps.

Why didn't you smile at me?

You're smiling at everyone else through these mind-numbing speeches. You're smiling so beautifully when they show you the inside of the building and the outside. You're smiling when the gem cutters show you the implements they use. You're smiling even though all you have to do is open your hand, and gems will fall from your palms should you want them to. Your smile is a thing of wonder. It's not the humourless, cheek-aching thing any ordinary face would have congealed into by now. Instead, it's a full-faced, fresh, sweet, cheek-bulging, bright-eyed smile.

The gem cutters are working, rasping away, using a spinning wheel to polish the rough diamonds, patiently coaxing the facets into being.

I want you to turn *me* into a diamond.

Cut the impurities away. Hold me up to the light. Not in the next life. Or the afterlife. Not even before afternoon tea, but now.

What's wrong with this moment?
All I want from you is the truth.
Who am I?
And why do I feel like this?

***

After the removal van left me in Clondalkin, I remained in the dark for a long time. I sat on the stairs in the hallway, hugging my knees and staring out to where a dim street light flickered. I'd left the front door open, reluctant to close it as if it would have been a confirmation of whatever sentence I was to serve here. There were no houses opposite me, just a deep black void hiding empty, unloved fields of scrub. I didn't want to close the door. I didn't even want to turn on the light. This virtually empty, cold house was supposed to be my new home. Instead, I felt as if I was intruding on the bare floorboards and walls, emphasising how alone I felt.

Eventually, I got up. It was getting cold. I went into the living room to organise the clutter of my life. The street lamp outside gave enough light to colonise this one room. I opened up my sofa bed and tossed my blankets onto it. While doing this, I was acutely aware of how dark the rest of the house was. All the other rooms were without lightbulbs. In those shadows were memories that weren't mine. Those memories had the smell of strangers on them—memories that were cold and unfamiliar to me. I rummaged in my bags for a couple of lightbulbs I'd had the foresight to bring. I screwed one into the socket and flicked the switch. The naked bulb exposed me to the world outside, so I used a bedsheet to cover the window. There was some curtain wire already in place. I put the radio on to keep me company while I made the bed.

I put the other lightbulb in the kitchen. The cupboards were empty. The gas cooker still held the cold, grease-laden smell of someone else's cooking. I got myself a pan to boil up some water and then realised I had no matches and no lighter to light the gas. I still had my jacket on, so after patting myself down and making sure I had keys and money, I went out and searched for a shop.

I walked through a sprawling housing estate lit by piss-yellow street lights. Out of habit, I avoided groups of people. Wide stretches of grass for playing fields meant I didn't have to walk on the pavements. The further I walked without finding any shops, the more I began to think Clondalkin looked like Ballymun without the Towers. The streets all looked the same to me, held together only by the architect's evident love of monotony. It was like an alternate Ballymun in which the towers lay down and died from boredom, and Clondalkin was what they called the remains.

I saw a lad walking toward me across the field. As he got closer, I called over to him.

'Any idea where I can find a shop at this hour?'

'Nothing open round here. Not till the morning, then you'd have to go in that direction about a mile.' He gestured over his shoulder with a thumb.

'Thanks,' I said, 'would you have a couple of matches on you?'

'No. Sorry. I don't smoke.' He walked on.

I stopped for a moment, indecisive, wondering if I should walk until I found someone who'd give me a match. Then, behind me, a familiar word emerged out of the distance.

'Nigger!'

It cut a jagged groove in me. The contempt dripping from the edge of that word felt like poison. I walked in the direction of the voice because that was the straightest way back to the house. I couldn't see who said it, but it didn't matter. There was an endless supply of people like that in Ireland. Knockdown one, and there would always be another. Always one more. Like dogs barking in the night, there was no stopping them.

I suppressed my anger and sense of hopelessness, smothering them until they stopped kicking. A cold, numb feeling took hold of my insides. By the time I reached the house, I could scarcely breathe. I closed the door and stood with my back against it. The radio was still playing, but the music slowly sank into the hiss and crackle of static. I had to bend forward with my hands on my knees, pulling oxygen into my lungs.

'Oh, God,' I said to nobody in particular.

I felt like I'd escaped from the pit that was Ballymun, only to go and walk back into it.

I remember thinking this is going to be very bad.

***

I've assumed that being near Swami Premananda would intensify my spirituality, but here I am now, darkness rising. What light there is doesn't feel like a revelation of my sacred Self. It's more of a distress flare, and in the lurid light, it seems obvious that the spiritual path isn't for me. I should just step aside. Let those who are dedicated and pure of heart and mind come here. I've been defeated by myself and do not belong in an ashram or even with those who are sincere in their desire to live a spiritual life.

But the idea of giving up, being unfit for the journey and standing by the wayside is awful. It evokes feelings of abandonment and desolation. I'm sure of one thing, though. I'd rather be abandoned and left behind than walk on the path as a fraud.

If I can't even deal with a smile being withheld, then fraud is what I must be. How can there be any spirituality in such insecurity? Such a need for approval does not lend itself easily to having a spiritual backbone. How have I deluded myself into believing I'm anything more than one of the multitude, stumbling in the gloom and mumbling prayers?

I find myself looking at Swami. Look at him over there, still smiling with no effort. Something pure and joyful is pouring from his heart like light from the sun. Yet he walked away from me yesterday when a smile was all I wanted. I just wanted something to say that the universe knows I'm trying to do my God damned best.

> But no —
> You have smiles for everybody else.
> None for me.
> It hurts.

***

The radio was hissing a thin, mean static into the air, like gas escaping from a pressurised pipe. I reached over and slapped the off button. That was what dragged me out of my sleep on my first morning in Clondalkin. I lay with my eyes closed, remembering the early days in Ballymun and the feeling of dread that always came with waking up in that damned tower. The dread feeling was back with a vengeance. It was a peculiar thing, that feeling as if I'd swallowed my heart, and it was forever falling through the length of me, falling as if I was hollow. I was falling like rubbish through a refuse chute in the guts of a tower. Falling through the numb sensation of subdued fear.

Fuck this, I thought, kicking the blanket off and sitting up.

Get up, and open the curtain. Welcome the day. Whatever it brings. I'm not a victim. I'm the one who decided to stay.

I got to my feet.

Pulled the curtain open a crack — Jesus! I leapt back from the alien glare of a massive eye above giant teeth. Stumbling over my bags, I fall backwards —

***

Like a leaf in autumn —
> I've fallen from the Tree of Life into oblivion.
> Nowhere, in a deep, deep sleep, I abide without myself.
> Sleep itself becomes weary.

It drifts away —

—and now I'm looking up at Lesley.

'Are you awake?' she asks.

I nod.

'Come and eat,' she says.

'No. You go. I'll have something in a bit. I don't feel hungry now.'

'You're sure? You've been very quiet since we came back from the gem cutters. Are you okay?'

'Yeah. Fine. Just tired, is all.'

'I could bring you some food if you just want to stay here?'

'No. Thanks.' I sit up and smile to prove I'm okay. She goes. I flop back down, my mind wandering back over the morning, tasting itself.

***

A horse! In the garden!

It was a great big thing, aloof and on the hoof, looking at me with big brown eyes. I picked myself up and pulled the sheet from the window. The horse was licking the grass, big thick tongue, smearing mud with lascivious strokes. Manure dropped from the other end. Beyond the horse, dozens of untidy caravans were parked up in what had been an empty field. A small, tousled-haired boy jumped onto the garden wall. He called the horse, and the horse followed him.

While I'd been sleeping, dozens of caravans had turned up and camped in the field. Or maybe they'd been there already, and I hadn't noticed them in the dark. Either way, I was severely pissed off. At that time, travellers had a lousy reputation in Ireland for thievery. So my immediate reaction to their presence was to start worrying about someone breaking in and stealing the 4-Track I'd borrowed from Joe.

For fuck sake.

What next?

I went around the house, checking the back door and the windows to ensure they were all locked.

***

Looking back over the morning, lying on my bed in the koothi, I feel worse than I did earlier. I get up, head out into the sun, and pace the Ashram grounds. The special abhishekam for those who will soon be leaving India will be taking place later. I don't want to be feeling this bad during the ceremony. I've got to sort my head out. I also need a clean dhoti, which happens to be the one I'm wearing. I go back to the koothi because walking is making me sweat.

Inside, Lesley's reading a book. She says, 'They're still serving food. Why don't you get something?'

'I'm still not hungry,' I say.

Lesley puts her book down beside her and asks, 'What's the matter?'

'Nothing. Go back to your book.'

'I can't concentrate with you moping around. Come on, sweetheart. What is it?'

'I don't know. It's hard to put into words.'

Lesley doesn't say anything, obviously expecting me to try and explain myself.

'I feel like I've spent most of the time here falling to pieces.'

'Oh, dear. It's not been that bad, has it?'

'No. It's been amazing. Really. The thing is, we'll be going back to England soon, and I'm still just me.'

Lesley chuckles.

'Who were you expecting?'

'A better me.'

'Yeah. I know what you mean. I went through that, too,

when I first met Swami. My advice would be to give the experience here a little time and space. You never know what might happen. Swami's like that with his teaching sometimes.'

I shrug. 'Sure. But I can't help feeling disappointed. It's like travelling to see Santa and being given an awful portrait of myself in a plastic frame instead of a new toy. Or a new me.'

'You're not sorry we came, are you?'

'No. I'm glad we came. No doubt about that, but perhaps I expected too much.'

'From Swami?'

'No. From me. Swami's turned out to be something other than what I expected. Something I never imagined. Something far better. But I thought I'd be changed by meeting him. I thought I'd be — I don't know — less like me and more like him. But I'm still just me.'

'Aren't we all, sweetheart.' Lesley smiles wistfully. 'But as I said, give it time.'

'Yeah. I know. You're right. And what time doesn't heal the memory buries, so — any idea how long it'll be before Swami will do the abhishekam?'

She shrugs. 'If the rest of the week is anything to go by, it could be hours or minutes away. You know the story. It'll be now but later.'

'Yep. Faster but slower.'

'Here, but there.'

She chuckles and lies down. She spreads her book across her face, blocking the sunlight filtering through the edge of the louvred window. The fan above slowly turns. The fridge shivers. Outside, the water pump clunks up and down like an arthritic knuckle. Children are laughing. Up in the roof, something rustles—a lizard in a grass skirt, perhaps? The smell of food grows faint. The scent of incense becomes stronger. I lie down too. For a long time, we wait. Long enough for me to start drifting —

Lesley speaks, almost to herself, whispering like paper.

'I keep wishing we could stay longer. But, in a few days, we'll be back at work.

I'm saying nothing, but I feel it too. This will disappear. The world will swallow us whole.

Almost as a long sigh, Lesley softly says, 'I feel so safe with Swami nearby.'

***

With a fist full of loose change dug deep into my pocket, I walked across the playing field near my house in Clondalkin. There were thick clouds in the sky, gathered to plot rain. I was hunched into my overcoat, pushing into a biting wind. I was coming back from the shops. The walk there and back took maybe an hour. I don't know if anyone called me a nigger. I can't remember now, not after all these years, but I do know I waited for it with every second that passed.

I felt like I was back in Ballymun.

I felt as if leaving had only been a dream.

Here I was, back in the nightmare that had been living in the shadow of those seven towers. There were no towers in Clondalkin holding up the grey slab of the sky, but they were there, inside my head. James Connolly tower was embedded in my heart, like a bone stuck in my throat, and I couldn't remove it without help.

I got back to the house in a cold sweat.
Closed the door
Locked it

***

Abruptly the door is opened.

'Lesley!'

We both jump off our beds. It's Mataji, a sense of urgency about her. She's slightly breathless and says again, 'Lesley!'

'What is it?'

'You must come. Quickly! Adrienne and Rekha are leaving. Come and say goodbye.'

Lesley looks at me, the urgency puzzling her. She follows Mataji out of the door. But what about me? Adrienne and Rekha are old friends of Lesley, and I barely know them, but I like them both. Why am I not invited to say farewell? I feel glum, then feel contempt for the silliness of such feelings. Sighing, I lie down and settle my head into the warm nook of my arm. I'm tired of myself. I'm going to sleep until the feeling passes.

I'm concentrating very hard on not being awake.

Laying here

Thinking

Outside I hear Lesley and Mataji laughing. They're coming back, giggling like girls. They open the door. I lie still with my back to them, not wanting to engage in conversation.

'I'll pop the kettle on,' Lesley says, ' and — ' lowering her voice, whispers, ' — Paul's asleep.'

'Bless him,' Mataji says quietly. I hear the one chair creak as she sits down. Hear Lesley open the fridge door. The sound of bottles clinking makes me thirsty. She's filling the kettle.

Mataji says, 'Now, I'll tell you the *real* reason why I called you.'

The noise Lesley's making stops abruptly.

Mataji continues. 'Swami said he wanted to have a look at you.'

'Really? At me?'

'Yes. I thought if I just called you out and told you why you'd start flapping.'

'I would have done, but — why did he want to look at me?'

Mataji sounds as if the whole thing is tickling her.

'God knows,' she says.'

I hear a match being struck. Lesley says, 'Now you mention it, I *did* look over to where Swami was standing, and he *was* looking at me. He gave me a huge smile. You know the way he does — '

No, I'm thinking. I bloody well don't.

' — but because I was so preoccupied with saying goodbye to Adrienne and Rekha, I didn't pay him any attention. So I didn't get self-conscious.'

Another match is struck. This time it's followed by the muted *'whump!'* of the camping stove being lit and the faint smell of gas.

'You shouldn't feel uncomfortable around Swami. You've known him for as long as I have.'

'I suppose so, but I've not seen him in person for years. And don't forget, the first time I saw Swami all those years ago, he looked at me as if I was something he'd trodden in and was looking for somewhere to wipe his shoe.'

'You've got no idea the compliment that he paid you. He went straight for your ego.'

'Well, that's what I gather now, but back then, I was crushed. I wanted to crawl into a hole and pull the earth in on top of me.'

'Straight for your ego, as I said.'

'I'd much rather he'd started with a simple hello, perhaps followed up with *'brace yourself.'*'

They're laughing. True to the tradition of spiritual masters throughout the ages, the only reason one will stroke your ego is to find the best place to crack it.

I hear the cups clunk and water pouring — the clink and

swirl of a spoon.

'Thanks,' Mataji says. 'It took years before Swami started to do the same thing to me. Only then did I get an inkling of what he put you through and why? With you, he didn't waste time applying the anaesthetic. With me, there was a lot of preparation beforehand.'

'Maybe with you, it took longer because he wanted to drop you from a greater height to crack the ego. Who knows? But you can understand why, figuratively speaking, I duck when he walks past.'

'Yes. I certainly do. But he's treating you with kid gloves this time around.'

'I know. I keep expecting a clip around the ear, and instead, I get a pat on the head and a big grin.'

I'm still listening, pretending to be asleep. Yeah. I feel like I'm getting a pat on the head too, but mine's fallen out the back of a —

***

Horse's arse.

Regularly — in my garden.

I'd pull back the curtain, and there it would be. It summed up Clondalkin and the turn my life had taken.

If, as I suspected, Ballymun was the arsehole of Dublin, then Clondalkin went one better. It went to the trouble of presenting me with an actual arsehole with a horse on the other end. I'd bang on the window. The horse would turn his big old head slightly to look down his big old nose at me. Then, with a derisive snort, the son of a mare would take his rump back to the traveller's camp across the road.

This regular morning visit always felt like an omen. I had a sense of being under siege. Sometimes it was just a subtle feeling, but inside, I felt as if life would pounce if I let my guard down. Maybe, if I'd arrived in

Clondalkin without having been primed to expect the worst by Ballymun, I wouldn't have faced each day with a growing sense of dread. It gnawed away like the rodents in Echlin Street. It lurked like the cockroaches under Corby Street, waiting for the light in me to fade away.

On the surface, when I met with the band, I appeared calm and ready to smile.

Under the surface, I was already running and just like in Ballymun, going outside had become problematic. If I had to leave the house, I didn't just consider the weather or distance but how much of my self-esteem the walk to the shop would cost. Not that I went to the shop often. I usually had very little money left after paying my bills. I got money from the dole, but most of it went on rent and my share of a P. A system the band had bought up in Belfast. To make my share of the payments, I lived frugally. Discounted cans of dog food wagged their tails at me as I wandered through the shops looking for cheap food. The only thing that stopped me from eating dog chunks in questionable gravy was the thought that I'd not only be waking up to a horse's arse but probably be eating one as well.

I wrote as if the only way I could escape from Ireland was through music, but, of course, it wasn't. I could have left at any time, but I didn't. I wouldn't. Not while there was a chance I could transform our experience in Ireland into something worthwhile.

Most prisons in the world exist in the mind, and few people will ever see the bars. I made a prison for myself from the bars of the songs I wrote. My attachment to a particular outcome held me in a place and situation that caused me great anguish. The early morning hours saw me drinking coffee, writing, listening, analysing and recording. I wrote lyrics feverishly, scratching at a pad with the one-pointed grim intensity of a prisoner scraping at a prison wall with a knife. I broke songs like a man breaking into oysters, looking for a pearl. By the time I went to bed, I was usually strung out on caffeine and hope.

Under the bed, I kept a small, thick length of metal I'd found in the backyard. It was about a foot long. Rust-like blood made it coarse. It was cold but comforting to the touch on the nights when I woke up, spooked by some noise in the house. I'd get up quietly, holding the bar to check the doors and windows. If anyone tried to break in while I was dreaming of breaking out, they'd be sorry.

***

Mataji's going. She's got some work to do for Swami. She's saying, 'Listen out for the bell. It'll be the call for the special abhishekam.' The door closes quietly.

'How long do we wait?' I ask.

'I thought you were asleep,' Lesley says.

I roll over and sit up, saying, 'I was just resting my eyes.'

She offers her cup of tea to me, which I take and have a swallow, nodding my gratitude.

'It could be minutes. It could be hours. You know how it goes. Hurry up and wait.'

'Yeah.'

'Can you pass me that book off the top of the fridge?'

I pass the book to her and the tea. She smiles sweetly and sips the last of it, looking at me.

'You okay?'

I smile and nod. Satisfied, she flips through the pages to find her place. I stand up, not sure what to do with myself. It's too hot outside to go for a walk, and I'm too restless to sit and wait. I walk around the room. My hands go to the pockets my dhoti doesn't have, so they hang by my side. I don't know what the fuck I'm doing. I wander into the backyard, where the sun is sharp and blindingly bright.

***

Summer must have come to Clondalkin, but I can't remember it. Instead, I recall long stretches of grey where a cold-hearted wind picked the rain up and threw it in my face. The breeze was never at my back, always in my face. The cold was so brutal at times that my hands ached like stones. I buried them deep in my pockets, balling them into fists, but the cold always knew where they were and found them. I was clenched like a fist myself, shoulders hunched, jaw tight, and teeth grinding whenever I left the house. Like a cat carrying a pitiful corpse to lay at its owner's feet, life brought racial slurs with mindless monotony. The tension between each incident would stretch, becoming narrow and sharp, waiting to snap. It was almost a relief when something happened.

Almost

But then the waiting would begin again.

Even though it didn't happen with the same frequency as Ballymun, for some reason, it sunk deeper. I was so weary of it. I had no idea these were the last few cuts before the tension would break. The self-control holding back the cold rage and flood of my sorrow and anguish would fracture. I quivered between the desire to run and the desire to fight and did neither.

Violence leads to greater violence.

Sometimes I attempted to converse with people who called out darkie, nigger, or coon. Some ran away, and others spoke with a smirk from the safety of the friends who flanked them. Some were aggressive, but I didn't react to that unless I had to defend myself physically. That was their dance. The odds were all stacked in their favour. I walked at my own pace, neither avoiding trouble nor seeking it but resigned to its inevitability. Trying to reason with them was like showing a dog a card trick. They didn't understand, or worse, they didn't care, which was worse than anything. It meant nothing to them, and yet the damage it did endured. It echoed within the hollow of my heart long after they had forgotten the words they spat out.

I endured it like a boy lying awake at night, waiting for a dog in the distance to stop barking.

Waiting —

***
***

Waiting —

I'm sitting in the sharp-cut shade in the backyard, sheltering from the sun. The air is swollen and bruised with heavy, sullen heat.

Why hasn't the bell rung?

I feel each second slowly passing as if each one is playing for time. Minutes are stalling, rubbernecking the 'Now' before moving on.

A bead of sweat on my left eyebrow is waiting to drop.

Not yet.

Waiting.

Still there.

Tickling.

I wipe it away. Get up. Pace the yard. Too hot here. Go inside. Walk there instead.

***

Waiting for the bus.
Waiting for the rain to stop.
Waiting for the wind to stop blowing in my face.
Waiting for the dogs to stop barking.
Waiting to be called nigger.

***

Lesley abruptly shuts the pages of the book she's reading. It made a little 'whump' noise like the stove earlier.

She sighs. 'I'm going for a walk.'

'I'll come with you. This waiting around is getting to me

too.'

'It's not the waiting that's bothering me, sweetheart. You pacing up and down is putting me on edge.'

'Oh — sorry.'

'You sure you're okay?'

'Yup.'

'Well, then, give me a minute. I'll change out of these clothes. I want to keep them clean for the ceremony.' She takes a Punjabi suit out of her case. It's slightly less immaculate than the one she's already wearing. She changes into it, grabs her cigarettes and heads for the open door.

The bell rings.

Time to go to the Prayer Hall.

***

Months passed. The fifth horse of the apocalypse stopped grazing in my garden. He moved on to pastures anew with the travellers. I continued to trade sleep for songs about peace, love, and conscience. We took those songs out and gave life to them in dark beer-stinking smoke pits. I looked for validation in those dimly lit places with cramped stages, tacky underfoot from sweat and beer. Behind the applause, which was sometimes rousing and occasionally paltry, derisive even, I heard the voice of salvation, and I stumbled toward it, climbing over everything else in my life.

***

Here we go! The bell rang! Lesley rushes back into the clean outfit she'd changed out of moments ago. We don't want to be late. Being late is *very* bad form. If you're late for a special abishekam, you miss out on the blessing. That's why she's hopping on one leg, trying to get her foot into the leg of her suit trouser.

So, we leave the hut, walking briskly toward the Prayer Hall. It's hard to walk fast in sandals. Grit slips in and bites the soles, but I don't care. I find a place to sit in the hall just in front of the wooden seat Swami will sit in when he comes out. Of course, it's not just me. All the other people who are to be blessed with this special puja are alongside me. A few hours ago, I thought I didn't belong, and now look at me. I'll be right by his feet when he gives us our special blessing. Being so close to where he'll be, gives me a feeling of belonging. Perhaps even redemption. Silly, I know, but tell that to my ego, silently purring as I sit in the lap of the gods.

Slowly at first, the purring slows.

Probably something to do with this long wait, sitting here. Just — waiting.

And now, the purring stops. The feeling of redemption turns sour. One of Swami's helpers appears and tells us Swami will not be here for some time.

We should all go and wait to be called.

I'm looking at his empty chair and feeling foolish. How could I have thought sitting here would mean anything? I look around at the faces of the other people. Young and old, man and woman. They get to their feet with good humour and patience, but not me. How easily I fooled myself into thinking I belonged here.

Me —

The person at whom Swami Premananda wouldn't smile.

Outsider —

***

In Ireland, inside my room, inside the house, inside my head, tight as a wire, hardly able to breathe, tension quietly crackled inside me like ice under running water.

Nobody knew.

Nobody.

Not even my family. I was able to see them for a few days. Ma sent money to buy a ticket so I could get to Manchester. I think she was under the impression I would leave Dublin for good once I'd gotten a taste of home. For so long, England was my Jerusalem and my Kansas. Sure enough, it was great to see Ma and my brothers. I also spent time with my dad, Desmond Donaldson. He married and started a family a few years after my parents went their separate ways, and his new family was as welcoming as my own. On my last evening in Manchester, Tony and I went walking with Desmond. Jason was at home with Ma.

I was happy to be near my father. It gave me a feeling of comfort and belonging, something I'd not had since moving to Ireland.

We passed four lads and a girl standing by the low garden wall of a corner house, talking to each other. It was here Tony said goodbye. He shook my hand because I was leaving in the morning, and he went toward his flat.

Dad and I continued across the road to the pavement. We walked the length of three houses when the word came through the air —

Nigger

I stopped and turned. The four lads and the girl were sniggering.

'It's nothing,' Dad said. 'Just ignore them, son.'

I walked back. I wanted to make sure Tony was okay. As I got to the corner, he was walking back to check on us.

'You okay?' I asked.

'Yeah. You?' he replied.

'We're fine. Shall we —?

'Sure,' he said, and without breaking stride, we smashed into the lads on the corner —

***

* * *

The sun is falling slowly, slipping from the sky. The bell tolls again. Once more, we leave the koothi and head to the Prayer Hall. How many times is this now? Four times? Five? I can tell you this for nothing. It's winding me up. Even as we walk over to the Prayer Hall, I know it's a waste of time. We'll wait a while before being told Swami will be with us later because that has been happening for hours. We've been going back and forward like a metronome.

    Tick and Tock.
    For why?
    Why?

***

The violence was brutal and overwhelming. My first punch broke the jaw of the lad nearest me. He went backwards, arms flying out to catch himself. He caught hold of the lad beside him, and they both fell over the wall. I jumped over it to start stamping on them. I raised my boot above the face of the one I'd punched to end the threat —

***

    Light and shadow conspire in corners.
  Moon above.
    The bell rings again.
    Again we leave the koothi.
    We're sent away again.
    And again, we trudge back.
    Tick
    Tock
    Time
  Wasting

This
Is
Madness!

.

***

Oh God

The look in the eyes of the boy —

I lifted the rough sole of my boot to stomp him but saw the look on his face. The eyes were wide open. Full of fear. Asking for mercy.

I don't want to hurt anyone, so why does life do this to us?

'Stop it. You're mad,' he whined.

Why am I smiling at them, I wonder.

'Jesus —' said the other.

'Stop it! What're you doing?'

Shiva dancing —

I stopped. Shocked.

I pointed at them. I said stay down, or I will fucking kill you. I spat on the ground to express my contempt, but it was all an act. The look in their eyes and the fear in their voices soured the exultation of my little victory. I felt bad for them and ashamed of myself. I stepped back over the wall. Tony was walking toward me. He'd caught one lad with a swift boot in the balls and gone running after the other.

The girl was still standing by the lampost. We ignored her.

'You okay? He asked.

'Yeah.'

He looked at the two on their backs in the garden and nodded in appreciation of what I'd done.

'How about you?'

'Fine,' he said.

We parted as if nothing had happened. That moment of unity felt good, and I was proud of my big brother. It had always felt like we'd have to fight half the country in Ireland, and there were just too many *faces to punch. But there were only four in England that night, and we'd gone through them.*

Dad was shocked at the violence.
I can still hear him saying, 'Lord Jesus —

***

— Christ, Almighty! Again! The bell rings, and we're going back to the Prayer Hall.

I say to Lesley, 'This is ridiculous!'

Quickly, she's washing her face with lukewarm water, burying her face briefly in her towel and then patting her skin dry.

'I know,' she sighs. 'Maybe this time Swami will be there?'

***

Clondalkin welcomed me back from Manchester with a cold embrace, icy fingers frisking through my sleeves and collar. The rain came and froze my hands. I bunched them into fists and dug them like moles into my pockets. Life went on. Day after day passed with the monotony of an identity parade where all the suspects looked the same. We rehearsed endlessly. Gigs came and went erratically, like a pulse on the heart monitor of a patient who was in an intensive care unit. Our musical career showed only faint signs of life, but I held on to them. Our demo was played on the radio. We had a few write-ups. It was nothing much but enough for me to keep going. It was enough to nourish my longing for something other than being a colour. Perhaps my ambition of being a successful songwriter was too much to ask of my modest talent, but it seemed a more realistic prospect than walking down the street without being called a coon.

***

***

Lesley hands me the damp facecloth and urges me to wash my face.

'You should at least freshen up. You'll feel better.'

She's right. I feel awful. I pour tepid water from the kettle into the bowl, push the cloth down beneath the surface, and hold it there.

'Come on, sweetheart, ' Lesley urges. She's holding her hand out for me at the doorway.

'I'll follow you over,' I say. She hesitates in the doorway. I wipe my face with the cloth and wave her on. 'Go,' I say through the course material. I hear the door close. When I look, she's gone. This special puja and the blessing have wound me up so much that I'm fuming. We've been back and forth to the Prayer Hall many times over what feels like hours for *nothing*. I'm *not* rushing over again. I'm not falling for it this time.

I will not be mocked.

Anger swells like a tumour.

***

I'd been sitting upstairs on the bus returning from the city centre. I had strings for my bass and groceries in two heavily laden plastic bags. The bus was packed. I would've walked the 10 kilometres or so to avoid sitting with the other passengers, but I was too tired. Too cold. Too wet and weary.

I knew there would be trouble as soon as I climbed the stairs. A bunch of lads at the back of the bus were being loud and disruptive. Ten minutes into the journey, they started throwing rolled-up bits of paper forward. It wasn't even at me, just toward the front of the bus, but I took it personally.

Why wouldn't I?

I looked back over my shoulder at them.

***

I'm walking toward the Prayer Hall. I see the light within it, warm and bright, yellow like honey, flooding out onto the steps. This is it. Swami is *finally* going to grace us with his presence. I can feel something sacred in the air. Even in my less-than-reverent mood, it's palpable. The closer I get to the steps, the more I feel it.

I stop.

I stand on the edge of this warm light.

I'm suspended between light and darkness, acutely aware of my anger, this rage burning furiously.

I can't move.

I can *not* bring this dreadful thing inside me into the Light of the Prayer Hall.

I can't.

I will not.

Like the fingers of a blind man looking for something dropped in the darkness, my mind is running frantically over the emotions in my heart. It touches these things, probing and pushing into them. These things I feel — anger and fear and self-pity — even hatred, I know all of these things intimately. They're all mine but —

Where is the love?

I'm searching, fumbling numbly for this one precious thing.

Searching —

I can't find it.

This thought slams into me with the gravity of a judge's gavel hammering down onto my cold heart. If there is no love in me, what is there for Swami Premananda to bless?

What is there to preserve if there is no love?

I stagger back from the golden light into a shroud of enveloping darkness and down the deserted road to the rusty gates of the Ashram. I walk alone. My consciousness continues to probe, tasting that through which it experiences itself. There's something bitterly cold, like a metal filling on the tongue.

My heart?

Where is the Love?

I'm shocked to find there is none.

Only cold, furious anger.

I hear a voice.

It calls my name.

***

Nigger.

There it was.

They had waited until they were getting off the bus.

Nothing happened that whole journey after I looked at them. Sure, I heard sniggering, but that was an old acquaintance by now, almost a shadow. And I knew something bad would happen, but I had to wait for the hammer to fall. But I was ready. Oh, Jesus, I was ready. My adrenaline rushed around, tightening and sharpening, secretly trembling, an animal in anticipation.

Come on, you bastards.

The bus came to the second last stop. That was my chance to leave. Get off and walk easily back to the house. But I didn't. It would have felt like I was running away, so I sat and waited. Waited for them to get to their feet. I kept my knee out in the aisle, so they had to brush past, daring them to say something, but they kept their mouths shut. Finally, as the last one passed, I felt an incredible relief. I almost laughed, seeing he wore a pair of trousers with a red tartan pattern, like Rupert the Bear.

As they got off the bus, the doors were closing, and I was sighing with relief, Rupert the Racist shouted.

Nigger.

Something in me died.

***

'Paul!'

Lesley is calling me.

I turn and see her. She's standing in the arc of light outside the Prayer Hall, looking out into the darkness, searching for me.

***

I walked back to the house over the field where I'd heard the first 'nigger' thrown at me in Clondalkin. I put my shopping down in the unlit gloom of the hallway and knelt beside my bed. I reached underneath for the metal bar I kept as a weapon should anyone break into the house. Nobody had tried, but I took it out now because I couldn't keep the bastards from breaking into my heart and my head.

Enough.

Something was broken, and I could not put it back together. All warmth was gone from me. The future was a cold slab falling toward me, and nothing mattered. Not any more. It was almost a relief to be so dead inside that nothing else could hurt. A cold metal bar grasped in my hand, tucked up my sleeve, I went back into the night.

Rupert the Bear had better fucking well run.

I was going to bury this bar in his skull. For Tony and Jason. For everyone who had to put up with bastards pawing their dignity with slurs and cheap laughter. I would make this point. Just leave other human beings in peace. You be you and let me be me. Be kind because your words may be the straw that breaks the camel's back. Think before you dehumanise the next person with your dumb-fuckery because you may turn that person into something less than human.

Every insult, every little cut into my sense of worth as a human being, every nigger, coon, sambo, blackie, packie, nig-nog, darkie, jigaboo, and spear-chucker had condensed into the metal in my hand. It was heavy with the bile and casual contempt strangers had thrown at me. They did it as thoughtlessly as the superstitious throwing salt over one's shoulder, not caring that it fell into an open wound.

I was going to give it all back.
I had to because I could endure no more.
No more.
No more.
No more.

***

I hear my name again. Lesley's calling me back to the Prayer Hall. If I turn my back, I'll be turning away from whatever light there may be within me. I know this, but it isn't this that makes me turn back. I begin walking toward her because I'm worried she'll miss out on Swami's blessing if she comes looking for me. So, I follow her voice down the road. I see her turn back into the light and the Prayer Hall.

And so, I enter with my cold heart and fury. Candles flicker ahead beyond the crowd, shadows slipping and shivering along the walls. Devotees sit in rows before me, a harvest of gently rounded backs. Soft pastel shades of cotton contrast with bare shoulders, glistening with oil and sweat.

***

It never occurred to me that I wouldn't find them even in the dark. They were outside a house, standing in a diffuse cone of piss-yellow light. I scanned them for the one with the red trousers. I assumed they had forgotten what had happened earlier because it meant nothing to them.

Well, I thought. You'll remember this.

***

I'm supposed to go to the front of the Prayer Hall and sit with the others, but I can't. Not feeling like this. Not in this profane state. So, I pick my way forward. Sit down a few rows back, clutching my knees to my chest, watching from that fragile rampart as Swami performs the special abishekam. One of the Mataji's, moving along the people at the front, ties a piece of red thread around the right wrist of each person. At the end of the line, she looks around. A strand of red thread is in her hand.

'Where is the boy?' she asks.

The other devotees point at me.

Behind, a voice urges, 'Go forward!'

I can't move. Will not move. I am rooted to the ground, a sapling that will be blessed where I am or cut down.

The Mataji comes along the aisle with the thread. I hold my hands out, the left supporting the right, and she ties the thread around my wrist. Bowing low, I touch the floor at her feet with my forehead. She returns to the front of the hall, and now I'm sitting amid a murmur of disapproval. Many will have seen my refusal to move as disrespectful. It only lasts for a second or two. Naturally, the devotees are more interested in the Mataji than the young man in their midst. She's moving along the hall, bare feet padding past as she sprinkles us with water blessed during the abhishekam. She draws it from a small brass pail, watering the little seeds of divinity in the field of flesh and bone.

I sit in utter silence.

Who am I?

***

Stepping out of the night, the lads saw me and started backing off. Voices were raised, shouting and jeering. Some woman standing in a doorway shouting, 'Don't be coming round here causing trouble.'

Me?
Causing trouble?
You don't know what trouble is yet.
I laughed at them.
Fuck you all.
I let the bar slip from my sleeve and snugly into my grip. I stood in the road, looking from one face to another, looking at what they were wearing, looking for the one whose head I would smash with the bar.

***

Sitting in silence in the Prayer Hall

I shatter like a clay pot.

Thoughts, feelings and memories explode outward and away.

I see fragments

Emotions

Memories

Physical sensations.

All my pain and sorrow.

All of them are nothing but fragments.

All I assume myself to be is breaking apart in a silent explosion.

I'm here in this nothing-and-nobody state as my former self breaks apart like the shell of a coconut. All I took myself to be, identified as is rushing away from —

From me?

This experience of ideas, emotions and physical sensations which pull and push endlessly is not me. Collectively, they are the movement and emotions I know as Paul. But I can see with the utmost clarity I am not them. They bind me as fog in a headlamp. Their grasp is illusory. I am aware of them, but they are not aware of me. They come, and they go. Everything comes and goes in the presence of this —

This what?

I have no words for what I am.

I am untouched.

I am before I am.

***

The voices of those souls in Clondalkin that night all melded together as they shouted at me. The pack started to circle, gathering their courage. I didn't care what they were doing. All I wanted was for one of them to bear the weight of their collective guilt, to take the weight of what I held.

With no rage or fear but with something cold and unfeeling, I watched them stalking around me, to and fro, wanting to step over the line between fight and flight. I paid them no heed.

My eyes were searching for red trousers.

Where are you —?

***

I am nowhere.

I am nothing.

I am Nobody.

Profound emptiness.

Within the emptiness of myself, I try to turn within myself, but there is no one *to* turn to and nowhere to turn.

I look for my 'real' Self, for something blissful and radiant within my consciousness.

    I find
Nothing
Formless
Nameless

***

Where are you?
    The one I was looking for was nowhere to be seen.

***

Paul is gone, and yet I am still present. Nothing I am came, and nothing that I am went.

Paul has no more substance or longevity than a dream when seen from this state which is always present.

Waves of experience come and go.

Paul is the collective expression of these waves.

I am that which is aware of this movement.

The waves themselves have no awareness.

'The light shone in the darkness, and the darkness knew it not.'

Paul is sound within the Silence.

Movement within the Stillness.

The dream and the dreamer are the same, but I am neither. The dream occurs.

It just is what it is.

***

Rupert the Bear was gone. Who could I give my pain to without him? I couldn't be sure the lads surrounding me were the ones on the bus. He was the only one I could identify. Without him, what was I at that moment?

I was the aggressor.

I had become what I hated. I was a stranger about to inflict fear, pain, and sorrow upon strangers. I was making them the receptacle into which, in my ignorance, I could pour my sorrows. My anger drained away like rain in the gutter, and I burned with shame at what I had been about to do. I turned my back and walked away as they laughed and jeered. The rusted edge of the bar bit into my flesh, drawing blood, but I was the only one it would hurt because I was the one holding it. I would hold on to it in one way or another for many years, and it would continue to draw blood until one night in India.

***

In the cave of my heart, the stone rolls back, and nobody is within waiting for the resurrection.

The tomb is empty.

I've fallen to the earth on wings of fire and shattered at the feet of Swami Premananda, only to find —

Nothing

Shattered fragments of identity return, fusing, and the recurring dream known as Paul occurs again.

Swami Premananda is in front of me, holding a small basket of sweet prasadam. The saint who wouldn't give me a smile gave me something far more precious. He gave me nothing and, through grace, allowed me to see that it is everything.

Humble, I mumble his name, and he moves on.

CHAPTER SEVENTEEN
And The Point Is?

And so here, I guess, is the point of this book, if it has one. My past haunted me. It caused much suffering, and through the years, my approach to alleviating this pain was to try and deal with the trauma directly. With some of my internal wounds, this seemed to work. With other mental and emotional injuries, all I managed to do was forget they were there until something exposed them. Some trauma just followed me around like a sad-eyed, persistent hound. No matter what form my troubles came in, I never looked at what lay at the centre of them all. Into what cup did these sorrows pour themselves?

Who was it that suffered so from the past?

Throughout my life, years after leaving Ireland, I went back in my head and heart and forgave those I could recall who gave me pain. The men that called me nigger as I sat on the back of the flatbed truck at the foot of Connolly Tower? I went to them in my mind, brought my heart to them, and forgave them. I forgave myself, too, for sitting there, young as I was and taking it. The man who almost cut my throat?

Forgiven. I returned to the night in Clondalkin when I was so convinced and entangled in my story that I was one pair of trousers away from committing a terrible crime. I took myself back in time and forgave them all. I embraced them as if they were my children. I asked forgiveness for all the bitterness my memory had held for them through the years. After the incident with Rupert, I'd returned to the house and wept. My future self returned to the past and sat with my younger, wounded self. We sobbed together. Then I forgave us both.

During this experience, I had been sitting up in bed to concentrate on bringing the memories back in vivid colour, sharply defined in all its detail. So deeply was I immersed in the painful recollection that I was in the fetal position by the end of it, unaware of having moved during the process. I emerged from the utter absorption of this experience with a violent inrush of breath that coincided with something rushing from my being. It was part rebirth and exorcism and felt like a profound release from the past. Yet, I still carried my wounds with me. Without realising what I was doing, I smuggled my wounds from the past through customs and brought them to India.

India brought a new perspective. If I was nobody, who was sinned against and who is there to forgive? If other people are as I found myself to be, they are as I am. Empty. Like me, they have the habit of identifying with a process known as whatever name they were given at birth, but that doesn't make them any more of a separate entity than I was. It doesn't make them somebody other than a nobody who mistakenly thinks they are an individual of consequence. And whose fault is that?

Nobody.

No matter the problem, if nobody is at its centre, there is also no problem. It's so sublimely simple. So look and see who is at the centre of this turmoil. Leave your trouble where it is, and look at who is troubled by it.

Who is there?

Creation comes out of emptiness.

You emerge from the emptiness of your dreaming and bring the world with you. What does it mean? It means whatever you want, but know that only the ego requires it to have meaning. The ego reaches for the future and, at the same time, is hanging onto the past. You are the tug of war between these, the knot formed by this tension. Let the rope break. Let go of the past and the future, and there you are.

Unbound.

All of my experience at any moment *is* the definition of what it means to be *me* at that moment. Not just the physical boundaries of my being but the air I breathe, the noise I hear, the thoughts, the sun in the sky, the bird in the tree, and the book on the table. Good and bad, up and down, left and right, hot and cold, big and small are all part of this manifestation, regardless of whichever aspects with which I may choose to identify. All of it is the 'I Am' ness of me. Everything that makes up *the experience* of being Paul *is* Paul.

And if Paul is an experience, then who is the experiencer?

'It' can be nothing that can be touched, tasted, heard, seen or smelt because they are also experiences. They occur within something greater. So what is that *thing* which is not a *thing* in itself? If it were, it would simply be just another thing that must occur within something greater.

This is so simple.

Realising this is the equivalent of slipping on a banana skin. It's funny in itself and needs no explanation. But, as soon as you start explaining the joke, it's no longer funny. It becomes madness, poetry, religion or prayer.

Love others as yourself is a statement of fact. Everything is you. You are everything. You're 'I Am'ness is the manifestation of everything you are experiencing. And the 'I Am' occurs in the presence of something untouched by all sound and movement. It remains constant but ever fresh because it does not age, project forward into the future, or cling to the past.

It knows thirst but is not thirsty.

It shines in the darkness, but the dark knows it not.

Am I in any way enlightened?

No, because who is there to be enlightened?

Enlightenment would suggest a change of some sort from my previous unenlightened state. However, there has been no change whatsoever in that regard. Paul is still the sum total of any given moment experienced through that perspective. For this reason, I lost all interest in enlightenment and even spiritual practices. There is nobody here to enlighten. Having a spiritual practice would be like polishing my shoes in a dream so that when I wake up, I'll look presentable.

Far from being enlightened, I would describe the period after my return from the Ashram as one in which my ego was subtly attempting to gain ascendancy whilst simultaneously being consistently hammered. This continued for a few years before it decided to gallop for the finishing line. It was almost as if, having found this emptiness, my ego rushed to fill it or at least cover it. Eventually, it fell into the nothingness, but not before I had done a lot of damage, particularly to those I love.

The shock of what I experienced that night was so profound that I couldn't even think about it except in passing for many years. I am as I am now, not through thinking about it any more now than I did then, but through virtue of my ego/mind being absorbed by the overwhelming stillness within which everything occurs. The silence is so beautiful my ego can't help but stop and listen. The reasoning mind is drawn to it somehow because it is fascinated by what's there. What it sees is something consistent. It's like seeing someone standing still in a crowd as the people rush around. The face of this person comes to your notice because of their stillness. Every time you notice the figure, they are still there, relaxed and looking directly at you. You get carried away with the crowd, distracted, contracted and harried at every turn, but once more, there is that figure, that peaceful face in the crowd.

Eventually, you realise the stranger is you. You begin to see yourself through the eyes of the stranger. And seeing yourself from this new perspective, you understand the nature of the smile on the onlooker's face and why it was so full of love and so benign, and the eyes twinkled with humour.

Everything I experience when I am awake, goes away when I sleep. Sure, it comes back in the morning, until at some point, it won't. It's a dream within a dream, but even in sleep, there is that which knows sleeping but does not sleep. Even in death, there is that which knows it too but is beyond death. It is already perfectly empty. Perfectly full.

Nobody was born, and so who is it that will become unborn?

The Presence which became apparent in the Ashram is still Present. Everything else has changed. Nothing remains but this. Life occurs through the grace of this Presence. This awareness, this sacred light, illuminates the air through which time ticks away. The metronome goes forward and backwards, projecting forward into the future and returning to the past. Only in the *now*, in the midpoint between those two dreams, is the music waiting, and when you hear it, it turns out to be the most sacred Silence.

The outward breath has that dry, parched odour of the past. The inward breath is ripe with the future, which will remain on the vine. The space between the two breaths is where the truth is. It was always there, but I never knew it. At least Paul never knew it. Still doesn't. The dream of Paul goes on like a wheel turning after the power has been cut. There is drama, laughter, sadness, and all that makes the human condition. The metronome goes back and forward but always comes back to Nothing. Always settles into Silence.

Every crisis subsides into peace.

So do I

So will you.

It took many years to dream myself into this particular moment where I'm writing this, but in all that time, only the thing which is not a thing has remained constant. Peaceful and content. Complete and yet empty. All else comes and goes, including the dream and the dreamer.

All that I am *not* comes and goes.

All that remains is that ever-present witness in front of which eternity passes.

The future is the mind.

The past is the mind.

I am not in the past or the future but am this moment.

I never *was*.

I will not be present later.

I am, now.

And in this moment, everything is complete. All things are the perfect expression of themselves. The mind turns them into longings or aversions. The mind tells stories because without the mind doing this, the mind ceases to exist. The mind is also the ego, and the ego is the story of ourselves that the mind compiles, and we believe in our innocence. And why not. The stories are compelling with a cast of thousands, and no expense is spared with all of creation as both audience and cast members on a stage that stretches as far as the eyes can see. So convincing is it that I would have killed to preserve my character and the part I thought I was playing in the drama. I spent so long trying to heal or distract my presumed self from the past that I missed the actual 'Self' which existed in the present and is free from troubles. Instead of being myself, I was trying to perfect the imprint my footsteps left on the beach, oblivious to the tide coming in.

Is the drama above at the beginning of the play or the middle, or the end? It doesn't matter. It's just your mind doodling a plotline. It does this because it exists in the process and ceases to exist when the process stops. It's like the picture of a pair of hands drawing themselves.

Stop looking at it and stop being drawn into the story.

Ask yourself, who is watching this?

Who is listening?

And when you get the answer, if there is one, and you return your gaze to the story as it unfolds, it isn't the same.

It's better.

Like being awake in a dream in which I'm —

Falling

Falling

Falling

On wings of fire

Falling towards the earth.

Looking for words to describe the indescribable beauty of it all.

I've enjoyed sharing my journey with you and would be happy to keep in contact should you wish to know more. I can be contacted through my website.

HTTP://www.thetempleofwhom.co.uk

You can find many photographs of the events in this book. I kept a photographic record at the time without knowing I would write this book someday. You can also find details of the charges and trial of Swami Premananda.

To contact me directly, please use the following email.

templeofwhom@hotmail.com or deuxducks@hotmail.com

Made in United States
Orlando, FL
07 December 2023